京都大学史料叢書
16

吉田清成関係文書七　書翰篇5　書類篇3

思文閣出版

写1　晩年の吉田清成

写2　吉田清成がワシントン駐在中にスクラップした魚雷艇についての広告用印刷物(本文51頁)

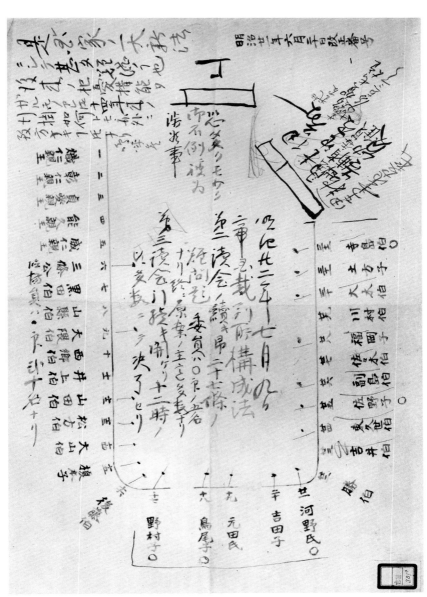

写3　枢密院本会議の座席表とメモ（本文224頁）

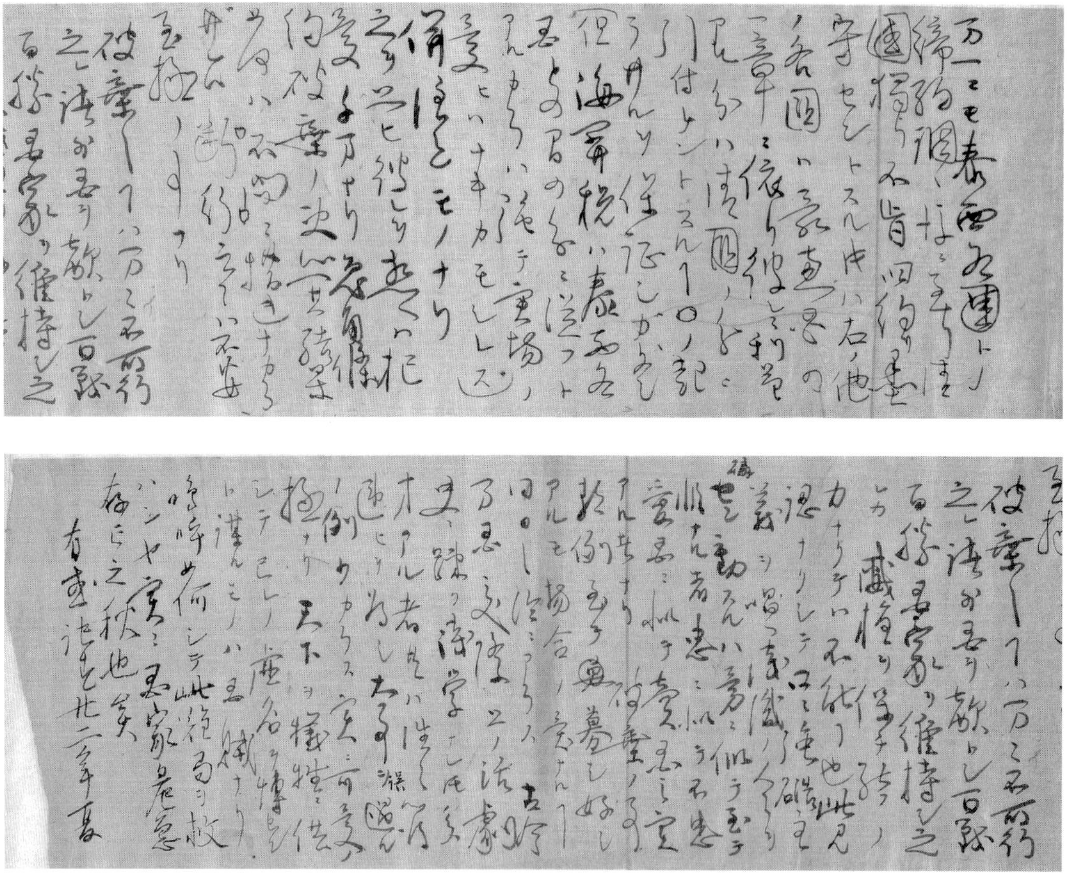

写4　大隈重信の条約改正交渉に反対する吉田清成の覚書（本文300頁）

凡　例

（一）　『吉田清成関係文書』は全七巻構成とする。第一～四巻までを書翰篇、第五・六巻を書類篇とし、第七巻は書翰篇・書類篇の二部構成とする。

（二）　書翰篇は、まず個別の書翰を日本文と欧文に区分し、本シリーズはさしあたって前者を対象とするものとした。これを吉田清成宛書翰・吉田清成発書翰・第三者間書翰に分類し、第一～三巻に吉田清成宛書翰（差出人判明分）と吉田清成発書翰（受取人判明分）を収録した。第四巻は吉田が駐米公使時代に作成した書翰のコピーブック、受信した書翰のスクラップブックの収録巻にあて、分量的に収録できなかった分は第七巻（本巻）に続けて掲載することとした。このコピーブック・スクラップブックには欧文書翰も含まれる。

（三）　本巻（第七巻）書翰篇には、まず第四巻の続きとして、スクラップブックの「洋歴一千八百八十年　雑書張貼」と記された頁以降の書翰群を収録する。続いて個別の第三者間書翰を収録した上で、差出人不明書翰（吉田清成宛）・受取人不明書翰（吉田清成発）を収め、最後に補遺として、第一～三巻公刊後に発見された未収録の吉田清成宛書翰（差出人判明分）・吉田清成発書翰（受取人判明分）を収録した。

（四）　スクラップブックの目次には差出人名を掲げた。不明のものや覚書類については〔　〕内に編者の注記を入れた。スクラップブックの書翰は、受信順にほぼそのまま綴じている順序通りに収録したので、年代が混在している部分がある。

1

（五）第三者間書翰と補遺は、それぞれの発信人の五十音順に配列し、同一人物の書翰は差出年月日順とした。差出人不明書翰・受取人不明書翰は年月日順に並べた。

（六）書類篇は基本的に作成年代順の配列とし、吉田清成の経歴を基準として、次のように区分した。

一　留学生時代

二　大蔵官僚時代　Ⅰ

三　大蔵官僚時代　Ⅱ

四　大蔵官僚時代　Ⅲ（外債募集のため海外渡航）

五　特命全権公使時代　Ⅰ

六　特命全権公使時代　Ⅱ（前アメリカ大統領グラント接待のため帰国）

七　特命全権公使時代　Ⅲ

八　外務大輔時代

九　農商務大輔・次官時代

十　元老院議官・枢密顧問官時代

十一　年代不明

本巻（第七巻）書類篇には、十・十一に相当する時期の書類を収録した。

（七）原題のある史料は、これを「　」付で表題とし、原題のない史料については、適宜表題を付した。作成者が判明する史料については、／で区切り、表題に続けて記した。

（八）すでに他で公刊されている史料については、その旨を注記し、表題のみを収録した。

（九）書翰篇・書類篇ともに、年代については、史料における表記や内容に即して、明治五年十二月三日以前の分については陰暦表記、それ以後については陽暦表記とした。推定年月については（）を付して示し、とくに多少疑問が残るものについては（カ）と表記した。推定しえない分については区分の末尾に収録し、区分も不可能な史料は十一に収録した。

（十）書翰篇・書類編ともに、文章表記に関しては、次のような措置をとった。

1　旧漢字・異体字は、原文の意味をそこなわない程度に、いわゆる通行の字体を用いた。ただし、別字体などは、原文にしたがって両用したものもある（例、島／嶋など）。

2　適宜、句読点を付した。原文に句読点がある場合には、とくに注記することはせずに、それらを尊重しつつ調整した。

3　明白な誤字・脱字等については、〔ママ〕〔　カ〕〔　欠カ〕で傍らに示し、訂正の場合には〔　〕で傍注を付した。当時常用されていた表現については、あえて示さなかった。

4　一般に片仮名表記されるものを除いて、原則として平仮名に統一した。また、変字体や〼・ヒ・ゟ・〆などの合字も通常の平仮名に直した（とき、とも、より、して）。

5　闕字は一字空けて処理し、改行は原文通りとした。ただし、擡頭および謙称の小字などは採用せず、前者は闕字の形で表記した。

6　破損・虫食などによる判読不能の箇所は、□や▢▢で示した。

7　朱筆や鉛筆書などについては、（　）で傍らに注記し、当該部分を「　」で括って示した。

8　外国地名の漢字表記の場合、（　）に入れて片仮名のルビを付し、原文のルビと区別した。ただし頻出する

3

アメリカ国内の地名については、本文中において煩瑣とならないよう以下にまとめて記しておく。

ワシントン……華（あるいは花）盛（あるいは清、聖）頓（あるいは都）、華府など

ニューヨーク……紐（あるいは新）育（あるいは約克）、紐府など

フィラデルフィア……費拉特立費、費（拉）など

サンフランシスコ……桑港など

9　書翰篇収録の英文中、活字印刷されていた部分についてはゴチック体で表記した。

（十一）用箋の種類が判明する場合および使用している筆記具、印刷の種類については、〔注〕としてそれぞれの末尾に注記した。

（十二）人名等についての編者注記は、〔　〕で傍らに示し、また参考になる事項は、〔注〕としてそれぞれの末尾に注記した。

（十三）別名・変名等を使用している場合には、一般的に知られている姓名を見出しに採用した。

（十四）最終巻の本巻には、吉田の年譜および編集の経緯を収録する。

（十五）吉田清成関係文書研究会構成員（本巻編集時）は次の通り。

（代表）山本　四郎　神戸女子大学名誉教授

　　　　伊藤　之雄　京都大学名誉教授

　　　　飯塚　一幸　大阪大学大学院文学研究科教授

　　　　田中　智子　京都大学大学院教育学研究科准教授

　　　　谷川　穣　京都大学大学院文学研究科准教授

齊藤　紅葉　　三重大学人文学部非常勤講師

久保田裕次　　京都大学大学文書館特定助教

萩原　　淳　　琉球大学人文社会学部准教授

西山由理花　　日本学術振興会特別研究員

水野貴久子　　京都女子大学卒業生

竹村　房子　　京都女子大学卒業生

※以上の他、鈴木栄樹、松下孝昭、大石一男の諸氏らが解読・整理の作業に協力された。

目次

凡例

書翰篇5

スクラップブック（続き）

203 Williams, G. B. ……………	('80カ)年1月17日……	三
204 Williams, G. B. ……………	('80)年3月17日……	四
205 中山寛六郎…………	('80)年（ ）月（ ）日……	五
206 中山寛六郎…………	'80年6月26日……	七
207 中山寛六郎…………	('80)年7月1日……	八
208 吉田清成………	('80)年6月29日……	九
209 竹下康之………	'80年4月16日……	九
210 柳谷謙太郎………	'80年5月8日……	一〇
211 菱川文哉………	('80)年（ ）月（ ）日……	一一
212 〔差出人不明〕………	'80年4月16日……	一二
213 井上要之助………	'80年5月5日……	一三
214 Earp, T.………	'80年5月7日……	一三
215 Carman, E. A. → Lanman, C. ………	'80年5月11日……	一四

目　次

216　Lanman, C. ……………………………………'80年5月10日……三四

217　Corps Cadets of West Point ………………'80年6月10日……三四

218　Richter, C. J. ………………………………'80年5月12日……三五

219　〔馬車販売の広告パンフレット〕…………'80年2月（　）日……三七

220　Gregory, H. D. ……………………………'80年5月17日……三

221　Northrop, B. G. ……………………………'80年5月18日……三

222　〔差出人不明〕………………………………'80年5月23日……三

223　Gregory, H. D. ……………………………'80年6月5日……三

224　Lanman, C. …………………………………'80年6月13日……三四

225　五十嵐文次（カ）……………………………'80年5月12日……三四

226　五十嵐文次（カ）……………………………'80年6月4日……三五

227　佐和　正 ……………………………………'80年7月12日……三六

228　Johnston, W. W. ……………………………'80年7月13日……三七

229　川崎寛堂 ……………………………………'80年6月1日……三六

230　〔行楽先についてのメモ〕……………（　）年（　）月（　）日……三〇

231　〔グラント関係電報①〕……………………'80年6月20日……三〇

232　〔グラント関係電報②〕……………………'80年6月19日……三

233　〔グラント関係電報③〕……………………'80年6月17日……三

234　〔グラント関係電報④〕……………………'80年6月18日……三

235　〔グラント関係電報⑤〕……………………'80年6月18日……三

236　〔グラント関係電報⑥〕……………………'80年7月18日……三

237　〔グラント関係電報⑦〕……………………'80年6月18日……三

238　〔グラント関係電報⑧〕……………………'80年7月18日……三

239　Edwards, S.→吉田貞 ………………………'80年6月17日……三五

目　次

240 Edwards, S.	'80年7月1日	...... 三七
241 Edwards, S.→吉田貞	'80年7月5日	...... 三七
242 Edwards, S.→吉田貞	'80年7月10日	...... 三八
243 Edwards, S.→吉田貞	'80年7月11日	...... 三九
244 Edwards, S.→吉田家〔カ〕	'80年7月12日	...... 四〇
245 Edwards, S.→吉田家〔カ〕	'80年7月13日	...... 四一
246 Edwards, S.→吉田家〔カ〕	'80年7月14日	...... 四二
247 Edwards, S.→吉田家〔カ〕	'80年7月15日	...... 四三
248 〔メモ〕	（　）年（　）月（　）日	...... 四三
249 橋口文蔵	'80年6月24日	...... 四四
250 橋口文蔵	'80年6月24日	...... 四六
251 〔馬車メンテナンスの広告チラシ〕	（　）年（　）月（　）日	...... 四六
252 〔B. G. Northrop による日本の進歩に関する New York Tribune 宛報告（賞金関連）〕	（'80カ）年（　）月（　）日	...... 四七
253 〔魚雷艇の広告チラシ〕	'80年3月25日	...... 五一
254 〔ミートジュースの商品説明パンフレット〕	'78年12月1日	...... 五三
255 〔芳香剤の商品説明チラシ〕	（　）年（　）月（　）日	...... 五九
256 〔馬車修理の広告チラシ〕	（　）年（　）月（　）日	...... 六一
257 二郎	（'80）年11月26日	...... 六二
258 小倉治郎	'79年11月26日	...... 六二
259 天野瑚次郎	'79年11月26日	...... 六三
260 Dickinson, P. T.	'80年1月5日	...... 六三
261 Young, J. R.	'79年11月20日	...... 六四
262 Henry, H. A.→吉田貞	（'79）年7月16日	...... 六四

目　次

第三者間書翰

263	Antisells……………………………………………………………（'75）年７月21日……六五
264	〔食用亀肉等購入についてのメモ〕…………………………（　）年（　）月（　）日……六五
265	吉田清成→伊藤博文……………………………………………（'75）年１月（　）日……六五
266	吉田清成→大久保利通…………………………………………（'75）年１月３日（　）……六六
267	〔計算メモ〕……………………………………………………（　）年（　）月（　）日……六六
268	Henderson, H. C.→吉田貞……………………………………'75年１月15日……六七
269	〔米国州知事・議員選挙に関する報告〕……………………（'75）年（２）月（　）日……六七
270	〔Fish, H. 書簡写し〕…………………………………………（　）年（　）月（　）日……七〇

第三者間書翰

一　伊藤圭介発宮本小一宛………………………………………明治（10カ）年１月18日……七二

二　伊藤博文発井上馨宛……………………………………………明治15年11月10日……七二

三　伊藤博文発井上馨宛……………………………………………明治（17）年３月12日……七三

四　井上馨発山県有朋宛……………………………………………明治19年12月17日……七三

五　井上馨発山県有朋宛……………………………………………明治20年４月13日……七三

六　井上毅発山県有朋・井上馨宛…………………………………明治（15）年８月30日……七三

七　井上毅発山県有朋・井上馨宛…………………………………明治（15）年９月３日……七六

八　井上毅発伊藤博文・井上馨・吉井友実宛……………………明治（17）年12月24日……七七

九　岩倉具視発グラント宛…………………………………………明治14年３月31日……七六

一〇　岩倉具視発石橋政方宛………………………………………明治（　）年６月27日……七六

一一　岩村高俊発柳谷謙太郎宛……………………………………明治（　）年10月23日……八〇

一二　大隈重信発吉田二郎宛………………………………………明治（７）年４月11日……八〇

一三　大隈重信発吉井友実・伊藤博文発上野景範宛……………明治（　）年６月24日……八一

一四　大倉喜八郎発渡辺宛…………………………………………明治（　）年９月４日……八一

目　次

- 一五　大倉喜八郎発志田喜衛宛……明治（　）年（　）月二六日……（八一）
- 一六　岡田令高発志村智常宛……明治（　）年四月二七日……（八三）
- 一七　岡本健三郎発井上馨宛……明治（　）年一月五日……（八三）
- 一八　海江田信義発島津家令扶宛……明治（　）年六月二七日……（八四）
- 一九　加藤静儉発松方正義宛……明治（　）年一〇月九日……（八四）
- 二〇　北代正臣発志村智常宛……明治一二年一月六日……（八六）
- 二一　北代正臣発志村智常宛……明治一四年一二月一七日……（八六）
- 二二　北代正臣発志村智常宛……明治一四年一二月五日……（八六）
- 二三　北代正臣発佐久間克宛……明治（　）年一二月五日……（八七）
- 二四　黒田瀧発吉田貞宛……明治二一年五月二九日……（八六）
- 二五　小谷静治発志村智常宛……明治（　）年六月一五日……（八六）
- 二六　工部省会計局発松田栄宛……明治（　）年八月一九日……（八六）
- 二七　小松原英太郎発吉田勇蔵・志村智常宛……明治二四年八月五日……（八六）
- 二八　西郷清発吉田貞宛……明治（　）年六月二六日……（八九）
- 二九　税所新次郎発吉田須磨宛……明治(22/23)年一一月二四日……（八九）
- 三〇　鮫島慶蔵発吉田貞宛……明治（　）年（　）月二五日……（九〇）
- 三一　沢井熊次郎外十四名発ガーフィールド宛……明治一四年六月（　）日……（九一）
- 三二　渋沢栄一発井上馨宛……明治（　）年一月五日……（九二）
- 三三　渋沢栄一発大倉喜八郎・益田孝宛……明治二〇年一月三〇日……（九二）
- 三四　渋沢栄一発種田宛……明治（　）年二月二四日……（九三）
- 三五　志村智常発肥後七左衛門宛……明治五年一月二一日……（九四）
- 三六　志村智常発吉田貞宛……明治八年一月（　）日……（九四）
- 三七　志村智常発吉田貞宛……明治八年二月一八日……（九六）
- 三八　志村智常発吉田貞宛……明治（8）年六月六日……（九七）
- 三九　志村智常発吉田貞宛……明治8年7月28日……（九六）

目　次

三九　志村智常発吉田貞宛……………………………………………明治10年1月20日……一〇〇

四〇　志村智常発吉田貞宛……………………………………………明治10年2月9日……一〇一

四一　志村智常発吉田貞宛……………………………………………明治11年5月18日……一〇二

四二　志村智常発吉田貞宛……………………………………………明治11年6月30日……一〇三

四三　志村智常発吉田貞宛……………………………………………明治11年8月15日……一〇四

四四　志村智常発吉田貞宛……………………………………………明治14年1月11日……一〇五

四五　志村智常発吉田貞宛……………………………………………明治14年12月23日……一〇六

四六　志村智常発岡田彦三郎宛………………………………………明治（　）年7月28日……一〇七

四七　志村智常発吉田貞宛……………………………………明治（　）年（　）月（　）……一〇八

四八　高橋新吉発宮本小一宛……………………………………明治（　）年8月26日……一〇九

四九　高峰譲吉発渡辺洪基宛………………………………………明治（21）年2月8日……一〇九

五〇　立嘉度発熊谷武五郎宛………………………………………明治（　）年4月4日……一一〇

五一　田中章発岡田彦三郎宛………………………………………明治（　）年5月14日……一一〇

五二　谷口安定発田口将之宛………………………………………明治（　）年5月17日……一一一

五三　種田政明発山沢静吾宛………………………………………明治（　）年2月3日……一一一

五四　寺島宗則発渡辺宛……………………………………………明治16年6月20日……一一二

五五　徳大寺実則発吉井友実宛……………………………………明治（　）年1月9日……一一二

五六　中村五郎発岡田彦三郎宛……………………………………明治22年1月4日……一一三

五七　新納刑部発町田久成宛……………………慶応（2）年6月7日（'66）年7月18日……一一四

五八　新納刑部発町田久成宛……………………慶応（2）年6月7日（'66）年7月18日……一一五

五九　新納刑部発竹隠宛…………………………慶応（3）年3月12日（'67）年4月16日……一一五

六〇　二橋元長発遠藤宛……………………………………………明治（21）年5月31日……一一六

六一　三島通庸発奥宛………………………………………………明治（　）年2月23日……一一七

六二　三島和歌子発吉田貞宛………………………………………明治（21）年5月30日……一一七

目次

空　湯地定基発渡辺千秋宛……明治（　）年（　）月（　）日……三二七
竺　吉田家執事発吉田別邸執事宛……明治（　）年八月二三日……三二六
四　吉田二郎発井上馨宛……明治一七年七月二六日……三二六
空　吉田勇蔵発吉田貞宛……明治一七年二月二三日……三二三

差出人不明書翰（吉田清成宛）

1　明治（4）年九月一八日……三二二
2　明治（6／7）年（　）月（　）日……三二二
3　明治（22）年（10／26）日……三二二
4　明治（　）年四月三〇日……三二二
5　明治（　）年五月一二日……三二二
6　明治（　）年七月一八日……三二二
7　明治（　）年八月九日……三二四
8　明治（　）年九月一八日……三二四
9　明治（　）年一一月七日……三二四
10　明治（　）年一一月三〇日……三二四
11　明治（　）年（　）月一五日……三二四
12　明治（　）年（　）月（　）日……三二五

受取人不明書翰（吉田清成発）

1　明治（7）年（7カ）月（　）日……三二六
2　明治21年五月27日……三二七
3　明治22年（　）月（　）日……三二七
4　明治（　）年（　）月（　）日……三二六
5　明治（　）年（　）月（　）日……三二九
6　明治（　）年（　）月（　）日……三二九
7　明治（　）年（　）月（　）日……三三〇
8　明治（　）年（　）月（　）日……三三〇

補遺

［吉田清成宛］

一　浅井新一
1　明治（6）年10月24日……三三二

二　阿部潜
1　明治（6）年九月三日……三三一

三　五十嵐文次
1　明治（11）年七月五日……三三二
2　明治11年七月28日……三三三

目　次

３　明治（13）年６月18日............一三六

四　井上馨

１　明治（７）年６月21日............一三六

２　明治（12）年８月６日............一三七

３　明治13年９月30日............一三七

五　井上毅

１　明治（17）年12月24日............一三九

六　井上雅彦

１　明治（21）年５月20日............一四一

２　明治（22）年９月25日............一四一

３　明治（　）年５月25日............一四二

七　穎川君平

１　明治（　）年12月15日............一四三

２　明治（　）年12月18日............一四三

八　奥　青輔

１　明治（19／20）年２月12日............一四四

九　鹿児島県詰役

１　明治（　）年９月19日............一四四

一〇　金子謙〔カ〕

１　明治（　）年９月12日............一四四

一一　川崎祐名

１　明治（12）年３月15日............一四五

一二　北代正臣

２　明治（　）年９月12日............一四六

１　明治（4／6）年11月24日............一四六

一三　郷友会事務所

１　明治（　）年９月25日............一四七

一四　熊谷武五郎

１　明治（19カ）年（　）月９日............一四七

２　明治（21カ）年（10カ）月24日............一四八

３　明治（　）年（　）月15日............一四八

４　明治（　）年（　）月26日............一四九

５　明治（　）年（　）月............一四九

６　明治（　）年（　）月（　）............一四九

一五　佐久間克典（カ）

１　明治4年12月17日............一五〇

一六　志村智常

１　明治（　）年（　）月23日............一五〇

一七　世古延世

１　明治（　）年11月13日............一五〇

一八　寺師宗徳

１　明治（　）年２月１日............一五一

一九　長谷川方省

１　明治（4カ）年12月17日............一五一

二〇　富田鉄之助

１　明治3年５月６日............一五一

二一　奈良原矢太郎

２　明治（　）年３月31日............一五二

目次

書類篇3

1　明治（21カ）年8月12日 ……一三二
2　明治（21カ）年10月21日 ……一五二
3　明治（22カ）年5月30日 ……一六六
4　明治（23カ）年10月26日 ……一六七

二二　橋口直右衛門
1　明治15年5月2日 ……一六六
二三　室田義文
二四　吉田二郎
1　明治（15）年10月25日 ……一六○

1　明治13年7月30日 ……一六一

［吉田清成発］
一　西郷従道
1　明治（9）年（　）月（　）日 ……一六二
二　花房義質
1　明治（　）年（　）月（　）日 ……一六二
三　吉原重俊
1　明治（　）年10月11日 ……一六二

十　元老院議官・枢密顧問官時代

1　株券に関する覚書 ……一六七
2　吉田清成宛当座預金引出の件／東京第三十三国立銀行 ……明治20年7月19日……一六七
3　「意見書」／谷干城 ……明治20年9月……一六八
4　吉田清成・貞宛宮中観菊会招請状／土方久元 ……明治20年11月2日……一六九
5　高知県人建白書抄録／吉田清成（カ）……明治20年11月5日……一七○
6　鎌倉郡内戸長役場宛吉田清成借地に関する神奈川達（写）……明治20年11月30日……一七○
7　吉田清成宛借地に関する通知／鎌倉郡内戸長役場 ……明治20年12月2日……一七一
8　「拝借地返納之件」／吉田清成 ……明治20年12月……一七二
9　条約改正問題等政治改革に関する意見書 ……明治（20～22）年……一七三
10　吉田清成宛参賀申入書／土方久元 ……明治21年5月23日……一八七

目　次

11　三条実美・黒田清隆・大隈重信・松方正義・大山巌・森有礼宛廻覧状／農商務省………明治21年5月28日…一八六

12　山田顕義・榎本武揚宛廻覧状／農商務省………明治21年5月28日…一八九

13　伊藤博文／山県有朋宛廻覧状／農商務省………明治21年5月28日…一八九

14　西郷従道・谷干城・三浦梧楼宛廻覧状／農商務省………明治21年5月28日…一九〇

15　吉田清成宛参内申入書／鍋島直大………明治21年5月28日…一九一

16　吉田清成宛勲位録送状／賞勲局………明治21年5月28日…一九一

17　領収書／尾崎弥五郎………明治21年6月2日…一九二

18　吉田清成家執事宛取調申入書／警視庁会計局用度課………明治(21カ)年6月2日…一九三

19　吉田清成家宛回金申入書／宮内省内匠寮………明治21年6月6日…一九三

20　宮内省内匠寮宛入費精算帳／畑戸源二郎………明治21年6月…一九三

21　吉田清成宛陪食の沙汰申入／土方久元………明治21年7月13日…一九四

22　井上毅宛参内達／井上毅………明治21年10月8日…一九四

23　吉田清成宛通知／井上毅………明治21年10月12日…一九五

24　吉田清成宛叙勲通知書／賞勲局………明治21年10月16日…一九五

25　日清間続約草案………明治21年11月16日…一九六

26　吉田清成参賀申入／土方久元………明治22年1月21日…一九六

27　吉田清成宛練兵式先着申入書／鍋島直大………明治22年2月7日…一九六

28　吉田清成宛金銭借用証文（写）／吉田昇二郎………明治22年3月31日…一九九

29　第三十三国立銀行宛借用金証書（写）／岡田彦三郎………明治22年4月2日…一九九

30　第三十三国立銀行宛抵当承諾証書控／吉田清成………明治22年4月2日…二〇〇

31　家計元帳／吉田清成………明治22年5月5日～9月30日…二〇三

32　「借憶簿」／吉田清成………明治22年5月21日～25日…二一四

33　「次第不同万留　壱号」／吉田清成………明治22年7月1日～21日…二一六

目　次

34　伊藤博文宛枢密顧問官定員に関する通牒／黒田清隆…………明治22年7月3日…………二八三

35　枢密顧問官座席表…………明治22年7月9日…………二八三

36　「次第不同万留　弐号」／吉田清成…………明治22年7月22日～8月12日…………二八五

37　「元帳」／吉田清成…………明治22年7月26日～12月24日…………二八七

38　「日記　次第不同万留　三号」／吉田清成…………明治22年8月13日～9月2日…………二八五

39　草道家廃戸主及相続についての願書…………明治22年8月…………二九〇

40　帝国臣民身分法修正案…………明治（22）年9月…………二九四

41　条約改正についての御前会議開催意見書／後藤象二郎…………明治22年（10）月…………二九四

42　「久光親話紀を奉るに就て上申」／島津忠義・島津忠済…………明治22年11月19日…………二九六

43　島津久光建議附書（写）／島津忠義・島津忠済…………明治（22）年（11）月（19）日…………二九六

44　三条実美宛意見書／島津忠義・島津忠済…………明治22年11月…………二九六

45　雑メモ／吉田清成…………明治（22）年（12）月…………二九九

46　条約廃棄論批判の覚書／吉田清成…………明治22年…………三〇〇

47　磯御邸宛請求書／堀之内勘五右衛門…………明治23年1月29日…………三〇一

48　島津忠済宛意見書／高崎正風・海江田信義・吉田清成・寺島宗則…………明治23年4月24日…………三〇一

49　「旅行願」／吉田清成…………明治23年7月18日…………三〇二

50　吉田清成宛議案送状／枢密院書記官…………明治23年8月21日…………三〇二

51　吉田清成宛東宮参賀申入／曽我祐準…………明治23年8月25日…………三〇四

52　「非分県陳情書」／長野県下伊那郡飯田町住人二十四名…………明治23年9月17日…………三〇六

53　非条約論者および大隈重信らの扇動に関する抜萃書…………明治23年9月…………三〇八

54　「出納簿」／吉田清成…………明治23年11月…………三一〇

55　尾崎朝景宛照会／枢密院書記官…………明治23年12月6日…………三一二

56　外務大臣宛と枢密院の内談に関する手続き案…………明治（23／24）年…………三一八

57　「清市に対し目的を立候以来続て外務省へ奉職後今日迄の概略」／町田実一…………明治（23／24）年…………三一九

目　次

58　「無罪放免判決書之写」／伊東巳代治………明治24年3月30日………五三一

59　「英国覆案に対する意見」／伊東巳代治………明治（24）年5月2日………五三五

60　吉田清成宛賛成依頼書／日本諸新聞切抜通信舎………明治24年5月9日………五三九

61　病床日誌A／吉田清成………明治24年5月13日～24日………五四〇

62　病床日誌B／吉田清成………明治24年5月19日～6月5日………五四四

63　「廿四年辛卯五月病痾中当座備臆簿」／吉田清成………明治24年5月26日～6月7日………五四八

64　大津事件に関する上奏／東久世通禧他十二名………明治24年6月1日………五五二

65　病床日記………明治24年6月6日～7月19日………五五五

66　「廿四年五月より御床臥中御薬及御飯食物御手扣」／吉田清成………明治24年5月28日～8月2日………五五八

67　病床記録／吉田清成………明治24年5月28日～6月30日………四八六

68　「殖民意見書」／榎本武揚………明治（23）年………五〇六

69　三十三銀行失敗始末………五〇七

十一　年代不明

1　金銭受取に関する覚書／吉田清成………明治（　）年7月（15）日………五六

2　支払いメモ／島崎………明治（　）年8月15日………五七

3　椎野正兵衛領収書………明治（　）年12月22日………五九

4　度量衡改革についての吉田清成覚書………明治（　）年………五九

5　横浜港石炭積入場所調………五〇

6　英米との通商条約に関するメモ／吉田清成………五二

7　英金俸給高に関するメモ………五三

8　華氏気温表………五三

9　条約締結に際しての国是確定意見稿………五四

10　人名表………五四

目　次

11　人名表…………………………………………………五六
12　人名表断片……………………………………………五六
13　政治体制に関するメモ／吉田清成………………五七
14　「島津家譜歌」…………………………………………五八
15　「人は同等なる事」……………………………………五九
16　「藍壺の法」……………………………………………五〇
17　「桐樹発生地」…………………………………………五二
18　藍の製法………………………………………………五二
19　公債買入に関する覚書…………………………………五二
20　吉田清成宛農地経営に関する報告／岡田彦三郎（カ）………………………………………五三
21　家政に関する覚書／吉田清成…………………………五四
22　買入品に関する覚書／吉田清成………………………五七
23　吉田貞買入品に関する覚書／吉田清成………………五八
24　支払覚書…………………………………………………五九
25　刀装具目録……………………………………………五一
26　松植木代金メモ………………………………………五五
27　書状文例／吉田清成…………………………………五六

吉田清成略年譜…………………………………………五七

京都大学史料叢書（第一期）『吉田清成関係文書』全七巻の完結にあたって………………山本四郎………五六九

吉田清成関係文書七　書翰篇5

スクラップブック（続き）

'80年1月

203

Williams, G. B.

（'80 カ）年1月17日

Hotel des Anglais
Menton, France,
Jany 17, '79.
［マャ］

My dear old Yoshida:

I hope you will not think I have forgotten you because I have not written you, but the truth is that since poor Doc's death I have not felt in the humor of letter writing. Neelie wrote to Tei, however, &（吉田貞）so you have had information of our doings. Firstly let me say that Mrs. Arnold is still improving and that while she is still confined to her room we hope she will be around again all right in the course of a week or two.

I saw Matsugata at Paris only once. The day after I saw him I heard poor Doc was dead & so I did not see anybody for some time afterwards.

In London I saw Minami, who was getting along very well. He said Irwin was there as the agent for the sale of the government rice & that he was endeably making a very good thing of it. Minami thought there was no occasion of Irwin's presence or all the business would be done through respectable Rice brokers. I presume, however, that Enouye stand behind Irwin. Campbell of O.B.C. informed me that none of the bank people had seen Wooyeno for over eighteen months. Wooyeno does not keep his private a/c at O.B.C. The government a/c is, however, kept there as usual.

Panmure Gordon, whom I saw at O.B.C. says that the Japanese Loans are in good hands at permanent (i.e. to hold until maturity) insertment & consequently but few operations are recorded. Japanese credit is A/- as good as any government's.

I have nothing in the way of news to say to you. Just before leaving home we elected Mr. Orth again to Congress & of course he will again be in the Foreign Affairs Committee of the House of Repre-

3

sentatives. He will of course have a good deal of influence with the State Department and if I should want to be Consul General to Japan there would be no difficulty. I don't want it, however, & only mention it en passant. If the Consul General could be of any service to Japan it would be different but as he cannot I will let it go.

Much obliged for the boys sent to Lafayette & left with my sister at Washington. You are always remembering me in some pleasant way, but I will get even with you some day.

I will meet you again before long & get you to do one or two things for me. I owe Mr. House for the Tokio Times, and also want to give a little present to one of our former Japanese servants & before you return to America will get you to make payment for me & I will repay you.

Let me know how you found things at home. Who has taken Okubo's〔大久保利通〕place in influence & importance & how do you find your own status.

Give Tei & the little one a great deal of love from Neelie & myself & believe me my dear Yoshida. Always the most sincerely and affectio-nately.

Williams

My address is still at Lafayette—as I don't know how long we will remain here.

204

Williams, G. B.

（'80）年3月17日

Hotel des Anglais
Mentone, France〔ママ〕
Mch. 17.

My dear Yoshida:

I have been hoping for a word from you giving me some idea of affairs in Japan, and particularly how you find thing affecting yourself since my arrival here I have seen no Japanese papers & so am quite lost for Japanese news. I observe, however, that Okuma〔大隈重信〕has recently published the actual expenditures of the Empire for the year 1876. I am glad this is being done—as it will eventually serve as a good check upon financial affairs.

I observe that many of the American papers—particularly the Chicago Tribune—are criticising

'80年（　）月

the United States Government for making the new treaty with Japan operative only when European Governments make similar treaties. The drift of sentiment is that the U. S. should entirely cut aloof from Europe in its intercourse with Japan. By the way, have you seen Blaines letter on the Chinese question? Fearing you have not I enclose it herewith & call your attention particularly to that portion discussing the power of a nation to abrogate a treaty without the consist of the other contracting party. Why will not Japan accept this view & wipe out envy old convention?

At Rome the other day I saw Nakamura, the Japanese Chargé d'affairs. He informed me he was trying to do something with the Italian Government about the treaty, but was not succeeding very well. It occurred to me that he was not a proper man for so responsible a position—not having enough push.

I sail for America by the "Brittanie" in May 15th and will go immediately to Lafayette. Mrs. Arnold is progressing very favorably toward recovery, and we hope will be quite well again by summer. My dear wife is as well as a wish.

205　中山寛六郎

What is your programme? Do you purpose returning to America? Or will you remain in Japan? I hope you will not fail to inform me of your intentions, as I want to know exactly your purposes. By the way, when you return I hope you will bring for me a thousand or two of the best Manilla Cigars. I want cigars, as I don't like the cheroot.

I wrote you some time of thanking you ever so much for your thoughtfullness of your friend Georges when leaving Washington for Japan. One of these days I will have the chance of reciprocating.

Duckie & I think of you often & wonder how Tei and Foomi are. Duckie wrote a long letter to Tei some time ago. Kiss them both for us and belie me my dear Yoshida ever.

Yours Affectionate friend
Geo. B. Williams

I enclose you a newspaper clipping regarding your old "friend" Harris. Write to me at Lafayette.

（'80）年（　）月（　）日

'80年（　）月

Requested <u>to</u> <u>be</u> Cambridge Mass.

<u>Personal</u>

Mr. Yoshida

My dear Sir

With a sincere hope that your generosity will not regard my writing to you as a mere matter of audacity on my part, because of your having seen me only once, I own a courage to humbly ask of you a favor of condescending to listen to my private wishes which are in brief as follows:—

I left home three years ago with the cherished hope of studying law at Harvard; which I did. In fact I have finished my studies and, in April, on entering the examinations required for the admission to the Suffolk bar which, as you are aware of, has the reputation of the highest standing in the country, passed them satisfactorily, so that I could practice law, had I been a naturalized citizen. The last three years, I spent here, were necessary and exclusively devoted for the legal study and the acquirement of the language which scarcely left me any leisure to study the people.

My educational fund is private; that is, I receive it from my father who has many claims besides myself upon his income. Thus I have been studying here. But, after all, my wishes are only half realized and on the arrival of the time for the harvesting of the healthier knowledge with the greater ease by the aid of the better handling of the language and of the closer familiarity with the customs and manners, I must quit the field of education without rummaging, to any satisfaction, the object of search—solid knowledge. Alas! alas! Knowledge to gather is immeasurable; while the fund to sustain me in the pursuit is limited. What help can there be for me? From whom can I expect a sympathy and material assistance in realizing my humble but earnest wishes to elevate myself to the forward position occupied by my patriotic country men?

Under the present circumstances, a man of common education is not of a great benefits to Japan. There are already many students at home, who have honored themselves with the accomplishment of their studies in arts and science abroad. But among them, there are only a few who completed their education by the acquirement of any practical knowledge, so as to be able to explain readily the political complications and the multifarious development of social phenomina [ママ] of the country where they have been resident and studying. Surely enough, they have some knowledge; but scattered and superficial and not enough to enable them to philosophize the analogous cases happening before them, so as to meet the demands of the progressive people of home.

It is my earnest wish to prolong my stay in this country. But my father's words are Medes [ママ] and Persians [ママ], so long as I have no other means. He generously allows me to travel a little in Europe before I go home. But this is not enough. To think over the subject is mere moping. But amidst this crowd of prostrations, I entertain only one hope; and it is in your power. If your sound discretion advice you to read my earnest wishes thus laid before you, and find me adequate to fill some office at the Legation in Washington so as to learn first of all diplomacy under your careful directions, I shall pledge all my faith to endeavor with my utmost to realize my cherished and earnest wishes. How long I shall stay at the Legation, I do not mind. So long as my duty requires me, I shall obey.

Humbly waiting for your generous answer for my there earnest wishes, I remain.

Faithfully and Respectfully
Kanrokuro Nakayama

206
中山寛六郎

'80年6月26日

Cambridge Mass.
26th June 1880

Mr. Yoshida
My Dear Sir

Though my mind is fraught with the fear that you may consider me as an unreasonably impatient lad, yet the pressure of the circumstances to which I am the helpless victim, compels me to wear the immodest mask of boldness to advance you solicitingly these few lives with the intention to inquire if your public duty has not yet favored you with a leisure to cast your lenient thought upon my hum-

'80年7月

ble wishes, which bear a vast deal of importance to my private longings, that I already begged your permission to lay before you. Situated and actuated as I am, human fragility is keenly felt. At one moment, the hope for a favorable news from you, though, of course, yet entirely audaciously presumptive, lighten up the gloom of my anxious mind; while, at another, the yet premature may needless discouragement founded upon a probable disappointment in the actual realization of my earnest wishes swells the bosom intently. Though the labyrinth passing between these imaginary walls of joy and painful anxiety, I am nursingly tottering. Get I proudly own a priviledge to entertain a cheerful hope for my longings. My wishes are humble but sincere; and such sincere wishes, I can not help believing, you ever encourage among your young countrymen. Whether I shall be buried in the depth of discouragement and sorrow, or lift myself in the air of hope and expectations for the performance of various duties overous upon the Japanese, it entirely rests with your acute discretions, which, I humbly hope, you will, in this case, exercise in my

favor to encourage my grad wishes.

Wishing you to pardon this unmannerly impatience and let me hope respectfully to hear a joyful answer to my earnest wishes. I remain

Sincerely and Respectfully

Your humble Servant

Kanrokuro Nakayama

P.S. I respectfully thank you for a note from your secretary, improving me your condescending and kind acknowlegdement of my letter.

207

中山寛六郎

（'80）年7月1日

芳函難有拝読仕候。陳は拙願難相達、身御多端之節御懇諭奉厚謝候。過日来内願に及候通り小生義は私費之学徒にして僅に三年之在学にて宿志之幾分はたす、今日既に帰途に上るに至れり。公使館に望処は不成、他に無策、嗚呼夫れ小生之不幸にあらすして何ぞや。貴意中何か御佳策あらは示諭あらん事を希望此事に御座候。小生過日来願候は分外之望を望候にあらす。只

'80年6月

当国に在留之出来候を望候事故、何なりと身分相応之
用事を務め在留相成候策あらは御示諭の程奉懇願候。
公用御多忙之処如此私事を以貴意を労し候は実恐縮之
事候へ共、小生之心中を御推知被下様奉希望候。早々
頓首々々

七月一日

　　　　　　吉田清成

吉田清成様

中山寛六郎様

208

吉田清成

（'80）年6月29日
日付なし六月九日
の郵便役所印あり

本月初旬之貴書　　　正に相達、以阿久沢一
応及御挨拶候後、引続き多忙にて結局之御答致遅延候
処、重て廿六日付之御書束到来、是亦熟読御懇望之旨
趣逐一致了承候。然処当公使館之儀は当時満員且つ拙
生において附属之役員相命候権無之候間、乍遺憾難応
貴願之趣候。此段乍遅々貴答まて匆卒如此候也。

六月廿九日

　　　　　　吉田清成

中山勘六郎様
〔寛〕

209

竹下康之

'80年4月16日

謹て奉啓す。先は海上無恙被遊御着候事と奉慶賀候。
御出立の節は却て御賓客の御妨と恐察仕、態と御無礼
申上候段幾重にも御宥恕奉願候。扨て其後は兼て御取
計置被下候旨に付、外務省え被相雇候儀と屈指相待居
候処、今日に至るまで未だ何たる御沙汰も無之候間、敢
て相疑候義には無之候得共、如何なる都合に御取計置
被下候哉、長岡殿に致面謁同公より外務大少輔の方々
を始め問合せに相成候処、右は尊公よりは鄙生の義に
付御出立前に何たる御沙汰も無之由に同公より回答有
之、如何の間違に可有之哉。併しながら一旦尊公の御
引受にて御都合たりとも素願相叶候様御取計置被
下候との御事に付、定て他に御都合被成下置候事と恐
察仕候得共、鄙賤の一書生別に便りて素志を陳述すべ
き人も無之甚た以て当惑仕奉存候。固より不肖の康之
には候得共、一旦外務に奉仕する以上は飽まて之に罷

'80年5月

勉致し洋行の素願相遂げ誓て尊公の御望に負かざるの

覚悟に御座候間、定て尊慮に協はざるの所作も可有之

候得共、何卒寛大の思召を以て御助勢の上御試験可被

成下候。就ては思召の程も恐入候得共、猶又急に外

務大少輔の方々か或は塩田公に御申立被下、且又御当

地公使館を始め諸領事館等に好機会も御座候節は乍此

上御仁力の程偏[ママ]に奉願上候。恐懼恐懼頓首謹言

十三年四月十六日

　　　　　竹下康之[三郎]

　　　　　東京麻布市兵衛町
　　　　　二丁目八十五番地

吉田全権公使殿

謹て追啓す。若し御差支も無御座候はゞ塩田・

中井弘の二公に前書の儀に付、別に御添書被成

下候儀は相叶申間敷や、乍憚相伺候也。

〔注〕「竹下蔵版」とある罫紙を使用。

210

柳谷謙太郎

'80年5月8日

去る四日御一同御無異御着之電信拝承欣賀之至奉存候。

拠当地御滞在中は特別之御芳遇を辱し、加之御懇篤之

御諭示を蒙り感銘之至御座候。且亦御出発も火急に相

成何等御饗応申上候義も無之、不本懐之至御寛恕為

在之幸甚之至候。頃日は定て今閏令児にも御壮健御安

居被為在候義と奉存候。荊妻よりも宜く申上候様申出

候へは御致声之程奉願候。途中ハンボルトにて御発之

尊信正に拝承、モールス氏へ之寄贈品は出来合品無御

座別段註文[ママ]、本日同氏へ相届置候。同氏は去る四日便

にては出発不致、是迄之通オレゴン地方航海いたし候

趣に御座候。右烟管は雛形之通にて代金は拾弐弗に御

座候。

ウヰリヤス氏へは御指命の如く寄贈仕置候。何れ同氏

幷カピテンモールス氏より答詞可申越奉存候。但しウ

ヰリヤス氏へ之物品代価付紙別紙入御覧候。

フレートにて御携帯之貨物横浜より之□□[破レ]は払済と存

居候処、また之由に付、相違之義は有之間敷奉存候間、

払入置候義に候。

御滞在中御依托之件々は先つ前書申上候儀に止り候義

と奉存候。右等は疾く申上度奉存候へ共、御出発後河
瀬氏之為めに奔走且日本邦郵船出入にて多忙、不得止遅
延仕候段は宜御了承被下度候。

河瀬氏にも去る一日当地出発相成候へは不日貴地にて
御面晤被為遊候義と奉存候。同氏滞在中種々注文之取
調件も御座候へ共、滞在日短く且館務等もあり充分之
義請求に応し兼候義も御座候哉と懸念罷在候。乍去不
得止義に候へは宜御含置被下度候。

先は右迄申上度、余情后便に譲拝陳可仕候。頓首謹具

十三年五月八日

　　　　　　謙太郎拝

吉田公坐下

尚々、御貨物第四号の内花瓶等取出跡に詰合せ之
為め荀罐詰数個差入候間御笑味被下度候。以上

Confidential

As to the affairs of the class in Consulate I
am extremely glad to have had your excellency's favorable consideration for which please
accept my sincere □□. Now I respectfully ask
your excellency's □□ to the minister of our

Dept. to send （以下省ヒ）

211
菱川文哉

（'80）年（　）月（　）日

五月二十三日讒劣不肖生菱川文哉謹再拝白、全権公使
吉田公閣下、生北越一賤児固非有知閣下特聞其賢明博
識不堪欣慕、則欲求一謁、退而思之方今都書生愈漫風
儀、其甚至有屡赴貴権之門施騙欺之術故、其嫌忌書生
甚於狐狸書生到其門不論其善悪不問其情意、悉使閣者
辞去嘗無許見由、此如愚聞閣下之芳名雖欲一遂謁奉其
教聴其高論恐与似盗之悪生同視将進而不進也。既而閣
下奉朝命赴米国濤浪千里又不能遂謁、而欣慕念日長一
日不能忘焉間、上書以求謁于内務大輔前島公嘗以所挟
持於心者喋々与輔公弁論言辞失礼、而輔公笑而不各焉、
且曰吾子宜求知于吉田公使公者則一世之傑士可必加礼
遇也、生欣躍拝跪辞而返于家愈慕閣下而不能已也。則
陳卑情閣下能察焉生之辞家也。則遊于新潟三年学英学、
卒而来于京入芳野金陵翁之門又三年矣。雖然天資魯鈍、

'80年4月

今年雖及十八一業無修一事無成自思之則将愧死也。　幸
而聊有報固之念夙欲委身陸軍、年十六始為陸軍幼年生
徒学仏学二年余、今春転入於士官校稍似得成業之発程
矣。　然聞道日尚賤所学之業一無所得也。　故識力矇昧無
憑以可開達、仮令後日出校奉士官之職恐無為人長之智
徒辱校名已況立功天下報国思之厚哉。　是以日夜汲々思
志学而如無書何哉、生家貧窶加之弟妹数輩皆就学、父
之費於資於学者月数十金、於貧愈貧而窶益窶、生一愈
毎及于此覚〔カ〕涙之泣然而下也。　幸而過月謁前島公也、公
憐生之愚衷則許所好之漢籍尽以与于生、可謂餓者得食
也。　而生未能得英仏之書也、生聞之父母去遠不遊而生
去親遠而為日久矣。　親之念我不忘也必矣、嗚呼欲帰家
而尽孝則道不得聞欲聞道、則憂無書与師生望於閣下者
乃是而已、孟嘗養
鶏鳴狗盗之〔ママ〕之為而自謂非之比生平日未志失其元也、又
敢将于卒伍而不辱閣下之顧命也。　仰願閣下垂涵養之徳
使生得五車之書、則又敢不呉下之阿蒙而止也、日月垂
照則朽木又華江漢送流則涸魚又游、是生所以不堪懇望

也。　頓首再拝

生や、閣下の大任を抱ひて一小生に云々す可から〔る脱カ〕
ざ身なるを知ると雖とも万里を遠とせずして卑情
を演ぶ。　蓋し大に閣下に望む所あればなり。　然り
而して生が乞ふ所の成不成は徒に閣下の意中に決
し、其成不成に因て生必ず届するの意なし。　切に
乞ふ閣下其の乞の許と否とに拘らず、速に玉簡の
芳報を来たし玉はん事を。

日本東京

陸軍士官学校生徒

菱川文哉拝

212

'80年4月16日

〔差出人不明〕

Imperial Post office,
Yokohama; April 16th 1880

My dear Mr. Yoshida,
About three days before your departure, I gave
to Mr. Takahashi, five bibs for your baby, with the

'80年5月

request that he would be sure to give them to you, or to your goodlady, before you left. This, for some reason, he failed to do, and I therefore take this, the first occasion to send them to you, although it is too late for them to be of any use on the trip. I send them as a registered sample.

You have, by this time, almost reached your destination, and I sincerely trust the trip has been made without too much fatigue, and in good health. The Takahashi's and ourselves are well, and unity in hardest regards to you and yours.

With best wishes for your welfare

I am

Always faithfully yours

Sani, em, Shya,

213

井上要之助

'80年5月5日

Annapolis, Md.

May 5, 1880.

My Dear Sir,

I am very glad to hear of your safe arrival at Washington, and hope you and the family are not very fatigued after such a long Journey. Please give my kind regards to Mrs. Yoshida.

Yours very truly,

Y. Enouye,

214

Earp, T.

'80年5月7日

No. 217 So. Third Street,

Office Hours:

From 11 until 2 o'clock.

Philadelphia, May 7th 1880

My dear Sir,

Mr. Takahashi wrote me by the last steamer, and asked me to let you know the address of Mrs. Parvin.

It is —

Mrs. Parvin.

Care of Mr. M. B. Buckman.

No. 570 Marshall St.

Philadelphia

Mr. T. said that you had a package to send to

'80年5月

her.

His Excellency
K. Yoshida
Japanese Legation

Very Respy Yours
Theodore Earp

sold thousand's of dollar's worth to be Le Due & I
will get heni to make up a nice lot for you for
tomorrow mail.

C. L.

215　Carman, E. A. → Lanman, C.

'80年5月11日

Department of Agriculture,
Washington, D. C., May 11, 1880.

Chas. Lanman Esq
Dear Sir;
Yours of this date requesting in behalf of Mr. Yoshida a package each of flower and vegetable seed is recd. I extremely regret that we have not a seed of any kind in the Depts our supply being entirely exhausted.

Very respectfully
E.A. Carman
Chief Clerk

There is a seedsman in Georgetown who has
[以下裏書込]

216　Lanman, C.

'80年5月10日

Dear Mr. Yoshida:
I send you a small bottle of quinine, with two papers containing 3 grains each-merely to show the size of each dose. My plan has been to take 3 grains at night & 3 do in the morning. Try this treatment, and I hope it will make you feel better.

Truly yours
Charles Lanman

G. T. May 10, 1880
5 P.M.

217　Corps Cadets of West Point

'80年6月10日

[封筒表] Jushie Yoshida Kiyonari and Family

FAREWELL TO '80 FROM '81.

The pleasure of your company is requested at the Farewell Hop, Given to the Graduating Class

June 10th 1880,

West Point.

HOP MANAGERS.

EDWIN ST. J. GREBLE.

SAMUEL E. ALLEN.

JAMES H. WATERS.

EDWARD O. BROWN.

GUY E. CARLETON.

JOHN BIDDLE.

HENRY C. HODGES.

LYMAN HALL.

ALBERT S. Mc. NUTT.

HOMER LEE BANK NOTE CO. N. Y.

〔注〕士官訓練の絵入りのカード。Compliments of the Corps Cadets. と印字された別カードあり。

Richter, C. J.

'80年5月12日

Brewster・&・Co.,

(Of Broome St.,)

Carriage-Builders,

Gold Medal AND Decoration of the

Legion of Honor,

Paris Exposition, 1878.

Bronze Medal AT THE International

Exhibition, London, 1862.

BROADWAY, 47TH AND 48TH-STS.,

New-York, May 12th, 1880.

Chas. Lanman, Esq.,

Georgetown, D. C.

Dear Sir;—

We are in receipt of your esteemed favor of the 10th inst. and in reply beg to offer you our thanks for your efforts and kind words in our behalf to your friend. We are aware that you can purchase carriages at prices below our own, but we believe in the end that ours are cheapest than the lowest priced ones in the market offered at any time. We sell nothing except work of the very best class, and strictly of our own build to the very smallest

'80年5月

details, making our own locks and all the fittings about a carriage which are so necessary to add to its durability and to give satisfaction, as a family vehicle.

Please find herein enclosed drawing of some of the latest styles of Landau. We send you one with a glass front like No. 3554, and the other with leather top No. 3559. We also hand you our price list, on which we have noted the prices of both kinds of carriage.

This is the most fashionable family carriage how in use. We make about an equal number of each kind, both being very handsome and equally convenient. The one with the glass front makes more of an open vehicle when the top is up and does not obstruct the view in front as in the case of the leather top.

The most fashionable linings now are morocco for the lower parts, with cloth combined in the top and on the doors. The dark shades of maroon and green are the most preferred, and occasionally dark blue, which also makes a very handsome carriage, although this color is not so much called

for within a few years back.

The tops of these carriages are made of the very best imported leather, which is celebrated for its great durability, making this part of the vehicle, which generally gives out first, wear about as long as any other part of the vehicle. It does not get hard, not near so soon, or shabby, as the very best American leather, which we are able to get. It is tanned specially to order abroad from carefully selected hides of young cattle, so as to secure the greatest amount of durability.

The trimmings are all selected with the greatest care and are the best imported goods. All the plating and lamps are made of extra manufactured stock, all hand work; the plating is all very heavy and of extra fine quality.

We use the celebrated Rubber Cussioned axles on all our carriages. This adds much to the comfort in riding and obviates greatly the jar and jolt in rough reads. We make these carriages after the foreign style, with stout important looking wheels, as a rule.

We make them in several sizes. The large and

C. J. Richter

〔注〕署名以外はタイプ文字。

219

〔馬車販売の広告パンフレット〕

medium carrying with ease and comfort four good sized people. The smaller size, of which we are now building two, has a little smaller front seat— makes a lighter and more compact carriage,—the front seat being capable of carrying two good sized young people. The back seat is about as usual.

We should be pleased to sell your friend a carriage and if favored with his order he may rely upon our best efforts to give him one that will meet his expectations fully, and we believe that after he has used it a little while he will never have reason to regret the additional cost.

Yours truly,

Brewster & Co.

◆◆◆◆◆◆◆◆◆◆◆◆◆◆◆◆◆◆

PRICE-LIST

(UNIFORM TO ALL)

OF

CARRIAGES AND ROAD WAGONS,

Of Standard Quality, Manufactured by

BREWSTER & CO., 〔OF BROOME-ST.〕

BROADWAY, 47TH AND 48TH STS.,

NEW-YORK.

'80年2月（　）日

March 15th.

Advanced 〔朱字〕 Prices,

ROAD COACH			$2,400	
PARK DRAG			2,600	
LANDAU ..... Leather Top .... Elliptic Springs..Collinge Axles,		1,650 〔以下での列朱字〕		$1,700
" .... Glass Front .... " ...		1,700		1,750
" .... Leather Top .... " " Double Suspension,		2,500		2,600

'80年2月

Carriage	Springs		
BROUGHAM ..3 Sizes, Hard Wood Finish	Elliptic Springs	2,550	2,650
" ....Glass Front	"	1,300	1,350
COUPÉ ....Circular Front, Small Size	"	1,375	1,400
" ...... Medium Size	"	1,400	1,450
GRAND D'ORSAY	Double Suspension	2,250	2,350
COUPÉ	"	1,900	1,950
" "	"	1,450	1,500
LANDAULET, Size A	Elliptic Springs	1,500	1,600
" " B	"	1,550	1,600
" " C	"	1,700	1,750
COACH	"	1,600	1,600
" ....Glass Front	"	1,600	1,650
" ....Curtain Quarters	"	1,550	1,600
VIS-À-VIS	"	1,250	1,300
BAROUCHE	"	1,350	1,400
"	Double Suspension,	2,000	2,050
CABRIOLET ..For Single Horse, Small Size	Elliptic Springs	975	1,025
" ..For Single and Pair Horse	"	1,075	1,125
VICTORIA	"	1,200	1,250
" ...with Rumble	"	1,300	1,350
" ...with Rumble	"	1,650	1,700
" ...with Rumble	"	1,750	1,800
" ...Grand, Detached Boot, and Rumble	"	1,900	1,950
COUPÉ ROCKAWAY, Best Finish	Elliptic Springs	1,100	

'80年2月

CURTAIN ROCKAWAY, very Light, Plain Finish	Three Springs	935	975
SIX-SEAT " " " "	Elliptic Springs...1,100 to 1,450	700	725
STANHOPE PHAETON	" Collinge Axles,	1,000	1,025
DEMI-MAIL " "	" "	1,100	
FULL " "	" "	1,400	
PHAETON, Extension Top, no Arch	3 Elliptic Springs	675	700
" " with Arch	3 "	700	725
" Half Top	4 "	900 to 1,100	
" without Top	4 " "	700 to 800	
" on Side Bars		500 to 550	
" with Doors	2 Elliptic Springs	525	550
T-CART	Collinge Axles,	800	825
DOG-CART, Two-Wheeler, with Shifting Apparatus	Collinge Axles,	$725	$750
" without " "	Collinge Axles,	650	675
PONY-CARTS, Large Variety		235 to 325	
" Small Size, Plain Fiishn [プレーン]		500 to 550	
WHITECHAPEL CART	Collinge Axles,	800	
STANHOPE GIG	"	575	600
LADIES' DRIVING PHAETON, Leather Top and Rumble	"	1,050	
PONY PHAETON, without Top	2 Elliptic Springs	350	
" " " "	3 "	400	

'80年2月

GIG PHAETON, Four-Wheelers, and ⎫ Large Top, Side Lights and Hoods;
WAGONS for Physicians,   ⎬ Full Trimmed 460   480
" " " with Leather Top " with Rumble 3 450
" " " " " 4 725
" " " " " 4 900

HOWELL GIG PHAETON, with Top, Open or Close Sides 440   465
ROAD WAGON.....Standard Style; Shifting Top; with Shafts................. 425   450
"   "   "   " without Top;   "   " 310   325
TRACK WAGON, All Weights... 185
SULKY.. 125
WAGON POLE...Plain Whiffletree Tips...................................... 40
        Extra, for Full Plated Tips..................................... 5

POLE STRAPS FURNISHED ONLY WITH STANDING POLES.
The best Imported English Leather used for Tops of all heavy vehicles.

◆◆◆◆◆◆◆◆◆◆◆◆

Coats-of-Arms.................................... $10 to 15.
NO CHARGE FOR SIMPLE CRESTS OR MONOGRAMS.
Boxing for Shipment will be charged for in all cases, the cost varying (according to size)
from $10 to $40.
Boxing Mail Coach,.............................$65.

NOTICE.

Special attention is called to the fact that we use "*The Rubber Cushioned Axle*," only; and our experience in the use of over two thousand sets confirms the claim that it is the most important improvement in wheeled vehicles ever made.

It lessens greatly the disagreeable jolting, vibration and concussion, and largely reduces the wear and tear.

BREWSTER & CO., [OF BROOME-ST.]

Broadway, 47th and 48th Sts.

P. O. Box 3956.

New-York, February, 1880.

Correspondents will please bear in mind, in addressing us, that the above is our *only place of business,* and that we have no connection with any other concern using a similar name.

〔注〕すべて活字印刷。"TO BE RETURNED TO BREWSTER & Co., OF BROOME STREET, BROADWAY, 47th & 48th STS, N. Y."と印字された馬車の図面二枚付。価格表部分のみもとの体裁を尊重し一段組とした。

220

Gregory, H. D.

'80年5月17日

Blair Presbyterial Academy.

Blairstown, N. J.

May 17th, 1880.

To his Excellency Kiyonari Yoshida,

Minister Plenipotentiary from his Majesty,

the Emperor of Japan,

Dear Sir,

I hope that you have had a safe and pleasant voyage, and that your abode with us may be long and happy.

To-day a letter from my highly valued friend Dr. K. K. Mayeda, which had been forwarded by the gentlemen of the legation, tells me of his health, and that because you are his warm friend you were about to do me the kindness to bring with you from Japan something which he wished to send to Mrs. Gregory. For this, I thank you very much, and ask that you will be so kind as to let me know if there is any thing which I can do towards its safe transmission to my wife at this place.

The railroad to Blairstown begins at Delaware, N. J. a station of the Delaware, Lackawanna and Western Railroad, which starts from New York. We can also come from Philadelphia to the same place. I usually receive in safety articles thus directed

Via Delaware,

D. L. & W. R. R.

H. D. Gregory,

Blairstown,

N. J.

In sending from Washington, it might be best to put before the above

Via Penn'a R. R.

It may be, however, that you have at hand in Washington, a better knowledge of Directions than mine.

Please to（ﾏﾏ） let me know of any thing to be attended to on my part, and believe,

Under great obligations

Yours truly,

H. D. Gregory

Ans;
（以下異筆）
Dear Sir.

17th inst. your favour of the 17th inst. was rec'd with pleasure. Many thanks for your kind expression for our welfare. Mr. Mayeda's letter in question was forwarded by me. The package he entrusted me with for your good lady has not arrived in Washington. It will however reach my hand about beginning of June with our personal effects etc. as they are on the way from S. Fco to this city.

So soon as it reaches me I will have great pleasure in forwarding forthwith to you.

221　Northrop, B. G.

'80年5月18日

State of Connecticut,
Morgan School,
Home Office of Secretary of Board
of Education,

Clinton, May 18 1880.

Hon. Yoshida Kiyonari,

My Dear Sir,

I congratulate you on your prosperous journey & safe return to your important & responsible portion in Washington.

I sent you my paper just printed on "Rural Improvement".

Possibly you may find time to glance at the articles it contains. See "Contents" p2, on "Tree-Planting" "Recuperation of Sterile lands" & "How to improve the Homes & Home life of the people"

Most truly Yours
B. G. Northrop

222　〔差出人不明〕

(’80)年5月23日

尚々、折角御身御愛護専一と奉存候。

御当府へ滞在中は通常の如く無例之御心身を蒙り更に不知所謝也。尚爾来非常の御苦労も不被為在御精務中ならんと遙に奉歓喜候。愛輔并に野夫に於ても在御安着以来碌々勉励罷在申候間乍余事御安意可被下候。いまだクラーク氏には面会いたし不申候得共、いづれ不日見舞に差越御伝言等可申述含に御座候。先は御礼まで荒増以禿筆奉得尊意候。謹言

五月二十三日

吉田清成閣下

223　Gregory, H. D.

'80年6月5日

再伸甚恐縮之至に御座候得共何卒御令閨様え可然様御鶴声可被成下候。敬白

'80年6月

Blair Presbyterial Academy,
Blairstown, N.J.
June 5th, 1880.

Dear Sir,

You will be pleased to hear, that the package which you were so kind as to take charge of reached me to-day in perfect condition.

Renewing my sincere wishes for your health and happiness, I remain under obligations,

Yours very truly,
H.D.Gregory.

To His Excellency
Yoshida Kiyonari,
Minister from the
Empire of Japan.

224

Lanman, C.

'80年
6月
13日

Georgetown June 13 '80.

My Dear Mr. Yoshida:
Thinking that Mrs. Yoshida might relish some fresh currents I send over a few.

I also send over for Foomi a bit of cake which
〔吉田文〕
was made by Ume.
〔鎌田梅子〕

If you have decided the Lot question, you might send me the result and I will notify the Superintendent to day, — so that he can give his orders tomorrow morning. Hope you are quite well again.

Sincerely Yours
Charles Lanman

H.E.Mr. Yoshida

P.S. Should the currents prove to be too—acid they might be stewed with a little sugar.

225

五十嵐文次〔カ〕

('80)年5月12日

何なりとも御用被仰越候はゞ難有至極に御座候也。

別封川崎祐名老台より小倉への一封乍恐縮御渡被成下候様奉願上候。

去る四日海陸無滞華府へ御安着被遊候趣今朝の新紙に相見へ大祝恐賀至極奉存候。然は閣下御脱錨爾来本邦異事も無少候へとも紙弊〔ママ〕の下落随て物価の騰貴下民の

迄差上拝借之儀御聞済被成下候はゝ無窮之大幸
に奉存候也。

苦悩不一方由に御座候。何にか良薬もなきものかと至
る所囂々然たる事に御座候。又国会開設論者も集会条
例に障られ当時は泣寝入の姿に御座候へとも却て種々
の密会の盛ならんかも難斗由に御座候。去る八日は招
魂社祭礼にて例の相撲相催され退出掛け寸猪〔ママ〕と相覷き
候処梅ケ谷と武蔵潟の取組は余程揉合長くして喝采震
動遂に梅ケ谷の勝と相成申候。尚引続き回向院にて去
る十一日より相催居候由に御座候。閣下本邦御在府中
何時なりとも参館　尊顔を拝さるべくと御不沙汰勝に
罷在候処、御脱錨爾後愚児の慕意切々として誠に心細
く相感し日夜閣下御帰朝の速かならんを祈念罷在候。
追て暑気相催候処折角時下御保護被遊候様奉希願候也。

誠恐頓首

　　五月十二日

　　　　　　頑児又次百拝

　　吉田公使閣下

尚々、乍末奥様御愛子様へ御伝声偏に奉上候。
甚た恐縮之至に御座候へとも御残し置に相成候
御書籍之内経済書等大切に取扱候間証書志村様

226　五十嵐文次〔カ〕

（'80）年6月4日

追て薄暑の候　御隻様始め弥御壮栄の御儀と奉恐賀候。
扨内国之諸品騰貴の折柄とは云ひ至て平安之姿に御座
候間御安意可被遣候。頑児儀も公務精励罷在候。既に
川崎老台に乞ひ爾後被服課に転し三四月中は千住勧農
局製絨所へ絨地質の検査法及ひ同品取扱方習錬之為局
長に言上外二名と共に罷越、目今は陸軍在庫数万の絨
及綿類に毎年縮綿并に手入を人夫にて為せし所、今度
は製絨所の器械に倣ひ人力にて運転せしむる一二の器
械を設置せんと自ら課長に謀り昨今頻りに奔走罷在候
処、有識者も成功の保証も為すに付将に着手を乞と欲
する処に御座候。弥成功するに至りては莫大の人力及
金円を省き申候。頑児性来の愚痴は勿論実に浅学にし
て世上に一切を奏する能はず、爾来少々経済学に心を

'80年6月

用へ余間に勉強罷在候へとも児が果して読書位にて（ママ）は奏功益難しと右之被服課に転候次第にて、則ち倉庫数百庫有之内外の物品にて十二聯隊の予備及ひ常備常用共其数の莫大なるに驚入申候。然るに一般物品の精粗を知るもの少き而已ならず定額金の重且つ貴きを知つて物品の要目つ貴きを問ふ者少く実に歎すへく、尚倉庫数多の人夫を使用するが有て是又大に研究の一助と相成申候。然るに要用なる物品貯護の方法荷渋き運（ママ）搬の軽便其他器械等に付川崎老台よりも屢尋問に相成候へとも、如何せん経験も無之而已ならず別に工夫を凝すの寸気も無之唯愚意を労する而已に御座候。尚又内国の事情を聞見するに農業起らず工業敢て盛なるに非ず、諸器械或は内国の物品に付発明力を養ふが如きは敢て問ふ者なく、実に我皇国より政体の美良なるを欲すと雖とも如何せん弾丸黒子の地工業盛大ならされば決して対等する能はず、当時輸入愈盛大なり誠に不肖の身随分苦慮罷在候。就ては頑児右等粗官民の事情も相分り帰朝後一ケ年半余の経験せし処にて多少之相

違も無之事と愚存仕候。只是の上は今一度洋行して前件の事情等を実験見聞せんと欲するの意切々として寝食を忘るゝ事に御座候。此段追々大蔵省商務局有識者等の説を聞くも専ら同説にて弥愈愚意切々たり、伏て希くは　閣下既往の罪を顧みられず特別の御憐愍を以て偏に御尽力を奉伏度、前件の目的を達せんと欲さば願くは領事館に如かずと愚存仕候、伏て米国なり英国なり再行仕度　閣下非常の御愛顧を垂れさせられ井上（馨）卿閣下へ添書一通次便下賜度決して　閣下の御尊意を煩すに非ざれば成就せざるの儀にて　閣下の御添書を頂戴せし上は井上西郷閣下等へも相願ひ是非と（従道）も相願遂げる意に御座候間幾重にも　閣下特別の御愛顧を以て次便必す一通御添書候間志村様迄御封入被成下度、（道）頑児生来の大願に御座候。児品行の義は昨年来父母同居既に妻対も仕り児が不品行より一家一葉の風波を生せし儀も無之候。児今三ケ年外出するも陸軍は不申及一国の事業を助けんとするも決して遅きに非さる也。実に児昨今の熱心するや愈切に御座候。

26

閣下旧来の罪業を顧れず昔日の児は今日の児に非さる

とし幾重にも児が目的貫徹仕候様偏に奉歎願上候。

閣下御在府中も児が奉願上度存候へとも未た二年を経すし

て事情に通せさるの御教示も可有之と差控居候。然る

に爾来少々見聞を広くするに愈再行の要用なるを知り

実に安居する能はす呉々も奉歎願上候也。　誠恐々々頓

首

　　六月四日　　　　　　　　又次百拝

吉田公閣下

乍末奥様へ宜く奉願上候。何にか御用も被為在候

はゞ被仰下度奉願上候。

尚々、前件の歎願は偏に御聞済の上次便御取斗奉

仰上候也。

227　佐和　正

（'80）年7月12日

謹啓　私共一行六名英国より一昨十一日当港え着来

る丗一日桑港出帆之郵船にて帰朝之筈に有之候。明十

三日夜之汽車にて其府え罷出直に十四日朝参館可仕候

条御縫合御面会被下度。　此段申置候也。

　　七月十二日　　　　　　　　少警視佐和正

吉田全権公使殿閣下

〔注〕New York, Westminster Hotel 用箋。裏面に吉田朱書

で以下の書込有。

「十四日朝参館、佐和、林、小野田、万中、藤井、納富、

以上六名同道大統領へ紹介し快話数刻にして辞す。国務

大輔大蔵大輔海軍卿代理へ各紹介しパテント役所へいた

り夫より議事堂見物せしめて帰館、此日暖度殆と九十度

なり。

　　　　　　（カ）
昼飯をリダスにおひてすゝめ夕飯は宅においてす。十

五日朝皆発。」

228　Johnston, W. W.

'80年7月13日

Delaware Water 90h.
（ﾅ）
July 13 1880,

Mr. Yoshida Kiyonari,
My Dear Sir,
Your letter was forwarded to me and imme-

diately conate to S. M. Cornes. He will care & see the children & tell how he can be sent for in case his services are needed. I am glad to hear that Mrs. Yoshida & the baby are doing well. I shall soon be in Washington & may be able to aid you in the search of a nurse, but, at present, I do not know of one.

I have no doubt that Mrs. Yoshida will be able to leave for Deer Park soon after I return, and it will be better for her to do so than to remain in washington. I hope until I see you, that you are way keep well.

Your's resptfully
W. W. Johnston

229　川崎寛堂

'80年6月1日

一簡拝呈、倍〔ヤヤ〕御清穆御起居奉恭賀候。頃日は航路無御滞御着米相成候由伝承拝賀之至奉存候。却〔カ〕説当地御出発前は種々御厚意を蒙り万謝紙上難尽爾来書中可奉窺候処、日々紛忙に打過乍存御疎濶相成候段御海容万乞仕候。御地之近況如何新聞紙等にて領知仕候得は方今イレクシヨオン之段如例騒紛を極め申候形状左も可有之想像仕候。就ては彼馬関事件も如貴説弥本年之国会には行れ申間敷と奉存候。依て本年十二月集会之期を希望仕候外有之間敷、而して其期に先ち御施策之次第も可有之兼て愚考之辺熱心難止御座候間何卒尚御厚配之処為公私万希仕候。御地之形状は追々御了知可被為在候得共御出発後之形況を慨述候はゝ左の如し。民間には自由主義之論弥よ盛にして国会論者（真偽はさてをき）と云もの至る処に散満す（中には国会の何物たるを知らず只の熱に浮かれたるものも多かるべし）片岡謙吉等の建言書御却下後又一層反動を起し過激者を増殖せし形勢なり。しかし官にては厳重なる集会条例発行ありて種々沈圧に御配慮なり○貿易の形状は日に衰へ輸出入の平均などと云事は何時視得べきを知らず、商人社会は頃日銀貨取引所米商会所の停止にて人心胸々、一片の御布告にて株〔シェヤホルドル〕主は其財産の半を損失し一時金銭財布の大騒動

'80年6月

を醸し殆んと所謂パニックなりし、例へば倫敦のロヤ
ールエキスチェージ又靭育[ママ]のヲールストリート之買売
を一日停止せは如何なる影響を起すべきものなるべし
と嘆思す、方今銀貨と紙幣の差は三十二銭より五銭迄
位なれとも是れ全く大蔵省より売出し銀貨あるゆへ也
○新任の Minister of Finance 大なる勉励のよし、銀
貨の差は四十銭を越さす可らずとの御決心なりと風説
す、然れとも天然の相場は稍もすれば五十銭以上の勢
なり○大隈は実に心痛の形状なり、左もあるべし、野
人の語には該氏をして退かしめんと企つるものありと
世評なり○世上にては種々の風評あり、或は渋沢が銀
行のクレジツトを以て「ライスヲ買入たり銀行は云々
云々との説か立ちそれがため該行より預け金を引反す
もの多く渋氏の栄誉[ノール]にも関し気の毒なものなり○市中
ウェートペルソンは何をなす事も出来ず当惑を極め候
事無限也○米価は騰貴々々と唱へて都下の市民は困難
の色を顕せり、然れとも其実際に至ては米価のために

困するものは敢て想像するほどにも非る由、之に反し
田舎は近年米大に富を増し田畝の価非常に貴き由、本
年の麦作も只今の景状にては上作のよし、国の為賀す
べき事なり、茶は本年豊作且売れ方景気よし、生糸の
市場平穏にして且価低下なり、工業少しも進まず僅か
に繁昌を致すものは「マツチ」製造所のみなるべし。
各省又定額減少の説あり、或は減員又は事を大簡にな
すとの風評、しかれとも内閣に色々議論あり、とかく
一定せざるとの事也。

前文拝陳仕候通り弥本年十二月国会之期前自然御着手
相成候は丶国家之大幸、且小生熱心之情御採用も被成
下候は丶乍不及心力を尽して聊か報国の一端を表し度
奉存候。しかし小生之微力何之成功如何んと痛心仕
且又其内命を蒙り候も小生力之及ぶ所に無之、到底閣
下之御愛顧御保護を蒙り不申候ては成就難相成次第有
之、只々只管　閣下に哀訴仕候義に御座候。何卒微志
御憐察被下置若可然時期を以て　閣下より其筋へ御照
会相成自然小生嘆願之義御許容相成候は丶実に小生終

（　）年（　）月

身之大幸と奉存候。依て此義此上とも御賢慮を万希仕
候なり。
先は右爾来之御左右窺度旁拝陳如此御坐候也。拝具
頓首

　　　　十三年六月一日夜於
　　　　東京蠣殻町二丁目廿四番地

　　　　　　　　　　　辱知
　　　　　　　　　　　　川路寛堂㊞再行

　古田公使閣下
　　恭呈

尚以時季折角御保愛為国奉祈候。当地小生相応之
御用も御坐候は〻何卒御命令奉希度奉存候也。

230
〔行楽先についてのメモ〕

（　）年（　）月（　）日

Narragansett Pier.

Leave in the morning—six hours to N. Y.—go directly on fine boat—pleasant night on the sound & next morning, after an hour or so in the cars arrive at the Pier.

231
〔グラント関係電報①〕

'80年6月20日

Blank No. 1.
THE WESTERN UNION TELEGRAPH COM-PANY.

This Company TRANSMITS and DELIVERS messages only on conditions, limiting its liability, which have been assented to by the sender of the following message.

Errors can be guarded against only by repeating a message back to the sending station for comparison, and the Company will not hold itself liable for errors or delays in transmission or delivery of Unrepeated Messages.

Same air as Newport, but more quiet;—good cottages; many picturesque attractions; several best physicans [ママ] from Baltimore and Philadelphia have cottages there;—hotels frequented by refined classes; and N. Y. morning papers reach the place in afternoon. Fishing, if desired, and many things to sketch. Many interesting places easily reached.

'80年6月

This message is an UNREPEATED MES-SAGE and is delivered by request of the sender, under the conditions named above.

A. R. BREWER, Sec'y. NORVIN GREEN, Presi-dent.

Received *at Telegraph Office in Palmer House, June*

Dated Washington D. C. 20 1880

21

To Yoshida (Japanese Minister)

Palmer House

Madame and all doing very well. Cable from Enouye says Kuroda requests you to answer about Grants stallion.

Akasawa

Forwarded from Galena Ill

22 Collect 83

Send your telegrams to the Palmer House Telegraph office.

READ THE NOTICE AT THE TOP

〔注〕イタリック体はスタンプ。

232 〔グラント関係電報②〕

'80年6月19日

Dated Washington D. C. 19 June 1880

Received *at* Galena Ill June 19 4. 33 PA

To His Ex. Mr. Yoshida

Japanese Minister

Care Gen Grant

All first rate, The boy yourself to Gen Grant mentioned in todays Herald

Lanman

13 paid NS

〔注〕21と同一様式につき印字部分は略す。

233 〔グラント関係電報③〕

'80年6月17日

Dated Washington DC 6/17 1880

Received *at* Union Depot Pgh 440pm

To His Excellency Mr. Yoshida

Japanese Minister

Nchgd Ex gorngwesh

'80年6月

Care Depot Master

Doctor at twelve said both improving nothing
new.

Lanman

8 paid

〔注〕231と同一様式につき印字部分は略す。

234

〔グラント関係電報④〕

'80年6月18日

Dated Washington DC 18 1880

Received *at Telegraph Office in Palmer House,*
June 18

To His Ex Mr. Yoshida–Japanese Minister
wife says she is much better both improving no
news.

Lanman

10 paid cy

Send your telegrams to the
Palmer House Telegraph Office.

〔注〕231と同一様式につき印字部分は略す。イタリック体は
スタンプ。

235

〔グラント関係電報⑤〕

'80年6月18日

No. 29

Dated Galena Ill 18

To Yoshida, Japanese Minister
Care Cal Fred Grant

Rec'd at cor. Lasalle and Washington Sts.
CHICAGO, Ill. June 18 1880

Will be glad to see you. Yanada will meet you
and bring you directly to my house.

U. S. Grant

17Dh a

〔注〕231とほぼ同一様式につき印字部分は略す。ただし冒頭
に（ANSON STAGER, Vice-Pres't. Chicago, Ill.）の名の
印字もあり。

236

〔グラント関係電報⑥〕

'80年7月18日

Blank No. 2
THE WESTERN UNION TELEGRAPH

COMPANY

ALL MESSAGES TAKEN BY THIS COM-
PANY SUBJECT TO THE FOLLOWING
TERMS:

To guard against mistakes or delays, the
sender of a message should order it REPEATED;
that is, telegraphed back to the originating office
for comparison. For this, one half the regular
rate is charged in addition. It is agreed between
the sender of the following message and this
Company, that said Company shall not be liable
for mistakes or delays in the transmission or
delivery, or for non-delivery, of any UNRE-
PEATED message, whether happening by negli-
gence of its servants or otherwise, beyond the
amount received for sending the same; nor for
mistakes or delays in the transmission or delivery, or for non-delivery, of any REPEATED
message beyond fifty times the sum received for
sending the same, unless specially insured; nor in
any case for delays arising from unavoidable
interruption in the working of its lines, or for
errors in cipher or obscure messages. And this

Company is hereby made the agent of the sender,
without liability, to forward any message over
the lines of any other Company when necessary
to reach its destination.

Correctness in the transmission of messages
to any point on the lines of this Company can be
insured by contract in writing, stating agreed
amount of risk, and payment of premium thereon
at the following rates, in addition to the usual
charge for repeated messages, viz.: one per cent
for any distance not exceeding 1,000 miles, and
two per cent, for any greater distance. No
employee of the Company is authorized to vary
the foregoing.

No responsibility regarding messages at-
taches to this Company until the same are presented and accepted at one of its transmitting
offices; and if a message is sent to such office by
one of the Company's messengers, he acts for
that purpose as the agent of the sender.

Messages will be delivered free within the
established free delivery limits of the terminal
office—for delivery at a greater distance, a special

'80年6月

charge will be made to cover the cost of such delivery.

The Company will not be liable for damages in any case where the claim is not presented in writing, within sixty days after sending the message.

A. R. BREWER, Secretary.
NORVIN GREEN, President.
READ THE NOTICE AND AGREEMENT AT THE TOP.

Send the following message, subject to the above terms, which are agreed to.
To Japanese Legation

Washington D.C.
Arrived here Nine half; will leave Nine. This evening reaching Galena Six tomorrow.

Yoshida

July 18 1880

237
〔グラント関係電報⑦〕
'80年6月18日

0556 No. 401 233pm

Dated Lafayette Ill. 18
To His Excellency Jushie Yoshida Kiyonari—Japanese Minister—at some hotel
Rec'd at cor. Lasalle and Washington Sts.
CHICAGO, Ill.　　June 18 1880

Telegraph me when and where you will be at Chicago as I am hungry to see you.

Geo B. Williams

17 paid Gi
〔注〕235と同一様式につき印字部分は略す。

238
〔グラント関係電報⑧〕
'80年7月18日

THE AMERICAN UNION TELEGRAPH COMPANY is not to be liable for damages aris-ing from any failure to transmit or deliver, or from any error in the transmission or delivery of, an unrepeated telegram, beyond the amount received for sending the same. But, to guard against errors, the company will repeat back any telegram, for an extra payment of one-half the

'80年6月

regular rate, and in that case it is not to be liable for damages, beyond fifty times the amount received for sending and repeating the telegram.

THE AMERICAN UNION TELEGRAPH COMPANY is not to be liable in any case for damages, unless the same be claimed, in writing, within sixty days after the receipt of the telegram for transmission. And this company is not to be liable for the act or omission of any other company, but it will endeavor to forward this telegram over the lines of any other telegraph company, necessary to reaching its destination, but only as the agent of the sender and without liability therefor.

LESSEE OF THE DOMINION TELEGRAPH CO. OF CANANDA, AND CONNECTING WITH THE FRENCH ATLANTIC CABLE.

July 18 1880

To Genl. U.S. Grant
Galena Ill.

Have just arrived here intend to arrive at Galena tomorrow morning.

Will it be convenient for you to see me then & there?

best compts. to Mrs. Grant.

Yoshida Kiyonari

〔注〕裏面に「六月十七日発カリナ行途中電信往復」とあり。

239

'80年6月17日

Edwards, S.→吉田貞

Strasburg Penn'a
June 17, 1880

My dear Madame,

I will do now what I have wanted to do ever since I knew you were in Washington, but I thought I would wait until you had become thoroughly rested, and felt somewhat at home.

I heard with great pleasure indeed that you had arrived with your little family. I cannot tell you how anxious I am to see you. Mr. Yoshida, and darling little Foomi〔吉田文〕, not forgetting the strange little gentleman, whose acquaintance I guess I could soon make.

There has not been a day since you left Washington that I have not thought of you all. You

'80年6月

have occupied a large place in my heart ever since I learned to know and love you, and I have greatly treasured the kindness and lose you always showed me while I made my home with you.

I trust that you and your family enjoyed good health while in Japan. I suppose the time passed very rapidly to you.

To me, it seems so long; enough has occurred to make it appear like years instead of months.

After my dear father's death, of which I wrote you, my health was very poor for months, my nervous system was completely prostrated, but through good medical treatment, and change of air and scene I recovered, and am now in my usually good state of health.

Miss Ball writes me, you are not so well. I am very sorry to hear it, I hope our good doctor Johnson will soon make you well.

I suppose Foomi has changed much since I last saw her, let me see, it is a year and a half. On Saturday next she will be three years and seven months old. I hear she shatters altogether in Japanese. She will soon pick up English care should be taken that she does not learn it incorrectly from her nurse. Has old "Mamsie" come to see her? I hope you have a good nurse, and will have no trouble with any of your household arrangements, it is very annoying when they go wrong.

I was exceedingly surprised when Miss Clara Ball wrote me of Mr. Takahashi's marriage, I think they both acted foolishly, I was not favorably impressed with Miss Erp when at the Legation.

I gave Mr. Takahashi credit for too much good sense to act so indiscreetly. I suppose the girl he married is the same that visited you.

But I must stop writing, or I will weary you. I have been wondering whether my little "father" and "mother" missed their "big daughter" and if they felt quite at home without her. I do not think I have changed much. I am a little older and a little wiser I trust. Kiss Foomi and the little one for "Kattie".

It would be a great pleasure to hear from you. Love to Mr. Yoshida and your own dear self.

Your affectionate friend
Sallie Edwards

To Madame Tei Yoshida

240　Edwards, S.

'80年7月1日

1953 Nth 7th st.
Philadelphia Pa.
July 1, 1880

My dear friend

Your telegram has just been received forwarded me from my home.

I thought I would write as I could more fully explain my long silence in answering your dispatch. I have been here for several days, having my eyes examined. The vision is very indistinct of the left eye. Will be compelled to remain probably two or three days longer under treatment.

In the meantime could I know more explicitly as to your desire for my presence. If urgent, I might arrange matters so as to come on. Will hope to hear from you. Excuse poor writing, have belladonna in both eyes and am hardly able to see what I am doing.

1953 Nth. Seventh st. Phila. Pa.

Your friend S. Edwards

In great haste & much love

P. S. Telegram says "three children" and yourselves "are well". Can it be possible? If so I send my heartiest good wishes.

S. E.

241　Edwards, S. →吉田貞

'80年7月5日

Strasburg, Penn'a
July 5, 1880

My dear friend

Your very kind and pressing letter reached me in Phil'a. As soon as I received it, I made immediate preparations to return home and just succeeded in making the train. I have concluded to accept your kind proposal but will need a day or two to make preparations for leaving. I shall come by way of Phil'a, where I shall have to halt to see the Dr. I left rather abruptly and before his business with me was quite completed. You did not say what time you would probably leave Washington. I will try to be with you on the 8th. or 9th. hope it will be satisfactory.

I am very glad to hear that you and your little one are so well.

There will be time for me to receive any word you might possibly wish to send me.

Affectionately your friend Sallie Edwards
Madame Tei Yoshida

Two children (以下異筆書込) must be sent to Deer Park tomorrow or Thursday but I can not go with them. This was the reason I wanted you to come up at once if at all you will come to us.

If you can't come at once we will have to engage other person to go with my children to Deer Park as I can't as yet take them myself. The weather getting so hot that I would not like to have them in city any longer. I am daily awaiting your arrival as I wish you to take my 2 ch. to Deer Park being myself nor strong enough yet. If you can't come immediately some one will have to take them at once the weather getting so hot that we would no longer wait & keep them in city.

telegraph back

Mrs. Yoshida.

〔注〕異筆書込部分は吉田貞返書案ならん。"Reason I telegraphed & requested telegraphic answer was". "Mr. Yoshida though very busy will go with them" などの抹消箇所あり。

242

Edwards, S.→吉田貞

'80年7月10日

Deer Park Pa.

July 10, 1880.

My dear friends

You received my telegram reporting safe arrival. The ride was about as agreeable as could be expected.

Haru was taken sick almost as soon as we got fairly under way and was dreadfully so the entire way. I fortunately kept firstrate and waited on all hands. (吉田文) Foomi was as good as a kitten, took a long sleep. Kiyo took two naps fretted some until be got (吉田清閲)

accustomed to his new bed. Katie did admirably. I took Foomi with me to supper, Katie gave her her bath and both are now asleep. I ordered tea in the room tonight for Haru & Katie as she K. did not want to leave Kiyo. I feel the responsibility pretty heavily.

I have arranged for milk from one cow, to be boiled and kept on ice. There is no crib in the room, a cot can be put up but the room you mentioned to me for baby is too small, the central one would be better, as it is much larger. A cot will not answer, as baby could not be left in the bed alone. You will, I suppose have to send Kiyo's crib from home. Katie will have, in the meantime, to sleep on the edge of some bed. Thermometre registers 74° and will be down to 70. It is very pleasant. Shall I send soiled clothing home next week?

I deposited $25.00 in the office. I paid 3.00 to conductor for seats, 55cts. to porter, 30cts. for coffee at Cumberland, and 25cts. for oranges. I think you gave me $1.20 in small change instead of $1.30 I cannot find ten cts. I did not lose any. Katie says Kiyo sings "by by Mamma by by

Katie".
It is late and I must go to bed.

Write soon,

Love to all

Sallie Edwards

P.S.
I will keep you posted.

243

Edwards, S. →吉田貞

'80年7月11日

Deer Park Hotel

July 11, 1880

Dear friends

I suppose you will want to hear from the children again today. The baby's towels have been somewhat loose. He had five operations since we arrived last night at five o'clock, until five this evening. I had the Dr. come this morning. He said the baby would naturally feel the change, of milk etc. for a day or so, he left powders which were given him when not sleeping. He took a long nap this afternoon and afterward a ride in the Park in

Dear friends

Kiyo is much better no operation through the [吉田清風] night and best one this morning. Katie says he was very bright in the Park throwing kisses etc.

The air was damp early this morning. Yesterday (Sunday) the thermomete 82 at 2 o'cl'k. I think it was hot in the city. I telegraphed last night for crib, netting & bath-tub.

Kiyo is now taking his morning nap. 3 P.M. Dr. has just gone says he considers Kiyo a well boy. I hardly know how to manage about Foomi's [吉田文] meals. Haru thinks they must be just the same as at home.

In that case I would have to order them to be brought to the rooms. Dinner is from 1 to 3, supper at 7. I think Foomi could eat dinner, which is the heaviest meal, in the middle of the day with me, and for supper take simply bread & milk, which would be quite as healthful, and save useless expense of having meals served in room.

Yesterday Foomi slept all afternoon, and consequently could not go to sleep very early in the evening. Haru thought it was supper, when the his carriage he was out this morning too. Katie is very attractive and watchful. I had her dinner [オ] brought to the room as Kiyo [吉田清風] was fretting and I shall do so whenever he is. There is no occasion for you to feel troubled. The baby takes his milk and enjoys it, he drinks it altogether from the tumbler. The ride yesterday was very disagreeble, we were swung about dreadfully, which was enough to disarrange the baby's stomach for a little while. I think he ought to have his crib. The doctor will come again tomorrow.

Foomi keeps very well. I stick to them closely [吉田文] I tell you, and do the best in every way I can. Dr. said he had not heard from Dr. Johnston.

Will write again tomorrow.

Affectly

Sallie Edwards

Deer Park. Md.
July 12, 1880

'80年7月12日

Edwards, S. →吉田家〔カ〕

'80年7月12日

child eat very simply.

If you will tell Haru what to do or me I will be glad.

The children have gone out now after thin naps.

Affectly,
Sallie Edwards

245
Edwards, S. →吉田家〔カ〕

'80年7月13日

Deer Park Md.
July 13, 1880

Dear friends

Children are well. Baby looks firstrate. No occasion for woriment.〔ママ〕 Foomi takes breakfast 〔吉田文〕 with me, and lunch and supper in her room, will so continue until you come.

This hall is very noisy. You may make some change when you come. I think for the present I will have a cot put up in the central room which is the largest, now occupied by Foomi & Haru. The housekeeper informs me, as well as Mr. Dennis, that I can get no crib, not even at Oakland. Had the telegram been punctuated you would have understand. "Express Crib, netting, & bath-tub. Sheeting is available here". There are no mosquitoes, I believe, but flies are very troublesome. It seems we can get little here, there are few conveniences. I can get sheeting, but none of the other three articles. There is no laundry connected with the Hotel. I have given the clothing to a woman outside. I do not know yet how she will do. The hotel sends working to Cumberland which I think would be inconvenient. You can get carriages here suitable, large or small, without horses, so if you please you can bring your own horses.

4.30 P.M.

Dr. has just left. He is a very pleasant man. Kiyo takes wonderfully to him. Dr. carried him 〔吉田清風〕 around a long time. He left powders as Kiyo had two movements today which were quite loose.

He will be in again in the morning. I have not been quite well. I got powders from Dr.

Will be wonderfully glad to see you, we are lonesome too. Foomi sends kiss to Papa & Mam-

'80年7月

ma & "Chesi" baby. Foomi says "Kiyokasi too". Kiyo says he loves papa "in there" pointing to his heart.

Mrs. was glad to hear from you. We can get no bananas about here & Foomi seems to crave them.

Affectly,
Sallie Edwards 〔マ丶〕

S. E.

246

Edwards, S. →吉田家〔カ〕

'80年
7月
14日

Dear friends

Deer Park, Md.
July 14, 1880

All doing well. Baby took a splendid nap and is bright and good seas out in the park this morning and Foomi and he are now out.〔オ〕 Netting〔吉田文〕 cannot be gotten nearer than Bolt, so this "Romeo" proprietor told me, so I thought Mr. Akasawa might buy five or six yards of cheapest kind, double width, and you can bring with you.

You might order some bananas Bryan would do them up so they will keep nicely.

You ask my opinion about the place. It is what Lake George would be without the Lake.

It must be healthy here, and it is so quiet, still the few people who are here manage to make considerable noise on this floor. The table is tolerably good, but the room appointments are very meager. Then the waiters here have been exasperatingly slow in executing an order, but that is improving. Dr. Mclomas says there is considerable complaint about the hotel. It changed proprietors since the spring.

That Mr. Adee sat at our table one evening for supper. It seems he was here but over night I have not seen him since.

I am glad the shoes came I spoke of them before we left. The weather here for a few hours in the middle of the day will be quite warm but the evenings are very cool mornings also. I think the children will thrive while here.

Mr. Dennis has just told me boarding for horses is $500 per head a week. The carriage, a side-

'80年7月

seated one he referred to, he could not tell now, could be fixed when you come.

So Dr. Johnston is coming with you? I feel quite forlorn and lonely at table.

Foomi & Kiyo send kiss to Papa & Mamma. [吉田清風]
I think Madame will like it here. Give love to her. [ヲ]

Affctly,
Sallie Edwards

Bring Foomi a doll-baby this one she has is comming to pieces.

247

Edwards, S.→吉田家〔カ〕

'80年7月15日

Deer Park Md.
July 15, 1880

Dear friends

I have not much to say but think you will look for some word. Your long letter was received this morning. The thermometer at the hottest here I believe was 87° or thereabouts, on the porch. The nights particularly are quite cool. Dr. comes every day and sometimes looks in twice a day. He read a letter to me today from Dr. Johnston. Baby is doing well considering his complaint, two operations today. He sleeps better now, both children seem to have gotten accustomed to the noise, and sleep right along notwithstanding the orchestra plays near by in the vestibule where you enter.

Telegram received Gentleman not arrived yet, will perhaps come in late train.

Kiyo laughed over the photos, and kissed & bit [吉田清風]
it. But I have them two in my trunk. I want say what I did. I don't know whether I will get to Oakland. The Dr. says I ought to go at 10 A. M. and take dinner & return at 2 P. M. and if I missed the train he would send me back in his carriage. I could then tell about the table, but I wouldn't like to leave babies so long.

I have not said anything about changing our rooms. He will have the opposite ones opened tomorrow.

If it is not too much trouble I would like you to bring me a pair of slippers suitable for walking; not to pay more than $2.50. Size 3½ C. my shoes are

( )年( )月

not very comfortable.

P.S.

My clothing I left for washing Madame will
please bring.

The small crib would answer but Katie thinks
baby can do now, I had a cot put beside the bed and
it does very well.

The same can be done for Foomi if you think
best.

With love to all
Sallie Edwards

S. E.

S. E.

248

〔メモ〕

( )年( )月( )日

1 Pr. Bronze Vases —— Parlor
1 Set of New Photographs —— Mr. Y.
1 Fine Painting of Peacock —— Office
1 Lacquer Box—Octagon —— Parlor
4 Ps Embroidery —— Mr. Y.
a Pressed Picture —— Mr. Y.

249　橋口文蔵

'80年6月24日

謹て奉呈愚簡候。先以て尊公にも此内は数日間御旅行
被遊□〔候力〕由、炎天之折柄嘸汽車中等御退屈千万被為在
候事ならんと奉遠察候。併し尚無御違変御精務被遊御
座候半奉歓喜候。抑過日差出申候一愚書は疾く御掌握
被下候半と想像仕候。然処今午後一字比愚弟より電報
を以て申越候には、今般私程久敷希望せし欧行之企を
御許諾不被下候と承り実に愕然然失望とは此事、唯々天
を仰き尊公の御許認被下ざる之御趣意を拝誦仕度、次
報を足をそばだて待而已に御座候。いづれ此事件に付
ては深く御思召のありての事に相違無御座、抑是は私
一身上に付き不充分なる行状等有之に因る乎、或は其
外に御思召に不叶事ありての訳にや、如何程勘
考仕候ても想像付き兼申候。元来私が此欧行を企し事
は一時疎考之結果には更に無御座極々素志にて、殊に
唯々手を懐にし欧洲諸国を回遊し耳目を楽しむる

'80年6月

為めに行くのとは断然天地の差違にて、勿論一書生の
身上御座候へば金等も余計には無御座訳にて、譬へ望
んでも遊山抔といふ事は出来ざる訳に御座候間、ケ様
な希望は更にいたし不申候。第一私の希望する所は外
国に留学する間に普仏の両国へ差越御熟知被遊候彼ビ
ート砂糖製造等専ら実地上に学び充分にやり付け申決
心に御座候。然らばやがて本邦へ罷帰りし上は幾分か
其製造等に尽力し、随て一ケ年八百万円許の輸入の巨
額も追年減少し、夫のみならず折々は其輸入之惣高を
外国へ仰がさる様相成り申に於ては、国の為め一大利
益ならんと愚考仕申候。勿論最初より御許諾無之内は
我侭勝手にする考は更に無御座候得共、よもや御異論
はあるましきと推察し当校長はしめ其他クラーク氏等
へ私の目的を物語り申候処、いづれも夫を慂慂〔悪〕し是非
其砂糖製造方充分に学び得て日本へ帰らば莫大の利益
ならんと申候に付、昨今旅装最中之処、豈計哉斯の如
き尊命を蒙り頓と筆頭に尽し難程の失望に御座候。其
上来年中には此学校を卒業する決□〔心カ〕に御座候へば此夏

の如き好機会も再び来不申、且つ何国に居ても相応之
入費に及び申事ゆへ僅欧州往来の旅費を投ち尤便益あ
る所に此休業を消光し私の素志を遂げ度と斯くは相□
申候。其見込にて昨年中は非常に節倹を勤め少々儲
蓄□あり、殊に憔悴なる事には彼ミシガンのホープ
カーレヂよりの□金も数日前に相達し申候ゆへ欧州
へ暫時留□金と旅費の事に付ては今更少も心配する
に及不申候。夫故□□恐縮之至りに御座候得共彼開拓
長官殿への愚生の願□□御取消被下度奉伏願候。勿論
金が充分にあれば其□□事は無御座見る物も多く見ら
れる訳に御座候得共、また一方之点より見れば却て金
が充分にありて余程人品が卑賤に成る而耳ならず、厭
悪害を引き起す元因と成る事其例不少、一書生の為め
には充分にあるよりや不充分にある方遥か優れりと愚〔ママ〕
考仕申候。先は以禿筆荒増私の目的を寸時も早く申上
候。何卒乍恐縮今一応篤と御勘考被下候て私の心中を
御憐察之上別願書を御許認被下度、唯々旻天に号泣し
奉歓願候。恐惶謹言

'80年6月

明治十三年六月二十四日　開拓使生徒

特命全権公使

吉田清成殿

橋口文蔵

250

橋口文蔵

願書

'80年6月24日

〔注〕□は破損により判読不能。

頓首

折角〳〵御身御愛護之上御勤務被遊度遙に奉祈候。頓首再拝

申候間、可然御取計被下度奉歎願候。

是は私の誤謬に御座候間、又々別願書相認め差上

再敬白此内差上申候件は届書に相認め申候得共、

私儀自費を以てビート砂糖穿鑿之為め当夏休業中或は

時機に依ては四五ケ月間欧良巴洲へ罷越度御座候間、

此段御免許被下度奉歎願候。恐惶謹言

明治十三年六月二十四日　開拓使生徒

特命全権公使

吉田清成殿

橋口文蔵

251　〔馬車メンテナンスの広告チラシ〕

（　）年（　）月（　）日

AMMONIA.

An accomplished chemist, engaged in applying his science to the needs of manufacturers, writes as follows, in answer to a request for a brief account of the effect of ammonia upon varnish:

"When a varnished surface is sponged over with even the weakest solution of ammonia, then washed and exposed to the weather, it cracks in two or three weeks, although the most durable of varnishes may have been used; and the ammonia evolved from the manure of stables is responsible for many cases, otherwise mysterious, of the rapid decay of varnish exposed to its action.

"The pungent alkaline gas unites with the oil of the varnish, forming a soap which, being soluble in

〔B. G. Northrop による日本の進歩に関する
New York Tribune 宛報告（償金関連）〕

252

（’80 カ 年（ ）月（ ）日

CHINESE AND JAPANESE INDEMNITIES.

[The following paper from the *New York Tribune* is timely, as the bill for returning these Indemnities is now pending. Any influence you may exert for this measure, with your member of Congress or through the press, will further a worthy object.]

WONDERFUL DEVELOPMENT IN JAPAN.

An earnest letter from the Hon. B. G. Northrop, Secretary of the Connecticut State Board

of Education.

The report of the Committee on Foreign Affairs just made in favor of repaying to China and Japan the unexpended indemnities so long held by us, calls for information in regard to them. The Chinese indemnity was essentially an overpayment made more than twenty years ago. Every President from Buchanan to Hayes, and every Secretary

'80年（ ）月

water, is removed by washing, leaving the surface apparently uninjured, but poorer in oil, and consequently less durable.

"The expansion caused by the sun's rays; and subsequent contraction of the new brittle varnish, soon produce cracks, which show especially on the upper surfaces and salient angles, and the same parts of the vehicle are most subjected to the influence of the ammonia by the falling on them of particles of dust impregnated with the gas.

"In all cases where a carriage has been standing in an atmosphere of ammonia, I recommend sponging with a *weak* solution of vinegar in water, to be followed by a thorough washing in pure water."

ANDREW J. JOYCE,
Carriage Manufacturer
Nos. 412, 414 and 416 Fourteenth Street,
WASHINGTON, D. C.

〔注〕活字印刷。

of State from Cass to Evarts has held that to use this money for our sole advantage would be derogatory to the honor and dignity of our country. Our Ministers to China, including Burlingame, Ward, Low and others to the present time, have all expressed the same sentiments. His imperial Highness, Prince Kung, when consulted on this subject, said that self-respect and National pride would forbid his doing anything that could be construed into a request, being content to leave it to the American Government to follow its own sense of justice, but the return of this indemnity would be highly honorable to the United States and advantageous to both countries.

The Japanese people justly regard their indemnity as an extortion. The Daimio of Chosiu, who warned off foreign vessels from the Straits of Shimonoseki—for this was the offence—was then "a rebel," for whose acts the Japanese Government was hardly more responsible than ours was for those of Jefferson Davis during our rebellion. The Japanese Government promptly expressed extreme regrets for those "outrages on foreign commerce,"

an apology which would have been accepted from any European Government. The Japanese might have contended that this narrow strait—at some points less than a mile wide—was an inland arm, subject by the laws of nations to their own control, even to the extent of excluding foreign vessels, and that therefore no offense had been committed.

So far as I can learn there is but one opinion among intelligent people conversant with this subject as to the injustice of this exaction. In December, 1872, I sent to the Faculties of all the colleges and prominent educational institutions of this country a form of petition to Congress in favor of returning these two indemnities, requesting their signatures. This request received a general and prompt response. This collection of names was as remarkable in quality as in quantity. When pasted together, this grand list of "petitioners" was presented to the House of Representatives, Jan. 27, 1873, by Gen. Joseph R. Hawley, where it was found long enough to stretch quite across the large hall of that body. This petition, with the names of all the signers except mine, was printed and presented to the members of Congress.

I also sent a small tract, prepared for that purpose, to the leading journals in all the States. With one exception, so far as I could learn, the comments of the press were favorable to the return of these indemnities. Since then, lecturing on this subject in ten different States, I have found ample proofs of the growth of this sentiment in various parts of the country. Several successive Committees on Foreign Affairs have recommended that this money be refunded. A bill for this purpose once passed the House of Representatives. In 1872 another bill, remitting the balance then unpaid, was passed unanimously in the House, but was not reached in the order of business in the Senate. Their return has long since seemed to me to be only a question of time. But the present time is specially opportune for this movement. The present is a critical time in the history of Japan, so long treated as if she had no rights which the great powers were bound to respect, and thus brought to the verge of National bankruptcy. The Japanese have been the victims of frauds and spoliations from foreign Governments as well as foreign traders and contractors. They have also made enormous outlays in their grand system of internal improvements. At one bound Japan has jumped from the fifteenth to the nineteenth century. Railroads, telegraphs, light-houses and light-ships along their vast sea-coast (far exceeding ours—Atlantic, Pacific and Alaska coast all included), war steamers and iron-clads, dry docks, hospitals, iron suspension bridges and a national army of 30,000 men, drilled in French tactics and equipped with breech-loading rifles, are among the many signs of material progress.

The moral and intellectual advancement is still more remarkable as indicated by the new and general thirst for knowledge, especially of Western science and civilization, the introduction of modern inventions and all forms of internal improvements, the organization of an admirable post office system, letters prepaid with penny "1 sen" stamps like ours, a mint rapidly coining gold and silver corresponding in size and value to our own and far more elegant, daily and weekly papers—some of them illustrated—adoption of our calendar making Sunday the rest-day in the mint, post office, custom house and all Government offices, and prohibition of the sale of obscene books and prints. According to the report of Postmaster-General Mayesima for the year ending July 1, 1879, the number of letters, newspapers, books and samples sent through the post offices the last year was 55,775,206, giving an increase of 18 per cent over the previous year. There was a marked development of their news-paper enterprise. The number of Japanese journals mailed in 1879 was 16½ per cent more than in 1878, and 52 per cent more than in 1877. Though there has been during the year a large increase of post routes and 135 new post offices, 635 new stamp agencies and 487 new street letter-boxes, the income of the Department exceeded the expenditures by $122,978. The *Tokio Times*, of January 31, 1880, well says: "The Japanese Post Office, now thoroughly and systematically founded, shows, in pecuniary results, an excess which has not been achieved by similar establishments in any other part of the world."

But of all the progressive movements of Japan, her educational plans are the most significant. Realizing that ignorance has proved a source of waste and weakness, they have now learned that knowledge is power—the source of individual thrift and of national strength and prosperity. When in February, 1872, Arinori Mori, the former representative of Japan to this country, sent me from the Legation in Washington a formal invitation (which was not confirmed by the Home Government) "to accept a position under the Japanese Government which would give you the supervision of education—al affairs, and make you an adviser of the Government on all those subjects in the Empire of Japan", he enumerated among the duties to be performed, the aiding in organizing eight colleges, 256 high schools or academies, and 53,500 public schools. Much as has already been done, this magnificent scheme is still in abeyance,—not from any reaction or diminished appreciation of education, but solely from the financial embarrassment consequent upon their remarkable efforts to introduce all modern improvements in the briefest possible time. Though still prospective in many of its details, this

'80年3月

grand educational ideal is an inspiration to the Nation. Ardent and enthusiastic, perhaps the Japanese consider less the obstacles to be overcome than the advantages to follow the introduction of such a system of universal education.

The new measures must of course meet opposition. Conservatives are still found who deprecate foreign influence and recount with all the force of glaring facts the many wrongs already suffered from Europe and America. They glorify the past and denounce the ills unknown in the good old days of isolation, and foremost among these wrongs in the honest judgment of all Japanese and indeed of all honest minds conversant with the facts is this indemnity outrage. But in the face of manifold spoliations from abroad and difficulties at home, a new era has opened for Japan,—the noblest in all her long history, and indeed this revolution is the most remarkable that ever occurred in the world in the same limits of time. As an act of justice and an expression of National sympathy, and what is still rarer, an illustration of National conscience, the return of this indemnity would exert a moral influence of greater value than the money refunded, removing existing prejudice and increasing American influence and commerce, for England, France and Holland are involved in the same wrong, in which England was indeed the prime mover. No nation ever more needed or merited the sympathy and encouragement of the world than Japan in the present crisis of her affairs. Never in all our history have we had the opportunity of aiding so easily in the regeneration of a great nation. This plain duty, or rather this privilege, we cannot afford to neglect.

（注）活字印刷。

〔魚雷艇の広告チラシ〕

'80年3月25日

THE HERRESHOFF

PATENT IMPROVED

REPEATING TORPEDO LAUNCH!

Manufactured of the best material and workmanship under the direct personal supervision of the Inventors and Patentees,

253

and ADOPTED by the GOVERNMENTS of the UNITED STATES, RUSSIA, and GREAT BRITAIN.

D. D. CONE, General Agent, 1305 F street N. W., WASHINGTON, D. C., U. S. A.

The Herreshoff Torpedo Launch has been greatly improved and its destructive powers more than doubled during the past twelve months, and now possesses many advantages over all others, being, in fact, the only *Repeating Torpedo Launch* in the world. Its armament consists of *four spars*, each carrying a powerful torpedo, *arranged to strike the enemy four times in rapid succession,* above or below the water as may be desired, and without stopping for one instant to reload. Extra spars and torpedoes can be carried, and readily adjusted while in action, to strike eight or ten times in rapid succession, if necessary, and without returning to the ship or land. One Herreshoff Launch will, in fact, *do more than four times the execution of any other.* It bears the same relation to other launches that the Winchester *repeating rifle* does to the ordinary single breech-loaders.

The steam is supplied by the Herreshoff patent steamgenerator invented by the Herreshoff Brothers, and the subject of two patents in the United States, Great Britain, and other countries, which will raise one hundred pounds of steam within six minutes of the time the fires are lighted. It consists of a coil of pipe three hundred feet long, is less than half the weight of other boilers, and absolutely safe from explosion. Guaranteed speed, eighteen miles per hour, over a measured course. Larger engines and boilers will be built by special contract to drive at a higher speed, if required. The peculiar construction of the boiler and engine adds greatly to the lightness of the launch, *enabling it to be hoisted on davits with wonderful facility.*

At competitive trials with other launches one year ago in the United States, Russia, and Great Britain, the Herreshoff Launch was unanimously decided to be the best in every essential particular. It gets up steam in six minutes as against *fifty minutes* by the next quickest competitor. In general agility of movement in the water, stopping, turning, going backwards, &c., and in maneuvering torpedoes, no other launch could for one instant be compared with it.

In regard to the Herreshoff Launches in use at the United States Torpedo Station, where naval officers are instructed in torpedo practice, the Secretary of the Navy reports that "*they are fulfilling all the conditions required*," and that one of them "*has made a run of twenty miles in one hour, and for short distances a speed of upwards of twenty-two miles per hour has been attained*."

The reports of the Russian and British Admiralty Officers who tried the Herreshoff Launches purchased by their respective governments, a year ago agree in substance with that made by the Secretary of the United States Navy.

Since the above-mentioned trials, the Herreshoff Launch has been greatly improved, and its improvements thoroughly tested and proven, and now it is safe to say that it will *more than* fulfil the expectations of its patrons. Each launch is furnished complete with booming out engines, four poles or torpedo spars, electric apparatus, all necessary tools and spare parts, six torpedoes, and five hundred exploders, all complete and ready for instant service. Percussion or electric torpedoes may be used, and either or both kinds will be furnished to order in quantities to suit purchasers.

We usually have one or more launches on hand complete, with all necessary appliances for service, *ready for inspection, trial, and immediate delivery*; and are prepared to build them to order *at the rate of ten launches per month*, if necessary. They are made of the very best material and workmanship, and are tried and proved before delivery. For further particulars apply to or address—

March 25, 1880. WASHINGTON, D.C., U.S.A.

D. D. CONE, General Agent,

〔注〕活字印刷。

254

VALENTINE'S
PREPARATION OF
MEAT JUICE.

'78年12月1日

〔ミートジュースの商品説明パンフレット〕

TRADE MARK.
LETTERS PATENT
GRANTED
APRIL 25TH, 1871.

AWARDS

International Exhibition,
PHILADELPHIA, 1876,

"For excellence of the method of its preparation, whereby it more nearly represents fresh meat than any other extract of meat, its freedom from disagreeable taste, its fitness for immediate absorption and the perfection in which it retains its good qualities in warm climates."

UNIVERSAL EXPOSITION,
PARIS, 1878.

RICHMOND, VIRGINIA, U.S. of America, Dec'r 1st, 1878.

The circular which was issued in 1871, and has been used since as a wrapper for the "Meat Juice" bottle, is now enlarged, so as to enable me to offer, besides extracts from the important testimonials therein contained, Hospital, Army, and other reports. Thus affording evidence for seven years regarding the applications of the "Meat Juice."

After seven years, therefore, during which time I have been engaged in perfecting the "Meat Juice" and establishing the principle involved in its production, I find that beyond a record of my labors, there is but little required to be said by me, since distinguished evidence has so fully and fairly estimated the value of the "Meat Juice" and determined its applications, that there seems nothing wanting to an understanding or appreciation of it.

I desire, however, on this occasion, to invite attention to the concurrent testimony that, extending through a series of years, sustains opinions from first to last, and general confidence in the preparation:—indicating with the maintenance of the character of the "Meat Juice" uniformity of results have been obtained; and that all I could have hoped for in my original thought and intention in the conception of a nutritive principle had been realized.

I shall, therefore, simply submit the evidence to which I have referred, with the remark that, during quite an extensive intercourse and correspondence with eminent medical and scientific parties in Europe and America, I have been greatly stimulated and encouraged in my efforts by the deep and sincere interest manifested by them in the momentous subject of foods, but more particularly foods for the sick, and that it will be always agreeable to me, as occasion may arise, to have suggestions from experienced and well-advised authorities regarding my product.

Mann S. Valentine

The Medical profession recommend that the following statements be made:

The two-ounce oval bottle, adopted for the "Meat Juice," contains the concentrated juice of four pounds of the best beef, exclusive of fat; or the condensed essence of one and a half pints of the pure liquid juice which is obtained from the flesh of beef.

The "Meat Juice" has been subjected to heat, and the fluctuations of different climates without change in its character. See testimonial of Dr. Trueheart. The Meat Juice does not freeze.

The use of the "Meat Juice" does not interfere with the administration of any medicines, but it would not be advisable to mix acids or alcoholic liquers with it, as they may impair its nourishing qualities. Take the "Meat Juice," therefore, a short time before remedies. The use of hot *water* with the "Meat Juice" *changes its character and injures its value.*

The use of seasoning for the "Meat Juice" has been wholly abstained from, leaving to the medical adviser all directions in this respect required for the sick.

It has been recommended that, whenever the stomach from irritability fails to retain food or medicines, the "Meat Juice" be employed to prepare that organ for, or reconcile it to, other nourishment and remedies.

Time for taking the "Meat Juice," as recommended.—before meals, (see Dr. Weisiger's manner of using it,) on rising in the morning and retiring at night, and with debility, during the night.

Regarding the application of "Meat Juice" in the *nausea of sea sickness*, see testimonial of Dr. Bradley, of Cunard Line of Steamers, and reports of surgeons of American and Red Star lines.

Its application after excessive or habitual drinking, see testimonials of Drs. Miller and McSherry.

For its use hypodermically, see note of Editor Va. Medical Monthly.

MODE OF ADMINISTRATION.

The minimum dose in extreme cases should be a half-teaspoonful, diluted with a tablespoonful of water, *cold or tepid*—increased to two teaspoonsful, diluted in proportion. A further dilution has been advised of half-teaspoonful to one and a half, or even two tablespoonsful of water, or infants. In the administration of the "Meat Juice" by *enema*, the directions are the same as for the stomach, except that the quantity should be larger.

METHODS OF PREPARING AND INCORPORATING THE "MEAT JUICE."

The best way to take the "Meat Juice," rendering it an inviting and grateful drink, is by the use of cool or cold water with it. If preferred, use ice in it.

The "Meat Juice" may be warmed on a water bath to the temperature of 130°F.—but as this requires *great care*, it would be advisable to so prepare it only when positively necessary.

Stale bread, crumbled in the "Meat Juice," makes a savory diet for the sick, while it constitutes a safe advance toward solid food.

Where Cod liver oil is objectionable to the stomach, the "Meat Juice" commends the oil to its acceptance and digestion.

Glycerin may be employed with the "Meat Juice" when directed by a physician.

（中略）

VALENTINE'S MEAT JUICE WORKS.

[Extracts from notices of Richmond Press.]

Among the industrial institutions of Richmond

whose onward progress has been watched with pride, is one which, apart from its merits as a manufacturing establishment and a source of revenue, has contributed to the honorable distinction of Richmond in other respects.

The Meat Juice Works of Mr. Valentine have again been removed to more commodious quarters. A building has been constructed and adapted to Mr. Valentine's special purposes and provided with all the elegant machinery and appliances demanded by the increasing popularity of the Meat Juice.

Hundreds of thousands of pounds per annum of the choicest beef are now required for the production of the extract. The large cattle pens and slaughter house for the Meat Juice are situated on 25th street and Nine Mile Road. There all the preferred portions of the beef are selected and the bones and fat removed previous to delivery at the Works, where the meat is submitted to Mr. Valentine's processes for the elaboration of the Juice,

We would state that those portions of the animal which are not used for the Meat Juice—as the ribs and other pieces, the tallow, hides, bones, &c., are each and all readily disposed of to the various co-operative enterprises of this city, while the *pressed meat*,—residue after the extraction of the Juice, known as "Meat Cake," is in great demand among our farmers, who feed it with corn meal and vegetables to their hogs and fowls.

As a consequence from this important enterprise among us, a large quantity of material also, is required for marketing the Meat Juice, in the form of bottles, wood and paper boxes, printed matter, &c., that contribute to the general welfare.

As was seen by us in the opening of the New Works, yesterday, there was a striking contrast between the contrivances employed since the commencement of the great enterprise and the now new and elegant machinery and appliances demanded by the increasing popularity of the Meat Juice.—*Richmond Enquirer.*

Our object is to call attention to the fact that a discovery has been made which has been hailed with gratitude by invalids in all parts of the country, and challenged the admiration of all physicians and scientific men, and that the production of the

'78年12月

Meat Juice here in Richmond is to constitute a not unimportant branch of the varied industries of our city, with its now population of 79,000.

The valentine Meat Juice Works are fitted up with improved machinery, adapted to the work to be done. During our visit to the establishmen, we were particularly struck with the neatness and cleanliness of the employees, and the great care taken with the preparation at each stage of its production. No kitchen in Richmond presents a nicer appearance than the apartment in which the beautiful machinery performs its varied work, while the superintendent and his assistants are engaged in their several delicate and peculiar duties.—*Richmond Dispatch.*

Not only is the Meat Juice used in case of sickness, but as an article of food in compact form, as a Summer drink instead of liquor, and a beverage at the table of the wealthy, it has grown into great popularity. It is carried on ocean steamers, and has found its way into many lands—its portability rendering it especially valuable to explorers and travellers.

The beef used for the production of the Meat Juice is reared on the extensive pastures of West and Southwest Virginia. Mr. Valentine, after having made trial of cattle from all portions of this country, Texas, included, finds the Short-horn Durham stock, raised on the nutritious grasses and in the genial climate of the Virginia pastures, the most perfectly matured, largest juice-yielding, and all things considered, the most economical and satisfactory material for his product. He uses only heavy, muscular animals weighing from 1,500 to 2,000 pounds.—*Richmond Whig.*

SPECIAL.

The "Meat Juice" is prepared by intelligent and experienced labor, under my personal observation. Only the best material is used for production, and its purity and identity will be maintained.

The "Meat Juice" is put up in bottles of only one form and size: *a two ounce, oval, amber bottle,* with two labels. On one label is printed my signature, and on the other my trade-mark. The "Meat Juice" is sold directly to the trade. I have no

(　)年(　)月

travelling or other agent, except Mr. IRA W. BLUNT, who is located with me in this city.

MANN S. VALENTINE, Richmond, Va.

AGENT'S NOTICE.

In response to the increasing demand for Valentine's Meat Juice, and with a view to the more extended production of this dietetic new Meat Juice Works have been erected. They have been arranged for our special use with improved machinery and appliances for the more satisfactory prosecution of our advancing home and foreign business.

From February 26th, 1877, therefore, our office will be on the spacious Court, entered from 11th street; our Works may be approached either from Cary, 11th or 12th streets; our cattle pens and slaughter house, as before, 25th street and Nine Mile Road.

The "Meat Juice" may be obtained from the druggists, wholesale and retail, throughout the United States, Canada and Europe.

IRA W. BLUNT, Agent for Valentine's Meat Juice, Court, bet. Main & Cary & 11th & 12th Streets, Richmond, Va., U. S. of America.

（注）活字印刷。中略部分は医師98名分の推薦文。

255

〔芳香剤の商品説明チラシ〕

(　)年(　)月(　)日

EUCALYPTINE.

A TOILET PREPARATION OF ACKNOWLEDGED EXCELLENCE.

CLEAN AND AGREEABLE IN USE.

Eucalyptine is a balsamic compound based on products from the Eucalyptus trees of Australia, imported directly for its manufacture.

Eucalyptine preserves the natural softness and flexibility of the skin, and maintains it in a healthy condition at all times.

Eucalyptine protects the skin from the injurious action of cold and windy weather.

Eucalyptine is an infallible healer of chapped hands, rawness of the nostrils due to cold, cracked lips, and cold-sores. It is emphatically unequalled for these purposes.

Eucalyptine immediately removes that disagreeable dryness and roughness of the hands which is occasioned by household occupations, gardening, and similar employments; it may be frequently used in small quantities after such work.

Eucalyptine is a specific for cuts, scratches, and abrasions, acting as an emollient and antiseptic, with gentle stimulating properties.

Eucalyptine is an invaluable remedy for Hemorrhoids. It cannot be too strongly recommended to those who suffer from them, as it gives rise to an immediate healthy reaction which terminates in a complete cure.

Eucalyptine cures burns, mosquito and other insect bites, and sunburn; also, irritated and inflamed surfaces generally, produced by chafing or other causes.

Eucalyptine is very beneficial in many forms of eruptive disease; it allays itching, is antiseptic and healing in its action, and excludes the air.

Eucalyptine, for the above reasons, is especially useful in the treatment of cutaneous troubles in childhood. It may be used, moreover, in any quantity with absolute safety.

Eucalyptine is an admirable toilet article for application to tender or chafed feet, soft corns, bunions, &c. Its perfect cleanliness, antiseptic and lubricating properties, especially adapt it for this purpose.

Eucalyptine is most serviceable and agreeable applied in small quantities to the face after shaving.

Eucalyptine has a strong, somewhat camphoraceous odor, inseparable from it, which is refreshing and pleasant. This is the same fragrance which pervades the great Australian forests. It is the dissemination of these volatile, antiseptic substances which undoubtedly gives that country its immunity from zymotic disease.

Eucalyptine can be applied to the hands and face *at all times*. It is delightful in use, not only on account of its healing and soothing properties, but also because it is entirely *free from greasiness or clamminess*, and will not soil the clothing in the least, or interfere with any occupation.

Eucalyptine differs from all other toilet articles in these important properties as essentially as it differs from them in composition and effective-

( )年( )月

ness. Those persons who use it once will continue to do so.

Eucalyptine is sold by all druggists—Price, 25 cents.

W. A. VARIAN & CO.
212 Delaware Avenue,
WASHINGTON, D. C.

〔注〕活字印刷。

256
〔馬車修理の広告チラシ〕

( )年( )月( )日

NOTICE!

CONCERNING REPAIRS.

Carriages for summer use needing repairs should be placed in our hands in MID-WINTER, and WINTER CARRIAGES as soon after the 1st JULY as possible. This will insure better attention and better work, and give time for the hardening of varnish before use.

Carriages received for repairs *are not insured* against loss by fire and the elements, unless specially agreed upon.

Storage will be charged on all Carriages remaining in our shop two weeks after notice is given of their readiness for delivery.

Freshly varnished Carriages should be washed frequently, and exposed to air and light, and should not be covered until the varnish has become hard. MUD LEFT TO DRY UPON FRESH VARNISH WILL LEAVE SPOTS.

ESTIMATES.

In submitting estimates for repairs, we aim to make them full and complete, so far as an examination of the carriage before it is taken apart will permit, but in the case of very old Carriages broken and worn-out parts are often discovered when the work is being done, and these should be made good to secure safety as well as economy. These additional repairs will always be made, unless the owner directs otherwise, when the carriage is placed in our hands. Any item found in our estimates may be stricken out and notice given to that effect.

Customers are assured that all repairs will be charged at *regular and uniform prices*, whether

estimates are made or not, and that all work in-
trusted to us will be done in the best manner, and
with due regard to safety and true economy.

Orders may be left at my Factory,

412, 414 & 416 FOURTEENTH

STREET, N. W.,

Andrew J. Joyce,
Washington, D.C.

〔注〕活字印刷。

絵入新聞に右形容を載せ有之候間差上申候。先は取急き右まて申上候。草々拝具

　十一月二十六日

　　　　吉田清成閣下

　　　　　　　　二郎拝

257　二郎

　　（'80）年11月26日

拝啓　閣下幷に御挙家御清栄被為在奉賀候。当地もシーパンに向少しく賑々敷相成候。本月十九日本館近方の14th st. Circle にゼネラールトーマス氏の銅像を建立し各地方より多分の兵隊来会建立式を助け候。多人数の群集近来稀有之事にて有之候○グラント氏の名望甚た盛之様子にて改進党中明年大統領に挙けん事を欲するもの不少由、或はニカラグウハ運河会社のプレシテンドたらん事を望むものありと、同氏に関し昨日の

258　小倉治郎

　　'79年11月26日

尔後御佳勝之御事と奉拝賀候。追々御送致申候グラント氏欧亜回覧実記次編第十一十二三本今便拝呈仕候間、乍憚御落手可被下候。

一別紙受取書之通昨週ウォームリーより払方願出候処、仕払可然者に候哉難相分候に付、御幸便之節否御報知願申候。同人事は頓に御帰任相成候儀と心得近頃迄遷延仕候訳之由申出候。尤も右之趣閣下へ可申通旨同人へ申置候。

一先便治郎昇級之儀不取敢御吹聴申置候処右に付今便更に拝謝申述度候。治郎事帰朝之念更に無之現在之地にて事務勉強仕度志願にて罷在候間、其辺御含将

'79年11月

来たりとも不相替治郎身上に関し万端不悪様御掛引
被下候様願申候。
右御見舞旁陳述仕度候。草々謹言

　　十二年十一月二十六日
　　　　　　　　在華府
　　　　　　　　　　小倉治郎再拝
吉田清成様閣下

259
　　天野瑚次郎

'79年11月26日

小書謹呈仕候。然は閣下愈々御清康拝賀此事に有之候。
小生義も無事在勤罷在候。去春以来遂に一封之拙翰を
も拝呈仕らす久濶之罪幸に御海恕被下度候。小生義今
般外務二等書記生に被任再ひ華盛頓公使館在勤被命候
に付、謹て拝受仕候間、此段御吹聴申上候。右昇級云
々義は小生欣然拝受する処に候得共、唯其任に堪へさ
らん事を恐れ候のみに御座候。此一条に付ては固より
閣下に於て種々御尽力被下候事と存候間、右は閣下に
対し小生之深く陳謝する処に御座候。此事たる曩に新

官拝命之後次便早足御礼可申上候処、本省行公信発出
之際殊之外多忙に有之候より遂に遷延して今日に至り
候段、真に不相済義に候得共、幸に御仁免可被下候。
当地格別異事無之候、唯我公館近傍にある小公園即ち
第十四街「ソルクル」と唱へ候地へ頃日故ゼネラール、
トーマス氏之銅像設立之儀式有之、大統領を始め内閣
官員大審院判事各国交際官員陸軍武官及ひ其他之諸人
之に臨み、甚た盛大なる儀式に有之候。我公館よりは
小生臨席仕り候。先は謝詞旁御通知如此に御座候。頓
首再拝

　　十二年十一月廿六日
　　　　　　　　　　天野瑚次郎九拝
吉田公使閣下

二白、閣下御令室へ宜敷御伝声奉願候。先達て御
子息□□有之候由、右御祝儀申上候。以上

260
　　Dickinson, P. T.

'80年1月5日

179. Bluff

'79年11月

Yokohama
Jan 5/1880

To His Excellency
Mr. Yoshida
Minister to the United States
Sir

The enclosed Letter of Introduction from Mr.
John Russel Young reaches me per Steamer Gailic.
I have the honor herewith to transmit it to your
Excellency.
And to be Yours Very Truly
P. T. Dickinson

261

Young, J. R.

'79年
11月
20日

New York Nov. 20, 1879.

My dear Sir:

I take pleasure in introducing to your acquaint-
ance Mr. P. T. Dickinson, of California, who visits
Japan for the purpose of seeing the country. Mr.
Dickinson is a gentleman highly esteemed on the
Pacific Coast, and any courtesy you can show him
will be a great favor to me.
Yours very truly,
Joe Russell Young

To His Excellency Mr. Yoshida.

262

Henry, H. A. →吉田貞

(79)年7月16日

Many thanks, my dear Mrs. Yhosida, for your
generous gifts received yesterday. They are very
beautiful, and have given us much pleasure, and
will ever be a source of gratification as indications,
of your kind remembrance of us when absent.
I hope, you will soon be removed from the heat
which must oppress you and that when you return
we shall have the pleasure to see you and the babies
often, in renewed health and strength.
With the respects of our united household to
Mr. Yhosida & yourself.
believe me
Yours most sincerely
H. A. Henry
Washington July 16th.

（　）年7月

263　Antisells

（　）年7月21日

Mrs. Antisells compliments to Mr. Yoshida and receives with many thanks his lovely little gifts, anything coming from his country is so acceptable. She hopes to have the pleasure of thanking him in person.

July 21st
1311 G st
(ﾏﾏ)

264

（　）年（　）月（　）日

〔食用亀肉等購入についてのメモ〕

Copy

The Japanese Minister
to James Warnley, Dr.

1878
Feb 21	To 3 Cooked Terrapin	900
Mar 26 〃	Terrapin	1000
〃 〃 〃	1½ Doz. Rolls	25
		────
		$19.25

265

吉田清成→伊藤博文

（'75）年（1）月（　）日

〔注〕ペン書、罫紙。本文書以降は"Letters uncopied"とある間紙の後に綴じこまれている。

新年之佳慶千里同風乍恐　聖上益御鎮坐被為遊御楽々大賀至極奉存候。老閣依旧御安泰御加年被成御軫掌候半、奉雀躍候。二に迂生同断、乍憚御降神被下度。僕出立も度々遅延之後漸十一月九日に発帆いたし、海陸無恙通行、去月十六日華府安着、同十八日大統領面謁相済直後より公務担当、碌々消光仕候間、乍余事御休神可被下候。

支那之関係も終に無事平定いたし邦家之美事何か是に過きん他国之傍観者之欣然之至に候。是全憂国之徒余あるか所以ならん当地においても両国之為御言を演る者不少、御賢察可被下候。尚此末内地無事を保候様御注意被成下度、偏に所希望御座候。御存之通当地は至て閑静之地にて殊に頃日議院も休暇にて閉鎖之折、何

'75年1月

も新報珍説無之候。実に僕之当職は緩々充分之余暇有
之候故、久々怠惰之業務も振起せむには是より難有職
務は無之候。御賢察被下度候。是れ少くも三年程は被
取置候様御添力所希候。吉田書記官始一列一統別条な
く幸に御降神被下度候。右年始之賀言且つ安着之御一
左右申進度急々如此御座候。頓首

〔巻村〕
伊藤殿
「伊藤 参議」

〔注〕墨書。

266
吉田清成→大久保利通
（'75）年1月3日

清成

新年之佳慶 聖上益御静臨被為遊御高座老若益御多吉
御加年被成成奉大賀候。扨一簡拝呈仕候、支那之役も終
に首尾能御所分相成、我邦之名誉も益海外へ轟候様に
御談判相立、是全我国民之尊王愛国之真情余溢あるに
基とは雖其器にあらされは、或は万全之策行はれかた
きか、偏に老閣所有自得之深慮、真操以此役を遂くる

に至れり。是我全民之所深謝なり。這般は既に我兵も
退陣相成候事と奉察候。実に此一挙は他国人之内にて
も言路あるものは極冷評相憂候程之一大難事に候へは、
談判相済事平穏に帰せしとの新報を閲し、両国之為祝
言を唱へ候者不少、御賢察所祈也。随而迂夫にも去十
一月九日横浜表を発帆し、海陸無恙通行、十二月十六
日華府安着仕、同十八日大統領へ面謁相済即日より公
務担当、歳末歳始之弐等にて少く要務も有之候へ共、
格別之事にも無之、是よりは追々当政府之各省寮局成
立等今一層視察いたし度心組に御座候。当時議院も休
暇にて格別之珍事無之、下之関償金は是非日本へ惣額
返却すへく、又は半額を返却して残りは日本人、或は
米国壮年輩を撰ひ日本語を学はせるは彼我之浩益とな
るへしとの見込、大統領之題言に相見得申候。併右は
当年暮之議会にて投論可有之と申事に御座候。
近日布哇島之王来米条約改正之二周間程滞府、大ひ餐
応を受けて去る。当時カナダ近辺巡暦最中に御座候。
大統領へ謁見之御国書を附候節下官演舌義、大統領よ

268

Henderson, H. C.→吉田貞

'75年1月15日

Legation of Japan
for the United States of America.
Washington, D. C. January 15, 1875.

Madam:

I write this merely to say that I would be glad
to consult you, in regard to the furniture matter,
whenever it may suit your convenience to call at
the Legation.

Very respectfully yours

Mrs. M. C. Henderson
Alexandria Virginia

〔注〕罫紙、ペン書。ただし全体に対して赤色ペンで「×」
と抹消し、上部に「To be filled in private file book」、中
程に「This was not sent Y. K.」、そして下部に以下のよ
うに記す。

Sent us follows:

Mr. Yoshida will be glad to see Mrs. Henderson when
convenient to her, in order to listen to her wishes
with regard the furnitures of the Legation as he
remembers having once heard her to express her

り返詞和訳為致置候間、奉入御内見候。当政府之人々
依旧親睦之情を厚くし我邦之安穏を切に好する等、或
は他邦に異り候、御賢察可被下候。
先は年始閣下無事御帰朝之祝賀まて申上度、如此御座
候。恐々謹言

〔注〕墨書。

大久保様

一月三日

〔計算メモ〕

267

( )年( )月( )日

85,000,000÷7 ＝ 595,000 Fl.
19,000,000÷11 ＝ 209,000 〃
2,600,000÷22 ＝ 57,200 〃
Total ＝ 861,200

£ 71,766 @ 12fl. per £
〃 72,000 about—

〔注〕鉛筆書。

( )年( )月

desire in keeping them—

'75年2月

269

〔米国州知事・議員選挙に関する報告〕

〔異筆ペン書〕「当国近来珍説之摘要を書取備貴覧候也」

'75年(2)月( )日

去る一千八百七十二年ルイジアナ州に於て知州事其他州官及合衆国議員撰挙の時に方り、夫のデモカラト守成党とレポブリカン改革党両党に於て各知州事を撰みしに、デモカラト党はマクエネリー氏を撰み、レポブリカン党はケロツグ氏を挙けたり。マクエネリー氏は六万五千五百七十九の投票を得、ケロツグ氏は五万五千九百七十三説を得たり。両党の投票を較計するに、マクエネリー氏の投票ケロツグ氏より多き事九千六百有余なり。又同州の議員を撰挙せしに同じくデモカラト党の員多きに居れり。是に於てケロツク氏は州議院集会の期に先ち合衆国地方裁判所へ訴て曰、マクエネリー氏多数の投票を得る所以はレポブリカン党の為に説を出すへき黒人を脅かし其投票を妨けて、以てレポフリカン党の投票を減し自己の党をして多数を得せしめたるデモカラト党欺罔の所為に出つれば国憲に抵触する旨を述へたり。而して華盛頓政府も亦此訴訟に関与し命をルイジアナ州に在る華事に下たし、若し裁判に服せざるものあれは合衆国の兵力を以て之を抑制すべしと、蓋し地方裁判所をして裁断の旨趣を徹底せしめん事を欲してなり。又マクエネリー氏はケロツク党の撰挙を認許なからん事を大統領に控訴す。因て大統領はアットルニーセ子ラル（表法院長）に托し其当否を監別せしめ、マクエネリー氏の申請は允准しがたき旨を指令したり。是に於て合衆国議員の論も二党に分かれり。国会に於ては其議員中より特にルイジアナ事務取調掛を撰み、其事を探索せしめたるに、ルイジアナ州の人民は真に米国政府の抑制を免かれざるの議を（此は大統領の措置の排議する）事務取調掛より報告せり。復た一千八百七十四年同州々議員を撰挙するに方り、前次撰挙の如くデモカラト党多数の投票を得たる事を主張すと雖とも、レポブリカン党はデモカラト投票の内若干数を除却して自

己の党多数を得たりと唱へり。何んとなれば是れは投票の内幾許は僅に数年前まて全く奴隷たりし黒人種の投票によりて其多寡あれはなり

黒人投票の自由を妨けされは、必すレポブリカン党の為めに投票すべしとの想像に起れり。是に於てレポブリカン党とデモカラト党に於て同州内に在る黒人の投票を妨けんか為め多人数を殺害せしめたりと云事を責問せり。果して此会も一千八百七十二年の撰挙に異ならす、大いに紛擾を醸せり。又一千八百七十四年十二月に至り、州議院集会の時に方り一千八百七十二年の如くレポブリカン党はデモカラト党の欺罔を責問し、其州官に就かんとする者を目して乱賊と称するに至れり。因てレポブリカン党より其事由を華盛頓政府に申請せしに、政府は遂に其請にまかせ、ゼネラルセリダンに兵を附し同州に遣はし、兵威を用て議員五名を州議院外に放逐したりと云ふ。是に於てデモカラト党は米国政府に於て州事を左右するは甚た米国の政体に悖戻する事を主張し、大統領及ルイジアナ州出師の隊将セリダン氏等大いに非議を蒙れり。デモカラト

党のみならす数年来大統領に左祖せし有名なる者も此措置を非難し大統領に与せさるより、国会中各執を生し両党有名なる議員等各其党の為めに論弁を尽せり。当時大統領より国会に答弁する所の詞気最前に比すれは稍妥穏なるか如しと雖も、猶已むを得さるの事あるに方りては兵威を用て制止するの権を有する事を固執すと云ふ。抑此紛議の原由に溯るに、デモカラト党に於て人民投票の自由を妨けし事と各区より報告せし投票の員数真正ならさるとに由れり。然れとも両党州政を握るの権利果して孰れに在か、頗る反対の激論あれは其曲直未た知る可からさるなり。此論議未た穏かならさるに、復たアルカンザス州に之に彷彿たる騒擾を醸せし新報によつて更に一層の紛議を生せり。其原由は若し不得已の時に当りては兵を遣すへき旨を大統領の同州のレポブリカン党に約せしに由るなり。次て一千八百七十五年に至り、ピンチベッキと云ふもの華盛頓に来りルイジアナ州の撰挙を得るを以て米国上院の議員たる事を主張すれども、米国上院の議員たる者は

（　）年（　）月

州議院の撰挙を経る事国憲なれは、斯く紛擾の際に方
り確定せさる議院の選挙を得たるものを以て真正の議
員と認むるや否、目今議論中にてピンチベッキ氏は未
た其席に就く事を得さる由なり。

　　　続き

ルイジヤナ州にて選挙したる米国上議院の議員ピンチ
ベッキ氏を真正の議員と認や否の議に於て、一千八百
七十五年二月十七日上議院中頗る激論ありと雖とも、
同氏は遂に国会に於て拒絶されたり。同氏はレポブリ
カン党派の州議院即ちケロツグ党議院の撰挙を経るも
のなれは、若同氏を真正の議員と認むるときは則大統
領の兵力を用て関与するの策を賛くと云べし。故に
此議に関しては大統領党の議員も多く之を拒絶するの
説を述へて、以て大統領の措置を輔けざりしなり。又
アルカンザス州の紛議も全くルイジヤナ州事と同一に
して、一千八百七十二年知州事其他撰挙の秋に方り、
ブルーク氏改革党当年より一千八百七十七年までの間

270

〔Fish, H. 書簡写し〕

（　）年（　）月（　）日

Sir,

〔注〕在米国日本公使館用箋、墨書。＊欄外に「ピンチベッ
キ氏は黒人種なり」とあり。

凡そ一年、大統領はバキストル氏の設置せし州政府を
真正の者と認可せしに、今茲一千八百七十五年一月八
日に至り、更に上議院に報告して曰、ブルーク氏即ち
真正の知州事なり、然るに同氏は暴動の為めに其権利
を圧制せられたるなり、抑此紛議を裁定するの責は国
会独り之に任し宜しく大統領の責任を解放すへしと云
々。

知州事に在任すへきとの選に当れり。因て米国道審院
亦同氏を証認せり。茲に又バキストル氏守成党も同時
知州事の選に挙られたる事を主張せり。是に於て両氏
各知州事の職に就かん事を企謀し、両党各自に州兵を
以て両氏を護衛し両党各州議院を設置せり。今を距る
*

I have the honor to announce my arrival at Washington in the capacity of Envoy Extraordinary and Minister Plenipotentiary of His Majesty the Emperor of Japan to the United States of America. I enclose herewith a copy and an translation in English of the letter of credence addressed by His Majesty the Empelor to the President of the United States and I beg you, M͞r Secretary, to take the directions of the President and to inform me, at your convenience, of the time at which the President may be pleased to give me an audience for the purpose of delivering to him the letter of my sovereign.

With respect & consideration.

Hon. Hamilton Fish

Secretary of State.

〔注〕ペン書。上部に赤鉛筆で「not used」とあり。さらに別の箇所に以下の異筆あり。

Draft of the proposed letter from Y. K. to the Secretary of State on arrival in Washington—not used

Prepared by S. Smith of foreign office

（　）年（　）月

第三者間書翰

一　伊藤圭介発宮本小一宛

明治（10ヵ）年1月18日

謹呈。春寒料峭、台候清健欣忭々々。挹今回吉田公使より到来之由にて米国植物書類五本幷種子数多分御寄贈被下、海岳奉感謝候。右内には奇品も可有之相楽申候。時気相考官園へ培養相試可申と奉存候。先は右御礼之義、御序之節吉田君へ御伝語厚奉願上候。

一、右培養仕候。付ては生長之景況追て委敷可申上候様可仕候。何れ其内晋謁可申上候得共、不取敢御礼着報迄、匆々如斯候也。

　一月十八日　　　　伊藤圭介再拝手

宮本小一先生御案下

二　伊藤博文発井上馨宛

明治15年11月10日

朝鮮の独立は必要｜〈用〉なり。我々の為には実際の扶助を与ふるは甚た利益なり。若し彼れよりの扶助を求むるなれば、彼れは〈先づ〉再び独立を唱ふる為めには、

先つ我が将来の扶助政略に名分を与ふる為に、我々に向て公然の宣言を為すを必要とす〈又同時に於て彼れは

強固なる政府を基因と為して我が扶助に依頼す可し〉。

彼の外交上に付〈際の点に至〉ては、〈彼れが〉頃〈傾

日支那の所属と自ら宣言〈告〉して外国に与へたる国書をば取還すを要す〈戻さざる可からず。如何なれば〉斯る国書は〈恐くは〉向来彼の独立論に関し〈宣言に向て〉多分非常の矛盾〈重大なる撞着〉を来す憂ある〈為す〉可し〈き故なりし〉。

先頃、〈外国と結ひ聞き〉たる彼が外国と締結せし条約は、外廷の批准せざるや必定なり〈する所と為らざる可し〉。多くは〈甚しく〉彼れの勝手〈利〉となる可き条

三　伊藤博文発井上馨宛

明治（17）年3月12日

爾来御清穆敬賀之至に奉存候。去説〔却〕一小事に御坐候処、汚高聴乞明裁度、彼の後藤象二郎之嫡子猛太郎と申者、予て官途何処にても奉職執業致さとて受依頼居候処、勿論以欧学従事するの外無之英学〔独逸学〕、充分と申には無之候得共、且々間に合候丈け之事は可有之に付、外務省中佐々木之嫡子の類例に做ひ、当分御入置被下候儀は相叶申間布候。若し御不用に相成候節は小生御引受可仕、此段一寸願試度、乍御手数吉田大輔へも御談合之上御取捨之程宜布御願申上候也。

　　　　三月十二日

　　　　　　外務卿殿　内願

　　　　　　　　　　　　　博　文

〔注〕後藤猛太郎は同年に外務省御用掛に採用された。

款を多少含蓄するを以てなり〈掲けたる故を以て必らず〉。故に彼に取て最も肝要なる者は、成る可き丈け早く欧洲に使節を派〈差〉遣し、該国書を取戻し、幷〈及〉びに彼れは自助の方向を立てゝ〈彼を扶助する為に最も自由なる思考を以て彼れ自己に〉直接に条約の談判を為すにあり〈可し〉。斯る場合に際しては〈前顕の目途に拠れば〉、我と支那との葛藤は増加するなるべし〈せざるを得ず〉。〈故に〉先づ兎に角に臨時の滋事故を予防する為、〈海軍〉当今の情態に於ては、極力〈都て〉海軍の用意に着手すること〈をするを極〉必要なりと思ふなり〈とす〉。

　　　　明治十五年十一月十日午後九時発

　　　　　　於伯林府　伊藤

　　　井上殿

〔注〕原文書抹消分を〈　〉で、書きかえられた部分を傍線で示した。

井上馨発山県有朋宛

四　井上馨発山県有朋宛

明治19年12月17日

[一部朱印]
[親展送第八四〇号]

条約改正会議録第九、第十英仏文各三部つゝ差進候。
御落手有之度候也。

明治十九年十二月十七日

外務大臣伯井上馨[印]

農商務大臣伯山県有朋殿

（注）外務省罫紙。

五　井上馨発山県有朋宛

明治20年4月13日

[一部朱印]
[親展送第二九七号]

条約改正会議録第二十二英仏文壱部差進候条御落手有
之度候也。

明治二十年四月十三日　外務大臣伯井上馨[印]

六　井上毅発山県有朋・井上馨宛

明治（15）年8月30日

農商務大臣伯山県有朋殿

（注）外務省罫紙。

此書竹添へも伝覧被下候はゝと可奉存候。

廟堂之神算其宜に当り逐次之訓条其図を誤らざるによ
り一大事迅速結局に至候段慶賀奉存候。花房之談判傍
観いたし候処凛乎不可犯之色あり。其労不少と奉存候。
生事一個之満足にて何も用無き事に候へとも、幸ひ三
日間に了局に及へる一大談判に間に合ひ、責て花房之
文筆上之助力抔いたし候事本意之至奉存候。第一之報
告は中山帰朝に托し、猶両三日滞留京城一見いたし、
且調印後之事情も見聞いたし候上にて第二之報告も携
帯し品川丸にて帰朝可致奉存候。
支那人は大院を拘引し朝鮮内政に向ひ十分之干渉を行
ひ属国之名称に違はざる実力を施す之政略に出候とい

へとも、案外我か談判に居仲せずして、却て陰に平和
之結局を誘導したるは、全く外務省之黎庶昌へ対する
覆啓により少し念を入れ考へたるもの歟と被存候。但
し将来何等之変態を現し候も難斗、又朝鮮に対し恩威
並施し韓人をして益々右清左和之心を抱かしむる哉不
可知といへとも、或は却て干渉過度之弊後日収局に
困み候に至るも亦難斗と存候。故に縦令此際各外国に
於て何等之異論有之、我国之反対干渉政略を勧説候も
のありとも、我国は只管一条之針路を取り他に関係せ
ずして専ら朝鮮との和好を保続するの主義に出候事良
計歟と奉存候。右は花房も其意にて有之候。

或は又馬建忠之遠略にて黎庶昌に飛報し我国に於ても
内乱干渉に同意叶力候様之事を掛合候歟も難斗奉存候。
万一右様之事も有之候は〳〵、公法に依り痛く擯斥いた
し度ものと存候。

又朝鮮積衰之余一国独立之気を失ひ、一変して支那之
属国たる事を甘心し、我国に向ても米英に当てたる同
然之書面を送り、日韓条約之第一欵を削除する之希望

を提出するも難斗歟。若し此事あるに於ては実に交際
上之一大問題と奉存候。花房は彼のボアソナド答議之
意味一応御話いたし置候へとも、何れ其報之至候は〳〵
更に御庿議に有之候事と奉存候。

馬関より前日奉筆上候通、李裕元登庸等之事情に依
て見れは、将来は朝鮮之一国は全く李鴻章之掌中に
帰し候事と被存候。馬が所作に依り候へは属国論を
主張して我交際を妨くるに至らず候へとも、李か胸
中は未易測と奉存候。李か喪中にてきりてでる事能
はざりしは一之幸歟奉存候。馬は専ら総理衙門之意
を承け候ものと被存候。

一、賠償之金額に付ては少し過当とも可被恩召歟に候
へとも、是には花房も別に存意有之、何れ帰京拝謁
之上可奉口陳候。

一、王妃幷太子妃薨去に付ては吊悼之国書被差送度、
右は花房之嘱托により奉書上候。

一、馬之挙動分明ならず。一時弐百之護衛と共に京城
に入りし由に候へとも、或は韓使之後ろ仏けに成り

井上毅発山県有朋・井上馨宛

出没いたし候歟も難斗。尤可疑は償金之多額を承諾
せし事にて、是れも韓人は他人之ふところを頼みに
いたし候ものにては無之哉と被存候。明日生京城に
入りて馬之居処も相分可申歟と存候。
一、何れ将来之変態は朝鮮之事に付日清之関係愈々多
端に渉り可申歟と被察候。就ては此節之総理衙門よ
り回査を経たる照会に対せる我か覆照は尤も慎重を
要候歟奉存候。
其他は中山より委詳可奉言上、来月三日迄には生も東
帰発航之心得に付何も奉筆略候。頓首再行
　　八月丗日
　　　　　　　　毅
　井上外務卿殿
　山県参議殿

七　井上毅発山県有朋・井上馨宛
　　　　　　　　明治（15）年9月3日

中山帰京後別に異状無之候へとも、生丗一日済物浦を
発し、本月一日京城に入り、昨二日仁川帰港仕候。京
城にて見る所にては支那之兵多人数にて王宮に屯守し、
宮門外に木柵を構へ、又京城之外門を警戒し、其外に
水兵之記号を付したるものも道路に徘徊するを見たり。
公使よりも委細被申遣候通り、支那兵にて朝鮮乱兵に
着手し、拒捕人を殺死し、朝兵は多分逃竄したる等総
て支那人にて刑政を執行し、朝人は束手聴命之有様と
相見へ候。馬建忠之旅館を尋ね試候処折節不在にて、
留守之者之申す処にては、明日より〔陽〕即ち二日也いふ揚遠号に乗
り南易〔陽〕湾より天津に回り去るといふ。馬去て後事に任
する者誰れなる乎と問へは、呉欽差と答へたり。馬が
去るは定めて再来之積りなるべし。右之景況にて将来
之関係如何之変態を現すべきや頗掛念に奉存候。又支
那之屯兵も不紀律に相見へ候へは、我か兵員は十分に
警戒を加へ喧嘩闘争抔引起さざる様〔柄之助〕高嶋よりも注意し
居に有之候。彼の兵各処に屯営候分も今日は悉皆王城
に繰入れ候ものと見へ、大砲をも運ひ入れ候を見受候。
彼れは何辺迄干渉し、何処にて収局するに〔虫損〕□致なる哉

不審之事に有之候。右等之事情も有之、且今少し見物もいたし度旁々今一と便滞留し、花房京城に前往し愈々異議無き上にて小生は帰朝いたし度奉存候。朝鮮人は京城其外道中にても懇ろに接待いたし、公使は何つ頃再たひ入京なる哉、館舎之掃除等の手当いたし候。宜敷也抔申居候。人民は稍や安堵して業に就く様子に有之候。家具を背負ひ帰宅するもの陸続見受け候。猶詳細は赤羽松延より可奉口陳候へは略之、多分小生は七日八日頃和歌浦丸にて帰東可仕候。頓首再行

九月三日

毅拝

山県参議殿
井上外務卿殿

八　井上毅発伊藤博文・井上馨・吉井友実宛

別啓

井上議官来簡写

局外干渉の是非は姑く置て論ぜす、今度の争点は帰する所王命の真偽に在り。竹添の手中に「日使来衛」の四字と丼に国王より直付せられたる「大朝鮮国大君主李㷆 [大朝鮮国大君主宝] と白紙に鈐したるものあれは、前日の召命は国王の旨に出たる証憑とするに十分なるべし。但し一の弁解を費すへき事あり。彼れ外務衙門を経ざる王命は憑拠とならすといへるは欧洲の例に照すときは一理ある説と聞ゆ。然るに此説は全く「モルランドルフ」等の捏造にして朝鮮人の云ふへき論に非らす。其故は朝鮮は純粋の専制国にして親勅は最上の勢力ある命令たるは其慣例なるは疑なければなり。故に花房公使か十五年に再ひ京城に派し談判を開きたる時も直ちに国王に面謁して其親決を請ひ、然後に始めて領議政と商議の便を得たりしなり。然るに今更俄然立憲国の例に倣ひ外務大臣を経ざるを以て国王の親勅を無憑拠となし或は矯旨となさんとするは、巧に其時の事実を塗抹せんとするの論説に過きさるべし。

米公使の説に

井上毅発伊藤博文・井上馨・吉井友実宛

明治(17)年12月24日

縦令外国公使の入衛は幾分か兇徒に勢力を予へたるの効果ありたるにもせよ、朝鮮政府は此を以て外国公使を責むる権利なし

と云へるは尤も至当の論理なるか如し。

試に局外より双方を是非するの論者あらんと仮言せしに、竹添を党レ賊扶レ凶として交際上不レ認の罪を負はしめんとするは尤不当なるべし。何んとなれば竹添は一意王命を重んし王の躬を扞護するの行為に止り兇徒を煽動し又は聯合したるの情事なければ也。縦令朝鮮政府は竹添の入衛の為めに意外の損害を受けたるにもせよ、是を以て竹添を指目して扶賊之連累者なりとする事を得さるべし。

右は徐相雨派出接待否に付必要の一点と被存候に付贅述仕候。若し強ちに竹添の行為を認めざるの廟議にも無之候はゝ、縦令他に全権大臣を派出さるゝにもせよ徐相雨・穆爾蘭徳（メルレンドルフ）の使節は御引受無之方歟と奉存候。モルランドルフは各国公使并に領事の信用を失ひ、已に先日も各国使臣の異言あるを知り朝鮮の官職を辞し

再ひ京城に入らすと迄に明言し仁川迄帰途に就きたりしに、李鴻章よりの内意に由る歟再ひ京城に還り外務大輔の職に就きたり。米公使フート氏は竹添へ向ひ「モルランドルフ氏を除かされは和平の談判を為し難し」と朝鮮国王に言明せん事を勧めたり。右御心炬〔ママ〕迄に申上候。再拝

十二月廿四日

毅

宮内卿殿
外務卿殿
宮内大輔殿
外務大輔殿

〔注〕外務省用箋。

九　岩倉具視発グラント宛

写

明治14年3月31日

謹啓　爾来益御清穆奉賀候。毎時我公使迄懇ろに御伝言被下難有多謝の至に候。貴邦の事情は吉田公使より

岩倉具視発グラント宛

時々申報有之、逐一致承知候。偖台下此地御発程以来、歳月荏苒幾星霜を重ね候得共、台下御滞在中予幸に日夕相来往し、其清興今尚ほ依然永く譲れ難し。台下請ふ、予か未た能く英字を解せさるの故を以て、平昔疎濶の罪を怨せよ。但た吉田氏を以て台下の恒に健安隆昌なるを拝承し、欣喜不斜候。且台下の今日尚々として我帝国の為めに謀り、苟も其利害に関する事件に於て、便ち我儕を輔助せんと欲する尊意ある事を致了知、斯友愛なる高志を辱なふし、我儕感佩不過之候。誠に台下其人の若き有為者にして、我儕の為め周旋尽力を致す事此の如きあり。則ち寧そ美果を結はさるの理あらんや。是れ予の敢て聊も疑はさる所に有之候。台下に在ては、蓋し夙に吉田氏より御聞及被成候て、彼の琉球事件に付、日清両政府間に経過したる始末を詳細御承知の事と致遙察候。我政府に於ては台下の論旨に遵ひ、百方計を致して両邦の為めに謀り、即ち本件を平穏に調理して彼我双方の利益安寧を求めん事を庶幾し、因て我儕の清国人民を待つや、毎に友好親愛

〔ら欠〕

の情を致ささん事を勉め、蓋し遺す所も之れあらさるに、惜哉、彼方に在ては、肯て之れを認受せすして、事竟に画餅に属するに至れり。是れ固とに我儕の与かる所に無之、奈何とも詮方なき次第に有之候。我委員の北京出発前に於て、彼れと総理衙門との間に交へたる談判始末の覚書は、業已に吉田公使迄相廻し置候間、委細同氏より御聞取被降度候。

我皇帝聖体愈平安、邦家益静謐に有之候条、此段御省慮是祈、我皇帝には毎時台下の御噂さ被為遊候事に御坐候。

惟願くは貴邦愈安寧にして、新大憲の治平猶旧大憲の時に於るか若くならん事を。且つ台下な再〔ママ〕ひ斯貴位に昇るは、其日蓋し遙遠ならさらん事を希望致候。

布哇皇帝には全地球御周遊の序、過日本邦へ御立寄被遊、我儕乃ち拮据して御饗応申上候事に御坐候。

将又当地に御用事も有之候はゝ、何時も無御遠慮御申越可被成候。早速欣然措弁可致候。

午末毫令室並に台下へ同僚よりも宜敷申出候也。敬具

明治十四年三月三十一日　　　　岩倉具視

ゼネラール、ユー、エス、グラント台下

一〇　岩倉具視発石橋政方宛

明治（　）年6月27日

来翰一見、今日芝紅葉館に於てヨンク氏招請に付、午後二時より五時迄之間に出頭之趣、如命昨日吉田公使よりも通知有之、只今可及返書存居候処候。已上出頭可致候。此段吉田氏へも御通知有之度御報旁如此候。早々

六月廿七日

　　　　　　具　視

石橋政方殿

一一　岩村高俊発柳谷謙太郎宛

明治（　）年10月23日

昨日相願置候県下北陸銀行之義は、随分混雑之事件にて拝話中前後致候件も有之、御聞取難被成事柄も御坐候と存候間、別紙は此度大蔵省へ差出候請書之写にて、之を御一読被下候はゝ其大概御了察と存候間、差出置候に付、猶宜敷次官公へ御申上被下度、此段重て御依頼仕候也。

十月廿三日

　　　　　　岩村生

柳谷謙太郎殿坐前

一二　大隈重信発吉田二郎宛

明治（7）年4月11日

横文一通造幣寮キンドルより遣し候に付御廻し申候。至急翻訳之上吉田少輔〔清成〕へ御廻し被下度、此段申入候也。

四月十一日

　　　　　　大隈卿

吉田少丞殿〔二郎〕

一三　大隈重信・吉井友実・伊藤博文発
　　　上野景範宛

明治（　）年6月24日

〔前欠〕御求御取帰可被下候。

〜油断成かたく候間、自然其筋御参考之端しにも相
成候はゝ望外之至に奉存候。可然御取計可被下候。小
生も明后六日之飛舟にて馬関迄参候間、いづれ帰京之
上万縷可申上候。多分京城迄も罷出可申と奉存候。何
義も拝眉可申上。　早々頓首

六月念四日

　　伊藤少輔
　　吉井少輔
　　大隈大輔

上野大丞殿

一四　大倉喜八郎発渡辺宛

明治（　）年9月4日

〔封筒表〕吉田様閣下御親展
〔封筒裏〕大倉喜八郎

今夕五字よりデクルード氏ケネデー氏〔駐日英代理公使〕等参会之事に御
座候。同刻より必御繰合御光来被下度奉待上候。日本
風の料理に御座候。猫は小猫斗りに御座候。
手品遣へ〔ママ〕余興に参居候。右御謝迄申上度後刻拝眉奉待
入候。　草々

九月四日

　　大倉喜八郎

渡辺先生
　閣下

〔注〕封筒との関係は不明。

一五　大倉喜八郎発志田衛宛

明治（　）年（　）月26日

拝啓　先夜は甚た失敬御海容可被下候。然は其節御咄
申上候砂金場之一条、今日と相成候ては完全なる御約
条も取結に相成、稍六日之菖蒲とは奉存候へ共、ます

岡田令高発志村智常宛

廿六日

志田衛様拝復

一六　岡田令高発志村智常宛

明治（　）年4月27日

鶴彦

愛知人奥田マサカより
田中来た委細承知早く頼む

又今日同人より
何時出れるや返事

と申来。此方よりは昨日田中君へ向け
御手数深謝す知事公へ宜敷

今朝は永峰書記官へ一旦は断たれとも、田中氏も承知
東京之方にて応する事と相成たる由荒増陳述仕、田中
氏へ

今朝永峰へ咄した宜敷

と相発候次第。又廿四日附・廿五日午前発・同日夜吉
田より之御発簡三通共只今迄に一々落手、御書中之趣
委細敬承。今回之義に付ては

晩翠先生・田中君・老台之御深意御尽力被成下候段、
実以難有奉存候。田中君へは一昨日書状も差出置、老
台へも再度出状仕候。

拝啓　一昨日左之電報到来委細明瞭安心　三公之御尽
力深謝之至に奉存候。

間違の電報念の為め入封差上候。

　　　吉田公より
〔智常〕
昨日志邸の電信間違しと見ゆ。愛知の事は断然受る事
に決せり。

　　　田中君より

榎坂の電信にて承知あれ。愛知人近藤其他へは拙者よ
り弁解承諾せり。安心あれ。

　　　老台より

技師の方に運ひ中辞職には及はずと思ふ。

右にて一切氷解仕候。昨廿六日午前九時三十分発東京

キとサの間違より一時反対之事相と相成たる事申上置
候に付、御承知之事と奉存候。然るに貴地に於て一切

決意と相成、此上は至急上京、愛知人等とも万端の引
合且約束等取結候一段と相成申候。今朝永峰書記官へ
荒増申出候処、同氏も大に驚き小生之為には可賀事歟
も不相知候へ共、県庁の為には大に困る、何は兎もあ
れ知事方へも一書相飛せ可申と之事。其後県庁にて之
面談には知事は如何被申候歟は不相分候へ共、如此大
事業なれは拙者（永峰の事）は無止賛成の方に致す、知事へ
も其由申送ると之事。実は転任之事等も有之、事の決
行に及ひ吐露仕度とも存候へ共、夫ては余り突然薄情
之様にも相当候に付、内実は已に極たる後なれは寧ろ
予め発言の方万端よしと考ひ如此一発言仕候。併し日
々不相替県庁へ出頭勉励仕居、東京等之知人へは

昨日二十六日

と一回の分に対し返信差出、

不肖ながら担任する出京は成へく急ぐべし

今日は二十七日

県庁之方未済を成丈急く

と返信差出置候。何分此上ながら転任之方御急決被下

岡本健三郎発井上馨宛

一七　岡本健三郎発井上馨宛

在京知事へは田中氏より可然御取扱を乞度。其内には
出京小生面会可仕候。

右申上度。草々頓首

　　四月廿七日

　　　　梧園老台侍史

　　　　　　　　　令　高

今回之事は将来の為め随分愉快と奮発仕居候。

度奉願上候。此上は一旦独身にて出京、夫に引合等を
済せ夫より福島へ引返し、家族共召連上京之運に仕度
奉存候。何卒　晩翠先生及田中君へ宜敷御礼詞奉願候。

明治（5）年1月5日

新年奉拝賀候。爾后倍御清栄可被為成御起居奉謹賀候。
御発途後格別之事件も無御座先々御安念奉翼候。其中
御指揮可窺之条件は漸次申上候通の次第、猶又此回米
穀輸出之義に付、美代理公使より推而外務より掛合越
し、其回答案並に分析所之事務〔に付カ〕見込等夫々渋沢氏よ

り可申上運に相成居申候間、宜布御了得夫々御指揮奉冀候。外国負債之義も小野此頃横浜出張頻りに尽力にて追々相片付居申候間、右様御領承被遣度○東京府関門一条何分折合不申殆困却仕候。孰れ御帰京之上由利御直談奉願外無御坐と奉存候○伊万里県之事山岡〔鉄太郎〕相拝此度之郵船に乗組出県之運に相成申候。然る処昨日林〔友幸〕少丞より報告に追□〔破レ〕説諭を加へ、五六名程御□〔破レ〕使致し候段申出、其外之者とても結末何等之義をも不申立臘月廿日迄に一同引払相成候趣、誠に存外之次第にて御坐候。右之景況に候へは必す此末紛云之儀は有之間布、御安念奉念希候。則別紙林よりの書状二通差出し候。右にて悉詳御領承之訳と奉存候。右計早々何も御帰京之上可申上如此御坐候。頓首再行

正月五日

　　　　　義方

　井上大輔様

一八　海江田信義発島津家令扶宛

明治（　）年6月27日

拝啓　本日は例会に御坐候半、吉田氏参不参如何哉。前会之節所労にて罷帰候故同氏へ御手紙を以御尋被成候て可然哉。若難罷出候はゝ後の例日に御延被遊候方と奉存候。此旨奉伺候也。

六月廿七日

　　　　　海江田信義

島津家御令扶中様

一九　加藤静俒発松方正義宛

明治（4）年10月9日

一翰奉啓上候。漸々寒気之候、先以聖明倍御機嫌克被遊御鎮座候条奉賦万歳候。次陳台臺〔ママ〕閣下倍御清明王事鞅掌被遊候段、欣喜無涯候。賤軀儀海陸無恙広島着之段は、先鴻同僚共より微細申上呉候様申達おき候間、定て御了知も可被成下、爾后不取敢県情捜索仕候処、

加藤静俟発松方正義宛

封建之余習更に脱却不仕、万事私有之権を以政務取扱
ひ居、加之門地之陋習盛大にして、参事已上は多分門
閥家を以之に任じ、卒已下は大抵使部位に使用いたし
おき候位之事に御ざ候。今般暴動之一件も旧恩に感激
し、一時出駕を遮り候様も可有之候へとも、畢竟朝廷
之御趣意示方不行届よりして、無頼之奸民其機に乗じ
良民を煽動し、去月十三日広島町引続所々乱妨狼籍、
尾道と申処にて説論の官員を打殺し、其末兵力を以取
鎮め申候。未た人心折合不申、今日は家族一統東上之
筈に付、又々沸騰を醸すべき歟。詮する所暴動は下民
之挙動に候へとも、其実は官員一統之不束より起る事
に御ざ候。因て先鴻河野君より卿大輔之連名にて奏任
〔正道〕
以上惣免職、西本清助更に被任権大参事、其他官員黜
陟伺に相成申候。何卒至急御下知被成下候様、乍陰御
厚配被成下候様於小生も奉渇望候。
御沙汰次第夫々判任已下に波及し、職制等一層簡而軽
便、御趣意貫徹候様河野先生始昼夜勉励仕候。しかし
驚新狃故は民之常情、加るに沸騰之余燄未滅せす、旁

物議風聞等今必大沸騰いたすべく、無稽之小説自然御
聞込に相成候とも、必御採用不相成様御応援被成下候
様万々奉渇望候。

一、去月廿二日備後福山表暴動之由、趣意は広島同様
暴動之波及と申すべき歟。同県へも速に本省より御
出張、夫々御糺正有之度様奉存候。
〔ママ〕
倉鋪県於ても穢
多編籍之儀に付一沸騰を起し候由、右両条は篤と物
議聞糺、後鴻具に可奉申上候。

先は着御吹聴旁一応之事情可奉申上と如斯に御座候。
尚篤と取調後便に付与仕候。誠惶々々頓首再拝

十月九日
〔松方正義〕
松権頭尊官呈下執事
加藤静俟再拝

追啓　時下御自愛専一に奉存候。失敬之極に御座
候へとも吉田尊君、安藤君及中村・若山両君へも
可然御遁声被成下候様奉願上候。已上

しく奉存候。去とて毫も　吾翁至愛の慈教を不奉にあ
らす、只本邦の為右前段寸時も吾先生の休憩を伏乞す
る徹底の微志なれは、独り　吾翁時ありて頑児之為宜
しく先生に御伝述なし給はん事を頑児不勝恐惧伏願。

　　　　　　正臣頓首

　　　　　　正臣再拝

二〇　北代正臣発志村智常宛　明治12年1月6日

謹而奉祝賀

新年

改年万福御超歳成され万奉抃躍候。且説昨十二月卅一
日の尊書には晩翠先生錦街御移転の御垂示を蒙り、昨
夜は更に同先生良々御落合の端に就かれし御内告を拝
得す。実に前后　翁の慈懐深且切なる頑児泣感万謝不
竆、是際愚志の所在は素より独り　吾翁の憐愛洞知し
玉ふ如く同先生帰朝の尊報を拝し愚志融釈相覚候も、
畢竟此数月間夜白東望の余りにて今や却て愚志疲労融
釈如是、且頑児直に屢々先生の側に趨侍せさるものは
本邦の為寸時も休憩の永からん事を窃に先生の為、
即ち本邦の為に伏望の至情に堪へされは、日夕飛動の
心意を桔械し、態と相扣以て今後数日の処拝趨仕るま

十二年一月六日

　志村翁慈橋下

二一　北代正臣発志村智常宛　明治(14)年12月17日

寒気逐日相加候処、御一統様滋御清安被成御渉、千万
奉拝寿候。陳、其後は屢米国先生之御容子〔様〕御洩被遣難
有亦改奉拝祝罷在候。御額面壱個碁盤一面及碁石一対
御敷物一個合三種之御品永々恩借仕候。此御庇蔭を奉
蒙最早先生御帰朝之期を近日に得候事本懐不竆、過日
は謹而　膝下え拝還仕候。実以難有次第万謝是事に御
坐候。然処過般も粗上陳之如く頑児大坂上等裁判所詰
被申付候得共、抑法官たる職務は只盗賊と金貸之裁判
而已、其実何之苦労も無之、依而は此際何と歟因循消

日不遠先生御帰迄都合取計、断然不動之決心に御坐候

処、又如何にせん因循座過之景況頗る他に影響相及候

事実と相成、去迎此際疎忽に辞職致候半は先生之御志

にも有之間敷と兎角愚慮仕候ては、目下之処何となく

一と先赴任仕り御帰之頃迄彼地に於て万々心ならぬも

現職掌に従事仕居候事、其姿穏当なる可き歟と心志を

反覆仕り、所詮右様反覆仕候上は最早一日も踟躕可仕

に非らすと志気憤発、折節郵船之便有之哉に見受候に

付、突然本日出発之儀に相決申候。不遠先生御帰之事

故右之通一旦決然赴任仕候様相成る上は、奉対 膝下

将来之心事縷々御願も可奉申上置筈共万奉存候得共、

今更又事新らしく不申上共飽迄 膝下御体察被遣候儀

と相信じ、依之御暇乞にも拝趨不仕突然出発仕候始末

に御座候。只々娑婆界之事情無詮方行き掛りに御座候

得は不悪御聴分被遣、欠敬之段は深く御詫可被遣奉

仰願候。他日先生御清泰御帰朝之後は一日も速に御召

還被遣邦国之為微力之尽し甲斐御座候向え御救ひ出し

被遣候様、今日より予め 膝下迄外ならす御切願に不

倶に御封し込御差立方相願候。右御報如此御座候也。

と相信じ、依之御暇乞にも拝趨不仕突然出発仕候始末

に拝誦拝別之一言敬述不仕事甚遺憾に御座候。千万事

下逐日之寒威深御一統様御自護之程千祈万禱に御座候。

乍紙尾御一統様え宜く御詫御伝致可被降、乍去 膝下

情御垂憐奉願上。恐々不一

候。彼地着之上は猶追々御伺可申上勿論に御座候。時

候得は、呉々も先生御帰之時は千々万々宜く奉願上置

懐を杖也柱也前段之如く突然赴任決行仕候心事に御座

堪候。只此一事而已決て御忘却被遣間敷、到底右之慈

二二　北代正臣発佐久間克宛

十二月十七日暁燈下

梧園大翁膝下

頑児正臣拝具

拝見　陳は、大坂府へ懸合案写添候御用状則取調差進

候間、少輔公え御差出御異存無之候はゝ、直に本書御

認差立方御取計有之度、且今朝御依托いたし候二封も

明治（　）年12月5日

黒田瀧発吉田貞宛

二三　黒田瀧発吉田貞宛

明治（21）年5月29日

十二月五日

佐久間克様
別紙添

北代正臣

松田栄殿
〔注〕墨書。

拝復　来三十一日御邸内於て角力御催有之御寵招を蒙り難有奉謝候。当日御命刻拝趨可仕候。右御請申上候。

可祝

廿九日

吉田奥様人々

黒田瀧

二四　工部省会計局発松田栄宛

明治（　）年8月19日

御用有之候間、明廿日第十字正服着用出頭可有之旨本省より御達に付、此段相達候也。

八月十九日

二五　小谷静治発志村智常宛

明治（　）年6月15日

工部省
会計局

一書啓上仕候。薄暑之砌御家内中様愈御栄福可被為在候処、大賀不斜奉存候。其後愚書差上御窺可申候処、去春来不快に罷在快気後引続き郷村へ出張罷在候処、事務繁雑不得寸暇、乍不本意御無音打過不敬之段御用捨被成下度奉希候。陳は旧冬来歓願罷在候石神浜田之学資金云々、願之通御聞済可被成下様米国より被仰遣候旨彼等両人大いに安意勉励罷在候趣き申越、小生に於ても右御聞届被成下候段難有奉深謝候。扨当県之地租改正も漸く実地検査相済、道路修繕等も追々出来先つ外見は他県なみに相成候得共、人民之頑愚なるは実に恐縮に候。先は時候御見舞旁々右御礼迄、余は以後便御窺可申上

小松原英太郎発吉田勇蔵・志村智常宛

候。早々敬白

六月十五日

志村先生坐下

二伸

旧冬より恩借罷在候金子既に返納可仕筈之処、彼是
出費多く未た不都相成兼実に恐縮之至候得共、今暫
時御融用被成下度偏に奉歎願候。

小谷静治

吉田勇蔵様

二六　小松原英太郎発吉田勇蔵・志村智常宛

明治（24）年8月5日

拝具

八月五日

志村智常様

　　　　　　小松原英太郎

謹啓　子爵吉田清成御事兼々御病気被為在候処、御療
養不被相叶御薨去被遊候趣誠に驚愕之至御愁傷奉恐察
候。此品哀吊之意を表し度差出候。霊前に御備被下候
はゝ難有奉存候。不取敢御悼詞申上度如此に御坐候。

二七　西郷清発吉田貞宛

明治（　）年6月26日

〔封筒表〕吉田御奥様　貴酬　西郷清

華翰拝読、弥御清栄欣喜之至に奉存候。陳者明廿七日
午後第一時、於紅葉館蒙御寵招候段奉厚謝候。御来示
之時刻、必拝趨可仕、先は右御請旁得貴意度。匆々拝

答

六月廿六日

吉田御奥様御側中

　　　　　　西郷　清

二八　税所新次郎発吉田須磨宛

明治（22／23）年11月24日

時下益々御揃御安康之筈奉大慶候。降而拙夫にも消光
罷在候間、御休神被成下度。却説拙夫にも本日鹿屋警

鮫島慶蔵発吉田貞宛

察署詰を被命候に付は、意外千万なる事にて、如是病身にては退も難出来儀に付、直様辞表にても差出す含に候得共、只今辞表差出し候ては愛之助へ送金且つ家内を見殺しにするより外は無之、不得止一先つ住地之様明日発足する賦にて御坐候。就ては寒気に打向き差越し奉職致し候得は、又々例の持病相発するには無相違事に御坐候。只々愛之助出生の儀に付て返すぐ〳〵も残念千万、寝ても夢うつゝにて切歯致し候ても詮なき事、只なみだに暮れ居る事御座候。就ては今迄奉職罷在候も以前に山沢静吾君の御周旋に依り難有愛之助まても出生為致居候儀にて候。願くは御前様より又々清成君歟静吾君等へ右之事実御咄し被下候て、当地警察本部警部長久保活三〔村欠〕殿へ御知人も有之候はゝ、又々鹿児島警察之儀、帰署する様之事相叶間敷哉。八円の内より三円を引去り、又拙者鹿屋へ奉職するに於ては、又弐三円を費用残り一二円にて退も家内介抱は到底不出来儀にて候。又拙者身体にて旅行の奉職は是又見認めも無之次第にて御坐候。若し静吾君清成君より事実御憐憫察被下候て相叶儀も有之候於て大幸此上なき次〔カ〕第に御坐候。依て先つ此所にては辞表等も見合居り候間、何方にても御周旋の処清成君へ御咄し被成下度伏て奉願候。只今奉職を捨て候ては外に見込も無之、家内餓死するに外無之候間、御憐〔憫〕憫を以て奉伏願候。先つ此段要詞而已如是御座候。　拝具

十一月廿四日

　　　　　税所新次郎

吉田於すま様

追て、呉床之儀拙夫休暇にて一時帰家する含に御座候間、其時迄御待ち被下度。去る廿日又々女子出生致し御喜ひ被下度。

二九　鮫島慶蔵発吉田貞宛

任幸便一筆拝啓仕候。時下漸々冷気之候に相成申候得共、各位被為揃御壮栄に被為渉候半と奉遙察候。次に当地両家共無事消光罷在申候間、乍余事御休意可被下

明治（　）年（　）月（　）日

候。陳者今回近隣之者上京之便に付何にか差上度と勘
考仕候得共、山田舎之事なれば何にも無御坐、御当地
にも沢山御坐候品物なれとも唯た不取敢愚妻之寸志迄
鹿角菜壱包進呈仕度との事に御坐候間、御听止被下候
はゝ辱幸之至に奉存候。まつは此旨以乱文御左右迄如
此。艸々敬白

叔母様

　　慶蔵

二伸、志村氏え可然御鳳声可被下候。再尾

三〇　沢井熊次郎外十四名発ガーフィールド宛

明治14年6月25日

某等謹て合衆国大統領㑆[ガーフィールド]費徳公閣下に白す。頃者本
校の教員たる貴邦の学士曹爾多氏[ツルター]に因りて閣下の真
影を拝受するを得たり。未謦欬に接せすと雖も亦以て
泰斗の風采を想見するに足る。本校の光栄何を以て之
に加へん。実に歓喜の至に任へす。恭しく短束を奉し
て拝謝し併せて本校の撮影一葉を献す。誠惶誠恐頓首
再拝

神武紀元二千五百四十一年

明治十四年六月廿五日

日本長崎県長崎中学校筆生　薬師寺益三郎㊞

筆生　三輪与市㊞

助訓　森準平㊞

助訓　深浦重光㊞

準訓導　岡崎章介㊞

準訓導　上野廣太郎㊞

訓導　小高邦知㊞

訓導　田中小八郎㊞

訓導　山口勝吉㊞

同　穎原季善㊞

同　黒杭寛㊞

同　原賀福太郎㊞

同　北畠智謙㊞

同　桐野弘㊞

―――――

中学校長兼訓導沢井熊次郎㊞

合衆国大統領荘費徳公閣下

三一　渋沢栄一発井上馨宛

明治（5）年1月5日

拝啓　出納寮分析掛官員下阪可致に付、別封を以委細奉申上候得共、尚小生愚考之廉々及其地之事共左に申上候。

東京分析所は別紙申上候手続を以、予め精製出来候迄之目途相立候上にて、三ツ井組へ約定にて御任せ相成候方可然と存候。

但右場処充分之成業を望候はゝ外国人雇入候方可然候へとも、先成丈省略いたし、吉武其外両人にて間に合せ置候方、勘定向得失には相当可致哉に存候。右場処に於て分析出来候には、いつれ瑣少之増築可有之歟。右等之手続は幸ひキントル義東京へ罷出候都合に相成候はゝ、同人に両三日為見届候はゝ可然哉。

去臘廿九日附を以岡田平蔵分析所之義に付願書之件、其外にも精銅等之義も幷て申上候哉、何分可然御指揮被下候。右は御領掌被下候哉。

三井之少年御召連之義、同店京阪之都合等夫々御監視御督責被下度候。

神戸同店にて洋銀札発行之義御勘考被下度候。

一昨三日附之書状を以米輸出之義其外申上候処、もした御到手無之哉と奉存、別紙写さし上候。早々御指揮被下度。尤今日も外務卿輔へ面会頻に討論いたし、弥明日は英国公使引合可申と奉存候。さしたる懸念も無之候得共、別紙にも申上候通に付、何分御見込御差図奉祈候。

新分析所（大阪之分也）にて精製之仕事は相運候哉。先頃紀伊国屋万蔵方へ御貯たる金分析方申付候ては如何可有之哉と存、後藤より申談置候事有之候。随分割合もよろしく、精錬も可也出来候様子に候間、試として御申付候。

右等別書に相洩候廉々書添申上候。東京春来無異、別

段諸方よりも異聞無之、先平寧之姿に付、山岡（鉄舟）伊万里県行、明六日出帆赴任いたし候。同所も其後は平穏之様子、林（友幸）より来書有之、閣下へも両封有之候に付、既にさし上置候間、御落手と奉存候。于時春寒料峭、雪片霏々別て難凌候様相覚へ候。折角御調度専一に被相成候様為　邦家奉祈候。頓首
　　正月五日夜
　　　　　　渋沢栄一
　　井上閣下
　　　多忙間執筆前後不整、且乱毫之極失敬御海恕可被下候。

殿へ宜御申上被下可然御詮議被下度候。此段拝答如此御坐候。頓首
　　一月卅日
　　　　　　渋沢栄一
　　益田様
　　大倉様

三三　渋沢栄一発種田宛

明治（　）年2月24日

昨夕は初て拝眉失敬仕候。其節之高諭に明廿五日夕刻より日本橋近辺にて御出会之義被仰聞、則御約束申上候処、帰宅後小生幷小野善右衛門とも無拠用向出来、明夕は是非夫へ出会候様不致ては不相成義に付、何共恐入候得共、御日延し被下度候。尤委細は御令弟へ申上候間、御聞取可被下候。折角之高慮に応し兼候段は実に多罪之至に候得共、無拠業体筋之用向に候間、御海容奉祈候。吉田君（清成）同然御越にては却て恐悚之義と是も御令弟へ御答奉願置候間、是又御了承可被下候。右

三二　渋沢栄一発大倉喜八郎・益田孝宛

明治20年1月30日

尚々、只今本文之段申上候積之処へ御使被下候ニ付、乍失敬拝答仕候也。
今朝拝趨之御約束申上候処、昨夜来風邪気にて何分罷出兼候間、御違約之段不都合之至に候得共、吉田次官（清成）

は拝願如此御坐候。匆々

　二月廿四日
　　　　渋沢栄一
　種田老閣

尚々、何れ不日小生より申上、御一会奉願様可致候。御令弟義は飽迄御心得候間、御降心可被下候。今日より事務に処し御勉力被成候事に御座候。

三四　志村智常発肥後七左衛門宛

明治（5）年2月（　）日

未た緩々不懸御目候得共、弥御堅勝奉大慶候。然は先頃吉田[清成]少輔より御方へ相託し分析いたし候金銀地金之儀は、全体当人におひては売却之見込にても生し、金分析のみの望にて、其儀は御方へも示談申上置候哉にて候処、此節御方より御遣し被成候金子之儀は此方へ留置有之候得共、実は右地金御方におひて売却被成候儀は不本意之趣に候。一体右を大蔵省分析局にて買入候様之事に候得は、右地金之請取書は勿論、且つ浄算書書[ママ]等も有之筈は当然之事御坐候間、御手許に御坐候得は早々拙者方へ御遣し被下度。右は少輔より分て相託し置候儀に候間、此段一応得御意候。何分御即答被下度候也。

　申二月——
　　吉田少輔親族
　　志村工部大属
開拓使　肥後七左衛門様

三五　志村智常発吉田貞宛

明治8年1月21日

改暦之御祝儀千里同風申納候。先以御揃其地へ御安着被成候段、千々万々目出度存上候。横浜にて御別れ申候以来は、皆々気ぬけ致し、両三日之心持と申ては何ともたへよふ無之、日々噂さのみ申暮し候。吉田[清成]君にも是御心配被成候御様子に相さつし申候へ共、さすか大丈夫、写真にては一かさ御太り被成候様存候〇

志村智常発吉田貞宛

今般其地へ相越され候儀は、実に天幸此上も無之事に
付、まるで心を入替、万事無油断心得、寸暇には学文〔問〕
致し、朝夕之咄しもつとめて英語を用ひ、しらず
〲語学出来候様いたし、毛頭我まゝ気ずいのふる
まひいたさる間敷、帰国之節は心之錦を心かけ、人柄
之かゞやき候様日夜失念無之様祈念致し候○御祖母様
にも至極御丈夫に有之候間安心可被成候。色々上げ物
等被致、誠にゝ御悦ひに有之、拙子於ても厚志之段
万々忝なく存候○十二月三日紙幣寮十一等出仕拝命、
今般は大に勉強、朝は第六時より支度出勤、夕六時過
帰宅、調物等致し居候。兼之願之銀行取調役に当月被
仰付、洋算等入用之場所故、一入はまり宜敷、大元気
にて安堵いたし候。是皆吉田君之余光に有之候。
右申進度如此御坐候。余は次便申入候。めて度かしく

　八年一月廿一日　　　　　智常

　お貞君人々無事

猶々、折角御厭可被成候。別紙之注文品代書さし
進置候。此分は皆々進上品に有之候。

注文品代附

一金七拾銭　　上酒三升五合余
一金六拾四銭　　古味りん弐升
一金七拾五銭　　干柿弐箱分
一金六拾銭　　素麵百把
一金五十銭　　甘名納豆大箱一〔カ〕
一金八銭三リ　　布海苔
一金三銭六リ　　油落し十
一金七銭　　小豆壱升
一金六銭　　いんげん豆五合
一金五拾銭　　懐中しるこ
一金弐円五拾銭　　バラ美濃からし五
一金七銭五リ　　眉刷はさみ
一金三銭　　新暦一冊
一金廿五銭　　鋲釘〔カ〕
一金拾九銭五リ　　西洋上箱代荷造用

〆六円九拾四銭九リ

　外に

志村智常発吉田貞宛

一縮めりやす　五の内三つ　今日出来
此代弐円三拾五銭

二口
〆金九円三拾三銭九リ
此外に参通其外写真代

三六　志村智常発吉田貞宛

明治8年2月18日

一筆申進候。弥時かふ〔候〕御障りもなく目出度御儀存候。最早臨月にも相成候間、安産有之候哉と日々申暮し候。何卒無滞出産之儀祈り居候事に御座候。其節早速御申被遣候程待入候。此はみかき毎朝相用ひ候へは口熱去り、歯の根かたまり、至極よろしきよし、東京にて大分はやり候薬に付御廻し申候。兄君にも先日中より相用ひ大に宜趣に有之候○塩竈（シホカマ）様へは毎月十日御祖母様より御参詣被成候○先便に申進候御あつらい物品々は一箱に致し、此度之船便りにて相廻し申候。かち栗の衣かけ出来合無之候間、ほんの間にあわせ物さし進申候。中につまらぬ品入置候へ共、是は詰わらの代りに入候儀に御さ候。色々送り申度品も有之候へ共、運賃に相掛り、余り馬鹿〳〵敷御座候間見合せ申候。もし運賃に無構御望み被成候へは、猶御申越し可被成候○此度之一箱目方百○五斤にてワシトン迄運賃凡十円余之由に有之候○封し物にて竪壱尺巾廿五寸〔ツ欠〕迄厚さ壱寸以下に候へは、外務省にて引受無賃にて相届き申候。則此間差出し候手袋入之書状位之品に御座候○差立物こしらい候には男の手無之候ては中々出来不申、此私にても斗喜三郎と次郎と両人にて一日相懸り申候。幸ひに次郎は当方に留置遣ひ居候間、買物其外大に都合宜候○新富町番附差越候間御廻し申候。随分おもしろさふに有之候○臼井杉山おとと方にも相替り候儀無之候○昨日今日は東京は大風にて、宅などは庭敷内へ砂一寸位つもり、誠に困り申候。乍去巡査能く相廻り候ゆへ、市中に火事無之、尤少々之儀所々に有之候へ共、早速

消し候由承り候○お半殿には西洋服はきなじみ、沓も

御なれ被成候て、能御似合被成事とさつし居候。何

事も御修業に付、折角御しんぼふ可被成候。且高柳・

青山之御両所に付とも御替なく候間、其段御申上之事○縮

手袋弐つ相廻し候。此度猶厚き方にて壱つ代金三分弐

朱つゝに有之候○東京は旧冬より疱瘡流行、種痘いた

し候ものにてもふたゝびいたし候もの不少、それは先

にうるし気が薄く成りし故也。疱瘡流行之節は、早く

又うゑ候へは宜敷との趣左内申聞候まゝ、宅の子供は

先日猶又皆種痘為致候て用心致し候。横浜幷東京に居

候外国人にて疱瘡いたし候もの有之、既に開成所御雇

の教師は死去致し候○当月六日大風之夜七時頃、横浜

元町一丁目より出火、弐丁目迄焼失、九時半頃止む。

定て九蔵は類焼と存候。しかも山ガハ斗り焼候よし。〔側〕

右用事而已。余は後便に申進候。目出度可祝。

八年二月十八日

　　　　　　　　父より

お貞君人々無事

猶々、汽車中は如何哉と日夜心配致居、何卒無事

志村智常発吉田貞宛

三七　志村智常発吉田貞宛

明治（8）年6月6日

安着之吉左右速に承知致し度候なり。

一此度差立之酒其外損し等は無之候哉、次便に委

細御申越し之事。

追々暑さに向ひ候処、御揃いよく〳〵御機けんよく候段

万々目出度御儀存候。次に当かた何れも無事罷在候間

御安心可被成候。扨今般は和歌子写真御送り被遺、相

開き悦び、御祖母様は申に及ず、一同子供ら迄皆々大

声に悦ひ、しばらくの間大さわきに御座候。余は御察

し之通に御座候。実に大きく温厚にて、能吉田君に似〔ヲンコウ〕　〔清成〕

居申候。上野様にても大そう御ほめ被成、よくは分ら〔景範〕

すなきものにて、写真を見候へは猶逢見度、日々それ〔カ〕

のみ思ひつゝけ候〇寺嶋様・上野様へ之御文は早速差〔宗則〕

上申候。其内大鳥御家内へも一封御上け可被成候〇大〔重〕

隈奥様へも同様御文差上候様存候〇産後もいよく〳〵丈〔信〕

夫之由、附ては近々学問相始候儀と存候。右日夜勉強、是非とも成業いたし候様心かけ可被申、当地にても婦人方学問大にはやり、琴三味せんなどをやめ、一途に学問致し候者多く有之候。ゆめ〳〵油断被成間敷事○先便両度に色々見立差進し候間、最早相届候儀と存候。猶相好み候品有之候はゝ被申越候様存候。少々つゝ御用状便に差立可申候。手袋は気に入候哉。次便に否哉御申越可被成候。右申進度如此御座候。目出度可祝。

　六月六日
　　　　　　　　　父より
　お貞殿人々無事
　猶々、和歌子折角御保護、万端御心附可被成めて
　たくかしく

三八　志村智常発吉田貞宛

明治8年7月28日

先以御揃何の御障りもなくめて度御儀存候。六月廿五日御認めの御文七月廿四日相届拝見いたし候。次に当表清成君より先便は和可子の事歌共御贈り相成、御礼申中無之、呉々も此儀忘却致す間敷候事。共に付、須臾(しばらく)も高恩をはすれず報(むくゆ)るに勉強致すの外は無之、呉々も此儀忘却致す間敷候事。て通ひ参り候よし。誠に華族にも勝れ、此上もなき事少しもゆだん被成間敷様いのり居申候○学師は婦人に学問専一に相つとめ、又保養も肝要に候間、双方ともいかなる貴人も致し方無之候。此後ははたと打忘れ、のいくらも是あり。吉凶はすなわち世乃中の模様にてからばかりにも無之、世上にはかゝるうきめにあふもかとまよひをおこし、扨々残念の事に候。しかしみつも又思ひ出し、写真を見候へは、もしや夢にてはなき日を暮し申候なれとも、かへらぬ事とはあきらめ候て時は世の中にたのしみはなき物と存じ、只こつ〳〵と一と悲歎(かなしき)やるかたなく、園に出ひとり涙だにしづみ、も無之、そなたはもちろん、吉田君〔清成〕には嘸かしならん候よし、お知らせにて承知、其時は何とたとえんやう候。扨此程和歌子事俄に病気相発し終にはかなく相成御祖母殿誰にも無事相過し候まゝ、御安堵被成へく

志村智常発吉田貞宛

といゝ一しほ御愁傷被想像、甚心痛致し候。此上はお半殿申合御心をなくさめ候様心かけ被成へく候○納涼のため大暑中は八月頃迄北地へ御出之よし結構の事に候。追て其地の様子承り度候○喜代子学問之事御申越承知、尤に存候間、早速近辺にて師匠相尋候処、福沢と申有名の師御座候へ共、是は入塾同様に無之候ては修業相成不申、左候ては小学校之方稽古差支大に困り居候処、幸ひ田町より八丁余はなれ、麻布古川ばた方（松）様より少しに外国女の師有之由承りしまゝ頼かたく尋参り候処、津田仙（つだせん）と申人の世話、右の外国人学校を開き、いまた願済には無之候へ共、同人屋敷内にて女童を集（あつ）め、午後二時より夕方迄稽古いたし候趣に付、右へ相頼、小学校より直にかなたへ廻り、此程より稽古相始め申候○右に付思ひよらず津田仙と申人に面会候処、同人娘は其地に留学、其御方へ相越、日本語等色々そなたの世話に相成候由娘方より申越、誠に難有、且又毎々吉田君之馬車へ御乗せ被下、御懇切被成下候趣を申越なと咄し有之候。実に不思議之事に御座候○

当年は此地も暑さ強く、九十一二度位に候○此度は大倉やえ頼み兼て御申越の瑚珀織其外、別紙書付之品々一箱相送り申候。定て此手紙と一同にワシントン迄相届候はんと存候。猶好（この）みの品も候はゝ御申越被成候へは、よき便りの節に追々相送り候様致し候○先頃中相送り候二箱は相届き、中の品も格別損じ不申候段大悦ひに存候。是は不案内ゆへ色々心配いたし居候儀に御座候。しかし賃銭多分に相かゝり候由、是には困（こま）り入候○御ばゝ様の写真は此頃に取り相廻し可申候。色々取込延引いたし候○此間中よりしづ子がんろうの様に候処、暑さゆへか驚風（けふう）相発（おこり）、甚た六ケ敷、子供の病気には困り入候。しかし御案事は御無用に御座候。吉田君より何か御送り被下べくやの趣に候へ共、運賃相嵩（かさ）むるきに御座候間、御帰朝之節御みやけに戴き度く候間、其様御申上候事何もくめてたくかしく

明治八年
七月廿八日
　　　　父より

お貞との人々無事

猶々、折角暑さ御いとひ被成へく候。呉々も和可

志村智常発吉田貞宛

子之事思ひ切、此上は学問専一に御つとめ可被成
候。目出度かしく

三九　志村智常発吉田貞宛

明治10年1月20日

〔朱筆〕
（第三号）

御揃弥御多福被成御座、目出度御儀存候。二に此方一
同無事壮健に相暮し候まゝ、御安心可被成候。小児に
は当節は嘸々愛らしく相成、吉田君にも一入御愛し被
成候御事と毎々御噂申居候。先日西郷さん御事態々御
入被下、てうど在宿にて其御地之御様子とも委敷伺、
誠にく〳〵安堵且嬉しく大悦致し候。御同人御咄しに、
私日本之飯が好ゆへ奥さんへ願ひ、結び飯を持折々山
へ遊に住きたり、能き楽しみに有之、亦碁を打候処、
どちらが勝しやらわからず、いつも吉田君之裁判を頼み
勝負を知り候など、其内勘定ちかひにてかたれ候事な
どの御咄し有之、大笑ひいたし候。次にそなた学問之

儀心配いたし候間、実地之様子相伺候処、近来殊の外
勉強の様子、吉田氏同道諸方へ罷越、深更に帰り候て
もいつも勉学にて、当時は一段相進み、用事大小とな
く米語にて相弁し、随て読書および習字など立派に出
来候旨御申被来候。右は半分に伺候ても、拙子之悦過
分に候。向後猶無油断勉強有之候様に候。実に
是迄其地より被帰候人も多く有之候へ共、西郷さん之
様に御親切に御咄し被下候御方は有之。其方には種
々御世話に成、失礼のみ致し候まゝよろしく申進呉候
様御申聞有之候。

一本月十一日已来政府大変革にて、諸省官員数名相減
し、漸々相残り候ものは一段又は二段も相下り、其上
月給は是迄より相減し、百円取り七拾円に相成始末、
諸寮は御廃止局と改り、統計寮は丸で潰れに相成、夫
故左太郎も出仕不致、是にはほとんと困り申候。去り
とて惣体之事ゆへ何共いたし方無之、よつて今日より
大けんやく相始め、新聞もおきよの琴稽古も相止、都
て可成丈け費をはぶき可申積りなれとも、人数多、其

上乳母も居、中々骨折れ可申被存候。しかし無益之心配はけつして無用にて、今より如此心付居候へは、今日に差支候様なる儀は決して無之候。唯悦ひは臼井之儀、改て拝命月給も是迄丈け被下、是は大悦ひ、杉山も相残り候へ共、月給五円相減し、臼井同様に相成申候。高柳は免ぜられ大困り、お半さんも去暮より同所に居られ、嘸々心配之事と存候。日比野も免職、大よわり、同人は承知之通、勉強殊に御用立、是迄預り之御用向少しも滞り不申、十分に相勤居候処、今般之次第ゆへ甚た不平なれとも、せん方なく、毎日ねて居候由、実に此人などは気の毒に存候。左太郎などは寮を御廃し故、別段免職の御達しも無之、去る十二日一同出仕銘々の調物取束（ツカネ）本省へ相納め帰宅、其侭出仕不致候○料理茶や〔屋〕芸者など去年よりひま之所、此節は別て客来無之、官員さんの一件にて唐物屋始め人力車引迄大不景気、奏任官以上之人は馬車をやめるも有り、人力車を払、車夫の暇を遣すも有り、各夫々倹約相始め、一時之事には可有之候へ共、市中へは大にひゞき候様子に有之候○先頃中より外務省へ差出置候書状箱入之分、追々相届候半と存候。右に付当時差立候書状次第くに後れ候間、今度も御便にて差立申候。

右用事而已申進度、万々（ブン）めて度かし

　　十年第一月廿日出　　　　老父より
　　お貞君人々無事

猶々、寒気強候間、折角御厭ひ出生は精々御心付養育専要に有之候。呉々も本文の一事は決て懸念・被致間敷候也。

四〇　志村智常発吉田貞宛

米国公使館へ差立物
　九年
　十一月十日　　　紙包弐箇
　同　十七日　　　同　壱箇

〔欄外朱筆〕
副書

明治10年2月9日

同　廿三日　　同　弐箇

十二月九日　　紙包弐箇

同　廿三日　　同　弐箇

十年

第一月十日　　紙包弐箇

十年二月九日

〔注〕記名はなきも志村常の字。

右之通今日荒々御差立度候得共、都合次第にて相残候哉も難計候也。

四一　志村智常発吉田貞宛

明治11年5月18日

〔朱筆〕
第十二号

貴家御揃御壮栄御座候由、目出度御儀に存候。次に当地御祖母様初め、皆々無事相暮し候まゝ、御安心可被成候。抑此程は左太郎儀開拓使七等属被仰付月給廿五円、成候。一同大悦ひ、同人も今般は喜悦大勉強いたし居候。御悦ひ可被成候。誠に此度之儀は不存寄不意に被仰付、誰殿之御周旋やら更に相知れ不申、何れにも吉田君より之響（ヒヾキ）にて斯（カク）相運ひ候儀、万々難有存候儀に有之候。〇婦美子には益壮健成長之趣、朝夕之賑はひ嘸かしならんと想像致し候。帰国之事も相延ひ候様には候へ共、十月中旬に候へは二三ケ月之延ひに有之、猶楽しみを相増候と存候。追々暑さに向ひ候へは、近々レーキジヨルチエ又候参候はんと存候。其内は別て勉学一際（キハ）上達相成候様万々祈り存候。

右時候御見舞旁申進度、何も〳〵めて度候かしく

十一年五月十八日

父より

お貞殿

返す〴〵時候御厭ひ被成候様存候。

〔利通〕
一、大久保殿之御事は何共申様無之、吉田君には嘸々相歎（ナゲ）かれ候はんと夫のみ申暮し候。当方にても午後二時頃承り驚き、家内一同気色（ショク）あしく、日々奥方儀子供衆おゆうさん之噂なといたし候。委細

新聞にて御承知之ため、昨今之分弐枚手紙へ入れ
差進し申候。其余は後便に外務省より通し可申候。

一、大久保公一件の電信は何日何時参候哉、次便に
御申越候事。

間、此度は不申進候。

一、お喜代きたいに大久保さんひいきにて、此節にて
も折々申出、其時之大久保さん思召はどうであつ
たろうの、いらざる書生が国の大事のお方を殺した〔コロ〕の、
又先日も英国公使館え伊藤〔博文〕さんや大隈〔重信〕さんが参ら
れた抔〔ナド〕と新聞にあると、夫れらを見、大久保さんがい
らせれると一番に御出に相成るだろうになどゝ一々
たんそく致し候。それが為め自分も心痛〔シンツウ〕いたし候儀
に有之、御一笑〱。

一、左太郎も開拓使にては大に首尾好、日々精勤致し
居候。臼井も不相替精勤、此程御褒美を戴き大悦に
御座候。右申進度、如斯御座候。万々めて度かしく

十一年六月三十日
　　　　　　　　父より
お貞殿へ

猶々富美子には弥丈夫にて、旅館所々かけ廻り候
事と推量いたし候。折角心付怪我なと不致様呉々
も念入可被申候事。

一、帰国前は手帳をこしらへ何事にても一々書留

四二　志村智常発吉田貞宛

明治11年6月30日

〔朱筆〕
第十五号

大暑之趣如何御座候哉、御左右承り度一筆申進候。先
以御揃賑々敷御暮し被成候事、此上もなふ悦ひ入申候。
次に当方皆々無事消日いたし候まゝ御安心に可被成候。
当時は定て暑を避〔サケ〕候ため涼敷〔スゝシキ〕地に参られ候事と相察し
申候。

一、此程おたか参り、山々宜敷申上呉候様申聞、写真
一枚持参候まゝ相贈り申候。且雲丹〔ウニ〕一箱預り置申候。大久〔利通〕
食物類差出候儀は兼て御断に付相送り不申候。大久
保さん之御事咄し御座候へ共、先前申進候通りに候

四三　志村智常発吉田貞宛

明治11年8月15日

〔朱筆〕
第十八号

六月廿三日認められ候御書状八月十日到来、一覧いた
し候処、御揃ますく〳〵御壮健之由めて度御儀存候。次
に当方皆々無事安穏に御座候まゝ、御放念可被成候。
先便一寸申進候お喜世不快も追々よろしく、此節は常
之通に有之候間、御案事被成間敷候。

一、当夏はニヨルク之海辺へ参られ、海水をあびら
れ候由、養生には極宜敷趣兼て承り居申候。

一、九月十五日か十月一日頃桑港(サンフランシスコ)出帆之船にて帰国致
され候よし、さすれば遅くも十月末には帰着に相
成候半と、皆々大悦ひにて相待居申候。

一、兼て申進候通、所々めづらしき物とふ見候節は鳥
聞候。

置可被申候。学事は勿論に候事。返す〳〵目出
度かしく

渡書留、かどく〳〵いすぬ様いたし、帰国之上委敷咄
し承り度楽しみ居申候。

一、婦美子ハ(ママ)ます〳〵丈夫ニ育ち、此節は駆廻り(カケ)候由、
智恵の万事早き事おどろき入候。怪我なと無之様能
々心付、時々刻々守女(モリ)へも気を付可申候。

一、当時は帰朝之支度にて嚊々開敷(イソカ)、又諸方へ招かれ(マネ)
馳走に逢ひ、あるひは客来なと色々取込候事と想像
いたし候。

一、新聞紙は今便より差立不申、手前に留置申候。

一、帰途船中富美子困らぬ様、手遊物幷菓子なと用意、
又絵本なとも無之候ては退屈可致(タイクツ)候間、持参さる
べく候。

一、臼井にても一同無事、子供も至て丈夫に成長致し
候。此程は臼井も一段上り、七等属被　仰付、月給
も増し皆々大悦ひ、御祖母様も大悦に御座候。且先(精)
日も出情相勤るとて御褒美之外に御手当金を戴き、
此節大に都合よろしく、お花も宜敷御礼申入候様申

志村智常発吉田貞宛

右先日之御返事旁申進度如此御座候。あらゝめて度

かしく

　十一年八月十五日　　　　　　父より

お貞殿参人々無事

返すゝ時分折角相厭はれ候様存候。婦み子にも
此夏を過候へは、別て安心いたし候事に御座候。
一、今度御廻し相成候絵本は誠に珍敷、打寄拝
見いたし大切に仕舞置候。
一、婦美子帰り候はゝ日本之事皆始てに付、嘸々〔マヽ〕
驚き申候はんと存候。
一、先便拙老之写真三枚書状に封し入差立候間、
最早相届き候儀と存候也。目出度かしく

四四　志村智常発吉田貞宛

明治14年1月11日

第十八号

年始之御祝儀は別紙に申入候。其後御替なふ渡らせら

れ目出度存候。扨旧冬田町弐丁目之屋敷之望人有之売
渡し、同五丁目へ屋敷相求め候へ共、地借人家作致し
居、差向左太郎住居差支候に付、同四丁目へ借家住居
為致候処、何か手ぜま且日当りよろしからず、子供等
難渋之様子に付捨置難く、所々近辺相応之家作相尋候
へ共、歳末故か何分無之候に付、無余儀暫時之処当方
へ同居之事に取極、旧冬三十日に引移申、当女部屋大
掃除いたし、同所に住居させ、当年早々より諸方相尋〔さ欠カ〕
ね居、相応之家有之次第直に移転之積り、尤子供等之
儀は成丈け座敷之方へ参り不申候様申付、御祖母殿が
終日御世話、又御小言御察し可被成候。
右之段吉田君へ御断御申置之程頼入候。

一、旧冬勇蔵君より御送り被下候昆布上品に付、今便
御送り申候。且興津鯛も先便残之分相贈り申候。
一、御申越之半切紙今便少々差進申候。
一、此節東京は附火又盗賊多く、既に一昨夜小川町榎
本君宅へ忍ひ入、代金六百円程之品を盗み取候由、
誠に油断ならぬ事に御座候。一、梅ケ谷名代谷川年

始として入来番附持参候付、則差出候間御上け可被
成、何もく／＼めて度かしく
お貞殿無事

十四年一月十一日　　　　父

猶々、寒気相厭はれ候様存候。

一、旧冬十二月十七日之絵入新聞に左之通
　鮫島公使〔尚信〕が遠逝せられし訃音を聞て朝野惜み
　あへるに、在米国吉田全権公使〔清成〕も肺病にかゝ
　られ療養最中なりとの風説を聞けり。真偽は
　保証しがたけれど、若し実説なれは何卒快癒
　せられ候様にと祈るの外なし。

右新聞は更に不存、又絶へず御音信は有之平気
に罷在候処、逢人毎に咄し有之、少しく心配、
杉浦五郎君入来右之咄し有之、其地より之便り
之有無等問合され候に付、相談之上新聞本社へ
尋回りおよび候処、全く浮説之趣に有之、元よ
り左も可有之存候へ共、大に安心致し候事。

一、旧年差立候衣類は延引、嘸々不都合之御事と

申暮し候。其他之品々は気に入候哉、委細次便
に御申越し可被成候。

一、横浜にて高橋君へ依頼ブリイヤム氏へ注文之
　節通弁御座候処、是非十二月初度之便船迄に間
　に合せ可申趣之処、中々初旬は扨置、末之出帆
　前日に相成候ても届き不申、封し方とふ差支候
　に付心配により、同日午後より横浜へ出張取に
　参り候処、ゆるく＼当方へ差立候折柄にてあや
　うく当便に間に合せ候儀に有之候。

　新年之御題

　　竹有佳色

常盤木にまさるなしある呉竹は
もと末かけてふかみとりなる

右態と申懸候也。

平智常

四五　志村智常発吉田貞宛

明治14年12月23日

志村智常発岡田彦三郎宛

〔朱筆〕第四拾号に添

近々帰朝に付ては、餞別之為所々へ呼ばれ□□〔破レ〕は此方へ
招き候など、嘸々いそがしく候半と存候。拠婦女の身
にして又々其地へいたり候事は甚難き事にて、是迄数
年懇意になり、朝昼之様にゆきゝ候方々も、御互に万
里の波濤隔候事故、婦人どふしはまづ一世のわかれと
覚悟せねばならず、さすれは当地より其国へ出立之折
の別れとは大にことなり、殊に我国人と違ひ、外国之
方々ゆへ、先づ初めて其地へ渡り候節之事よりして、
数年来滞在中厚意懇心に預り候事共は勿論、倶に佳
興之事有之候節之事共礼謝し、或は打解かたらひ一も
おろそか事これなき様誰々にも極丁寧に相語可被申候。
実に日本婦女子が無智乃身を以衆人之愛を請候は無此
上僥倖に付、此際別して気を入れ、万事首尾好相はか
れ、後来米国に愛の不消様心かけ可被申候。
　此儀遙々申進候迄にも無之候へ共、老の寝覚に彼
れ是と思ひめくらし、婦人之身にして今般のわか
れは嘸かしつらからんと想像候まで、一寸申添か
しく。めて度可祝

十四年十二月廿三日夜認　　　父より

お貞殿

〔注〕吉田は翌年一月帰朝。

四六　志村智常発岡田彦三郎宛

明治（　）年7月28日

拝展　陳は御令閨御病痾兎角御勝れ不被成候由、嘸々
御困難之御事と御察申上候。就て吉田方留守邸之儀御〔清成〕
配慮云々御申越之趣御了承、拙子も日々見廻候含には御
座候得共、到低杉山壱人引受之姿に相成、駆者も居候〔ママ〕
得共、新参者故跡と当てにも致し兼候次第故、兎に角
一応唯今之都合鎌倉へ御通報置候方可然存候。該方に
ても心配に存候はゝ何歟御工風も可有之候。此段御回
答、草々不具

七月念八

岡田君貴下

志邨

猶々、酷暑之際、令閨君には折角御加養御坐候様
奉祈候也。

四七　志村智常発吉田貞宛

明治（　）年（　）月（　）日

副書

去る四日渓仙家内来車、今般自宅石室に製造取懸り候
儀之処、費用見積りよりは極外相嵩、仙造義は居不申、
私而已、誠に困却、勿論造作其他精々省略いたし候へ
共、元来手広、加之裏の方に往来道附、三方表構に相
成候故、案外石数相殖随て地形土台石等増殖、最早落
成間近に相成候へ共、資金に差支候儘、吉田様御留守
居右様之儀相願候ては恐入候へ共、何卒御助け被下、
金百五拾円御拝借被仰付度、勿論今日は所々旦那様方
へ願に出、彼是隙取夕景参上、何共恐入候段懇々相述
（為土産芝口蟹屋のカステーラ一箱持参）候に付、御申聞之廉々真に御察し申候。

乍去別段預り金迚も無之、適近本省より請取候共、必
用品取入候彼地へ相廻し候間、右代価へ仕払候折柄にて、
何分差当り不能其儀旨申断候処、正に証書差上、決て
御不義理等不仕候間、何と賖御取計御貸渡被下度条再
三申立、彼れ之事故諸家方へも出入致し居候儀に付、
一概に断付候訳にも相成兼候に付、篤と勘考いたし、
精々都合相成候様従是回答可致旨徐々に談合差返し、
再三愚考致し候処、是迄格別御懇命被成置候者之儀、
ケ様之節は必歎願可申上、彼れの目的に相違無之、殊
に此程の咄しに殿抔御出立前仰に、其方住居も近々石
造に可相成間、其節困らぬ様に為致と御懇に被仰下候
に付、千五百円丈は恪晴［ママ］いたし置候へ共、殆と右倍増
に相成候抔云々申聞直談、事情難黙止場合も御座候付、
彼れ再応不来内多少為持遣し候方可然と気付候間、左
の趣を以金五拾円貸附申候。

此程内話之金員之儀付、力及兼候得共、折角之依
頼難黙止候に付、精々不都合に不相成様思慮勘弁
いたし候へ共、御承知之通過日之大火災にて、知
己および出入之者等数員類焼、多少苦情申聞、是

非に不拘救助致し不遺候ては不相叶もの両三輩有
之、夫是何分差間候に付、真に気之毒には候へ共、
何分頼談之金員用立候訳には難相成、依て拙子差
繰金五十円用立候条申遣候処、差向受取方にて礼
謝申越、本証書は明日彼方持参候旨申越候　来一月
二日開
店見込。
之由。

右は何れに取計貴慮に相叶可申哉と再三再四愚考致し
候へ共、他に相談可致者も無之、痛心此事に御座候。
依て愚意之趣処右様専断いたし候。元より一己之取計
に御座候間、如何様にも取直し方有之候に付、否至急
御賢慮之程御通知可被下候也。
但証書差越次第写御廻し可申候事。

四八　高橋新吉発宮本小一宛

明治（　）年8月26日

回運丸便より呈啓仕候。御安泰奉欣賀候。陳者、漠城
より之報告疾に御地には事情御承知之儀とは被存候得

高橋新吉発宮本小一宛

共、適々探偵之者より申来候に付閣下迄申上候条可然
御取計可被成下候。外に点庵より之意見書奥村え宛
来致候に付御覧に入候。点庵は金剛山中之有名なる者
にて本願寺に帰向いたし、昨年元山津より来朝いたし
当時西京本願寺に罷居候。当地は別に相変り候儀無之
韓人も入館不致故、居留人民も困却を極候。扨回運丸
船長小島伴輔と申候者一昨年来より元山津えも数度航
海いたし候。就ては仁川又は元山幷当所に御用船回送
之儀有之候はゝ可被仰付段願出候間、万一御入用之儀
有之節は被仰付候て可然者と見認め候に付、左様御承
知可被下候。まつは此段奉得御意候。匆々再行

八月廿六日

宮本老台閣下

二白　千歳丸便より宝迫儀申進置候条、次便に何
分被仰越度候。

〔注〕朱筆にて「此伴輔に面し釜山の様子相尋ねしに何も異
状なしと云耳」とあり。

高峰譲吉発渡辺洪基宛

四九　高峰譲吉発渡辺洪基宛

明治（21）年2月8日

博覧会共進会例規之処に付、当省次官へ御書面之趣き
も有之に付、右取調べきの命に拠り外国博覧会に関し
たる諸書類［類］を調査し、其他右等之会へ派遣したるもの
両三名に就き取糾し候処、一地方限り開設の博覧会共
進会へ皇族親王家を総裁に奉戴したる適例に見当り不
申、又一地方に限たる内国之博覧会共進会にも其例無
之候間、右様御了承相成度小官より此段及御回答候也。

廿一年二月八日

高峰譲吉

渡辺洪基殿

五〇　立嘉度発熊谷武五郎宛

明治（　）年4月4日

間、尚正院へ相廻り候上は至急相運ひ候様時々は催促
奉願候。此程山田之一条抔は既に十六七日も相掛り実
以困怖之次第、右之辺可然御含置奉願候。以上

四月四日

立拝

熊谷様御親披

五一　田中章発岡田彦三郎宛

明治（　）年5月14日

拝啓　別紙第三十三銀行より相回候に付、夫々御調印
相成候様御取斗置被下度、明後日弥取引之節は、小生
御同行可致候得共、其内御取斗置相成度候。本日横浜
行は取止候得共、雅客多来旁参邸仕兼候間、宜敷御申
上置可被下候。明日は必す相伺候積りに御坐候。右用
事迄、早々

五月十四日

田中章

岡田彦三郎殿

此程は不快にて引入罷在、打絶不得貴顔。扨兼々御打
合［カ］願ひ置候神山之一件は、一昨日委曲伊藤へ申談置候

谷口安定発田口将之宛

五二　谷口安定発田口将之宛

明治（　）年5月17日

過般前田校長へ御托し御坐候御馬、御戻し方松田氏へ
御照会、即同氏より伝諭に依り牽せ差上候間御受取相
成度候也。

　五月十七日

　　　　　　　東京農林学校
　　　　　　　　谷口安定
田口将之殿

五三　種田政明発山沢静吾宛

明治（　）年2月3日

山沢静吾君閣下

本日退出より御出被下候趣奉承知候処、当日は退出よ
り脇方へ参堂〔九〕に付、何卒明四日午後四時比より御出被
下候度平奉冀〔ママ〕候。一昨日は御出被下候由、迂生被御尋
可申上筈候処、未其儀を不得、失敬平に御恕可被下候。
いつれ拝謁之上御帰朝旁々奉拝祝候。早々頓首

　二月三日

　　　　　　　　種田政明

五四　寺島宗則発渡辺宛

明治16年6月20日

芳翰細報を辱し、再四復読、本邦之近況如指掌之
至、賢兄弥御順康奉賀候。小生無異在任御放意可被下
候。曽て小子拙著差出候様相覚候。相達候哉。伏て叱
評所仰候。銀行条例改削新議尊案一応御垂示、尚熟読
可仕候。此等は其立法国に擬しなから其本を知らすし
て、フエノメナに区々たり。彼は其利あり、我と異な
る所以を知らさるへからす。之を知らすして効の同し
からんかを求るも得へからさる也。大銀行も亦同し。余
か愚著にも言ふ如く、ゼネラールアキシオムを脳裏に
蓄ふるもの鮮なきを奈何せん。若之を解せは本来のプ
リンシプルを存し、国情の差に因てアツプリケーショ
ンを異にすへし。斯く言へは黄口児も知りたる説法の
様なれとも、一向右之順叙〔序〕に進ますと見へて、頻りに

怨つにあらずや。抑々経済の理をして人間交生に其用を逞ふせしむる方法を講究するは英仏其他甚難しとする所なるに、我国之を擲棄するは大息之至、擲棄して居るには非すと惟ふときは更に大嘆息、纔に膚浅の説を献する者あれは雷同寵用、併し是れは我邦はかりにも限らす、第十八センチュリの初、仏にてもヂョンローに蠱惑せられ、其国財を大に失ふたる事なともありし。本邦の民情余程仏に似たるものあり。贅話は擱き、賢兄欧米に官遊の一望あるは幸なり。小生の後任に当ては如何。御心算肝要也。此等未発前外人に評せらるゝは不都合なれは、外務卿の外他言あるへからす。同卿よりも漫露せさるよう御添言可被下候。不要言れとも、外邦古今に可見の書甚多し。賢兄閑散の官暇多読なるも、或未足なるへし。外邦使臣の任は恰も読書界に流竄せらるゝか如きを幸とし、最其嗜好ある賢兄の如き、則前陳本源に遡らさるの大憾を除かは、本邦の福何過焉。此寸楮芳報の一辞に充る耳。時下折角御自玉所伏祈候。謹具

十六年六月廿日

渡辺議官殿

寺島宗則

五五　徳大寺実則発吉井友実宛

明治（　）年1月9日

（巻封）吉井殿　実則　請

一、為換手形　壱通

一、金三円七拾六銭　壱通

右唯今御到来に付、早速為持被下深難有存候。吉田氏へも宜御申入之様願存候。呉々御手数を相掛御面働（マヽ）存候。請取書差出候間宜御伝可被下候。猶面上可申解候得共、先御請而已如此候也。

一月九日

五六　中村五郎発岡田彦三郎宛

明治22年1月4日

皆々様御多祥之由慶賀不斜奉存候。去る二日付御書面之趣、逐一了承致候。右は此方より曩に国許草道家へ一書差出置候次第も有之候間、其回答次第御通報可致条其内は御手許置被下候様致度、右に付別段叔父へは書面奉呈不致候間可然御取計被下候様希望致候。先は貴答まて。　草々拝復

廿二年一月四日

岡田彦様貴下

五郎

〔注〕端裏に「廿二年一月四日五郎より岡田へ草道一件」との朱筆あり。

五七　新納刑部発町田久成宛

慶応(2)年6月7日((66)年7月18日)

英出以来追々御懇書時々御無礼も打過真平不得之至平に御宥免可被下候。拙にも無滞三月九日山川着船いたし候処、シンカポールより又々下血相初り余程相煩ひ、先月中旬比迄に漸く相治り申時機にて何分不気根、とんと力無御座候て出勤も出来不申候処、病中にミニストル職を奉し恐入次第、乍去此上は御互之事にも御座候へは、十分之勉職いたし候賦御座候。快気之運に相成（カ）候処、当月一日より出崎今滞崎罷在候。誠に難有仕合には御用透ホードエンえ相調丈薬用、是にて屹と全快候半、是にて已後罷在申候。偖又た拙之ベッポーイも弥仏行之賦当分出崎いたし居候。其上は尚又懸益御配意被下度平に奉願候。諸生中義皆々励勉御座候半、追々書状も相請取申上候へ共、右様之事にて是迄不得意こと計に候。何分不気根故実に不埒不本意千万、此節迄も様々答礼不相調幾重にも不埒千万御坐候へ共、乍憚貴君より宜御伝置被下度奉願候○偖又江戸板字引（カ）着直に相紕候処、此前之本は誤不少、当分は改本之調へ中御座候由追々申遣候へ共、未た出来不申候。開成所より追々願出候へ共何分一致方無御座候。決て油断不致候。一統困り致はは能遠察罷在候。先は乍延引御答礼旁寸紙奉呈候。頓首

第六月七日　　崎陽之客舎

新納刑部発町田久成宛

五八　新納刑部発町田久成宛

慶応（2）年6月7日（'66年7月18日）

上野君

石垣

京師も無事、長一件未た御所置不相成候。将軍も今に
滞坂如何可相成哉、筑前えは五卿衆未た守衛に諸藩よ
り出張り候〇滞欧中白山周旋之一条に存分　御英断相
承り展観出品アンバサトレ後電之通八月初旬には出帆
之賦に候〇御国許も当分改正中にて大混雑、御側御用
人も表御用人合幷町奉行御引取、御繰方御用人より兼
帯、寺社方も元当奉行所跡え引直し、御記録方造士館
え被引直、寺社方等之跡は砲術館被為立筈候。都之城
屋敷御用相承り海軍所御船手御引海軍所え合幷〇御殿
中に小手袖不苦、蒸気船方は都て其通年頭五節句麻袴、
其余は不相用筋被仰出候。乍然屹と度々御慶事等之節
は身明之事候。開成所より二等之列は大かた他国被仰

出候由にて当分出崎も多人数相成居候〇橋泉之所も御
国許之様着船候ゆへと出立迄は逢不申候〇此節は御国
は余程相開け候て横浜滞在之ミニストル被召呼幷其に
はアトミラルも同行之筈、最早当崎に四段備之大軍艦
其外にも滞船相成居候て三四艘も廻船可相成候半。其
上は磯御茶屋にて十分御懇意被為尽尚々深く御結ひ相
成筈、弥々能其折柄之旨海陸之調練御望相成筈御座候。
拙之出崎も貴君一列為替首尾且是より先之治定等之為
に御座候。又為替一件も先比懸合置最早相来候半〇偖
は我々列にも夫々銘々に掛被仰出皆一人つゝ被為宛候
て、桂御勝手方へ小海軍岩佐（大夫之　任あり）陸軍へ拙外国方、
其余之人数は都て定式方被仰出相成申候。日々之事御
用取扱に御座候。先比ホンコン差越之御国許より之問
合之儀に付ては委敷事情も相咄申候処、何分問合之通
にも参兼候事故、何れ□〔破レ〕出帆之夫衆え篤と御談被下
度、懸る事情難尽□〔破レ〕滞仏之白せんも同様に御座候。
尚又出帆之折には能く□〔破レ〕様可致候。近々之御書
中に相見得候儀にては余程□〔破レ〕意之由遠察罷在候。若も

114

新納刑部発竹隠宛

〔ママ〕被差急き事共御座候は、〻□分之御所置被成度候○御 〔破レ〕

交之遠航一条も已畢之事にて幕より一言之咎目無之、

既に先比は諸藩又は商人等誰人に不依遠航免許可相成、

且又展観所出品も勝手に相成り候様之勢候。御国許より展観所之勢に

咎目之勢に無御座候。御国許より展観所へ出品七分之

遣筈之由にて、拙生帰府之上は相究居米人も先日出帆

賦之筈にて最早江戸も買物出尽候。然処米魯蘭も被差

之由、蘭えは一人歟其外は三四人つゝと色々名も承り

候へ共急に取申候。追て可申越候○日本之事情等近々

申越候様承知之一条も是迄は何分届兼候事も有之候へ

共、前件通外国掛之名目相立居候事に候へは是より出

来申候。一ヶ月一度位之賦にて其向より仕出之治定い

たし置候○兵庫開港一件に付御国より何と申出も御座

候由、是は無相違其通に候。乍然余程意味有る事之由、

異人方も能々了解相成居候も無訳、既に此節は身明呼

入候時機相成候事にても何も御懸念之御廉更に無御座

候。不具

　第六月七日崎陽之旅舎

　　　　　　　　石垣

上野様

五九　新納刑部発竹隠宛

慶応(3)年3月12日((67)年4月16日)

誠御疎情罷過候処追々御懇情実に御深志之程不浅難有

厚謝候。偖若印も最早着も能く

運立候様暮々も祈居候。不相替貴兄以下一統勉励之旨

先々大慶至○先度も申上越置候通、京都も大変如何之

ものに候半、苦心罷在候。然るに　二之丸公も来る十

九日御発駕と相究御上京之旨、是にて後来之御企相

建候歟、何辺御手軽にて我々列之御供も無之御側役而

已に御座候。陸軍兵士一バタイロン、外に大砲一隊海

軍一隊之御供に御座候。此節は土佐侯にも御出懸之賦

に御打合相成候旨に存申候○小帯老も今以滞京、当分

之通にてはいつ下りの出来事に相成候半○五代にも不

相替多用、一昨日より又御出崎に相成申候。是は替せ

銀追々相届き出に付出崎なり○竹下にも大元気、集成

二橋元長発遠藤宛

館には異人参り居誠に日々盛之事に御座候。器械も十
分出来、拝見人実に数百人よし。夫故今日之細工出
来兼候処より、無拠二三日に相究り一ヶ月に三度つゝ
に相成可申候。堀壮十郎も通弁之為に集成館え参居今
暫時之滞在に候半。長崎生立にて嘸大屈之筈存候○磯
永には近々出来候由、親父にも極喜悦之至、実以無此
上事に御座候○米航人数も英地之様参候由、是は如何
に候半。懸て御配意も被成難有と存申候○長崎之カラ
ハにも来十六日比長崎出帆一先帰英之由、夫故才助も
尚以差急き申事に御座候○小子之スモールも着仏之由、
懇意之程も承知、誠に御懇情之程分て奉厚謝候。偖是
に付御奉行様方差上け等奉願置候処、先比御伺出候内
三百石つゝ我々列差上に付ては岩下并小子之スモール
は全く御構に被仰付候へ共、又々是非初之趣を相建候
筋に当分は申立中に御座候○仏語明要五本先比差上候。
残之冊出来候付差上候。余は出来次第直に可差上候。
因て仏之諸生には貴兄より宜く御計被下度奉願候。此
本は才助方え相渡置に付彼之家より差送可申、先々申

上度事共山々に候へ共幾〔カ〕く止め申し不日と存候。

三月十二日

竹隠君机下貴報

拙修〔カ〕拝上

一統之人数より折々英音も御座候共始終打過真平
不敬之至、宜御伝置被下候事乍余御頼申上候○岩印
初之人物も宜く。

〔付紙〕
「誠に余計之事御願申上嘸御困り之筈と奉存候へ共、
耳之不通成る者に物言ひの道具をキュッタにて拵候
見たる事御座候。是を御帰帆之折に何卒御土産に御恵
を願上度御座候。余り願上兼候へ共無拠入用に付遮て
奉願上候。宜御含み被下度、此段前広申上置候。」

六〇 二橋元長発遠藤宛

明治（21）年5月31日

尊書拝見仕候。向暑之節倍御清適御眠食之段欽慶。陳
は本日吉田様御邸に於て角力御催に付、御寵招被下難
有奉存候。是非拝見に罷出度心得之処、本日は兼てよ

り約置候無拠仕兼候。甚乍残念拝趨仕兼候。何れ不日
以参御礼可申述心得に御座候得共、一応之処宜敷御執
成被成下度、乍末久々御疎遠に打過不本意之至、其内
何れえか御供可相願、先は右拝願迄、匆々如此御座候。
不宜

　五月卅一日　　　　　　　　　二橋元長
　遠藤様侍史

六一　三島通庸発奥宛

　　　　　　　　　　　　明治（　）年2月23日

拝啓　御不快之由時分柄折角御加養専一と存候。陳は
兼て御内談仕候折田正介当庁へ転任之義既に上申相成
候間、至急帰京致居候様貴官より電報御申遣被下度存
候。此段得貴意候。敬具

　二月廿三日　　　　　　　　　（三島）
　　　　　　　　　　　　　　　　通庸
　奥老台

芳墨拝誦、来る卅一日角力御催に付小児召連参上候様
御紙面之趣案内拝承。然るに当時大磯へ入浴中に付、
乍遺憾参上致兼候条不悪御承知可被下候。右御答旁艸
々拝具

　第五月卅日　　　　　　　　　三島和歌子
　吉田子爵令夫人

再伸、乍御邪魔小児拝観に罷出候哉も難図、御含
み置被成下候様願上候。拝具

六二　三島和歌子発吉田貞宛

　　　　　　　　　　　明治（21）年5月30日

御聞取可被下候。偖根室県八等属吉田勇蔵儀貴県士族
切角御厭奉南山候。退て小宦儀無異在京仕候間乍余事
一翰呈上致候。未た冷気難凌候処愈以御精務被成御坐

六三　湯地定基発渡辺千秋宛

　　　　　　　　　明治（　）年（　）月（　）日

吉田家執事発吉田別邸執事宛

にて、当県へ奉職之者有之候処、此程中実父大患之急
報を得、為令看護帰省致候[ママ]候処、実父病症増進遂に死
去せし由に御坐候。就ては遠隔之地方へ奉仕候ては家
事向き目下困難を極め、其他内情に至難黙止儀有之候
趣に御坐候間、貴宦御配下欠員相当之場所へ御登用被
成下候様本人伯父吉田外務大輔より御依頼致呉候様懇
談承候故、何卒御聞済御都合被下度頻りに小宦より奉
願候。然るに吉田八等属儀は本県土木課員にて四五年
来性実奉務厚御用弁之見込も有之候処、何分難捨
置前件之情実に御坐候条を以突然軽子之御配慮相願
候得共、前段之次第に依り、旁御斟酌御厚意を以て是
非今回御採用被下度平に御願仕候。尚追ての御沙汰承
知仕度指向き右御願仕候耳。早々謹言

　　月　日
　　　　根室県
　　　　　湯地定基

　鹿児島令
　　渡辺千秋様机下

再伸、恐入候得共本文宣布御親披被下御繰合御加
対し翌二十四日乙号電報差立置候。去る二十一日付機

入可被成下、御模様不生に御教示被下度、貴報相
待候。敬白

六四　吉田家執事発吉田別邸執事宛

明治（　）年8月23日

別紙之通り、島津家扶東郷重持氏より本日午后七時郵
便にて被申越候間、此段及廻送候也。

　八月廿三日午后七時
　　　　吉田家執事
　吉田別邸執事中

六五　吉田二郎発井上馨宛

明治17年7月26日

機密第四十一号
〔欄外〕
「清仏間談判事件　八月十六日接収」

本月二十二日付甲号貴電同二十三日夕接閲仕候。右に

吉田二郎発井上馨宛

密第四十号を以て御送致申候総署照会えの回答其他一般の時事に関し、去る二十二日独米魯公使館に出会し、種々談話有之候中、右照会に対する返答振に関し説話有之候処、或は此度仏に於て八月一日迄談判に関し説話延し候に付ては、今暫く回答見合せ置候方可然と申候公使も有之、或は一応の回答致置候方可然と申公使も有之、帰する処近日の内一応の回答を致す事に相成候。尤総署照会中諸国竟に兵船を以て各口を滋擾し、以て貿易の阻滞財産の損傷を致さば一切諸国より独認賠補すべし、絲毫も中国に渉る事なしとの一節に対し一言せざる時は、或は仏艦開港場に迫るを辞柄とし、無頼の清人外国人の身体財産に損傷を致すとも清政府の責に非らざるとの誤解を生するの懸念も有之候に付、右様の乱暴を制止するは清政府の本分なりと総署の注意を催かし置く事に大抵同意、其他の点は各自の随意にて両三日中に照改を致す事に相成候。右の次第に付拙官も各公使回答振を見計へ、成る丈妥に措調照改致候積の処、甲号御電報に対し回電差進候趣も有之に付、

定て今日頃は何とか御指令可有之と存し、差扣罷在候次第に候。乍去右は独英公使等の振合に準し照改致し候とも我政府を約束する所毫も無之、若し上海談判不調と相成、仏艦開口を鎖さす等の時に方り、我人民財産に対し無暗に損害を加へざる様清政府の注意を請求候丈の事に止り候得は、別に不都合は有之間敷と思考候に付、若し今明日中に御指令無之時は拙官於ても一応の照改可致込に御座候間此段予め具申仕置候。尤右照会中以致貿易阻滞財産損傷一切応由諸国独認賠補云々拙官の電信余り簡略に過ぎ、仏より損傷を致すすす事に限り候様に相見候に付、去る二十四日の電信にて増補仕候次第に御座候。

両江惣督とパトノートル公使と談判可有之儀に付ては、別紙丙号電信安藤領事経由にて申進置候。右は機密第四十号を以て申進置候通り、曽国筌全権委員に命ぜられたる旨仏代理公使へ通知し、同時に尚五日の猶予を請求候処、曽氏於て償金一件丈の談判に渉る事ならは八月一日迄猶予す可き旨仏公使より回答したる趣に候。

119

吉田二郎発井上馨宛

安藤領事より電報に曽惣督は去る二十三日南京を発し
たる趣に候得は、清政府に於て何れ償金談判に渉り候
事に該惣督え指令したるものと被察候。各公使の意見
も、清政府は幾干か償金を出し、何か仏政府於て償金
の要求高を減すると其体面を損せざる丈の名を仏に
与へて、以て無事に帰するを謀るならん。仏も強て開
戦は好まざる処なる可けれは、尚協議の望なしと難言
と申居候。

去る二十二日別紙丁号写之照会総署より送来候に付、
翌二十三日独公使を訪ひ相談に及候処、同氏の言に、
仏艦福州港を侵す場合に於ては清政府之を鎖すの権あ
るは疑を容れす。然し未た開戦の前に方り、仏艦斯の
如き所為はある間敷被考候得共、総署より右様の通知
有之上は、其言ふ処に就て答を不可不致なりと申候。
其答振は、清政府は右の告知を為す以上は開港場に在
る独逸人に保護を加へらるゝ事、並に若し清人より独
逸人の身体財産を損害する場合に於ては必らす賠償の
要求ある可きに付、予め之を避くる事とに最注意ある

可き事と期望する旨に有之候。次で米公使を訪候に不
在に付、書記官に面し回答振問合候に、未た照改不致
趣に候。又昨日英公使を尋ね都合相尋候処、目今在福
州英領事に事情問合中に付未た照改致さす、総署に問
合たるに未た全く堵塞したる訳に無之様子なりと申候。
夫より露公使を訪候に、福州一件仏代理公使に尋たる
に、仏艦に於て清船の通行を妨くる等の所為ありし事
なしとの趣に付、未た照改不致と申居候。右一件は尚
各公使館へ打合の上不都合なき様照改可致と存し候。

右申進候也。

明治十七年七月二十六日

臨時代理公使　吉田二郎

井上外務卿殿

〔注〕駐清国日本公使館用箋。欄外に吉田清成外務大輔・竹
添進一郎駐朝弁理公使・外務省公信局秘書官斎藤修一
郎の朱印あり。

120

六六　吉田勇蔵発吉田貞宛

明治17年2月23日

左之通り之品々御手数千万之義と被存候得共、重より
購入方願上被呉候様願出候に付、御見立呉度願上候。
代金は少々不足之様に被察申候得共、昨年来より食ひ
残り溜候拾弐円丈より外無之趣に付、万一不足之廉有
之候はゞ、御手許にて御助力之程願上候。頓首

　　十七年二月二十三日　　　　　　　　勇蔵百拝

　　吉田家叔母君

　　　注文品

一、節糸織　弐反
　　内壱反は女角織壱反は夜具用に付、大ふしの荒縞何
　　れも御見立度候。

一、もめんうち　弐反
　　是は夜具裏用　色は紺なり

一、めんけつたん　壱丈六尺

一、着色きん糸　五匁

一、なき人寸志　八尺
　　是は大巾
　右之通り御座候也。

吉田勇蔵発吉田貞宛

121

差出人不明書翰（吉田清成宛）

1　明治（4）年9月18日

寺嶋外務大輔公え之別封早々届出取計候様御申越之段
承知いたし候。此段御直報および候也。

九月十八日

〔注〕裏面に「吉田租税権頭殿外庁」とあり。

2　明治（6／7）年（　）月（　）日

謹啓

少輔公閣下

夜来御近火折節烈風御心配被為在候儀奉察候。私共辺
よりは築地辺と誤認仕候より拝趨をも不仕恐縮仕候。
しかし御別条も無御座恐悦不已奉存候。

○

別冊は北代正臣より先つ閣下え呈し被下候様頼托に付
為持奉指上候。御一閲被為在候。御上にて内務及我卿
え御回し御座候様仕度との事に御座候。

○

本日は御風邪気旁御参省御断夫々申通候。且史官えも
御届仕候。大隈殿には昨日横浜御出張、夫より横須賀
辺え御越しと申事に御座候。御出省無之歟、又御届取
計申候。尤是は右各〔後欠〕

3　明治（22）年（10）月（26）日

拝呈仕候。昨今寒気相募申候得共、益御綏福被為渉奉
恭賀候。昨今は議長殿も被退、殊に御配慮の御儀と奉
存候。猶我国政治界之変動は之に止まらさる事と被想
察候。精々御自重御自愛奉千祈万禱候。井上伯〔馨〕山口よ
り神戸迄は近日帰ると、内閣へは不被帰抔噂云候とも、
神変不識之大将故如何や。外諸君は一先辞表御聞届無
之にて結局の様にも相見候。是亦何分のものに哉。此

際我工務局も局長更迭有之、本日斎藤修一郎氏商務局

長にて工務局長兼任相成、前田旧局長は農務局長
〔正名〕

農林学校長兼任相成候。官制発布前商工合併の小改革

を見申候。乍去人間及事務は改革の官制発表迄当分是

件奉願候次第に御座候。草々再越

　四月晦

　　　　吉田子爵閣下

5　明治（　）年5月12日

拝啓　昨夜は罷出御高話拝聴、且腹痛之為殊之外御心

配を豪難有奉謝候。御蔭にて本日は全回復仕候間、御

安意被下度、先御礼迄。草々頓首

　五月十二日

　　　　　　　　武再行

　　吉田清成様

乍憚御令夫人え宜敷御伝被下度奉願候。

世上時に閣下を某省大臣の候補中に相加候は乍蔭御嬉

敷奉存上候。当今〔後欠〕

○

高橋特許局長兼農林学校長は本日非職相成、世上に噂

高き白露国〔ペルー〕への鉱業に従事候為め、来月出発の筈に御

坐候。

〔是清〕

迄通の積に御坐候。

4　明治（　）年4月30日

先夜は参堂種々御高話共難有、深更まで御妨恐縮千万

に存候。扠、今一応御教示相願度、明夕か明後朝十二

時前参堂仕度候所御指支有之候はゝ御一報奉願度。御

指支無之候はゝ不及其義候。実は先や申上候如く来る

二日小集相催候都合に候間要領丈は十分相貯置申度前

度奉存候。尚内申可仕義出来候はゝ無怠可奉入尊聴候。

密啓

6　明治（　）年7月18日

本日も各大臣には内閣出頭集議有之候趣にて、山県大
〔有朋〕

臣には余程急きにて、巡査も間に合はさる位にて二時

過出頭相成候由に御坐候。本日之天気同様晴雨相分り

差出人不明

差出人不明

謹承拝上

七月十八日午後三時

晩翠公閣下

7　明治（　）年8月9日

昨八日御帰　朝に付別紙御届書被遣正に落掌仕候。正
院御届等夫々取計可申存候。此段可然被提上可申候也。

八月九日
　　　　　　　卿輔付属［ヵ］

吉田少輔殿　執事御中

8　明治（　）年9月18日

前刻は拝諭、偖、粗御予議之事とは存候へへとも一昨十
七日之臨時官報到来に付呈覧致候。匆々拝首

九月十八日後九時半
　　　　　　　　　　五人

吉田先生

9　明治（　）年11月7日

拝啓　尓後益御清穆被為在奉恐賀候［ヵ］。昨日は参謁奉謝

候。其節ねかひ候御書付御認にも相成御坐候はゝ被下
候様奉希上候。若も御用多にて未た御認にも不相成候
事にも被為在候はゝ、明日明後日にも被成下候様奉希
上候。先は昨日之御礼旁右迄、草々如此に御坐候。
頓首再行

10　明治（　）年11月30日

十一月七日
吉田君侍側　左右迄此相届

御清安奉賀候。陳は前日呈上之一冊猶又岩倉公一見致
度旨申聞に付明日迄宮内省え御投与被下度態と罷出候
処、御不在残念なり。両三日中一夕三嶋先生在京中御
一話相願度方奉面晤候也。

十一月三十日
　　　　　　　晩翠先生

11　明治（　）年（　）月15日

拝見仕候。鎌倉地所御拝借候義は、去る十二日頃に候

124

委細申送り置候処、今日に至り通行免状被差越候。因て直に当人止宿先き〔木賀村〕（かめや）え可相送候処、同人より閣下えの書束も御座候儀何とか御答も被遣訳に候はゝ、壱併差立郵便に付し申度、依て一同奉差上候。御答書被遣候儀に候はゝ、別紙え御封し込被遣度奉存候。

〔朱筆〕「郵便税未定に付跡払に取斗申候」

半荒田へ相托し差上候事と取覚申候。如何之行違ひにて今日頃御話に相成候得は、誠に不相済之説と恐縮平に御ゆるし可被下候。扨、早速可相窺之処、無據来客御座候に、いつれ早目と引取候はゝ参上可仕候。不取敢拝答仕候。頓首

十五日

清成公閣下

追て、過日は鎌倉より三橋与八参上候由、定て御建築之事を百事御聞取御都合と奉存候。

〇

閣下御俸金受取候に付、則為持差上申候。尤仕丁壱人差添差出し申候。此ものへ前件の概略差含め置申候間、御下命相成候はゝ謹奉可仕候。

〇

国債寮菰田謙助横浜より帰京、東洋銀行より別紙横文書被托候由、則奉指上候。

〔裏面墨書〕表書の通り慥に到着致候得共、東洋銀行之一書は不相見認候事。維れ通行免状は一書を添へ封込即刻仕丁へ

〔　　〕上

12　明治（　）年（　）月（　）日
〔朱筆〕
〔巻封〕少輔公御手許え

ウヰリアムス氏よりの書壱封メイゾンより預り置候処、本日閣下御臨省不被為在候間、則差上申候。且つ「パスポート」一条に付、去る十五日往復且熊谷大丞え伺の末、閣下御手許に御留め置相成、尤十五日には当人相渡候事。

差出人不明

外務少輔宅え罷越応接いたし、即時相弁し候様致し可申と申聞候事故、休暇に際し旁敢て意とせず、宿直え書記中

清成

受取人不明

受取人不明書翰（吉田清成発）

1　明治（7）年（7カ）月（　）日

発途以来横浜富貴楼にて大隈氏川村氏蕃地行の少将谷氏〔重信〕〔純義〕〔干城〕
なと昼飯を仕且午後三字波止場にいたり、オレゴニエ
ン船え乗船之頃三字半頃にて候乎。四字には出帆いた〔ママ〕
し、伊豆之沖辺より少々波立ち初め、終夜ゆられて難
渋を極め候。殊に二十二日之夜は少々斗り不快と云ひ、
安眠も僅斗にて労れを一入増し、廿四日は終日大風に
て、予航海中洋亜の辺に渡行之内、一度も当日之如き
荒き波間を凌き候事無之、殊に右オレゴニエン船は名
高き動き之強き船にて、さすが船好きも大小込り申候。
御察計可被給候よふ申候。其方が一緒にあらすして幸
ぢやと幾度も思ひやり申候。夜入時分より少々風も柔

き、殊に紀州之鼻を経て大阪之方え向ひ、稍々瀬戸内
に入りたる心持にて、終夜安眠も出来、廿五日早天四
字に起上り四方を望見るに、遠山之眺望、殊に旭の東
の方に上らんとする頃しも、一層の彩輝を加へ、兵庫
神戸之港は近きにあり、名にしおふ港河の廟は旭にか
ゝやき、明石灘一の谷の辺の樹木は青々と翠を含み、
職を魚漁に求むるものはおのがまい／＼漁舟を浮べ、
淡路島山は初秋を迎えんとて棚引朝霧に央は埋られ、
雲か霧が山か嶋かとも誤ては疑われたり。神戸上陸、
諏訪山の常盤楼とて近世高名の楼あり。此にいたり入
浴并せて朝飯を得、続ひて布曳滝にいたり、そのをと
に暫時之間納涼を極め、昼飯畢りて三字にもなりぬれ
は、神戸市中にある三の宮ステーションにいたり、四
字之汽車にて発途、大阪の北野の原に着せしは五字に
五分過ぎなり。迎の人々も余多参り居たれは、同道し
て直くに造幣寮迄人力といたし、十分斗にて着したれ
は、例のチムニーは煙を空にたゝよわし、小きロンド
ンの外様を為したり。

受取人不明

夜に入たれは難波橋辺の夕涼之大鼓の音は手に取るや
うにきこへ、月は人の想を増さんにや、雲なくさへて
昨夜のあらしもわすらしめ、月下に汲む盃も今はと置
ひて、十字頃休みてけさは朝ほらけ、東もいまた暗き
うち起き上り〔後欠〕

2　明治21年5月27日

〔欄外〕第三　三百五十枚　状袋共

一号
第弐なり

拝啓　陳は、本月三十一日白金志田町拙宅に於て小集
相催、小角力入御覧度候間、同日午後第一時御繰合御
来駕被成下度冀望仕候。敬具

廿一年五月廿七日
　　　　　　　　吉田清成
〔見合〕殿

追て、当日晴雨に不拘候。

3　明治22年（　）月（　）日

万一にも泰西各国との締約調候後に至り、清国独り不
肯、旧約を墨守せんとするときは、右の他の各国は最
恵国の一章に依り、彼れに利益ある分は清国の分に引
付けんとする事の起らさるを保証しがたし（但海関税
は泰西各国との間の分に従ふとあるからは強て実場の
憂ひはなきかもしれす）、併注意ものなり。
之を思ひ彼れを想へは杞憂千万なり。兎角条約破棄の
決心（其結果如何は不問に措き）なからされは断行云
々は不安至極の事なり。
破棄之事は万々不可行、之れ諸外国を敵とし、百戦百
勝国家を維持し、それか威権を保ち能ふの力なくては
不能事也。此見認なくして口に強碕主義を唱へ、浅識
の人々をせん動するは、勇に似て至て非なる者、忠に
似て不忠、愛国に似て売国の実ある者なり。破棄の事
類例至て募し、好しあるも場合の異なる事同日之論に
あらす。古今万国交際上の活劇史に疎く、浅学なれと
も多才ある者共は往々心得違ひを為し、大事を過るの
例少からす、実に可憂の極なり。天下を犠性に供して

受取人不明

己れの虚名を博せんと謀るものは国賊なり。嗚呼如何して此難局を救はんや。実に国家危急存亡之秋也矣。
有感記す廿二年夏

4　明治（　）年（　）月（　）日

一筆啓上仕候。久く御無音罷過候処、御揃御機嫌克被為渉候段は、勇蔵〔吉田〕其外より時々伝承仕居候処、頃日石神喜平次〔鮫島〕殿上京、御無恙候段委細直左右共承得慶賀不斜奉存候。随て弊屋一同瓦全消光罷在候間、乍余事御見得居候付、今般は多分東京見物として御上京相成候半と奉存候処、無其儀、稍々失望仕候。喜平次殿にも仕官之望有之由に候得共、京地にては中々六ケ敷、急に相運候模様も無之のみならず、到底存□〔分カ〕の等級等に出仕出来候訳にも至りかね、心配之事に御坐候。御推察可被下候。

却説近時は乍思御疎音申上多罪申迄も無之事は万も承知仕□〔居カ〕候得共、是無他、一は公私多用故日復一日と相送り、今日迄致遅延候。一は又勇蔵慶蔵両人之事に関し、彼是私の心意に適せさる事共有之、以書簡致上陳、御神配を醸候も本意なく奉存候、書状差上候得は、幾于か彼等身上に付私の意見を吐露不仕も却て恐多く奉存候付、当分差扣へ置き、自然は彼等之意向と私の心思と粗一定可仕、又否らさるも老兄公御上京とも相成候得は、親敷御相談可仕と困循仕居候次第に御坐候処、御上京も石神氏の口気にては近々無覚束、殊には頑弟儀目今帰県仕候事も不相叶、又当年中にも或は再ひ外国へ派出仕候も難測に付、不得止事、不適意の件三四御含之為にもと左に陳述仕候。

一、頑弟米国滞在留主中外籍志村智常〔蔵〕氏を相手取り、暴論強談を用ひし事、幷清成は不孝ものなり、我親（大兄を指す）に育てられたるものにして、更に恩義をしらす、帰朝の上親は義絶をすると云居る位の事也と、外籍志村氏〔蔵〕へ明言して罵る事。

一、同勇蔵より米国旅先へ無礼の文を送り金を乞ふ事。

一、拙生グラント氏為迎接長崎出張の留主中、婦人のみの家に来り、大酒の上中村五郎を相手取り諍闘に及ひ、硝子椀具を破棄し、一家中をして恐怖せしむる事。
但中村は遁逃の際、破れたる硝子の為に足を傷く。寸余にして医師を要催す。

一、目今も慶蔵は来客の有無を不問、食物の意の如くならさる時は、度々投棄する等の事度々あり。五郎山口などとは大に気の毒がりて居る事。

一、同人参宅の節は、私に対し朝夕の礼を為す事稀なり、況や刑妻に対しては面を合するも礼儀なき事多しと云。

一、同木錦夜具にては不足なりと拒む事。

一、付与したる物品を無にする事。

一、金は有余あるも書籍を求めざる事。

一、私帰京後
食事の麁抹なりとて来客（是は兄弟在宅中は毎日多数なりと云）〔厭〕或は下婢等の面前にて椀具食物等を蹴散す事婁々なりと云。

一、風呂入方の前後を争ふて、酒後志村氏と争論を促す事（是は拙在宅故教諭して押へぬ）。

一、頑弟え来客のある折、白昼大声を発して兄弟諍闘に及ひ、強は弱に傷け、泣哭んで家屋をして雲助社会の形情を為さしめ、来客或は親族の徒に向ひ、拙者の面皮に傷る事。

一、虚言偏見に基き一家の事を詐り、老公へ陳白する事。
衣服一切の外に毎月七円宛を付与すれとも尚足らすとして老公へ願ふ事、幷着金の事。

一、石見氏帰県の節、同人に托言して余一子をも拙生に不通、矢張従前の通資金を請ひ、一の書籍をも不求、徒に消費する事。

〔注〕草稿か。

5　明治（　）年（　）月（　）日

本月廿八九日比当地出立仕、直に紐育にいたり、一両日滞在仕り、文子疲労（ツカレ）無之候得は、汽船にてロングブランチ（是は海岸納涼之地にて、紐育より凡三十マキ

受取人不明

ル位の名所に御座候。前のプレシデントガラントは毎
年此地に避暑被致候。尤御同人には一家屋を所持被致
候よし承申候）え差越、両三日も休息仕、夫よりレー
キヂョルヅえ赴き候途中に有之候。サレトガと云名所
（名高き温泉の大そう有之候所なり）え三四泊もいた
し、夫よりレーキ迄都合僅に四五十マヰル、半日の間
に罷越、一ヶ月半程避暑仕候つもりに御座候。

　〔注〕草稿か。

　　6

　　明治（　）年（　）月（　）日

五日の手紙相達致被見候。皆々無事之由無此上事と存
候。今日は両人を誘ひ伊豆山へ小鳥狩に出掛候。少々
は猟も有之候。その方承知乎かの伊豆山ふもとの湯屋
にて昼飯共相進め候。やはりもとのいづさんに候へ共、
物価の騰貴せる事は先年に三倍の様子に被察候。
本日福岡（孝弟）参議も着、少く病気之由に相見得候。草道幷
勇蔵両人は明早天出立の仕度に候。直左右御聞取可被
成候。

　　　一左右のみ、早々不備

　　　　　7

　　　　　明治（　）年（　）月（　）日

芳筆拝読仕候。

御書拝読仕候。然は、来廿七日尊邸へ　臨御可被遊候
間。

　〔注〕草稿か。
　〔後欠〕

　　　　　8

　　　　　明治（　）年（　）月（　）日

〔前欠〕

しは予に稀成例にやと笑草の種にもと記し侍りぬ。今
日中は休暇の積なれ共、早天より客来余多、唯今少々
寸暇を得たる故、不取敢一左右申越候也。五代氏（友厚）へい
また面会は不致候へ共、使参り候故、土産物共は皆々
差遣置申候。
他は後便にて申送候。返す〱も毎日々々昼間には被
休度候。来月七日頃迄は人力馬車は不及申、歩引とて
も不致　〔後欠〕

130

補遺

【吉田清成宛】

一　浅井新一

1　明治（6）年10月24日

過刻御下命御座候仏公使館修繕之形行、土木寮中村五
等出仕へ問合候処、右は此程廻議面へ総裁閣下御決判
　　　　　　　　　　　　　　　　〔大隈重信〕
有之に付、直に達方取計申候趣に有之、即達案写差上
　　　　　　　　　　　　　　　　　〔孝禧〕
申候。
〔行間に朱筆書入〕
「然る処尚別属之通に相替り候趣、只今土木寮より
申越候間、是亦写取差上候也。」
一検査寮廻冊写し取差上申候。本職廻案は直に同寮へ
相達申候。

右申上候也。

十月廿四日

吉田大蔵少輔殿

　　　　　　　浅井新一

二　阿部　潜

1　明治（6）年9月3日

私儀理事官随行欧州経歴中、去る申十月英国ロンドン
バールスブラーデルスエンコの為替手形を澳国バンク
アンゴローに於て英金五拾斤引替候処、此度別紙写之
通り、彼地在留弁理公使より申越候趣にて、外務省よ
り達之に有之。即及問合候処、手形之儀は全く其人を信
用する処より、其人の裏書を以其手形を差支なく受取
候由。然る時は卑賤且一面も無之、我等を素より彼の
信用する理なし。全く重き政府の任を蒙むるの所以に
こそと存候。故に我等信を失ふ時は遂に政府の信を失
ふに帰するべくと恐入、深く心痛仕候間、各金子速に
　　　　　　　　　　　　　　　　　　　　　〔ママ〕
及返却度存候処、元来薄禄の私別に蓄財も無之、殊に

バンク閉戸之節、旅費の仕払に迫り月給三百円前借相
願候得共、何分仕払行届兼、尚彼地知己の者より二百
円程借用、漸く帰朝仕候程之仕合に付、只今差向一時
に返却仕兼、甚当惑仕候。畢竟私疎忽より西洋バンク
と承り候得は、何れも慥成者と心得、大切の御預り金
迄相預け御不都合相掛申候上、尚又此度奉願候も恐入
奉存候得共、右引替候金之儀は大蔵省御用中之旅費に
仕払候に相違無之間、何卒前文之情実厚く御推考事情
御洞察於大蔵省一時御立替、先方へ御返却被成下候様
奉願度奉存候。

酉九月三日

　　　　　　阿部　潜　印

吉田大蔵少輔殿

大久保大蔵卿殿

明治六年五月廿八日附、佐野弁理公使より書翰之抜萃
由利、阿部両人より当府ラーストアングローバンクえ
ロンドンボールスブラデルス会社為替手形売却候一件、
別紙翻訳文相添写之通申来候。其方にて御取紕御処置

有之度候。卑官取調候処には、為替手形之儀は自身
裏書致し候上は其最後之裏書人、之を請取候ものより
の責に任し、先より順番に相戻り之を出し候元に帰し
可申通例に有之候。

バンクより差出し候書翰之翻記文写し

以書翰得貴意候。陳は去る三月十九日、日本人由利、
阿部両人え澳国バンクアングローに於て、ロンドン
バールスブラデルスエンコ為替手形にて四十斤五十斤
弐口〆九十斤引替差上置、先方へ右御遣し之手形相廻
し候処、先方にて相渡し呉不申候間、何卒急々御取片付
候段奉願候。又ョーロッパ御在留中は政府之御入用
にて候得は、御差支も無御座候哉。猶以佐々木様御同様
分聊に候得は、御差支之事に御座候哉。何卒急々御取片付
之段是又奉願候。先は右之段申上度如斯御座候。謹言

　五月十八日

　　　佐野常民閣下

尚以右金子御払下け之節、ロンドンバールス為替手

形引替差上可申候様フランクより申出候間、此段宜敷御執成依て奉願候。已上

三 五十嵐文次

1 明治（11）年7月5日

（封筒表）JAPANESE LEGATION, WASHINGTON. D.C.
（以上印刷）
His Excellency Yoshida Kiyonari Japanese Minister,
Care of Willisford Dey Esq. Asbury Park, N.Y.

其後は御一門益御壮健にて御着之御答と奉恐賀候。当御館に於ては更に異事無御座候間、御安意之程願上候。高橋君にも今一時半に費府へ御発車に相成候て、尚又天野氏今朝御館へ御引移りに相成候事。御召使の者共も昨日は祭日故終日休職仕候とも、猶今朝より各之道を尽し洗濯掃除も殆と相済み、明日は各帰家の筈に有之候事。高橋君の命に依り紐府新紙は切抜き呈上仕度、昨夜は市中四方に花火風船の興あり、児既に四夏を経過せしも昨夜の如き美々敷花火は始てに有之候。当府昨今の暑気は一昨年に勝るの声何処も同様な程敬。折角御保護あらむ事と奉祈願候事に御座候。誠恐々々

七月五日
頑児
文次百拝

閣下

2 明治11年7月28日

（封筒表）H. E. Yoshida Kiyonari Japanese Minister Asbury Park. new Jersey. Private (Care of Willisford Dey Esq.)
（封筒裏）Return to Japanese Legation at Washington D.C. If not delivered within 5 days. B.E.

児昨今是を浅田氏〔徳則〕に聞けり、曰く「マサチューセッツ」農学校に於ては我同邦人は学費則ち教師料を省へて入校を免るゝと。児之を聞くや愚言此に傾して禁する能はすと雖とも亦鬱々と絶さるものあり。則ち既往を回顧すれは也。実に俯仰以て既往を回顧すれば、一身の不肖端正ならさるより素志に反し万重の愁患を閣下の尊意に醸成し今日の愛顧を忘却し未た閣下の寵愛に

飽かす、猶今愚言の有る所を奉呈して閣下に希願せ
と欲するも希願既に万回に過くるに至る、凡事物に際
限あるを知らは人心ある者の為さゝる処ならん。且つ
事理に基ひて国家に事を為す英雄の業跡を見るに、未
来の英業は前日に著しく不肖者既往の劣業を以て未
を推知するに足る。児重て一身の行状と事理とを熟思
すれば、其証著明にして愚意自ら疲屈し一身悚然たり。
然りと雖とも尚首を挙け古人の言を聞くに智者は投機
を尊ぶと、児今農校の一事を聞くも亦一機と云ふ可
らず、智者若し投機を尊はゞ愚者猶投機を尊ばさる可
さる也。児今既往の過科を忘去し赫醜の面皮を露披し
て以て閣下に希頼する所也、然りと雖とも今日既に閣
下に醸成せし入費煩労の巨大なると一身行状の確正な
らさるを回思すれば、何の面目有つて閣下に希願せし
や。縦令児の如き人心に乏しき頑奴たりと雖とも猶是
の上閣下の入費煩労を醸すか如きに至りては、児が決
して為し能はさる所也。只愚意躊躇して決する能はず
切迫の余却て温順ならす、麤暴に渡り閣下に対し不遜

に過くる有りと雖、今一回閣下の愛情に依り開拓使庁
の扶助を得て学業に就かんと欲す。児熟同校頭領クラ
ツク氏の意の有る所を察するに、彼既に我農校を札幌
に創起し爾来帰邦すると雖とも我国農業の急務にして
虧く可らさるを知り、然と雖とも蝦夷開墾の如きは入
費巨大にして其進歩の容易ならさると迅速ならさるを
憂ひ、猶古今万国の農業を顧さるの国は富強永続なさ（ママ）
るの経験より真情切々此に至りしならん。然るに蝦夷
開墾の初着より僅々十年に満たすと雖とも、幾万千金
を彼地に拋ち未た寸効ありを聞かさるは嘗て憂国者の
長歎する所なり。足元より建業直に其奏功を欲するは
決て為し能はさる所なりと雖とも、一は農業開拓其人
を得さるは不経験の士多きに期すや、昨年始めて実地
の農校を彼の地に設け十四五名の生徒を置くと雖とも、
噫功奏の日を待が如きに至りては長歎息せさる可から
す。是に依て見れば閣下の上進を以て開拓長官に依頼
するに至らば敢て嫌疑するの理無きが如しと雖とも噫
如何せん。児今日迄行状の醜悪なると其不肖なるとを

回顧すれば、閣下の上進に依りて政府の扶助を戴せん
と欲するは恰も閣下の尊顔を土泥にするに異ならさる
也。況や児元より奸悪の意あるに非され共、機に違ひ
訥言所思を尽す能はさるより屡閣下の尊意に触れさる
に至るも信用を得さるに於てや。是既往を回顧す万度
に至るも頑愚迂遠の為す所悔悟すれ共去らず唯天
地に附伏して号泣す。然りと雖とも機を見て取らす義
を見て為さるも亦男子の恥つる所、時機失ふ可らす壮
年の期軽ず可らず。児が是に凝滞して禁する能はず、
依て胆に意の有る所を閣下に奉呈す。児速に同校の規
則を一見するに縦令初心者たりと雖とも敢て試験の難
きを以て入校為し能はさるの厳例に非す、且つ雑費の
如きに至りては一ケ年三百元より三百五十元に至る、
猶学費を省くに至りては二百五十元に未満の額を以て
足るものの如し。然りと雖とも官生徒の名を以て入校
し学費を払はさるの如きは是為し能はさるの情実なら
ん。然し公に官生徒たらさるとも陰に通例の一貧生と
為すも何の妨か是あらん。児元より他官費生の如く千

有金を業上に要するは児嘗て恐るゝ所なり。是の希願
たるや其意甚た疎暴にわたり　閣下己の従者をして公
費以て就ゝ業かしめんと為して上進せしめんと為るは
却て閣下の盛績を損ふに似たりと雖とも、開拓長官に
一書以て其意の在る所を伺出れ能はさるか、噫是の言
意愚且暴にして閣下の尊意に触れんを恐る。猶今日
迄　閣下の愛情煩労に依り殆んと成就せし陸軍事務を
今烏有に附するも亦児か忍ひさる所、故に一時帰朝し
再ひ渡海するも何そ晩きに非され共唯其機を得さるを
恐怖す。噫偶男子に生れ国家の鴻恩に報ゆる能はす
非常の大功を建すして何草木と共に凋てんやと憤激、
胸中裂くるか如しと雖とも噫如何せん。不肖貧家の一
頑奴痴情為めに散乱する而已。伏て希くは閣下の明事
実の行はるへくして不理たらさるか、一時帰朝するも
再来の時機あらんか。偏に是希願の達するを祈る。依
て速に　閣下の言論の来るを謹て待つ。請ふ言意の不
遜を宥し偏に憐愍を垂れんことを、所思を尽す能は、[ママ]
誠恐々々頓首

尚他人の見を秘し給らんこと請ふ。

閣下

七月廿八日　　　　　文次百拝

　　　　　　吉田公使閣下

　　　　　　　　　　　　　　文次

3　明治（13）年6月18日

其後は追々暑気相催候処益　閣下始め御精栄之御儀と
奉恐賀候。然は内邦最も大平にして一昨日　主上も山
梨三重へ　御巡幸、人民毎戸国旗を挙け御安全を祈る、
実に君民の間未曽有之の美挙と謂はざるを得ざる也。
然なから閣下に於て江木書記官変死に付き彼是風評も
有之、定めて不一方御配慮被遊候御事と奉恐察居候。
就ては先便深く奉歎願候領事官附属に奉職仕度偏に奉
懇願上候。必す次便志村様迄御添書一封偏に奉歎願候。
甚た麁暴の言語文面に御座候所、今夕五時迄に郵便取
集めの新聞公告を見て驚駭仕候次第、乍恐幾重にも洋
行の上天下国家の為め愚児の素志を貫かる様に偏に奉
懇願上候也。誠恐々々敬白

六月十八日夕四時半

　　　　　頑児

四　井上馨

1　明治（7）年6月21日

梅雨之候候得共益御多祥御精勤と奉恐察候。野生儀碌
々消日候間御放慮奉祈候。別後呈書も不仕奉本背本意
候御海容是祈候。御地模様も於当地は真偽難認種々之
誤説斗候。併大久保先生大隈先生も四五前より御引
入との風聞、此先如何成行候哉乍蔭懸念罷在候。実に
外国え出師且内地人心之居合も未た確実ならす。諸先
御引篭真説に候得は誠に以恐入候次第に候。何卒危難
之間是非御担任御維持之策偏に処祈候。近来新橋之景
況如何被為在候哉。日々情義精密と奉想像候。当地も
格別面白事も無之御座候。陳は此一壺呈上候間、聊御
煩慮を御忘れ被成下候はゝ大幸と奉存候。先は御伺旁
呈寸楮候。草々謹言

六月廿一日

　　　　　井上馨

井上馨

吉田清成様

2　明治（12）年8月6日

奉拝読候。大将クラント箱根行に付馬車之義御下問被
下奉承知候。工部省に於ても不適当なる者斗故、過へ
ネシー箱根同行之節も横浜雇入候次第故、当度も於同
所御雇入之方第一手数を除き却て事容易に相済み可申
と奉存候間、自然御懸合等之都合も候はゝ野生方之接
対懸属官差上候ても不苦候。左候はゝ先之手続き等も
克承知仕居申候。
尚亦測量者之義被仰下い細奉承知候。明日午後二字歟
又は明後早朝歟不遠差出し可申候間、御留主にても相
分り候様御家来え御申含め置奉頼候。草々拝復

八月六日

　　　　　　　　　　馨

清成様

3　明治13年9月30日

（封筒表）吉田清成殿親展　井上馨

毎度御懇書御投与被下、従是は兎角世事に取紛れ未た
一呈も不仕恐縮之外敢て謝辞之方便も無之御海容被下
度候。既に八月八日附之尊翰も落掌仕候。先御着後は
御家内一統御安全之由、別て欣然之至に御座候。迂生
少々頭脳を痛み候故、七月十五日より御暇を願熱海え
行廻妻と会合、同二十一日帰東候て直に翌朝より上州
伊香保え転し去月十二日帰京、則追々公信を以申上置
候蘭公使と之不快なる争論最中、終不得止青木公使を
［ヘーグ］
ヘッグ差遣しリーコールを申入、漸過る十七日其終局
に到り、来る五日同公使も出立と相決し候様子にて、
一昨日其書簡を彼より差越申候。勿論上手際之作にも
不有候得とも、リーブアフセンスにても何んでも出板
せし事件として帰国せしめたるに相違無之、先々可也
之出来と御憐察被下度候。
御着後もイレクション旁以何事も其政府と御熟談にも
到り難き由御申越、如何にも左様と相考へ申候。又改
正事件米政府一先相済み候姿故、此度之新按を与ゆる

に付ても他公使とも相違候場合故、只ヒンハム〇えも

如何之手続きに致し候方都合に候哉と内談に及ひ候上

にて相渡し置申候。

誠に都合克老台国務卿え御面会之模様に依て推量候て

も、新ケ条持出しても敢て相談不致と刻付たる気味も

無之様相考へ申候。是則閣下之平常交際親密之致す処

ならん。敬祝仕候。カロシン油一件に付ては過日御説

明書御送り被下実に明瞭なる御示解にて、最初ヒンハ

ムえ遣したる意味と更に異変も之なく、尤名論と憾服〔ママ〕

仕候。尤両条共新大統領新任後に無之ては相談も纏り

申間敷、且改正一条は先諸国と談判を遂候上粗見込も

相立候上之方却て上策と相考へ申候。未た各国よりも

何事も不申来、只森公使より異見申越し候て答弁も致

し置候。則写差出候間御一覧被下度候。

江木狂死一条に付ては不一方御配慮別て御気の毒千万

に御座候。商務局長も在米せ〔斬〕ずは如期事件差起り申間

敷、又江木も正し所作とも難申候得共、如何に己に潔

くする迚も死に至る抔之事柄とも不被考、実に不幸之

至に御座候。兎角我国人同志は非常之極度迄不至て事

不為済気に往々有之候。

琉球事件も嘗てクラント君え御内談を御依頼の為書通

致し置候意にて宍戸公使え御委任に相成、七月初旬委

任状も差立、当節は談判最中に候て尓後之模様は夫々

写差出し候間、御承知之上は其大略丈セネラールえも

御序御報知置被下度候。最早余程ウィーキポイントも

顕然候故〔則日魯合従を世間、喋々するを疑ひ候気味〕、此機に乗し終局に到り候

様宍戸えも厳敷迫り立申候。

尾崎書記官一件は既に先公信を以申上置候得共、江木

之変あり又老兄え苦心を令増候様之処分致し候も不快

に候間、最早断然相聞可申候。尤御申越し之人物は差

出兼旁御高按当分書記生なしにて御不自由御忍ひ被成

下候方可然候間、左様御含奉願候。

御出足頃より相起り候会計方向も種々議論も有之候得

とも、先節倹主義にて先大蔵年々一千万円之余財を

生す〔則酒の増税四百万円余地方道路橋梁費凡毎年弐百万円国庫より出来せし分を相廃し諸省定額中より弐百万計り其他年弐百万円〕

減借紙幣之分は〔合計一千万円也〕を以て直接貿易を助け、又は地方之抵当

ある輸出副産物を限り低利を以貸し附る等に供し、其代り金輸出せし品に対する分を以て返納せしめ、其正金を以て漸々紙幣を交換すると粗決議に至り、方今着将始之顕索に御座候。尤定額は十四年度より減する之見込に御座候。併ペーパー之デブレシエーションは如何程にて止り候歟、方今之姿にては神なら〔ぬ欠〕身は定め難く候。此将来最早非常之困難を不起様只神仏え祈之外手立の無之候。内閣議論中には米納に帰せしめる論百出候て、大隈・伊藤・迂生等は殊之外ヲップホシションと相成、漸其論は相止み申候。兼て老台も吾国経済上には特別に御苦心も有之、実に前途如何様に相成候哉、則五里霧中之気色と妄想を起さざるを得さる形様に御座候。

其内時下兼々御自愛専一奉存候。謹言

十三年九月廿日

　　　　清成盟賢兄

　　　　　　　　馨

二白、上野大先醒も近芝金六町えスモルゴールト付家屋を与え先つ他之茶屋行は廃止之姿に候。永続すれはよいが。芳川こすく略事計勉め金を蓄ふる事上手に御座候也。

〔注〕外務省用箋。

五　井上毅

1　明治（17）年12月24日

井上議官来書写

千里懸隔の上に候得は、百般機会総て電信に托し候外無之、今次米艦に嘱し今廿四日付を以て長崎より発信は、飛電は別紙写の如し竹添の電申と共に御接手被遊候事と被存候。爾後定て神速の御決定有之候事と奉察候。馬関より呈書中には小官着韓後は暫く全権使節派出有無の決を待つ物を急かぬ方に可相心得申上置候処、韓人は頻に無礼の照会を送り、是に対し竹添に於て黙視すれは黙認の姿に当り、又文書にて答弁すれは我却て受身の位地に立ち徒に枝葉の争に渉り遂に要領を得るの時無かるへきに付、竹添も内訓に従ひ断然決意、明

日より京城に派し金宏集・趙秉鎬列序にて直接に談判
をなし、都合能く候はゝ彼より従前屢次の照会の失
敬を謝し取消しを請はしめ、然後に後段の結末談判を
為すへき下たる地を拵へ可申、又都合悪敷候はゝ一応十
分明快なる照会を送りて其儘仁川へ引取り朝命を待つ
筈に有之候。右の結果は大概廿八九日頃迄に蓬来丸を
以て飛電可申上候。護衛は態と減少し士官へ含め静穏
を主とする筈に付、其辺は御放意可被下候。朝鮮の事
情を約言するに、彼政府には一方には支那人の為めに
教唆せられ我れに向て傲慢無礼の言を吐き、以て支那
人の喜を買ひ、又一方には後難を恐れ国王及ひ金宏集
より密意を米公使抔に托し好意を表し甘言を通し陰陽
両端に計ことを為す有様に見へ候。彼れはモルレンド
ルフ及支那人の勧告により候歟、万国公法抔唱へ候
て、今度竹添の処置を軽し直ちに日本政府に訴へ公法
上の不ゝ認ニ公使ニ之例に依る積と相見へ候。此事に対
しては我政府は自から適当の御処分為在候事と奉存候。
可悪は支那人にて韓人を教唆し必至度竹添の処置を攻

撃し竹添をして交際上の罪人たらしめ、己れは日清兵
営偶然の口角というに托し、そしらぬ顔にて済す積と
見へ候。恐くは李鴻章か心算より出候歟と被存候。
大体廟議の決に至ては定めて已に神算遠計有らせられ
候事と被存候へゝは、今更愚見喋々不仕敬待下命而已。
頓首再拝

　　　十二月廿四日

　　　　　　　　　　毅

外務卿殿
宮内卿殿
外務大輔殿

〔以下別紙〕
電第一号

十二月廿四日発信　米艦に托す

私か済物浦に着いた廿三日夕、朝鮮外務卿は傲慢の書
面を送り竹添をして断して黙止すべからさるの位置に
居らしめたり。竹添は明日京城に行くへし、私も倶に
行くへし。

私等は深く内訓を守り疎暴の行為をなさゝるべし。然しなから私は信す、支那人は朝鮮人を教唆し務めて傲慢の言を吐き、竹添を称して賊に党するの罪魁となし以て自から其責を逃れんとす。故に此度の事は到底更に兵力を派し最後談判又は強迫に出てされは満足の結果を得かたかるべし。假令一時の和平を得るとも将来朝鮮より屢忍ふべからさるの無礼を受け、終に第三回の騒動を引起すに至るべし。

朝鮮に在る支那官吏は傲慢及詐謠にして黎庶昌の口気と反対せり。若し其官吏等を斥けさる前に東京に於て俄に支那の政府と和平結局の取組ありたらは、支那人并に朝鮮人は心に怡む所ありて遂に過を謝するの時なかるべし。

礼曹判書徐相雨全権大臣として日本に赴く之目的を以て今日当港に着したり。副使モルランドルフ跡より到着するを俟つて発行の積りと云ふ。朝鮮政府は駐在公使竹添を認めさるの目的なく、若し日本政府は竹添の行為を認むるならは予は政府か朝鮮の派出大臣を請け

取らざる事を希望す。

六　井上雅彦

1　明治(21)年5月20日

益御清安被遊御坐奉恐悦候。扨今般は枢密院へ御栄転被為蒙仰恐悦至極に奉存上候。右御歓奉申上度。草々拝具

五月廿日

吉田様御取次

雅彦

2　明治(22)年9月25日

謹上一書候。時下秋涼相催候処、閣下益御清健被遊御座恐悦奉存候。平素分て不奉窺御機嫌恐縮且不本意に御座候得共、侵威厳毎々奉信書も却て非礼共相心得御無音に罷過候。宜布御海容奉仰候。扨今般大林区々域位置共改正相成候に付ては、和歌山之如きは大阪新置大林区に被併雅彦等に於ては未た何等之罪も無之候得共、

廃官同様之身と相成、新置大阪大林区長は更に他人に
被命可申義と被察、是非も無き次第には御座候得共、
十有一年来効績は無之も無事相勤、其間地方官及地民
に対する官林紊乱を修め今日に至るも多少之辛苦も御
座候処、今日に至り改正之不可止義とは乍申、此侭廃
官に被属も実に遺憾云ふに耐へさる義に御座候。先年
已に廃物に属せんとするの際は　　閣下之御仁慈を以救
済之恩沢に浴し世間及知友に対し面目補高恩生涯不可
忘義、尚今日又尊慮を奉煩は恐縮至極に奉存候得共、
謹願くは今一度大阪大林区署長に転し本職今一回維持
候様不耐懇願候。

閣下雅彦等の内情御憐察被成下山林局長等之要路へ一
応御下命被成下度奉懇願候。書面を以軽々敷可相願義
には無御座候得共、自由に出京も出来兼且他に如此内
情吐露すへき先柄も無御座無拠侵尊厳此段奉歎願候。
最早大阪大林区長其人も撰定相成候義にも可有之欤共
相察候得共、内情色々議論も可有之義欤共相察候に付、
此際閣下御一言被成下候は〻山林局長等之其命を奉す

るは無論と奉存候に付、呉々恐入候次第には御座候得
共此旨謹奉懇願候。慢に胸情を吐露し汗顔之至に御座
候得共、従来分て御懇命を蒙る恩恵に乗し如斯に御座
候。宜敷御笑取奉仰候。恐惶頓首

九月廿五日　　　　　　　　　雅彦

正三位殿閣下

3　明治（　）年5月25日

〔前欠〕到底償却すへき現実を得さるに於ては別に良按
も難相立、就ては懇友之者窃に力を添へ過半之品は返
却を得る場合に相及候得共、総額に於て全く百円余と
相成居候に付、雅彦等微力之者力に叶ひ兼殆んと困却
罷在候。就ては実に恐懼之至極に御座候得共、同人に
於て他に可便先も無之趣に付、従来分て御恩顧を蒙り
居趣にも有之、何卒此回金五拾円丈け御恩借相叶候様
雅彦より歎願仕呉候様同人より願出、従来御高恩を蒙
り居尚如斯義を以奉汚尊聴候義は重々以恐縮之限に御
座候得共、同人之困難実に進退維谷之秋気の毒千万之

義に付、譴怒を顧みす此亦拝願仕候条、何卒患難危急
之情実御酌の上け被成下雅彦等上願之趣御採用之程謹て
奉懇願候。右は都合も御座候義に付乍恐岡田喜太郎へ
をも被命何分之尊慮御下命之程奉願上候。呉々も雑事
を以奉汚尊聴候段宜布御許容奉仰候。草々拝具

　　　　　　　　　　　　　　　　　　雅彦

　五月廿五日

　吉田正三位公閣下

七　穎川君平

1　明治（　）年12月15日

今般御発途に付、当地惣商估より御離盃差上度との趣
之処、頃日は追々御発途にも間近く、殊に時節柄御交
際上之宴会等も毎夕の御事とも拝察、忽然御案内申上
候ても迚も御操合せも出来間敷に付、何とか御操合せ
之相叶候時日私より予め相伺呉様被相托候。就ては
御迷惑とも拝察候得共、右御都合之時日何卒私迄御内
示被成下候様奉願候。尤右御都合之時日奉伺候上、商

估等より直に御招状拝呈候積之趣に候。先は此段奉伺
度如此。艸々敬白

　十二月十五日

　　　　　　　　　　　　　　　　　　　　君平

　吉田殿

2　明治（　）年12月18日

拝呈仕候。陳は、当地商估連より一夕御離盃差上度と
の事に付、昨今一連は協同会之名義を以て御案内致度、
又一連は惣商估之名目にて御案内致度と、二派に相別
れ、各連にて終に弐会之御離盃相催可申趣に付、頃日
は最御多忙之央故、却て弐会にも相成候様御迷惑に
も候半、是非何れにも相纏り、壱夕之御離盃に致候様
懇々申諭候得共、何分承諾不致是非弐連各自に御案内
致度趣にて、既に御招状も差出候段申候、如何にも御
多忙之央御迷惑之程畏縮之至に奉存候。極て右二連よ
り御案内状差上候得は御不審にも可被思召と拝察候間、
右両度に相別れ御案内仕候原因御含迄、此段御通知仕
候。尚又弥御繁忙之為御来車難相成候節は、右二連と

候。

奥　青輔／鹿児島県詰役／金子謙〔カ〕

も何に歟レメンブランスにも可相成品にても進呈可仕
との内議之由、粗及承候間、此段も御内報仕候。何れ
書余は何事も廿日には出京御面話可仕。匆々謹白

十二月十八日
　　　　　　　　　　　　君平
吉田殿

八　奥　青輔

1　明治（19／20）年2月12日

謹啓　昨夜は乍毎閣敬仕候段御仁恕奉希候。陳は、私
義本日は風邪気にて悪寒頭痛に付、甚恐入候得共今一
日丈引籠加養仕度御坐候付御聞済奉願上候。却説昨日
一寸御沙汰有之候欧州行随員属官之義は可然御工夫奉
願上候。差当適当之人物を得らるに非れは矢張局員下
島某にても又宜と奉存候。能々取調候処、英語には少
も差支無之文章も一通り出来候由なれとも、奥州産丈
にて俗に云気のきかない風あり。是は別に差支も有之
ましく、尤本人は将来水産之為熱心以て勉務之精神は

有之趣に付、局員なれは帰朝之上或は幾く之便益も可
有之歟と奉存候間、何分にも可然御指揮奉仰候。書余
明日も拝謁之上可奉申上候得共、其内乍略義以乱筆類
奉申上候。匆々謹啓

二月十二日
　　　　　　　　　　青輔拝
吉田公閣下

九　鹿児島県詰役

1　明治（　）年9月19日

〔巻封〕吉田太郎様　鹿児嶋県詰役

吉田慶蔵事御自ら御引受にて為物馴出府被仰付候旨
御県元より問合相達候間、最早其元へ着相成居候や、
何分御報承度此段御問合におよひ候。以上

九月十九日

〔注〕墨書。

一〇　金子謙〔カ〕

1　明治（　）年9月12日

今朝は浜田を以御報告書類正書之分一併被差遣、則熊

〔武五郎〕
谷大丞え申聞、不取敢大隈卿え差出申候。副書は今両

日程御留め置云々、委曲敬承仕候。是は御覧済之上丞

え差出候之心得に御座候。他一二浜田え話し置申候間、

同人より申上候儀と被存候。

扨報告一件も概略相済候に付、明日より御用中計算向

一切片付け、決を仰き候心得に御座候。精々勉強一両

日中参館万誦高論を戴候心得に御座候。先此御用此一

事相済候はゝ結局に至り候事と楽み罷在候。此段乍延

引御請旁奉申上候也。

九月十二日

謙再拝

吉田公閣下

一一　川崎祐名

1　明治（12）年3月15日

本月五日御認之玉章相達忝拝誦。御出発頃は参上之含

之処あれ是にて不果之義本意に背き、西郷氏と途中御

行逢之事を承候て御発程を存候。扨御一同も御無異に

〔従道〕
て御着熱之上は不二屋へ御宿離屋も御占に相成万事御

意に叶御遊湯之由、其上囲手御相手も無御不自由御消

光万々御都合之御事と拝察致候。尓来いよ〳〵御無事

御精浴之筈と想像欣喜仕候。粗御約之通生にも参向可

致に付御懇命難有可成丈罷出度思考致候得共意の如く

〔鞆之助〕
ならず、又高島子も二十七日頃乗船に相決候処色々談

置候事柄も有之、将田中光顕も不日より鳥渡旅行之筈

に候得共、一周日位の隙を得候義難整無拠時機御察

可被下候。何れ御帰家之上万事拝聴可仕候間、折角無

〔正義〕
御疲労御入湯御都合克御帰京可奉待候。松方氏も面会

御承知の通〇大先生方には条約改正とか輸入品を防厭

する趣法云々とか太政官中の改革にて何と歟色々咄も

有之候得共、拙輩取留たる事承得不申候間、何も御帰

京の上に相譲、先は御懇翰拝答又御動静伺等取束此旨

奉得鳳意置候。頓首

三月十五日

　　　　　　祐名

吉田賢台閣下

再伸　君は幾日頃迄御滞留之御見込候哉。御序に
拝承仕置度候也。

〔注〕青筆で「十二年」の書込有。

２　明治（　）年9月12日

華翰拝見、毎々御尋被下候由、失敬相働き御免。小生
にも未た寸功無之、故に甚御疎情罷過候。過日は無拠
用向にて大山家へ罷越、途中ちらと懸御目候得共心事
を不尽残懐不少。却説奈良原へは証人一条巨細御念入
拝承致候、聊差支無之候間御書入御直参、または客人
抔被下候てもよろしく調印可仕候。右拝答申上候。早
々。余不日譲御面唔置候也。　敬白

　九月十二日

　　　　　　祐名

よし田明府御坐下

一二　北代正臣

１　明治（4／6）年11月24日

過刻被下候御芳書於正院拝握仕候。漸只今点燈之後帰
省、別紙御詞令は於正院大輔殿より御言伝あり申候に
付指上申候。大輔殿には明朝十字迄外国人之御応接有
之、十字より尊邸迄省之馬車にて御出掛之筈に付左様
御聞置被下度候。愚弟は今夜帰省之途中何分昇殿之筈
に御座候得共、身命に相掛け柳橋之佳期厳約御座候侭
進撃仕候に付、孰明早朝迄に可罷出、此段御海容被下
度。草々拝述

　十一月廿四日

　　　　　吉田少輔様

　　　　　　　　　　　　正臣

一三　郷友会事務所

１　明治（　）年9月25日

今般鹿児島県下非常の風災に罹り、家屋傾覆作毛を損

し、為めに生業を失ふ者幾万人、其惨状不問に置くに
忍ひず。是に於て、鹿児島県在京の諸君と協議の上、
幾干の金員を義捐し、救助の一分に供し度、其募集金
取扱は、郷友会に於て担任候条、同感の諸君は、内桜
田島津家邸内事務所へ向御贈金有之度、此段及御通知
候也。

　九月廿五日

　　　　　　　郷友会事務所

一四　熊谷武五郎

　　1　明治（19カ）年（　）月9日

其後は御健在に被為入奉大賀上候。苑角［ママ］多事御無音恐
入候。生無事乍憚御降神被下度奉存候。

一近頃突然之申上方に候へとも閣下に非常之御保護不
願候とま［ヵ］けて不相成候。其訳は左の条項に有之候。生

と思召御仁憐是祈。　志村智風氏会計主任其任に不適哉
之趣、会計局長山内堤雲より内知有之候。右はもとよ
り不正ある訳に毛頭無之候へとも、是迄諸報告手をく

れ候間、相起り候と確信仕候、併し此議生より弁明一
時は相凌ぎ候も、固会計局長と密着之会計主任故、如
此会計局長に見込れ候ては、将来同人栄達之為め尤不
利益と奉存候。所謂此逓信省内に永住すへき地に無之
と同人之為めに生考定仕候。当管理局に定額金余り有
之候へは、又如何様とも他課え組替出来候へとも、実
に一文なし、考按に尽候。閣下御承知之野生性質堪
難く候へとも、又熟考候に、昔之客気を出し、是迄皆
様方御辛労相懸け一旦相忍候事、是か為今更水泡に属
させ候は不相済次第と深く注意堪忍仕候。何卒閣下此
事情御憐察被成下、只なとなしに同人御省いつれ之
局か課え御採用被成下候様に只管奉懇願候。十九年度
も最半に相成候間、廿年度に御採用被下候へは、至極
好都合に奉存候。もとより赴任致候時は互に勉強始終
を共にと奮発致候儀に候へとも、小官之悲さ、只会計
主務と申名号有之候故会計局より喙を容られ候時は如
何とも致方無之候旁閣下此度は生を救と思召御採用被
下度、呉々も願上候。右此儀志村氏えは極内々に致し

置キ候に付、此故も御含み、志村老人〔智常カ〕えも御話し御無用に被成下度奉存候。右之次第故、逓信長次官〔省〕は勿論、山内会計局長にも此儀に付御話御無用に被成下度奉存候。官海之風波致方無之、千緒万端共手紙に尽し兼候、いつか上京之時あれは可申上候。

右御内頼申上候義、前後可然御判読被下度奉存候。甚た恐入候へとも一寸御壱報奉煩上候。稽首

　　九日　　　　　　　　　　　　　　熊谷

　吉田様侍者

　　2　明治（21カ）年（10カ）月24日

御細書拝見仕候。益御健在に為入奉大賀候。
〇志村氏儀実に意外之仕合、全く心臓之仕業と存候。御愁傷奉遙察候。生儀生憎福島管区巡視中須賀川にて同人死去之電信に接し、幸帰途に就き居候に付、不取敢帰仙仕候。閣下電信及郵便拝見致候仕合に御座候。及丈けは御添心申上居候。志村老人〔智常〕も今日十字着に有之候。色々御相談之末、今日午後四時に火葬に致し、明日はあと仕末致し、明後日当地引払之都合致候。此段御領掌奉願候。

志村氏病中之景況は同人細君より申上候筈と存候間、喋々不仕候。実に人の性命は難頼事に御座候。右不取敢御報奉申上度候はゝ指置候。

　　廿四日　　　　　　　　　　　　　熊谷

　吉田様侍

乍憚、奥さまへ御悔よろしく御鶴声可被下候。

　　3　明治（　）年（　）月15日

今朝は御邪魔仕候。其時御命じ之川路之儀尚又卿え申上候処、更々無御差支御差出事に仕候。其砌御噂も被為在候通り、大蔵省事務御聞合無之に付取調方尤都合よく、即此省之大便宜と於僕は尚無此上雀躍之事に奉存候。其侭御入用之人も御用中被為在候はゝ吃度割愛さし上事に仕候。無御隔意被仰聞度、もとより卿も其含に有之候。

一、御尋申上候分課担当之件検査之件等、其侘にも何

此間無拠其都合相運ひ候と存居も、此際老閣にて非常
之御勘考被為遣御省え御採用被成下候儀相叶申間敷哉、
何分よろしく御工夫奉願候。傍非仰申立は見合せ一応
分閣下御見込み之積りを以て御談判只管御依頼為此
省奉懇願候。別条無之右要事、書余は又々其内参邸
方可奉申上候。稽首

　十五日
　　　　　　熊谷
　吉田様侍

4

明治（　）年（　）月15日

ウヰリヤム氏一件に付箱根入浴、左之通外務省より申
来候。右は僕顚末委詳承知不仕候へとも、外務右規程
を履行致候候外無之と愚考仕候。尚可然御指揮被下度候。
此段奉伺候。稽首

　十五日
　　　　　　熊谷
　吉田様側

5

明治（　）年（　）月26日

御健在被為入奉恭賀候。一昨日も一書申上候筈御覧被
下候事と奉存候。志村氏の儀に付何分行届兼ね、遂に
非職之申立不致候半て不相成候場合に立至り候。依て
御内慮奉伺候。
右多事。早々頓首

　廿六日
　　　　　　熊谷拝
　吉田老閣侍者

6

明治（　）年（　）月（　）日

拝閲仕候。
御下痢にて御出無之段拝承仕候。よろしく御加養専務
と奉存上候。
省務之事は謹領仕候。卿未参省無之候へとも何れ後刻
参候事と奉存候。其時は被仰申越候条件陳述可仕候。
右御報まて。匆々稽首

　即刻
　　　　　　武五郎
　少輔様老閣

一五　佐久間克典（カ）

1　明治4年12月17日

別啓奉申上候。御留守別事無御坐候。過刻御付与之
御書幷御伝言とも帰寓直に奥様へ御伝申上候。
馬渡殿へ之御伝言も夕刻造幣寮へ参り御面談申置候。
出納寮へ御旅費其外之儀今朝御談之通原田権大属へ相
頼置申候。右件々奉申上候也。

少輔様執事

辛未十二月十七日

克典拝具

一六　志村智常

1　明治（　）年（　）月23日

副書

昨日矢野氏に出会候処、意外御疎信罷過候段多罪、可
然申上候呉様演舌御座候。同人儀商法講習所森君創立
期引受周旋、然るに是迄一も規定相立居不申困却之由、

其節一寸話に、浅野子此節少々発狂体之由、在横浜同
人弟の咄に曰、何れより欤短刀を求来り、昼夜懐にし、
折節夜中呼子之笛を右短刀ヲ振〔ママ〕、細君を追廻し、同人
在米留守中不埒之儀有之趣なと糺問および、彼是県念〔懸カ〕
に付、当時細君は親戚方へ相預け候由。迂生本月初旬
同人尋問いたし候節は、右前之事故欤鬱々として談話
無之、先頃入来之節と大に容子違ひ、当節大に心配之
儀共有之、意外無沙汰之旨挨拶有之候。体裁尋常なら
すと見受候まゝ、帰宅後お半さんへも噂いたし候儀に
御坐候処、昨日矢野氏之咄にて案合致し候。前出浅野
氏舎弟之話に候へは、相違も無御坐儀と存候まゝ、此
段為念申進置候事。

廿三日

一七　世古延世

1　明治（　）年11月13日

貴墨拝見仕候。昨日は御用有之処横浜御出張、昨夕御

帰京候処御省向御用御召重り云々御書面之御旨委曲
拝承仕候。御都合次第にて明日にも御参　朝に相成候
はゝ可然と奉存候。一時は御帰京之御届云々之儀は宜
敷取計置申候間、御放念可被下候。書外期拝顔。匆々
頓首再行

十一月十三日

吉田殿閣下拝復

世古延世

一八　寺師宗徳

1　明治（　）年2月1日

拝復　先刻は罷出御懸之際御邪間仕候。抑其折願上
候書類は早速御回付被下、態々為御持之段御手数奉万
謝候。何れ一見之上更に御高指可奉伺候。将又富田氏
話之義は悉細了承仕候。決して御懸念無之様削正可仕
候。先は右御応まて、匆々得御意候也。　拝具

二月一日

　　　　　寺師宗徳

吉田高台尊下

一九　長谷川方省

1　明治（4カ）年12月17日

〔巻封〕吉田大蔵少輔殿　　方省拝復

尊翰奉拝見候。然は位階昇進之　宣旨御達被成下難有
拝戴仕候。猶又坂田伯孝同断之趣にて　宣旨一通御差
越被成下、同人事当地滞在にて伝達仕候様御端書云々
拝承仕候。右は当地え参り居不申横浜在勤仕居、既に
伴権助四五日前横浜出港之節も坂田事は彼地罷居候由
申事に御座候。則別紙伯孝え当る　宣旨は返上仕候間
御入手可被下候。いれ罷出御礼万縷可申上候へ共一
応御請旁申上候也。

臘月十七日

二〇　富田鉄之助

1　明治3年5月6日

富田鉄之助

Millstone N.J.

May 6th/70

過る廿八日夕に御着之御 Japes. 五名

右より附属

岩倉公子　龍小次郎（岩倉具経）
朝日小太郎（岩倉具定）

薩　折田　権蔵
長　服部　一三
　　山本　十助

右之通り何もN・B・（ニュー・ブランスウィック）にて御留学之由に承知致候。

以上

永井先生

2　明治（　）年3月31日
　　　　とみたてつ之助

華書難有奉拝誦候。御安泰被為入奉恐悦候。シーソン終り、少々御休息之時期、御快事いかにも奉仰察候。抑独国之模様は初めより難物に聞居候。今節は都て英政に同意之事不可疑。仏は鮫島公使在世中は、都て英政に反対せしむる策に有之に、昨今と相成ては右も水泡、全く英と同意之様子。伊国は縦令日本と多少之不和醸出候とも、英国之利益に難引換故、都て英政に随ふと申事、初より公然位に相分り居候。蘭は如何可有之哉、公使呼戻しより多少感触を害し候事有之間敷哉。露は独立の様に被察候得共、英政に反対、米国に尽力と申程に気込は無覚束候。来示之如く右等之強性を不砕は、終に本邦之体面を失し候事勿論にて、打砕く之策も可有之候得共、如何せん、政策貫徹せざる様之事間々有之、頭底首尾貫通不仕候得は、何事も甘く不取（ママ）行之一点に帰着候様愚察被仕候。夫等は御賢察之義に付縷述不仕候。青木公使も肺病にて一時は重病と伝聞仕候。フランクホルトの病院にて治療候に、追々快気と伝聞仕候。今節とても入院中に可有之歟、拝眉仕兼候義甚遺憾千万に奉存候。実は今朝迠御左右奉待居候。御用不為有よしに付、弥々当地より来る四日頃出立、桑港に走せ出候半かと予定仕候。昨今旧友間を奔走、頗る多端に消光罷在申候。先以御受のみ、此内乍憚御奥様えも可然様御機嫌窺御通来奉頼候。草々拝具

三月三十一日

　　　吉田公使閣下

富鉄拝具

尚々、ランメン氏より可然様御致声奉頼、本部え
送り物も候はゝ持参可仕候間、当地より回送候様
義宜敷奉頼候也。

二一　奈良原矢太郎

1　明治(21ヵ)年8月12日

出発以来海陸平安、去八日無事着熊仕候間、御安神可
被下候。横浜より筑前博多までは海上より、博多より
熊本までは陸行いたし候。

御闔家皆々様被為揃御清祥被為遊御座候半、大慶至極
奉存上候。矢太郎事着熊后直に御報知旁一封可差上相
考へ居候処、種々の事故に取紛れ意外に御疎濶に打過
候段、御宥免可被下候。当鎮台は猶士官乏しく為めに
事務繁忙、私事着隊当日より隊務を取扱ふ事に御座候。
去る十日の夜は非常演習(夜間不意に兵を集合し、非
常に備ふる為めの演習なり)有之、聯隊は皆集合し(時頃)各士官は軍装にて出頭し同一
時半頃出発して、黒石(熊本城を去る三里弱)と云ふ処まて夜行
軍いたし、同地に於て射撃演習いたし申候。此射撃は
毎年一度施行すへきものにて名誉射撃と云ふ者にて有
之、聯隊中各小隊毎に其小隊長之を指揮して一斉射撃
を行ひ、其の命中点の成績に優等依て一等及二等の賞
品及賞証を聯隊長より下賜相成候者に有之候。一斉射
撃とは其小隊を小隊長の号令にて一斉に射撃せしむる
ものに有之候。射撃する巨離(ママ)は一は千米突(メートル)、一は千二
百米突なり。其時私しの小隊は豈図らん多数の命中弾
数を得、二等の位置を得申候。実に意外の成績にて私
しの喜のみならず部下兵卒の喜び無此上程見受申候。
兵卒は休暇を貫ふを喜び一は己れの小隊の名誉なるを
喜ひ候義と察せられ申候。依て本日其の賞品及賞状授
与式有之候。賞品は火薬八吉羅(キロ)にて賞状とは只紀念と
して下賜相成候大形の証書の如きものに有之候。何に
しろ実に意外の手柄に御座候。可然御笑読被下度奉願
候。昨十一日は熊本城下の白川にて午前第五時より架

橋演習いたし候も白川は深さ二尺許なり。此日は炎熱殊に甚しき故士官及下士兵卒皆挙つて褌一つにて河中に入り作業いたし申候。此架橋演習は急造法を演習いたし、皆縄にて材木を結束し橋の脚を製へ其の上に木板を並べて橋の全体を為さしめしものにて、本邦にて架柱橋と名け仏国式のものに有之候。同午前第十時悉皆成就いたし候。其後暫時休憩いたし此橋上を各兵隊武装をなして列を正し之を渡るの演習等を為して帰営仕候。中々愉快至極此事に御座候。是又可然御笑読可被下候。隊務に於て野外の演習は前件述ふる如きものに有之候。御察被下度候。営内に於ては日々練兵場に於て操練の教授及週番勤務（営内に一週間づゝ宿直し品行上の監状被服類の修理及破損等の検査武器手入の監督糧食等我中隊一般の事務を監理するの責を帯ふ）及衛戍勤務（時して有之候非常に備ふる兵隊、火薬庫の衛兵、金庫の衛兵等を監視巡察するの勤務なり）大凡前述の通りの諸勤務有之候。只御心得之為贅言を顧みす御知せ申上置候間御笑読被下度候。私も出立の節着熊后直に一寸帰県いたす様御話申上候処、只今の有様にては私しの中隊には士官乏しく事務繁忙故、今休暇を願ひ

帰省候ては他人に対して少しく気の毒なる義も可有之と考え申候に付、暫時の間帰県のことは見合せ申候。尤も当八月の末か或は九月の上旬頃は他の士官も帰隊候ものも有之候様察せられ申候。其節能き折を見合せ休暇を願ひ一寸帰県いたす考に御座候。左様御心得被下度奉願候。又来る十月か十一月の間、当熊本鎮台兵は長途行軍を為し鹿児嶋に至り二三日間同地滞在候様間及候に付、私も隊兵と共に来鹿のことに候はゝ、其節に相譲り候ても宜しからんと相考へられ申候。此又御知申上候間御心得被下度候。御写真の余計なるもの有之候はゝ尊叔父様御叔母様及御子共衆の（クラント及清風のもののみにても宜しく候）もの幸便より御送附被下候様いたし度奉希望候。又御暇の節は御手の書を大形の唐紙に書置き御送附被下間敷や偏に奉願候。文句は何にても宜しく候へとも成るべく字数少なくして大字に奉願候（気度惟遠）なる四字を大書し賜はり候へは別して仕合の至に奉存上候。此の四字は志田町御自宅に在る有栖川宮殿下の御書にて王猛の語に録せら

154

追日冷気相催候処御揮家被為揃ます〱〱御清祥候半、大慶至極奉存候。降て矢太郎儀も其後無事精々服務罷在申候間、乍余事左様御休神被下度候。陳は私事着熊後直様墓参旁帰国候様予て御話申上置候処、隊務之都合に依り今日まて空く其意を得す、帰国之儀其叶不申候。来年夏の休暇にて帰国之賦に御座候。左様御了知被下度候。当師団も来る十二月一日より新兵入営いたし候筈に候へは私事も予て新兵仕込方を被命申候。士官一人にて西も東も知らざる土民を編入せしめて純粋之軍人を養成する事に候はゝ、一汗流さゞれは充分なる事は出来申さずと愚考罷在申候。御察被下度候。将又来月二日より別紙之通り加治木・福山・都ノ城地方へ長途行軍演習之筈、凡三週間の賦に御座候。右地方には初めての行軍に候へは面白事と存申候。左様御了察奉願候。

予て御願申上置候刀一本及御手書等御送与被下度奉合掌候。当時御繁忙之最中にて重畳恐縮之至奉存候へとも、矢太郎之秘蔵物に為し置度存し候得は、斯は尊厳れしものゝ結句に御座候。又幸便の節は御処持の来国光の刀か或一文字の刀の中一本は頂戴仕度候。先は到着の御報知旁如此に御座候。猶々時節柄御尊体御保養専一に奉祈上候。叔母様へ宜敷様御伝声奉願候。早々

敬具

八月十二日　　　　　矢太郎

尊叔父様膝下

再伸

写真のこと

御手書のこと　掛物になす為（私しの秘蔵物にする為め）

刀のこと　私しの秘蔵物也。

右重て奉願候也。

私しの中隊長は平井正衛と云ふ人にして熊本の人なり。昨年頃迄は士官学校に居りし人なり。依て同校の事情等御熟知のこと故私しも心易く別して仕合の至りに御座候。

2　明治（21カ）年10月21日

を犯し屡々遠き熊本より手紙上にて御願申上候事に御座候。御賢察被下度候。時下気候不順御尊体御保養旧に倍し専一に奉願候。先は安否伺旁如此に御座候。早々敬具

　十月廿一日

　　　　　　矢太郎

尊叔殿膝下

猶々、叔母様に宜敷様御伝声奉願上候也。

3　明治(22カ)年5月30日

追々暑気相催候処、尊叔父様を始御高閣御一統被為揃ますく御清祥被為遊御座候半、大慶至極奉存候。降て矢太郎にも無事奉務罷在申候間、乍憚左様御休意奉願候。陳は私事も当熊本に赴任後隊務等の為未た帰国の事不相叶、空く経過罷在申候。併し当来七月暑中休暇を以て弥帰国いたす考に御座候。

尊叔父様御存知の通陸海軍唯今の景況に就ては、私共の如き唯陸軍士官学校のみを卒業候者にては、実に将来の目途無覚束愚考罷在申候。依て従是又々東京なる陸軍大学校へ入学いたし度処存に御座候。尤右の事に就ては去年御地出発の際、川崎少将閣下より懇々御教諭を相蒙り候儀も有之候に付、同閣下の御懇情を空しくせざる様精々勉励、是非陸軍大学校に入学いたし度存申候。同校は隊附二年以上相勤めたる将校でなけれは入学試験御許可不相成御制規にて有之候故、私事は隊付新らしくして、後一年半も経過の猶予有之事に候へは、夫までの間精々勉励以て素志相達度存申候。左様御了承奉願候。就ては若し川崎少将閣下へ御面晤の節は、是非前述の儀宜敷様御通置被下度、伏して奉願上候。

寿屋方へは軍衣袴代価払の残金高三拾円位有之候趣、先日岡田彦三郎氏より承知仕候。就ては右残金は私処有之公債証書利子より御払込被下候様奉願候。当熊本にては私の月俸にて万事調弁して余り八石に御座候。

当熊本においては何も御通知可申上程の事も無之候。唯当地の招魂祭には私は始めての事にて、実に感入申候。東京の招魂祭より一層の賑にて有之様覚申候。

奈良原矢太郎

依て右公債利子の儀は皆寿屋方へ御払込被下候ても可
然奉存候。為念御通申上置候。右様御諒察被遊度存
候。

先は御安否伺旁申進候儀如此に御座候。尚々時節柄故
折角御尊体御大事に御保養専一に奉祈上候。恐惶敬具

五月三十日
　　　　　　　　　　矢太郎
尊叔父殿
　追伸　おば様可然御伝へ被下度奉願候也。

4　明治（23カ）年10月26日

謹啓　秋冷之候弥以御高閣皆々様被為揃御清祥之笋奉
恭賀候。降て矢太郎も無事奉務罷在申候間、御安神奉
願候。偖て此品は乍軽少進上仕候間、御叱留御風味被
下度候。別封はおすま様へ御送被下候様御依頼申上候。

清風・清能等は不相更精々勉学之笋不斜慶賀此事に御
座候。御家の普新〔ママ〕は如何、早や御成就之笋と奉察上候。
矢太郎御地出発の際御願申上置候西郷先生〔隆盛〕・木戸〔孝允〕・
大久保〔利通〕諸名士の手蹟は何卒郵便にても御恵投被下度奉

懇願候。おすま様よりの御手紙に依れは貴島巌は先般
一寸出京の由、就ては奇体なる注文を申入候哉承知仕
候。今より彼が如此処業には驚入申候。何んともかん
とも言はれんとは此事ならん。今後の有様思遣られ申
候。嘸々おすま様御心配の笋と察上申候。彦二及稲は
諸兄の擬をなさざる様ありたき者に御座候。

矢太郎事明廿七日より久留米地方へ長途行軍いたし、
来月十二三日頃帰営の笋に御座候。今度は師団演習に
て旅団と旅団との対向に御座候。赴任以来如此大演習
は今度が始めて有之候故面白き事ならんと察せられ申
候。

久留米より熊本まて鉄道事業は唯今着手最中に御座候。
来年四月迄に完成の由に有之候。依て来年四月以後は
馬関までは交通に相成候訳に御座候。
先は御伺旁如此に御座候。
猶々為邦家為御家御自愛専一に奉願上候。　敬具
　十月廿六日
　　　　　　　　　　矢太郎
清成様

二二　橋口直右衛門

1　明治15年5月2日

尚々、玉体御愛護専一に奉願候。

謹啓仕候。陳は三月九日、廿日并四月六日附之御書面

難有奉拝読候。大人始め御一同様御着後御健全被為入、

大慶不斜奉存候。大人には未た御栄転無御座候旨拝承、

折角早目相運申候様奉祈候。後任は寺島先生任命可相

成旨御知せ被下、此先生は兼て御申聞も御座候通経歴

有之人物に御座候得は、万端都合能き事と奉存候。同

人には本月十日前後に本邦発途之由、左候得は六月中

には当府え着之事と存し、徐々待受も仕度共御座居申候。

一、大人馬車之義は御出発後好望手を採立不仕候処、

先日漸く好望手を見出し、半は約束仕候処に先可見合

旨御指示被下、其故今まて売却不仕申候。併し四月六

日附之御書面にて売却可仕旨御申越被下、委細承知仕

候。依て近日売却仕候考に御座候間、左様御承知被遊

度、其他額弁諸器物等も取揃へ、ヲークショニヤーの

花盛に御座候。併し春日之長閑なるにも本国之如く花

手を経て夫々売却仕度奉存候。御出発後、諸払之儀は

実に莫大之高に相嵩み、実に苦慮之至に御座候。右に

関する請取書等は私帰朝之時悉皆取纏め持参仕可申候

間、左様御承知被遊度。過便米貨二千弗之額、本省

より御送致被下正に領収仕候。依て請取書は本省え廻

送仕置候間、自然御領収之事と奉存候。開拓使も被為

廃候に付ては、該使預け金引上け可相成と存し心配仕

居候処、誠に仕合之事に御座候。跡残額は諸器物売却

之上返償仕度奉存候。併し不足も生し候節は別途御回

金被遊候様仕度候。

一、馬之儀は其後ブラヲンより何たる挨拶も無御座候。

誠に失敬之至と相考申候。併し不日高平氏より掛合之

積に御座候間、左様御承知被遊度、若し相当之代価を

不収候以上は断然引戻し候ても不苦候儀と決心仕居申

候。

一、当地之情実等は委詳ランマン氏等より御通知之筈

に付、私は贅言不申上候。当地日々暖和能成、花園等

見等之興は無御座候。乍遺憾始終内籠にて読書之外無
御座候。是も一種之学問にて、先々我慢仕居申候。私
にも近比余程壮健にて不怠勉務仕候間、少も御掛念被
下間敷、折角御教諭に従ひ勉学仕他日些少なりとも御
国の為尽力仕度考に御座候間、左様思召被遊度、当館
も別段異状無御座候。をもしとかしと罷暮し申候。前
にも屡々申上候通り拙身上に付ては大人之御考に依り
如何様とも御下知被下度偏に奉願候。寺島先生の下に
居る事御適当と御考被遊候得は今より一年位は左様仕
可申候。併し又直に帰朝之方可然と御考被遊候得は其
方え御周旋被下度奉願候。併し一身上之事は些々たる
事にて如何様とも政府の辞号待つより外無御座候。乍
筆末御子供様方にも増々御生長被遊候由奉大慶候。先
日は湯地より委細書通致呉れ御子供様方之情実等承知
仕候。同人にも近比余程全快に被赴候由、誠に仕合之
事に御座候。御地も格別異状無御座候由折角官民共平
和を主とし御国の利益を計り度者と奉存候。板垣暗殺
一件は如何之源因よりして生し申候哉一向解し不申候。

恐々謹言

　五月二日

　　清成様

　　　　直右衛門

是迄は官員社会に暗殺流行仕候故是から民権社会え流
行可仕徴候かとも存申候。拠当地於ても最早交際時節
も相過き頓と閑暇に相成申候。併し折々役所之仕事は
相嵩み彼是繁忙を極め居申候。先は御返答旁申上候。

恐々謹言

　五月二日

　　清成様

　　　　直右衛門

追てマダム其他え宜敷御申上被下度奉願候。右は取
急き相認乱筆之至真平御海涵被遊度奉願候。（公使
館三階之物置にあるマンモントロンク中書籍と共に
一包の日本料理屋勘定書其他品川御殿山家屋建築締
書等御取集め、其当便に御差送可被下候様公使より
御通知有之候故、乍御手数宜敷奉願候。）右築田氏
　　　　　　　　　　　　　　　　　　〔梁カ〕
より通知御座候に付、直様右トロンク中角々まで探
索仕候得共見当不申、依て其他諸所も穿鑿仕候得共、
遂に捜出し不申、何とも遺憾之事に奉存候。尚後日
見出候節は御送致可申上候間左様御承知被下度候。
乍憚様築田氏より懇書請取申候得共後便返答可仕候

二三　室田義文

1　明治（15）年10月25日

奉拝啓候。時下益御清穆被為在御起居奉恭賀候。陳は、
前便申上置候敷物之義其後島村氏にも相談之上、嘗て
寺島殿等之ため織立候店に就き段々引合候処、当今之
相場にては白に藍紺之二色を以模様を添候一尺四方に
付洋銀三十五銭　等最上　同三十銭　等上　同二十五銭　等中　之割合な
れは、必す御意に相叶候様出来可申との事、尤広間之
方は四枚に次間は二枚と敷合にせずては出来難き趣且
右にて宜布候まま候被命候日より一ケ月前後を以織上
者候由、但此中等に値するものと雖も上海辺之出来合
即ち日本に渡り居候品杯には優ても決して劣り不申と
の事、又色模様は図本さへ御出候時は如何様にも出来
候趣候。右様御承知被下度一休最少之分なり。為見本
呈し度存候処、出来合之分は何れも両方即ち上海又は

日本送り之分にして下等品に付更に上中之度にて右二
尺四方之分一二枚注文仕置候間、出来次第幸便に附し
可奉呈候間、御急きにあらされは右貴覧之上御注文被
下度、又赤色等を織出し候分は蒙古地方にて出来北京
辺には折々売物に出候由なれ共、当地方には絶て無御
ざ由藍紺の二色なれは、当天津に限り候趣御座候。右
御報上之ため如此、当地着已来未た同宿も無之相分り
不申候得共ボリチック上に取りては追々御報上可仕義
も御出候様に推量仕居候。早々不一

十月二十五日

天津にて

義文拝

大輔閣下

〔注〕吉田清成文書のNo.一一二三と一七一四が同一の書状の
　　前と後を構成する。

間宜敷様御申伝被下度候。敬白

二四　吉田二郎

1　明治13年7月30日

Palace Hotel

San Francisco, (以上印刷) July 30th 1880

〔注〕欄外に Confidential と書き込みあり。

一書拝呈　本月念二日デーヤパークより御差出之貴書
過刻接手、逐件拝承仕候。先以閣下始め御家族方皆様
御健康被為在候由、奉忻賀候。小生儀、去る二十六日
無異当府着候処、幸に筑波艦碇泊中にて士官以下生徒
にも日々上陸余程賑々敷事にて御座候。今度該艦之来
航に付ては、士官以下乗組一同当府市民之気受甚た宜
敷、本邦之為可賀事に御座候。小生も屡々参艦調練抔
一見致候。是亦至極評判宜敷候。此程艦上に数百人招
待、盛大之レセプション有之候趣に承及候。
会計信第五号六号之儀御伺之通評決相成候様精々勉力
可仕候。帰朝之上模様早々御報可申上候。
小生後住書記官之儀に付御内諭之趣拝承仕候。然るに
当地にて或人より内々聞知候に、露国行尾崎書記官貴
地在勤長田二等書記官は引続露国在勤被命候積に本省
於て内決相成候哉之由、定て閣下にも公使にて右辺御
承知可被成とは存候得共、承及候儘御内報に及候。然
し右は真之私報に係り候事故、一概には信用難致候。
貴地出発前御示諭之趣旨は松谷〔後欠〕

〔章治カ〕
児玉大蔵便より被成下候尊札惣に相達致拝見候処、大兄にも愈御壮健当分は外国館におひて何歓へ奉務被成居候哉にて、僕共にも至り幸甚無事計候。折角再航可被下候。僕共には今に碌々下学罷在候事御坐候。幸皆々元気にて御坐候間御放慮可被下候。兄にも再航之思召にて候得共、未た其義不相調哉にて、午併当時之政府におひての御尽力、果国家之御為歟と奉存候。不遠野生等も一通り成業帰国仕り聊之微力をも尽し度奉存候。先は御報迄あらく〳〵如此御坐候。

永井五百助

【吉田清成発】

一 西郷従道

1
明治（9）年（ ）月（ ）日

統領始、国務内務其他内閣の諸卿へ御面会有之候方可然と被存候。是又御賢慮承度御座候。貴局事務之義は関沢事務官其地之勉強にて充分整成候哉に相見得、多幸之至御坐候。或は他各国事務官之内にも我国の事務捗進には稍々後れ候ものとて有之と被察候。右まて、不敢。草々抜首

吉田清成

西郷信吾様
侍史

二 花房義質

1
明治（ ）年（ ）月（ ）日

花房㒵様

三 吉原重俊

1
明治（ ）年10月11日

尚々、少々の支は押て御来駕可被下候。僕も差越度儀はいやなれとも〇旁考ふるに是非とも今度一会不仕候ては不相済候〇僕等も両度程集

吉原重俊

New Heaven Oct, 12ᵗʰ, 1869

会にて此段を呻せり。

永井兄も御来駕在候、愉快之程御推量可被下候〇抑僕

等にも次のサチュルデイ之朝則当月十六日也新約克に

集会を催促決定仕、「ニウフランセキ」生にも其段申

遣置申候。阿兄にも必々御操合可被下候。僕等も御存

之通無寸暇といへとも今度は押て差越事にて御坐候〇

併阿兄無拠御差支共御坐候は〻御報告早目に可被下候

〇新約克街に於ては Metropolitan hotel Broadway

に集会之賦也。

一僕等には爰許を三人同道にてフライデイ十五日夕出

立仕候て御許え来り御同船仕度候間、御待居可被

下候。先はあらく目出度。頓首

十月十一日

〔吉原重俊〕
大原令之助様

〔種子島敬輔〕
吉田彦まろ
〔吉田清成〕
永井和洲治
〔湯地定基〕
工藤十郎

Dear friends

Having seen this other page, I have no

any objection to go to New York, as you proposed

and I think the steamer leaves here for that city

at 11 o'clock p.m., so you must be at that time.

Shall I be at the depart or will you come up

to Mr. Newell's?

Your dearly

O, Re

〔注〕後半の英文は吉原重俊の返書。

吉田清成関係文書七　書類篇3

十　元老院議官・枢密顧問官時代

明治20年7月19日

1　株券に関する覚書

甲第壱壱〇七番

　弐百株　　　　　吉田清成

明治弐拾年七月拾九日交付

此券状之日付は

明治拾八年拾月壱日　森岡昌純

　　　　　　　　吉川泰次郎

第八回の利子札より第拾五回の利子札付

〔注〕墨書。

十　元老院議官・枢密顧問官時代

2　吉田清成宛当座預金引出の件／東京第三十三国立銀行

明治20年9月2日

東京第三十三国立銀行㊞〔朱〕

明治廿年九月二日

拝啓　陳は、兼て御預け入相成居候当坐預り金御引出し方の義は、何方も御名前下へ印影御押捺の上振出相成居候処、本日御振出しの第一号金参百五拾円の小切手へ御花押御記載相成少々困却仕候得共、通帖も御持参の義に付無相違事と存し仕払申候。何卒向后御引出しの節は御押印の上御振出し被下候様奉願候。就ては別紙印鑑紙へ向后御押捺可相成、御印鑑御押印の上郵便にて御遣し相成候様被成下度奉願候。匆々不備

吉田清成様　執事御中

〔注〕東京第三十三国立銀行用箋、墨書。

3　「意見書」／谷干城

明治20年9月

〔注〕農商務省用箋、墨書、表紙に「谷中将意見書写扣　明治廿年九月念日」と記し、「大山」の朱印あり。本意見書写本はもう一冊あり、墨書で末尾に「SK」の署名がある。『谷干城遺稿三』巻之六第一編第二十九文書に同じ。

4　吉田清成・貞宛宮中観菊会招請状／土方久元

明治20年11月2日

宮内大臣

皇帝　皇后両陛下の命を奉じ、元老院議官子爵吉田清成殿及令夫人を来る八日午後三時仮皇居禁苑に於て催さる

ゝ観菊会に招請す。

明治二十年十一月二日

フロック、コート著用、夫人は通常礼服或は西洋服著用

〔以下活字印刷添付紙〕
一皇居官門を入り御車寄に於て下乗すべし。

一参内の際案内状を持参して掛員へ示すべし。

一当日雨天なれは止む。

〔以下封筒に吉田書込〕
二十年十一月八日三時

〔朱筆〕
「両陛下　天機御潤敷被為居候。

両人共罷出候。昨年に比すれは御日割も疾やけれとも菊の盛りを過たるを覚ふ。第一は三百三十二花（但黄色）。外国公使連少数、加るに内外の夫人方昨年に比して少し。天気は快晴西北の風少々あり。華氏の計七十度に昇らす、穏暖と云べし。

五時前入御あり。

内外臣は五時前後退宮。

此日伊藤総理大臣鹿児島・沖縄其外へ向け午前九前半〔ママ〕の汽車にて新橋発、

〔厳〕
大山大臣
〔景範〕
・仁礼中将同断、見送る。
〔友実〕〔鞆之助〕〔島津久光〕
吉井・高嶋は従一位公病気為御見舞鹿府へ向け同時に発す。

其外数名発せしが見送の人数なし。」

十　元老院議官・枢密顧問官時代

〔注〕本文は菊紋入り印刷活字。宛先のみ手書。封筒表に「元老院議官子爵吉田清成殿　同令夫人」とあり。

明治20年11月5日

5　高知県人建白書抄録／吉田清成〔カ〕

〔親雄〕
元老院にて本田議官より請取たる高知県人建白書の内備忘の為記す　二十年十一月五日

一、明治十四年十月十二日を以空前絶後の　大詔を〔煥〕煥発し玉ふ云々。其内に　大政の統一を総攬し、又夙に立憲の政体を建て後世子孫継ぐべきの業を為さん事を期す云々。中略。

一、元老院は明治八年に之設けられ、府県会は同十一年に開かる。

一、新聞条例布告は明治八年六月なり。後十六年四月大に改正を加たり。

〔三〕
一、集会条例は明治十四年四月に布告し、又十五年六月を以更大に之改定す。

一、出板条例を以恣に著書刊行の自由を抑制し云々。請願規則を以陰に国事願望の通路を防遏するあり云々　（高知県人建白書の内に見ゆ。明治二十年十月）。

一、府県会議員の聯合集会往復通信を禁せしは十五年十二月第七十号布告を以なり。

〔注〕墨書。

達乙第三百三号

6　鎌倉郡内戸長役場宛吉田清成借地に関する神奈川県達（写）

明治20年11月30日

7 吉田清成宛借地に関する通知／鎌倉郡内戸長役場

7 吉田清成宛借地に関する通知／鎌倉郡内戸長役場

明治20年12月2日

庶第百壱号

先般拝借御使用相成たる官林芝地の内、字今小路通り今回道路新設許可相成候に付ては、別紙之如く達相成候条、速に御返地相成度、該書面は来る八日迄に御送附有之度、此旨及御通知候也。

　　　　　　　　　　　　　　　　　　　　　　神奈川県知事　沖守固㊞

明治二十年十一月三十日

其部内乱橋材木座村官林地及芝地本年九月農甲第二百七拾七号を以て東京府華族吉田清成へ貸渡候処、今回右の内前記反別道路に変換候条、来る十二月十日限り返地方取計ふへし。

一、反別壱畝弐拾八歩
第千百壱番の内
同郡同村同字芝地
一、反別三畝拾六歩
第千百弐番の内
鎌倉郡乱橋材木座村字大門官林

〔注〕神奈川県下鎌倉郡用箋、㊞を含めすべて墨書。

鎌倉郡小町村外十二ケ村
　　　　　　　　　戸長役場

171

十　元老院議官・枢密顧問官時代

明治二十年十二月二日

東京府華族

吉田清成殿

〔注〕神奈川県下鎌倉郡用箋、墨書。朱印には郡内全十三ヶ村名が列挙されている。なお、「華」の字を書き誤り、「関」の訂正印を押して訂正している。

神奈川県鎌倉郡小町村外十二ヶ村

戸長役場［印］　［朱］

8　「拝借地返納之件」／吉田清成

拝借地返納之件

鎌倉郡乱橋材木座村字大門官林

第千百弐番の内

一　反別三畝拾六歩

同郡同村同字芝地

第千百壱番の内

一　反別壱畝弐拾八歩

右予て拝借罷在候官林及芝地之内道路開設御用之趣御達に付、前記之反別致返納候也。

明治20年12月

明治二十年十二月

神奈川県知事沖守固殿

〔注〕墨書。

9　条約改正問題等政治改革に関する意見書

東京府華族

吉田清成

明治（20〜22）年

一今後政務の方針は国体を堅立し民性を発達し猥りに便宜取捨に流れさるへき事

維新以来百般の制度世勢の傾向に促かされ旧を廃し新を布き大に時機に応するの便益を得たりと雖とも、一利あれは一害之に伴ふは古今の通理、況んや鎖国の陋制を破り一時に世界の新事物に遭逢し、彼我の差別甚しきを見て事々物々旧体に安すべからざるより、僅に二十余年間にして殆んと旧時の観を一変したるは実に古今例少き実蹟にして、殆んと既往を顧みば我人共に呆然たらさるを得す。　畢竟此の如く大変化を来せしは時勢の推移にして人力の抑止すへき限にあらさるも、亦之か為め国性の傷け民情を乱したるの跡なしとせす。　故に今日に及ひて亦た擾々終に意外の変化を生するに至りしは、当初上下倶に志慮足らす計議熟せさりしか為めなりと謂ふへし。　是以て一事一物意外の変動を生し、為めに弥々旧法の廃すへきを覚り年々歳々改廃に遑なく、皆な悉く先規を欧米に採り人情風俗の特異を問はす一概に之を推及せしめんと欲するの勢には迫りたり。　故に事々物々更に定着の期なく常に擾々として今日に及ひしものにして、蓋其因ありて果を結

手　扣

十　元老院議官・枢密顧問官時代

ひしものと謂はさらんや。是れ現今政務の繁冗間断なく官民倶に生営の安堵を得さるの所以にして、当初兵馬控偬の際深く彼我の区別を弁するの遑なく、事物の緩急を忽にしたるの過なるべし。事已に過去に属して今更如何とも是非すへきにあらざるも、既往を鑑みて将来を慮るは政務の要領なり。況んや来る明治二十三年に及ひ立憲の政を布き国家未曽有の制度を行ふに及んては、又従来の如く単に時機に応変するの政策のみを以て国家の安泰を保維するに難かるへし。宜く今日に於て立国の基礎を定め、我帝国は万古不替の体性にして列国に特異なるの大本を存立して揺揺せさるの理由ある所以を審明し、以て国威を海外に発輝するの主旨を確立し、以て今後政務の進路は主として国粋を保存し大綱を失はす作新改良機宜を過つにあらさるも、従前の如く国民に先て改革を促かし事を設けて之を誘ふか如き処置を施さす、国性に害あり民生に利ならすとするも、事実に於て蔽ふへからさるの障害を現出するに至らすんは務めて其弊を拄き其欠を補ひ急激の変革を施さゝることを注意し、民心をして実着穏当国に報し　君に忠たるの精神を確めしむるにあらすんば、目下の情況を以て将来を察するに真に欧米の善風良俗之れ化するにあらす。　徒に奇を玩ひ新を喜ふの人情を生し只彼の悪習醜慣のみを模するに至らんかの杞憂なきにあらす。　果して此の如くなりとせは将来益々民心を揺動し延て国政を迷乱するに及ふや顕然たりと云ふべし。　況んや国本一旦動揺して上下帰向する処なくんは彼我各自の心慮に任せ、或は東に奔せ或は西に駆り南北皆人々の随意にして何の時か国家の方針を一定し、以て　帝国の隆昌を期すへけんや。　万一無識の輩一時の名聞を欲し危激の理論に沈酔し一呼一唱転々人民を鼓動するに及んては、今日の如き人心にありては之に響応する者尠からす、終に動乱を惹起すに至るならん。　然かるときは国家の典憲固より存すると雖とも、同胞相悪み同生相戕ふに至りては如何ぞ人心をして悲痛を感せざらしめん哉。　人情一旦相憐むの情に僻するに及んては終に事の正邪を判別するに違なく因縁相惹き終に国家の痼疾となるに至らん。　果し

174

9 条約改正問題等政治改革に関する意見書

て然らは何等の手段を尽すも又制すへからさるに至るへし。故に事末た発せさるに於て慎むは事を処するの良法なり。故に今日人心の紛乱殆んと破れんとするの機勢あるに当りては、一日も早く立国の大旨を定め　帝国の建礎に基き毫も他国の模型に化すへきものにあらす、只時態の宜しきを失はす国性民智の允す限りは務めて改良作新の方向を取るの要領を一定し、宜く　聖旨の在せらるゝ処を明示され、苟も内閣に立て国政を掌理に預る者は勿論、一般官吏より下人民に至るまて確然立国の大旨は　祖宗の典憲に基き毫も違背すへからす。只政務の緩急に至りては時宜に応して取捨措置すへきものたれは、目下政務の利弊に至りては之を論弁すへきも、立国の大体に至りては何人と雖とも喙を容るへからさるの観念を発せしめすんは、今日の如く政務の是非を以て立国の大旨を左右褒貶するか如き形跡あらしめは、終には云へからさるの極に至らんも図り難し。曽て西哲の語に曰く、凡そ国体とは恰も人体の如し。頭長しとて之を断つへからす。手足短しとて之を長ふすへからす。一国の歴史一国の慣行は是れ則ち国体の本原なり。故に身体を長短伸縮すへからさるか如く国体も亦変揺更革すへからさるなり。若し慮なく天然の体質を変換せんと欲し身体を毀傷せは反て患害を醸し身為めに斃れんのみ。軽浮固有の国性を更革せんと欲して国体を破壊せは反て紛乱を生し国為めに滅ひんと。実に的言と謂はさるべからす。故に目下寸時も踟躇することなく主として内閣大臣に於て各自心慮を定め立国の大旨を弁別し、偶々政務の方針を演述するに当りても異口同音毫も彼我均しく其意旨を異にすることなければ、尓他官吏に至りても自ら其体旨を服膺するに及ふべし。官吏の意思已に決せは自然人民の意思も定まるの期あるべし。是れ今日人心の紛々擾々を来せしは、畢竟政務の方針確立せさるを以て世人徃々理説に迷ひ、又は癖論に泥み各自随意の論旨を主唱するも更に其理否曲直を判明したることなきか為めなるべし。故に目下の急務は宜く建国の大旨に基き尓後決して軽挙外邦の模倣に失せさる旨を決議し、更に　聖裁を仰き各自服膺し身を以

175

十　元老院議官・枢密顧問官時代

て一般を率ひ自然尓他を風化するの実蹟を奏せられん事を期する所以なり。

一法令の改廃政務の得失は弘く諮詢を遂け私議に流れさるへき事

政務の得失は一時の便宜を考案取捨するにあらすして、現今適切の利害に止まらす永遠無窮の盈縮に関して最も軽んすへからさるの関係あるものなり。蓋法令の規定は主任の審査討議を経へ更に各官の熟議を尽し全体の得失を探討し、以て国家人民の為め利ありと判定せば宜く議案を備へて　聖裁を仰き而して下人民に令するの順序にして、固より典型遺漏なく法制厳正なりと雖とも、或は事の軽重を誤り或は緩急を失ふの患なしとせす。固より官制定まりて職守分あり。毫も上下の干犯なく従我の終錯なきは勿論なりと雖とも、千百の制令中或は彼に矛盾し之に復重するの実なしとせす。特に下民之を奉する者に至ては一令一法上司の令する処は従順せさるを得す。一指一揮官吏の命する処は遵行せさるべからさるを以て、万一法制を規定するに当りて遺議ありとせは頻次改補塡欠せさるを得す、終に当初の赴旨に基くことを得す。其実施に及ひ民間の情体に適合せさる時は勢ひ便宜に従ひ細目の条款規則を定めさるを得す。是以て上令偏に人民の安泰無事を期すへきものも、中間之を実施するに及んて益々緻密煩冗に流れ、下民其労苦に堪へさるか如く寛猛其実を異にするの跡尠からす。是以て一令の発する毎に廟議固より精密の討査を尽し議に遺漏なしと雖とも、百般の法令中或は其精神を誤るものなきを保せす。特に上司の督促厳急なれは下司意を迎へて只実施の蹟を競ひ、毫も人民の痛癢を顧みさるの弊を生するに至るへし。或は上司緩漫に過くれは各地実施の精粗均しからす、厳に過ぎ寛に過くるの弊を生し人民をして転々厚薄の念を起さしむるものなしとせす。故に一令一法民をして遵従の義務を随意にせしめは固より事に害なしと雖とも、苟も一国の典憲として国内に布くに至りては、只表面の利害のみを研究するに止まらす宜く表裏詳に影響する処を探究し、一点の損得と雖とも之を軽視せす一毫の故障といへとも之を看過せ

す、小心翼々深く慎み篤く考へ以て令示するにあらすんは、或は法令の精神を誤感し其赴意を誤用するに至らん。之れ実に天下に毒害を流すものにして国家の損亡[ママ]人民の愁苦計るへからさるなり。故に事苟も人民の利害に関するに及んては務めて弘く審査諮詢を遂け、一令を出すに及んては宜しく其実効を奏することを期せすんはあらす。若し朝令暮改の形跡を存し民心自然法令を慢り為めに之を重んするの心思薄きに至ては、政令何を以てか行はれんや。凡そ法令を破り規則に違ふ者多きは之れを忽視するに在り、或は千百人中法令の何たるも弁せさるものなきにあらさるも、要するに法令の尊厳犯すへからさるを慎まさるに坐するのみ。之れ法を出すに軽挙にして之を改廃するの頻繁なるか為めなり。若し法令を実施せしむるか為め強て違法者の夥多なるを欲すとせは果して法令の精神を得たりと云ふへき乎。反て施行の至難なるを証するものにして実に法令の尊貴を汚したりと云はさらんや。若し法令を布くか為め違背の多きを以て実効ありとせは法を作り人を駆り之を陥箄[ママ]に縛するに異ならす。豈に制法の要旨を得たりと謂ふへけんや。故に今後に至りては一法といへとも之を布くに慎み一令といへとも之を下すに軽忽にせさるは最も治国の要訣なり。況んや国家の大体に関し千載の治乱を定め民生の利喪依て分るゝか如き事件に至りては、特に既往の事蹟に鑑み将来の変遷を推し虚心平気に事物の利害を顧慮し一個人と雖とも異議なきに至るの覚悟あらすんは、必す中途紛紜の原となり当初の目的を果すに難かるへし。然かるに今回条約改正の議の如く世に伝ふる処れは一二当務者にありて議を決し

聖裁を仰きしものなるへし。果して如何は余人の知るへき処にあらさるも又深く顧慮すへきの事実なるへし。固より締盟和如[好カ]は一に　聖裁に存して臣民の得て是非すへき限にあらさるも、今回条約の如くは聞く処に拠れは単に和好通商ノ交際法を議定するか如きものにあらすして、我国是を変革し我法律を取捨するの関係あり。

乃ち　祖法を変通して内地雑居を允し我慣行を委棄して欧米の法理に基き法典を編纂し、或は裁判官を雇用し

十　元老院議官・枢密顧問官時代

て司法権を犯さるゝか如く、一旦改正条約にして批准せらるゝに及んては着々国民の頭上に利害を及ほし、今日の情体にありて説者の言の如き、改正条約にして成立するに及んては国性民情に対して何等の余響を及ほすへきや恰も一時に百雷の墜落するか如く、為めに何等の利害を感すへきや計るべからす。特に　聖意国土民生を統治し玉ふは所謂　祖宗の国土民生を害するに至りては決して軽んすへきにあらす。況んや要路大臣にありては克く国土民生を統へ　聖意を翼賛するの責任あるをや。若し議茲に出すして事を軽忽に決するの議を来すときは大臣の任職を完ふせさるの責を辞するを得す。終に　聖徳の煩を為し奉るに及んては将た何の辞か以て天下に謝せんや思はさるへからさるなり。条約改正の議は勿論尓他百般の法令に至ても今後は務めて内外の審査討議を竭し、廟堂部内は勿論事に直接の関係あるものは主務省に下し之を調査し、草案を編定するに至りても単に一個の委員の議に附するに止まらす、宜く実地の効否を探究し務めて事に遺漏なきことを期せんこと最も注意を要すへき処なり。況んや臨時政務の得失に至ては法令に異なり目下に施行して目前の便否を決し、或は将来の利害に関するものなれは最も弘く諮詢を遂け各人の意想を悉し交互の関係を詳かにせすんは事発して過あらん。若し一二の私議私見を以て天下の大勢を察し或は民生の利害を慮るときは、恐くは遺策を生し誤信を来し終に収拾すへからさるに至らん。故に今後は公私の議を区分し苟も公事に係るものは宜く政事堂に於て公言公議を竭く、十分に理否明白の判定を下すことを憚からさるへし。事已に発すへきものに至ては政府外に私議すへからす。仮令従来情実の存するありて私邸に審議するは事の円滑を保すへしと雖とも、今後政公議に出るの世に及んては決して従前の旧体を学ふへからす。宜く国政を諮議するの模範を示し、後来の政官をして政事を議するに於ては、宜く公場に公議するを憚からさるの道を開かれんことを希望する所なり。須らく内閣大臣に於ては

178

公私の議を分別し、国事を私邸に議し或は二三者の同議を以て大事を決するか如き軽易の挙動なからんことを期する所以なり。

一　要路大臣主として職を奉し任を尽すに謹蕭正明なるへき事

職守の高下は責任の軽重を規定する所以にして典憲の定まる処なり。何人と雖とも一回職守を奉するに至ては之に違非すへからさるや明かなり。固より官吏の職を奉するは職制の規定に基き毫も乖戻すへからさるの理なりと雖とも、尚ほ紀律を厳蕭にして其非横を検治し、以て国民の儀表たるに愧つる処なからしめんか為め、官吏懲戒例、服務紀律等を布かん。職守上の差誤に至ては悉く之を縄正したるの例は勘からす。其職を重んし任を完ふせしむるの道に至ては遺欠なしと謂ふへし。然れとも熟ら世体の実情を察するに、法令上に行はれて下に疎なるは稀有の例なり。多くは上に寛にして下に厳なるは普通の慣行、古今東西を問はす其弊習免れさると雖とも、苟も忠亮の臣議を建て非政を縄正し以て施政の清明ならんことを欲するに及んては、宜く上に行はれて下に令するにあらすんば何等の法令を布き以て職守の尊厳を箝束するも将た何そ官守を立るの要を得たりとせんや。若し官守の高下に従ひ法令亦た之に伴ひて寛猛ありとせは官守の尊厳を汚すこと幾千そや。上司の罪咎に至ては之を総攬するの主任なきを以て自然緩漫に流れ、或は交互の情義に繁かれ事実を隠蔽し、若しくは私情に泥みて軽重を取捨するの嫌なきを保せす。仮令下司の罪咎に至ては厳峻懲治の実を奏すへしとするも、亦上司の情弊を知るに於ては往々一時の災厄と認め毫も哀心に感銘するの実なきに及んては、将た何そ官守を立るの要を得たりとせんや。若し下司に至りても因縁結托して形跡を蔽ふに及んては亦た之を懲戒するの道なきに至らん。果して然らは百官己を脩め奉承の意に専なりと謂ふへからす。徒に職を弄して以て一身の利達を図るの道と誤認するに至ては官吏の腐敗已に極まれり。将何を以て政務の清明ならんことを期せんや。故に今後に至りては仮令要路

十 元老院議官・枢密顧問官時代

大臣と雖とも職守を欠く事あれは宜く自ら勅　奏して其過失を謝し、以て法制の厳蕭なるを示さゝるへからす。同僚亦た之を隠蔽庇護するの私情を去り明かに典憲を正し以て下民に観すにあらすんは、百官をして職守の重きを覚らしむること能はす。恰も官府を見ること私家の如く官職を思ふ事私業の如く去就軽易毫も慎重を主とする者なきに至りては豈に歎しからすや。夫れ官守は職任の高下ありと雖とも是れ皆法令を奉承して　聖旨を奉行するの任ならさるはなし。特に官守を帯ふる者は一般人民と異なり、苟も官命を奉承することに至れり。故に小官の職権小にして大官の職権大なりと雖とも、之を施政上に応用するに至りては大小軽重あることなし。仮令大官は国家の枢機を執るの大任ありとするも、其職分を分掌する小官に至ても又職守に軽重あるの理あること

なし。若し職任の大小は失過の軽重を来すものとせは、将何そ上官に重きの理あらんや。任大なれは責重し、職貴ければ咎軽からさるは理義の然かる処なり。特更人民に於て奉承の責任を論するときは官の大小軽重を以て順従の義務を異にするものにあらす。苟も人権を制し物権を推するに於けるか如く、決して軽からさるの事にあらすや。故に只官守の高下を論するときは官吏部内に限るか如きも、翻て人民の利喪を考察するに及んては決して軽重すへからさるを知るに足らん。故に官守を厳明にするは単に官吏をして其職守を完ふせしめ其身体を保全するの旨意に止まらす、職権を誤用し人民に影響する処なからしめんか為めなり。豈に何そ軽易視すへきことならんや。宜しく官守を厳明にし苟も法制に違ひ職務を汚すに至ては、官位の高下を論せす必賞必罰必す典憲を明にせは、自ら官吏部内の気風一変し職守厳明なるに至るへし。然らすんは今日已に世論の囂々を来し民心紛起に及ひしは、世人の伝ふる処に由れは政務機密内より発して外に伝はりしものゝ如し。或は新聞に掲載し或は人口に喧伝し、其原因は皆下官の疎漏にあらすして上官の軽卒に出るもの尠から

180

す。此の如く政務の機宜外間に漏洩するに至りしは、畢竟職守上司に厳ならさるの証跡にあらすや。然り而し
て独り下司に厳なるは将た政務の大要を得たりとせんや。是れ小事と雖とも因縁終に大事に及ひ国家を蠱毒し
人民を害傷するに至らは何を以て政令の厳明を保たん、何を以て政府の威厳を維かん、猛省せさるへからす。
故に今後は務めて要路大臣の職守を厳にし後来の儀表を立つること最も今日の要務なるへし。是れ職守の厳行
を期する所以なり。

一 要路大臣主として身を節し用を約し一般の奢風を矯治せらるへき事

勤倹の美徳は奢美の驕迭〔佚カ〕に制せらるゝは人情の免れさる処にして亦如何共為すに道なし。特に近来我国の風慣
に由り察するに、欧米誇奢の風漸次に浸潤し服飾衣玩亦た年を追ひて贅余を競ひ華美を誇るの情体なり。故に
一般の風潮又制するに由なく、一物を摸せは一物之に伴ひ蠡々として又制すへからsとす。故に上
下交々異観を争ひ歳々殆んと底止する処なく、陋巷の細民も又時風を追ひ僻〔僻〕村の農民も洋風を擬せすんは殆ん
と社会の交誼を繁くへからさるの観あり。是以て人々目前の嗜欲に迷ひ永遠の計を為す者少く、一日の奢楽を
貪らんか為め終生の難苦を覚らさるもの蠡々として一般ならさるはなし。是以て世風の鼓動する処因縁交錯転
々繁忙を極め人心毫も定着の心なく、一席一会の華美を競はんか為め千金を擲ち万金を投することも敢麗に異な
らす。是か為め無用の耗費年毎に加はり益々国力を衰残し凋弊日々に加はらんとす。仮令今日民間の情状昔時
に比し大に体面を異にせしか如きも決して実力を増加したるものにあらす。只聊か外面の虚飾を以て体面を妝
ふの風習行はれ、口腹既に饑ゆるも亦富奢を誇るの情ありと謂ふへきなり。此の如き潮勢にして果して底止す
る処なくんは殆んと国力を竭尽せしも将た近きにあるへし。故に此際上下一般非常の勤倹を務め以て本を養は
すんは、一旦災厄に遭遇するに及んては道路餓孚〔孚〕を以て満たさるゝに及はん。若し目前の安泰に泥み永遠の大

十　元老院議官・枢密顧問官時代

計を忽にするときは、必す囓臍の悔を貽すに至るや明かなり。仮令形貌文明を誇り粉飾開化を気取るも国力衰亡し民力凋落せは誰と倶に護国の精神を発揮せん。誰と倶に国基を維持せんや思はさるへからす。然れとも従来の推移今遽かに止むへきにあらす。海外の交通日々に頻切耳目の感触防くへからす。到底人力以て蔽ふへきにあらすと雖とも、若し今日の潮勢をして止まる処を知らさらしめは結局何れの処にか到着せん哉。今日にして有志の者之か矯救の策を講せすんは実に先途の実勢測られさらんとす。然れとも熟ら既往の実蹟に由り観察するに、今日上下軽浮の情勢を講せかし一般奢侈の風を長せしは概ね官吏の挙作に出る者勘しとせす。其一例を掲くれは年々土木を起し洋風の館宅を建築し或は官吏にして洋装を飾り、耳目鼻口の嗜好に至るまて挙て長短取捨の議論を唱へて一時を傾動したるより自然民間に波及し、商工農民にして毫も今日の生業に妨けなきものも旧風古慣時に容れさるの感をなし、相率ひて雷同し悉く上の為す処下之に倣ふの情体を馴致したるものにして、其原因を捜索せは蓋思半に過くること多からん。故に今日の弊俗を矯め国本を培養するの道を開かんと欲せは、宜く上率令して下之に順従するにあらすんは到底此の潮勢を挽回すること能はさるへし。特に今日国家危殆の情況を熟察し将来　帝国の独立を保持せんと欲せは、一時の措置以て此衰弊に頻するの弊習を矯正する能はさるなり。少く思慮を回し国家千載の計図を考ふるときは政府の任なり。若し国民艱難を極め将に塗炭に傾落せんとせは之を保抜救護するの任を果さゝるを得す。故に既往の失度を顧み今日に於て大に先途の大計を慮るに切なる心衷を以て主とし、内閣大臣各位より一身を節し用を約し勤倹の美俗を薫養せられんこと、蘯々たる下民之を暁すに道なくんは止まん乎。衆を率ひ道を教ふるは政府の任なり。然れとも豈に今日の急務にあらすや。固より一家一身の鎖事国家の大事に関係なきか如しと雖とも、俗を化し風を改むるには人心を感発せしむるにあらすんは其実効を奏し難し。況んや今日の国情は国家隆興の為め資財を投する

182

にあらすして、国力衰亡を促かすか為め民血を靡するか如きもの勘らすとせは、一輌の馬車一領の服衣も又軽きにあらす。況んや家室器什玩器飾器の類にして数十幾万を靡散して我に購ふも一人一個の贅余を誇るに止まり、尓他幾十万の凍餓を赦ふに由なきものをや。若し僻邑遠村生息を絶ち独り都下の民のみ華奢揚々たりとするも、決して国家の隆昌を得たりと謂はんや。須らく本根を養ふの道を開き今日の国力今日の民力に相応した程限を忘れす、分を守り序を越へす無用を転して有用に帰せしむるの主旨を以て務めて分外の贅余を節約し民生上有用の事物を輸入するの資に充て、先つ内閣大臣ハ断然日常の瑣事より節約を施し宮廷の盛儀を欠かさる限りは駟馬華車を軋らすの誇奢を慎み、質素簡朴を以て心とし馬上若くは歩行務めて倹徳を示すときは、自然下民の心情も又自ら愧る処ありて全般の風潮茲に一変し、耗費を惜み実業を興すに及へは人心自ら実着に赴き軽薄に流れす、国家の慶福実に図るへからさるなり。是身を節し用を約し勤倹の風を起すは目下の急務にして忽にすへからさる所以なり。

一　要路大臣主として上下を調和し民意を暢達せらるへき事

　上下輯睦し官民諮議するは上意下達の旨意にして政務の要領なり。昔時独裁統治の時代に於ても尚ほ古人は務を衆に問ひ敢て忽にせさりし例あり。維新の際御誓文中にも万機公論に決すへしと　宣せ玉ひたるより、尓来政務の要旨は皆民意を酌み民心を和するの方針に嚮かさるはなし。特に旧時に異なり官民の分界年々に密着し出入進退反して猥雑に乱るゝやの歎なきにあらす。是れ官民互に分界を固守して利害を同ふせさるの形跡にあらすして、上下の意想交通し官民の情誼濃厚なるの一証たるへしと雖とも、未た実情を尽せさるものにあらす。尚ほ上下の情意普からす、民情を容るゝの窮溢なる乎の疑なきを得さるなり。是一私人間の交誼を云ふにあらす、弘く民心を調和し上下敵抗の精神なく其人を信し其命を聞くに憚らさるにあり。若し夫れ今日の如く上令を出

十　元老院議官・枢密顧問官時代

せは下之を難し、官命を下せは下之を渋むの感なきにあらす。故に常に上下意思を均ふせす官民方向を一にせす、東に行くへしと云へは西に奔り南に進めと云へは北に駆けるか如く常に乖離の念を抱き、施政転々至難を加ふるに至れり。特に要路の進退を是非し大臣の陟黜を論し毫も顧念する処なきか如く、苟も聖命を奉して要路に立ち政務の綱を執る人に対しては、仮令何等の巧拙あるを問はす国民悉く慎思熟考以て進退の宜を得たるや如何を質すへきに、反て快然可否を公衆に広言して憚らさるの形跡あるは抑も何等の原因そや。是れ皆上下調和の道開けす互に情意の普からさるの致す所にあらすや。若し要路官吏の進退の如き人民の痛痒に関するものとせは如何そ斯の如く漠々に看過すへけんや。必す賛襄協議力を尽して以て補翼庇護せさるへからす。然るに要路大臣中二三子を除くの外は空々として一人も痛痒の談を為すものなきは豈に上下の意思和熟せりと謂ふへけんや。実に官は官たり民は民たりとの意思にして国民共同協力国家を愛護するの実ありと謂ふへき乎。此等の実況を目撃する時は実に日本人民の軽浮無識にして倶に国家の大事を托するに足らさるを難せすんはあらす。若し夫れ此の如く官民の情意相通せす依然将来に及んては、誰と倶にか国家を維持し誰と倶にか国威を発揚せんや思はさるへからさるなり。此の如く上下の隔意を来し官民の乖離を促かせしは果して何等の原因ありて然かるや、須らく思考を要すへきなり。固より人民にして国事を建議するものは元老院に提出するの道あり。又一私人にして私事を請願する者は請願条例あり。毫も言路壅塞の嫌なしといへとも畢竟民意の調和せさるは単に形跡上に止まるへからす。必す無形上人心に感得する処あるにあらすんば決して民心を一和し民意を暢達する者にあらさるなり。然かるに従来要路大臣にして民間の志士を遇するに稍々冷淡に過き、為めに情意を害せしこと尠からす。其一二例を掲くれは、民間志士にして要路大臣を訪問するものあれは容易に面謁を允すことなく、稀に面談を諾する者も心慮を置て意見を職取することを務めす、弁難排斥一席にして失望の念

184

を起さしむることとなしとせす。是以て幾多の苦心を積み煩労を極め僅に意衷を陳へんと欲するも、他事に托して之れを謝絶せられ若しくは知見なきを以て聞かれさるもの多し。偶々幾日数の煩労稍く面談の期を得へきも一席にして面斥を受くるに至りては豈に何そ情意を傷め得さるものあらんや。顧みて要路大臣の職任を云へは国家人民を掌理するの任なり。所謂志士を統轄誘導するの人にあらすや。然らは乃ち要路大臣は国民の主人にして国民は乃ち従者の如く、従者事を主人に訴へんと欲するに主人用に托して之を拒み或は之を斥くるに至ては何れに向てか意思を陳へんや、実に方向に迷へりと謂ふへし。然かるに己の職任を顧みす公用に托して面談を謝す、公用とは将た何事そや、実に事実矛盾の甚しきものにあらすや。若し志士来りて談せは慰藉して遣るへし、或は意見を出すものあらは親く閲覧して答ふへし。固より人民の上言する処悉く政務に実施すへきにあらさるは論なきなり。只己の職任は人民を統治するの任にして他なきを証するに於ては民心に感得する処深からさらんや。然のみならす大臣の要職は国家の機軸にして朝廷亦優典之を遇し玉ふは古今東西其例あり。是れ皆職任の尊重を表章する所以にして単に威厳を示して人民を虚喝するの謂にあらさるなり。然のみならす万一不逞の徒あり非行を行ふことあれは、民情を乱し国典を傷くるの失あるを以て出入倶に警備を厳にし安全を図るは亦た事情止むへからさる事なりと雖とも、今日の如く人心乖離を来さんとするの際に於ては、従て種々の迷想を起し誤感に陥るものなきにあらす。故に寧ろ目下に於ては民の為め職を尽し国の為め任を果すの精神確然動かさる所以を表明し、身体を捧けて以て誠意誠心人民の衷情に感得するにあらすんは、何れの日か隠殺暗害の弊を絶つの期あらんや。仮令何等の防禦を設け鑑察を下すも防衛厳密なるに随ひ隠悪の手段益々増長し防くへからさるに至るへし。特に恐るへきは今日の如き軽燥暴激の士多く世勢の艱難を加ふるに随ひ年月に同気相求め転々勢援を増長するの勢にあり。若し今日の民心をして僻癖邪念を長せしむるに至りては、一時政府の威

十　元老院議官・枢密顧問官時代

令之を抑圧するに足るへしと雖とも、一国人心に萌出したる発念は幾多の年月を経へ幾多の妨害に遭ふも決し
て跡を絶つものにあらさるなり。威迫を以て一時に強抑を下すときは種々形跡を変し終に出没究なきに及ふへ
し。万一露国虚無党の如き兇行を逞ふするに及んては実に国体を汚損するの大害を変生するものと謂はさらんや。
故に一夫の志と雖とも奪ふへからさるは古訓の戒むる処なり。況んや人情相憐み同病相予ふは普通の情感、政
府の威抑厳峻に過くる時は自然強を挫き弱を扶くるの人情より転々人心を激昂するの跡なしとせす。是れ従前
兇行者の形跡に就き考察を下すときは思半に過くるものあらん。特に時勢の変状恰も維新前各藩の浪士天下に
横行したりしときの如く、今日は名を壮士に藉りて稍々跋扈の色あり。甚しきは自ら浪人と称し公然人に誇る
の傾あり。昔時幕府に於て浪人を観る軽侮に過きたりしも、漸次党援を増し各地気脈を通するに及んては又制
すへからす。終に籠絡以て鎮撫を計り或は厚餌以て観心を買ふに及ひたり。此の如く時勢の変遷は人意の表に
出ること多く預計は常に為すに先て破るは天下の通規なり。故に今日壮士の気激盛ならす之を撲滅するに足れ
りと為すへからす。一圧一抗年月倶に根底を堅むるに及んては亦如何共施すに道なからん。故に君子は微を慎
むを以て規鑑と為す。目下の気勢を察するに亦宜く前轍を忘れさらん事を欲せり。慎ますんはあらす。故に今
日は務めて威厳に傾くの弊を絶ち大磊不羈の心慮を以て天下の人士を遇し、一介の士と雖とも務めて情意を傷
けさらしめんことを期するなり。然れとも人あり謂へり、政府は確乎として動かさるへし、要路大臣は飽まて
威厳を以て下に接すへし、然らすんは政府の弱点を示すなりと。之れ誤見の甚しきにあらすや。政府は人民を
統轄するの官府なり。何そ人民と相対して輸贏を争ふの処ならん。若し政府は人民と権力を争ふの府とせは恰
も一国内に一敵党を生せしむか如く、何そ人民統治の原理に背叛するの甚しきや。蓋政府の強弱は只理に存する
のみ。政務正理に合せは誰か之に抗せん。然らすんは挙国之に背離し一時と雖とも政府の体を維持するを得ん

186

や。或人の説の如く日本国強盛なり日本国隆昌なりと云ふにあらすんは決して正当の論と云ふべからさるなり。是を以て鑑みるに、今日に於て人心の紛糾を解き上下一致盛に経倫を行ふは実に目下の急務なるべし。若し此緊要の時期を空過するに於ては正に明治二十三年の国会開設の時期に頻迫せり。此時に及ひ擾々不定の人心にて経過するに於ては国家の安危預めトすへからさるなり。故に要路大臣にして身体を処するには、身を民間に下し心頭に止め確乎不抜の精神と公明正大の所為を以て人心の誤感を解き共同一和相俱に国家維持の大本を堅立せすんは、将た何れの時か安静の目的を達すへけんや。是れ目下に於て上下を調和し民意を暢達するは尤も緊要なる所以なり。

〔注〕墨書。

10 吉田清成宛参賀申入書／土方久元

明治21年5月23日

来る廿八日 皇后宮御誕辰に付通常礼服^{燕尾}着用午前十一時参賀可有之、此段申入候也。

明治廿一年五月廿三日

宮内大臣子爵 土方久元

枢密顧問官子爵吉田清成殿

〔注〕宮内省用箋、墨書。

十　元老院議官・枢密顧問官時代

11　三条実美・黒田清隆・大隈重信・松方正義・大山巌・森有礼宛廻覧状／農商務省

明治21年5月28日

別封御送付に捺印可然候也。

明治廿一年五月廿八日

公爵三条実美殿
　御家扶御中〔印〕〔朱〕

伯爵黒田清隆殿
　御家扶御中〔印〕〔朱〕

伯爵大隈重信殿
　御家扶御中〔印〕〔朱〕

伯爵松方正義殿
　御家扶御中〔印〕〔朱〕

伯爵大山巌殿
　御家扶御中〔印〕〔朱〕

子爵森有礼殿
　御家扶御中〔印〕〔朱〕

農商務省
宿直

13　伊藤博文・山県有朋宛廻覧状／農商務省

〔注〕農商務省用箋、墨書。

明治21年5月28日

別封御送付に捺印可然候也。

明治廿一年五月廿八日

12　山田顕義・榎本武揚宛廻覧状／農商務省

〔注〕農商務省用箋、墨書。

〔異筆線カ〕
伯爵山田顕義殿
御家扶御中
〔異筆線カ〕
子爵榎本武揚殿
御家扶御中㊞〔朱〕

明治21年5月28日

農商務省

宿直

13　伊藤博文・山県有朋宛廻覧状／農商務省

別封壱通御送付に捺印可然候也。

明治廿一年五月廿八日

明治21年5月28日

189

十　元老院議官・枢密顧問官時代

〔注〕農商務省用箋、墨書。

伯爵伊藤博文殿
御家扶御中　印〔朱〕
伯爵山県有朋殿
御家扶御中　印〔朱〕

農商務省
宿直

14　西郷従道・谷干城・三浦梧楼宛廻覧状／農商務省

明治21年5月28日

別封御送付に捺印可然候也。
明治廿一年五月廿八日

農商務省
宿直

伯爵西郷従道殿
御家扶御中　印〔朱〕
子爵谷干城殿
御家扶御中　印〔朱〕

農商務省
宿直

子爵三浦梧楼殿
　御家扶御中　印〔朱〕

〔注〕農商務省用箋、墨書。

15　吉田清成宛参内申入書／鍋島直大

明二十九日勲章授与式執行に付、為列立午前十時大礼服着用参内可有之候也。

明治二十一年五月廿八日

枢密顧問官子爵勲二等吉田清成殿

〔注〕式部職用箋、墨書。

明治21年5月28日

式部長官侯爵鍋島直大

16　吉田清成宛勲位録送状／賞勲局

本年一月一日調査勲位録印刷候付、別冊壱部及御回候条御領掌有之度、此段申進候也。

二十一年五月廿八日

吉田議定官殿

〔注〕賞勲局用箋、墨書。

明治21年5月28日

賞勲局

十　元老院議官・枢密顧問官時代

17　領収書／尾崎弥五郎

明治21年6月2日

御本省より志田町迄椅子卓子往復運送御入費

一、金弐円七拾銭　　荷車九輛
　　　　　　　　　壱輛に付金三拾銭
　　右代金正に奉請取候也。

明治廿一年六月二日

　　　　　　　　麹町弐丁め拾七番地

　　　　　　　　　尾崎弥五郎㊞

上様

〔注〕罫紙、墨書。

18　吉田清成家執事宛取調申入書／警視庁会計局用度課

明治(21カ)年6月2日

　記

一、全部毛布　　弐百九十枚
一、半部毛布　　弐百弐拾枚の内弐百拾九枚

右之通御返納相成正に落手致候。外に半部毛布壱枚不足相立候に付、御使之者立合之上種々取調致候得共発見不致候。就て御宅に於ても至急御取調有之度、猶当庁に於ても再調可致候。且中皿百枚は弥生舎へ向け御返却相成度候也。

会計局用度課㊞[朱]

明治21年6月6日

六月二日

吉田家執事御中

〔注〕警視庁用箋、墨書。

19　吉田清成家家扶宛回金申入書／宮内省内匠寮

　　記

一、金参円参拾四銭也

是は去月三十一日テント御拝借に付該品御邸迄搬送したる費用受負人高木善兵衛別紙精算書之通。

右金員早々御回金相成度此段申進候也。

明治廿一年六月六日

吉田清成殿

　家扶御中

〔注〕内匠寮用箋、墨書。

内匠寮㊞[朱]

20　宮内省内匠寮宛入費精算帳／畑戸源二郎

明治21年6月

高木善兵衛

十　元老院議官・枢密顧問官時代

芝区志田町吉田枢密院顧問官御邸へテントウ運搬并に御買上人足共御入費精算帳

合金参円参拾四銭　[朱印]「黒沢」
＊

テントウ　五張運搬

内訳

運送車　————　往返八輌　　壱輌に付参拾五銭　　金弐円八拾銭

鳶人足　————　弐人　　壱人弐拾七銭　　金五拾四銭

右之通精算相違無御座候間御下渡奉願上候也。

明治二十一年六月

内匠寮御中

〔注〕罫紙、墨書。＊の箇所に差出人の朱印押印あり。

高木善兵衛代
畑戸源二郎 ㊞[朱]

21　吉田清成宛陪食の沙汰申入／土方久元

来る十六日正午十二時御陪食被　仰付候に付、参内可有之旨　御沙汰候条此段申入候也。

二十一年七月十三日

明治21年7月13日

23　吉田清成宛通知／井上毅

枢密顧問官子爵吉田清成殿

追て着服はフロックコートに有之候也。

〔注〕墨書。

宮内大臣子爵土方久元

明治21年10月8日

22　井上毅宛参内達／鍋島直大

来る十七日神嘗祭に付

一勅任官の面々午前九時四十分参内

一奏任官幷准奏任及判任官以下にして従六位以上華族（除く）を勲六等以上の輩午后一時より同二時迄に参拝

右之通御達可有之此段及御通知候也。

明治二十一年十月八日

枢密院書記官長井上毅殿

〔注〕枢密院用箋、墨書。

式部長官侯爵鍋島直大

明治21年10月8日

23　吉田清成宛通知／井上毅

別啓及御通知候也。

明治21年10月12日

十　元老院議官・枢密顧問官時代

廿一年十月十二日

吉田顧問官殿

（注）枢密院用箋、墨書。

24　吉田清成宛叙勲通知書／賞勲局

[朱筆]
「送第四百四号」

先般及御廻候本年十一月定期海陸軍武官勲位初叙并進級の議案は新定の瑞宝章を賜はるへきものに候条、為念此段申進置候也。

明治二十一年十一月十六日

明治21年11月16日

吉田議定官殿

（注）内閣用箋、墨書。

賞勲局㊞[朱]

井上書記官長

25　日清間続約草案

明治（21／22）年

第一条

両締盟国の一方か其領地内に於て現時諸外国の施行する裁判管轄権を廃止するときは他の一方か該領地内に於て現に施行する所の裁判管轄権も亦廃止せらるへし。然る上は其国臣民は全く在留国の法律規則に服従し各般の事

196

項に於て該国政府及官庁の管轄を受くへし。而して法廷に於て権利を伸張し及保護するに於ては内国臣民の享有

する総ての権利及特権を享有すへし。現行両国修好条規及通商章程中本条の規定と抵触するもの、即修好条規第

八条第九条第十一条中〔又其本分を守り永住暫居の差別なく必す自国理事官の支配に従ふへし〕の一句并に第十

三条又通商章程第十四款第十五款中〔本人は理事官に引渡し処置すへし〕の一句は、本条の実施と同時に無効に

帰すへし。

第二条

現行両国海関税則は本続約実行と同時に互に之を廃止し爾後両国政府に於て適宜海関税則を定むる事を得。但し

何れの場合と雖も両締盟国の一方は他方の領地内の生産物若くは製造品に対し諸外国の同種の物品に対し課する

ものより多きか又は之と異なる税金を課すへからす。　又他の一方の領地内へ向け輸出すへき自国の生産物若くは

製造品に対し同種の物品か諸外国へ輸出せらるゝときに課するものより多きか又は之と異なる税金を課すへから

す。

第三条

両締盟国の一方の領地内へ別国の生産或は製造に係る物品の輸入を禁せさる間は他の一方の領地内の生産或は製

造に係る同種の物品を何れの地より輸入することをも禁止する事なかるへし。　但現行通商章程を以て特に輸入を

禁したるものは本条の限にあらす。　然れとも両締盟国は衛生上或は公衆の安寧に関し危害を生する事あるへしと

認めたるときは特に貨物の輸入を制限し若くは禁止する事を得。

第四条

貨物輸出の事に関しても前項の規定を適用すへし。

十　元老院議官・枢密顧問官時代

船舶の出入貨物の輸出入及其他一切の事項に係る海関規則及罰則、密商取締法及罰則丼に船舶の噸税及其他船舶より徴収すへき諸税金は両国政府に於て適宜之を定むる事を得。但し以上の事項に関し両締盟国の一方は他方の臣民及其船舶に対し常に最恵国各外国の臣民及其船舶と比しき待遇を与ふへし。

両国間現行通商章程中本条の規程と抵触するもの（第五款、第六款、第七款、第八款、第十款、第十二款、第十七款、第二十七款、）は本続約実行と同時に之を廃止すへし。

本続約第一条に依り両締盟国の一方か他方の領地内に於て施行する所の裁判管轄権を廃止する迄の間は其領事に於て本条第一項に掲けたる諸罰則を施行すへし。

第五条

両締盟国の一方の海関に於て納税済の他方の生産物及製造品か内地に輸送せらるゝに当り、之に対し両国の内地に於て賦課せらるへき税金は諸外国の同種の物品に課せらるゝものより多額なるか又は之と異なる事なかるべし。

第六条

現行修好条規丼通商章程中本続約の条款と抵触するものは凡て之を廃止するものとす。

第七条

本続約は成る可く速に之を批准し北京に於て批准書を交換すへし。

本続約は明治二十三年二月十一日より之を実行し現行修好条規の有効なる間効力を有するものとす。但し両国政府に於て本続約を改正するを必要とするときは何時にても右改正の要求を為す事を得へし。

〔注〕碧雲茗圃用箋、墨書。

198

26 吉田清成宛参賀申入／土方久元

〔朱印〕　〔朱筆〕
「太后」「甲第二九」号

来廿三日　皇太后宮御誕辰に付午前十一時通常礼服着用　青山御所へ参賀可有之、此段申入候也。

明治廿二年一月廿一日

　　　　　　　　　　　　　　宮内大臣子爵　土方久元

枢密顧問官子爵吉田清成殿

〔注〕宮内省用箋、墨書。

　　　　　　　　　　　　　　　　　　　　　　　　明治22年1月21日

27　吉田清成宛練兵式先着申入書／鍋島直大

来る十一日青山練兵場へ臨御之節供奉被　仰付候旨宮内大臣より申入相成居候処、其儀に不及旨更に被　仰出候間、同所へ御先著可有之、此段申入候也。

廿二年二月七日

　　　　　　　　　　　　　　　式部長官侯爵鍋島直大

枢密顧問官子爵吉田清成殿

〔注〕式部職用箋にコンニャク版、宛名のみ墨書。

　　　　　　　　　　　　　　　　　　　　　　　　明治22年2月7日

十　元老院議官・枢密顧問官時代

28

吉田清成宛金銭借用証文（写）／吉田昇二郎

明治22年3月31日

〔朱筆〕
「七月十三日記す。　印紙の手数なし」

〔朱筆〕
印
証

〔朱筆〕
印
一金弐百円也

右は差掛要用出来前書之金額拝借仕候処確実也。　返済之義は来る廿二年六月三十日迄に返済可仕候。
為後日証文依て如件。

〔朱筆〕
印

京橋区日吉町
弐十番地
〔ママ〕〔朱筆〕
吉田昇次郎印

〔朱筆〕
「印は吉田昇二郎」

明治廿二年三月卅一日

吉田清成殿

〔注〕墨書。

29

第三十三国立銀行宛借用金証書（写）／岡田彦三郎

明治22年4月2日

200

29　第三十三国立銀行宛借用金証書(写)／岡田彦三郎

借用金証書

金五円也

此抵当芝区白金志田町十七番地地券証弐枚

但利息

右之地券今般抵当に差入本文金額借用致候処実正也。然る上は明治二十二年七月三十日限り元利無相違返済可致
候。万一元金未納中抵当品の価格低落致候はゝ貴行の望に応し増抵当差入る歟、又は低落丈けの内金可致候。若
し又此抵当品に付非常変災災故障等相生し候へはゝ[ママ]、是亦貴行の望に応し更に右抵当品同価の抵当差入歟、若くは
即時現金を以て期限に抱[拘]らす返金可致候。尤も本人旅行又は失踪其他何等の事情にても暫時間にても不在する歟、
又は調金及ひ兼る等に係り右約定の義務負担執行難致場合は、引受証人に於て本人に成り代り直ちに此義務を負
担する事を特約し、毫末も貴行へ御迷惑御損毛相掛け申間敷候。為後日特約証人連印を以て差入れ置く借用証書
仍て如件。

明治廿二年四月二日

　　　　　　　　　　　　　　　芝区白金志田町八番地

　　　　　　　　　　　　　　　　借用本人　岡田彦三郎印

　　　　　　　　　　　　　　　　　　〃　　　十五番地

　　　　　　　　　　　　　　　　引受証人　御名　印

第三十三国立銀行
　　頭取
　支配人　御中

十　元老院議官・枢密顧問官時代

〔注〕墨書、裏書は吉田筆。

〔裏書〕
「四月一日夜」

30　第三十三国立銀行宛抵当承諾証書控／吉田清成

明治22年4月2日

扣　抵当承諾証書

拙者所有芝区白金志田町十七番地宅地弐百九拾九坪五勺、十八番地宅地八拾壱坪七合五勺、岡田彦三郎へ貸渡し使用を許し候に付、都合によりては他へ抵当として差入候趣正に承諾致し候。然る上は岡田彦三郎と債主との約定に依り自然右地所を債主其他の名義に書換候義に相運ひ候も決て異議無之、速に書換の手順を尽し譲渡証書を製し相渡すべきは勿論、債主に対しては負債主の約束に従ひ毫も拙者より故障等申間敷候。依て為後日証書如件。

明治二十二年四月二日

芝区白金志田町

十五番地

吉田清成

第三十三国立銀行御中

〔注〕墨書。

31　家計元帳／吉田清成

明治22年5月5日〜9月30日

202

31　家計元帳／吉田清成

〔表紙〕

明治廿二年
元帳
〔朱筆〕
「い号」
五月改　　吉田

五月吉辰改

五月五日

〇一金百円　　　貞渡

五月七日

△一五拾円　　岩越渡

手元より

五月九日　直下

△一金五拾円　岩越岩蔵

五月十二日夜

△一拾五円　　岩越

五月十四日

△一拾五円　　岩越

△一拾五円　　岩越

十　元老院議官・枢密顧問官時代

同日

〇一五円　　　　　貞渡
〔朱筆〕
「日々小仕用」

十八日

〇一四拾円　　　　貞渡
〔朱筆〕
「之れは直に岩越へ相渡候由別帳にあり」

同廿一日

〇一弐拾円　　　　貞渡

同廿五日

△一拾円　　　　　岩越渡
〔朱筆〕
「地学協会一月より六月に至会費払のとき」

五月廿一日

一拾五円　　　手元へ
〔朱筆〕
「成」
〔朱筆〕
「ん鎌倉へ松田と市とを連れ行き一泊入費詳細は別の手控にあり」

廿六日

〇一拾円　　　　　貞渡

同廿九日

204

△一拾円　　　岩越

同卅一日

△一弐拾円　　　岩越
[朱筆]
「下男共給料其外内渡の分あり」

同日

○一拾円　　　貞渡
[朱筆]
「下女共同断」

六月一日

一拾円　　　岩越代印

此日鎌倉へ家内一同召列

六月一日

一三拾円　　　手元

同日　　　岩越

一五拾円

同四日　　　鎌倉行

一拾円　　　貞手元へ
[朱筆]
「学資幷小仕」

十　元老院議官・枢密顧問官時代

六月五日

一拾円　　　　　　　岩越

同日

一四拾円　　　　　　同

同七日

一弐拾円　　　　　　岩越

　　　　ウ井セント云々

廿二年六月

十一日

一拾円　　　　　　　岩越

　　　華族同朋会一ケ年三円云々あり

十四日

一金拾円　　　　　　岩越岩蔵

六月十七日

一金拾円也　　　　　岩越岩蔵

六月廿日（Ｃ）の内より　［朱筆］

　　　但花房よりのミルク代の内「十八日に岡田引出す」

一一拾円　　　　　　岩越

31　家計元帳／吉田清成

同日

2　一五円　　　　貞渡
　　　小仕用

3　一五円　　　　岩越
同廿三日

清かパン云々のとき　岩越
廿四日
〔朱筆〕
「此日岡田へ百円の切手を相渡置候事」

六月廿六日
4　一五円也　　　岩越渡

六月廿七日
5　一拾五円也　　貞渡

六月卅日
下婢月給其他小仕用
6　一三拾円　　　岩越

六月卅日
下人月給其外
7　一拾円　　　　お貞渡

207

十　元老院議官・枢密顧問官時代

小仕用仕立代其外と云事なり

七月二日

8　一弐拾八円六銭　　岩越渡

但三十三国立銀行切手三十番

井上岩越与之

[朱筆]「小切手払」

同三日「Cの口より」

10　一五円　　　手元成

✓ ん小買ものゝ為
[朱筆]「10は手扣のみ記す」

✓ Okada

ＣＣ　岡田井上与之

七月四日

11　一百円也　　岩越

六月分諸払の内として

同日　　　貞渡

12　一五円也　　銀貨

同三日　別口六月廿四日引出の口より

9　一拾円　　　手元成

　　小買ものゝ為
　　［朱筆］
　　「七月七日に至り更に貞渡に取計算当相立候事」

同三日

一壱円八十銭　　　貞渡

市五郎一円

駅者庄吉　五拾銭　為手当

車夫　　　三十銭
［朱筆］
「右は貞手元より渡候事故に本文貞渡はなき姿に改めたり」

七月七日　弐百円の内より

13　一拾円　　　　　岩越

同日
［朱筆］
　　「之れは別口」

三田当町十七番金子屋滝次郎方より書箱二、壱個六十九銭つゝ払方の節

14　一壱円三拾銭　　岩越
　　［朱筆］
　　「13の払は手元より取計置たしに付、更に不渡とも元帳には免の姿に可取計ふ事」

七月七日　　弐百円の口より

15　一拾円　　　手元成

十　元老院議官・枢密顧問官時代

〔朱筆〕
「但仕払ひは別にあり」

同日四時同断

16　一五円　　　　　貞渡一件
〔朱筆〕
「Education」

同九日同断

17　一弐拾円　　　　岩越

同十日　弐百円の口より

18　一拾円　　　　　貞渡
〔朱筆〕
「日々小仕用」

七月十三日　清純の預け金引出したる口五十二円八十五銭の内より

19　一五拾円　　　　貞渡
〔朱筆〕
「吉田昇次郎謝儀の半額」

同日　弐百円の口より出す
〔朱筆〕
「△六月廿五日引出百円残の内より出す」

20　一五拾円　　　　貞渡
〔朱筆〕
「吉田昇次郎謝義之半額、右二口合壱百円也、本年一月以来の謝儀として即日貞子へ相渡」

二十二年

七月十四日朝

〔朱筆〕
「弐百円の口より」

21　一弐拾円　　　　　　貞渡
〔朱筆〕
「盆節季付届、家従手宛等の為其外小遣用」
×「七月十四日朝午前岡田承之」

同日　六月廿五日百円の口を了る之にて此口尽る

22　一弐拾円　　　　　　岩越
〔朱筆〕
「単に拾円也弐は過ちなり」

×七月十四日岡田

同十五日午後　弐百円の口より

23　一拾円　　　　　　　岩越
〔朱筆〕
「小遣用」必用〔ママ〕の分のみを可相払　〔朱筆〕「此時魚精とか云日本料理四月分二度五月分六度分取に来ると云」

同十七日午前
〔朱筆〕
「刀」一五拾弐円三拾八銭
綱屋総左衛門代　　　渡辺源八郎渡

同廿日
〔朱筆〕
「此処に弐百円入　吉田氏
返済同十五日朝」

十　元老院議官・枢密顧問官時代

24　一拾円　　岩越
対小遣用
〔朱筆〕「昇二郎先生返済の口を用ゆ」
同廿二日夕
25　一拾円　　　岩越
榛原総買もの届
三河屋フランネル等同

〔以下別紙〕
八月卅一日　三拾円入
内払
九月一日
一金弐拾円　　貞渡
更に井上渡
同三日朝
一金拾円　　貞渡於東京
本日帰鎌倉
九月七日
一金弐拾円　　井上渡

内　五円三橋へ遣す

　　拾弐円余同払

✓手元九の廿四

廿六日

五円　野元学資払の時此口より足す外十円は外の新口より出す

三十日

×市承知

弐百円吉田昇次郎へ貸す

九月廿六日

弐円　　　岩越へ

女下り候に付月給渡の時

〔注〕半紙四つ折り冊子。墨書。見せ消し、△・○、算用数字はすべて朱筆。吉田ほかの確認印多数あり。また一部に確認済を表すと思われる朱線・記号、区切り線あり。

十　元老院議官・枢密顧問官時代

32　「借憶簿」／吉田清成

〔表紙〕

廿二年五月

借憶簿

松廼舎

五月廿一日

一拾五円　　入

五月廿一日

一壱円七十二銭

品川より大舟まて上等一下等二

一新聞紙幷発車表　五六銭

廿二日

一六円弐拾八銭

稲荷山なるものに二円其外もあり。

三橋にて一泊観音坊主拠長留主番［ママ］　鶴見等参る故如此。

尤人力車代も此内にあり。

五月廿二日

明治22年5月21〜25日

214

一壱円七十二銭

大舟より品川迄三人分汽車賃上一〇六、一ッ此日伊藤伯〔博文〕園遊会三時より六時、故に朝汽車にて帰着せしは十二時なり。夫婦共三時頃出掛六時半頃引取、盛会なり。

重もに山水に因る。

此日応挙画展覧会あり（小伴与右衛門所持）午前より差越熟覧す、凡弐百四五十幅計也。感賞するもの四五、

二重県の人

一十銭　会場にて　茶代〔カ〕

同日

一壱円十銭　上野精養軒昼飯

五月廿六日

此日貞末松の新妻見舞を促す、同行して帰途勧工場に立寄り魚買入たるなり。

一十八銭　水さし一

一七十銭　靴下二つ

同日

一弐拾五銭　時計紐一

同日

一弐円　平戸焼茶腕〔腕〕五　箱入

廿五日

十　元老院議官・枢密顧問官時代

折田総監、高崎正風、伊達宗城、其外中村正直、西周、田中芳男、吉田昇二郎、大倉喜八郎（家内中）、大の

貞輔其他数多の雅客を見受けたり。

五月廿五日

一十銭　東京新図

〔注〕半紙四つ折り冊子、墨書。

33　「次第不同万留　壱号」／吉田清成

明治22年7月1〜21日

〔表表紙〕

明治二十二年七月一日

次第不同万留　清成

　〔朱筆〕
　「禁他見」

　〔朱筆〕
　「壱号」

〔裏表紙〕

二十二年七月一日

次第不同万留　清成

　〔朱筆〕
「石河正蔵へ公債証書一枚恵みたるは廿二

年一月廿六日の事なり。礼状等別にあり」

216

小田原の鴎盟館は片岡永左衛門方より海岸へ三丁位あり（伊藤議長七月十四日より家内引連相赴き、今（十六

日）も滞在中津田有賀より申来る。「大迫貞清桜川町十二番安藤則命赤阪丹後丁一番地」

七月一日　半晴

田中太七郎氏来る（築地二丁目角之中井氏邸」小島湾築切埋立の件に付事情を述ふ、左に。

七月二日　曇

七月二日前　曇

学習院補助費廿一年十二月可納分浅居候付、促ありて本日井上岩越に命し之を取計金弐拾八円六銭（小切手第

三十番）。

同日前

川西留五郎代来る。　払ひ代金は来月迄予猶之事を井上を以申含無異議承知の由。

同日前十時

吉田昇次郎師来る。　先生少々不元気之赴に見受る。十一時半去る。拙者・貞・文子」拙生本日大ゐに快し、平

日に不異草臥脳重きを覚ゆるのみ。食欲過る程なり。

同日八時五十分頃

前田献吉氏来、奈良漬を贈る。暫時にて帰る。去月卅日大森射的場開場式の模様を聞く。大臣は土方のみ、寺

島徳大寺元老院より四名程と云。

昨夕福島方へ梅四斗俵一を遣す。市五郎・乙吉扱之。

一七月十一日於紅葉館金子堅太郎の送別会を開く。議長始各顧問も揃ふ。同時に同航の中橋徳五郎（法制局参事

官）・木内重四郎・太田峰三郎・斎藤浩躬も金子の願にて同席せり。「中橋は生農商務十九年奉職中尽力して該

省に入れ置たる者と云。

一七月十五日午前十時半海軍省に至る。不在に付直様樺山氏鞠町八丁目十九番を訪在宅田実氏依嘱の硝石精製の
企を話す。委曲は一つ書に譲る。

同時樺山氏の言に鹿県党派は公民同志会と名乗らんと決したる由なれとも、之れは今般上京の者共一己の資格
にて決したる事故、帰県の上同志共へ協議の筈なり。右に付当十七日河島淳・野村清明・蒲生仙の三士同伴下
向の筈、是非甲乙丙等の数派に別れざる様尽力之つもりと云。

十四日の夕川村邸に会せしは樺山・伊集院兼寛・伊東中将・松方正義・仁礼氏等にて、郷友会将来の事を談せ
りと云。于時樺山氏常に持論之通会の子弟世話の事は充分負担すべし。政党の傾き等ありて方向を誤る様の義
に付ては、吉田氏伊集院などわかものにして御世話被下度ものと協議せりと樺山氏直話なり。樺山氏も成程武
官故尤之赴なれとも拙等も役職上甚困難の場合あり。御互には一己人の資格にて官制を不犯かきりは尽力する
は当然之事云々談せり。

一七月十六日午後樺山氏へ一封を致す。田実氏頼の硝石精製の一つ書五枚となし差遣したり。此の一つ書は此に
略す。

一七月十六日三時頃太田峰三郎（法学士、「明治廿二年」法制局試補、福岡の人、仏学のみ）今般憲法上取調の
為欧洲へ被差遣に付諸般の心得振承度との事にて二時間程も時を与へ充分欧米各国得失、英の倣ふべからす、
米は申迄もなし、孛のひた真似は我国に取り不益、仏の共和政治は外交上には弱く、且其外百年以上の歴史上
の結果を話して我国に必要と否とを明に研究する事肝腎なり云々。其外略す。

一斎藤浩躬（法学士「明治廿二年」〔朱筆〕外太田氏と同断）両人ながら大ゐに満足して帰る。五時二十分なり。当十八

日米邦船に投じて航する筈なり。

一七月十六日午前九時半金子堅太郎（枢密院議長秘書官）福岡の人、之れも取調に出発の暇乞なり。Geo. B.

Williams氏去年十〔消〕一月頃Austin Herr氏を紹介する二通之手紙を為見、充分分る様に言伝し置たり。金子氏

一々要点を筆記せり。大判事ミルラル氏へも篤く言伝置、且昵近になりて可然云々勧め置たり。

一七月十五日五時頃より浅田徳則氏見ゆ。九時頃帰る。重もに重脩の件と憲法発布に付帯する難問題を談す。于

時田辺貞雅嫡子当時商務局勤務二十四五才の人を迂生の秘書記にすゝむ。

井上陳政飜訳局にあり。二十四五才の人にて漢文に妙を得、通弁も右に出る人なかるべしと、之れも可然とす

ゝむ（得能良介氏支那に遣し置たる人なり）。当時大鳥公使引付け取調最中の由。〔圭介〕

一七月十七日ウヰルヤムスへ一封出す。金子其他の為が重きに居れり。細書にて十二三ペーヂ即五十ペーヂ余に

均し草稿あり、略す。

同日

一中村博愛氏見得寸暇なし。緩談を不許○貞伊藤の妻君を病気見舞す。上野おばゝ殿へ立寄ると云。〔朱筆〕「上等科の二」

一同十八日文子証書授与式に付貞子同伴七時発出掛十弐時過帰る。文子三級生に昇る。

皇后様臨御相成候事。

一大臣の内大隈・大山・西郷・松方なぞ見得たる由。〔重信〕〔巌〕〔従道〕

同日朝金子へ一封を遣る。市五郎品川ステーション迄持越。

同日

十　元老院議官・枢密顧問官時代

一吉田師参る。前十時頃容体を誉たり。清介も治療を受く。十七年上製梅干若干を送る。

同日

一梅ケ谷へ同断并大樽一は同年下製の分なり。

一清風・清張・清武試験昨日本日明十九日三ケ日なり。

同日

一貴嶋氏より弓掛一つ贈来る。之れは薩摩出来にて前約の分なり。

七月十四日

一七銭　　夜市にて鍋一

一同十五日　三橋へ渡分
一壱銭

同十七日

一拾五銭　ウヰルヤムスえ一封出す。金子堅太郎其外の為なり。

〃十九日夜

一拾五銭　XVS 散歩の時草臥用たる車。

同廿日夜

一拾七銭　銀座迄同断。

同日

一六拾銭　酒匂処「鹿児島屋」にて煙草弐百目求

一金　　次田店に椅子六脚相求凡拾弐三円位と認めし事

220

七月廿日

一　終日取調ものにて田口手伝ふ。重もに掛地書なと取片く。夜九時より三時間運働せり。

一　当日より池上弥太郎を仕ひ試用す。

一　来客は大抵謝絶す。昨日町田実一見ゆ。暫時面会せり。為差奇事なし。

七月廿一日

一午前取調もの。且つ東郷市介見に付暫時面会を許す。筑前石炭山即鞍手郡山田村の分を岸良彦七と共に借区の企なし願書差出たる云々。川村氏に関する話あれとも不面白に付略す。

一郷友会総集会に付山内五十番地新設の会場に出席す。樺山・大迫・有村・谷元〔景綱〕・柴山等四五十人なり。役員の改撰を行ふ。樺山氏会長に拙生も今度又々幹事に、折田平内・有村国彦〔国彦〕・川上操六等外略す。樺山至当の演舌あり。大迫同断〔道之〕、田尻〔稲次郎〕も少々なしたり。二時頃に始り五時過には御開散せり、于時微雨なり。今夜は草臥運動を止む………十二時前相休み安眠す」当夜岡田に命し捺印にヌメ地上に壱丈五尺を注文せしむ」安眠の為此の四五日間は薬用ポルトワヰン等を少々つゝ用、功ありて害を見す」午後より雨降路わるし。之れ散歩を妨くる所以なり。

〔朱筆〕
「日記次第不同万留弐号に続く」

〔注〕四つ折り半紙、墨書。

十　元老院議官・枢密顧問官時代

34　伊藤博文宛枢密顧問官定員に関する通牒／黒田清隆

明治22年7月3日

枢密顧問官定員の件

枢密顧問官は十二人以上と枢密院官制に於て定められ、其最上限を規定せられざるに付、右定員二十人と御決定

相成可然哉、茲に閣議に供す。

明治廿二年七月三日

枢密院議長伯爵伊藤博文殿

　　　　　　　　　　　　　　内閣総理大臣伯爵黒田清隆

枢密顧問官定員別紙閣議の通裁可を経たるに付、此旨及御通牒候也。

明治廿二年七月三日

枢密院議長伯爵伊藤博文殿

別紙枢密顧問官定員の儀、内閣総理大臣より通牒相成候に付、為御承知供回覧候也。

明治廿二年七月四日

　　　　　　　　　　　　　　伊藤枢密院議長

〔欄外〕

〔ママ〕二十二七月五日前九時半寺島副議長より廻達、即刻川村〔純義〕顧問官へ廻達取計候事。井上定次扱之。

〔宗則〕

福岡ヽヽヽヽヽヽ

川村ヽヽヽヽヽ

大木ヽヽヽヽヽヽ

土方枢密顧問官殿

寺島枢密院副議長殿

222

佐々木、、、、、、
副嶋、、、、、、
佐野、、、、、、、
東久世、、、、、、
吉井、、、、、、、
勝、、、、、、、、
河野、、、、、、、
吉田、、、、、、、
元田、、、、、、、
鳥尾、、、、、、
野村、、、、、、

追て、御回覧の上周尾より御返却可有之候也。

〔注〕墨書。欄外に朱筆にて「機密」とあり。

35　枢密顧問官座席表

明治22年7月9日

十　元老院議官・枢密顧問官時代

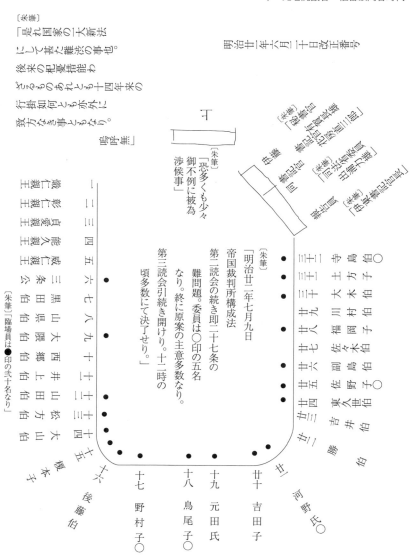

〔注〕コンニャク版。上、伊藤とその並びの部分は墨書。●や○は朱筆。鉛筆線の書込多数あり。臨場員は20名とあるが、●は19名にしか付されていない。

224

36 「日記　次第不同万留　弐号」／吉田清成

明治22年7月22日〜8月12日

〔表表紙〕

明治二十二年七月一日

〔朱筆〕
「同廿二日より用ゆ、外同類壱号にあり」

日記次第不同
万留

〔朱筆〕
「弐号」　禁他見　清成

七月廿二日小雨天　冷

早天

一川崎正蔵来る。氏は一週間前出京の由、格別之用なし、質疑の廉ありたるゆへ解聞せ置候。必竟大体に関する

事多し、中略㊀精養軒に滞留すと云、所謂御気之伺云々申出候。

〔吉田〕
一昇二郎先生十時頃入来、治療を受。文子・貞子・清風・グラント・清介同断。先生先日来と引かへ元気付居候。

一吹田屋より椅子六脚為持遣候請取置候。之れは重もに鎌倉用つもり、右すい田屋は新橋側竹川町角なり。

〔博文〕
一伊藤氏へ差越候処昨日より又々小田原へ赴たる由、妻君矢張微恙。

同廿三日小雨天　冷且暖

一元田永孚先生を訪、予て約束し揮毫相頼置候。尤留主故一封残帰候」神田区裏猿楽町一番地。

一前田就吉氏午後入来、海浜院え譲渡之（同人媒介に関る）約束に相成居候地所の義に付、長与専斎方へ足労し

十　元老院議官・枢密顧問官時代

不逢候。手紙を以申入候次第有之候由。先日三橋へも充分申聞置候哉に候。

一田中章氏五時頃より入来、十時頃去る。福島より廿一日に出京之由、公私混合之用ありと云々。毎之通公私内外之積話あり。略す。

先年来約束之桐木東京着し居候間、大体一個分は小生へ進むとの事に候。他一個極大の分伊藤氏へ廻す事に話置候。

一夜半まて取調もの致し直に安眠いたし候。

七月廿四日雨天　暖

一吉田師十時に来る、親子七人共診察を受く。拙大なに快く候。

一今朝五時半起上る。直に書類取調に加り八時前朝飯済。

一一時出門、田中旅寓神田淡路町二丁目一番地へ差越、同道にて駿河台鈴木町平本鎌徳方へ桐材を改めに行き、帰途小川町加藤良助と云へる指物屋へ同行、火鉢之事を依嘱せり。椅子一脚皮ふとん五枚枕一其外誂置帰る。五時帰宅之時は志村翁相見得居候に付、何事も不出来、九時罷帰候。本日少々草臥候ものと見へ眠相催候に付、十一時頃より相休み候。雨淒々屋中滋々加るに暑蒸難堪時候に候事。

一昨日宮内省官制改正あり、随て役員更迭も多し。先つ名義の変りたる位と云ふも過言に非さるべし。廿五日之官報に詳なり。

一昨今之新報評ては山県氏[有朋]を呼返しに再ひ電報を送つたなと云ふ。多分然らん。唯軽挙何の故か一向分り不申候。世中諸事如此んは真に杞憂に不堪事共なり。嗚呼無。

一先日来之新誌或社会之評判に井上を磯辺之別業に壮士等襲来強て面会を乞、強て之を拒み書取を以意見を聞た[馨]

226

りとやら何とやら、何か穏ならぬ様子にも聞へたり如何にや。

七月廿五日雨天冷且滋

六時頃起上り、如例身体を清む。天曇れとも気分爽快なり。

未明にうかみ候儘書留岡田親父七十の賀の祝に　寄松祝。

〽百年や越えてますく〱万代のいろこそまされ岸の松か枝　未定なり。
[朱筆]
「一本日は清国皇帝誕辰日に当るを以午前十一時半祝賀之為同公使館を訪ふ。公使黎庶昌氏各書記官等と共に出
てゝ各賓に応す。　露公使を始め蘭代理公使朝鮮同断榎本大臣其外と同時なり。シャンパン酒を各賓に饗す。異
なり」
　　[武揚]

一八貫町なる時計屋小林方へ立寄掛時計直しを命す。同銀時計壱個を購求す、価十五円なり。

一弥左衛門町なる〇一なる紙屋へ寄り美濃半紙等注文し置く。

一之より帰途神明前なる方にてつゝら五個求む。書類蔵置の為なり。

一三田指もの屋にて机壱個求鎌倉用三尺四方位のものしやうじにて製し価一円五十銭と申事也。
[朱筆]
「此数月間世間に噴々せし東京府会賦金廃止に付賄賂之濫受ありし云々、皆気之毒千万に思ふ処なりしが、終
に頃日に至り福地源一郎其外を拘引して昨今予審最中なり。若此事にして幾千たりとも実」跡あらしめは上も
なき落胆至極の事共なり。連類も不尠と申事なれは、不日拘引の数も嵩むべし。目下国中に有名なる学者を以
自ら誇り才弁達家政治学小説もの其他百般の事に付衆に越へたるの名を広ふする福地氏、しかも数年来府会々
員たり議長たりするの人に如此ならは、外又同事ならすや。連類の人名中にも類似の人不少候。全国中に
名を得たる者共にして夫れ然らは将来「我議会開設之時を如何せん、杞憂之極なり。之れ等は外国ても類なき
　　[朱筆]

十　元老院議官・枢密顧問官時代

に非されとも亦国体人情も素より異なる処あり、斯の如き悪弊より真先に輸入し彼の長処は深味を得さるの場合にも立至らは、遺憾の極と云べき事ともなり。　害国民傷之者は私利を専らにするより甚きはなしと云ふも過言ならさるべし」

七月廿六日晴天　　早天は曇

一吉田先生十時頃来る。　大抵唯治療を受く。　本日例の相火鉢吉田氏に見立たる分参り居、径弐尺四五寸も有之、見事のもの故同人にも大喜に候。　他加藤より誂もの皆来る。　即刻払取計候。

一〇一より紙類持参る、皆注文に叶ふ故為請取置候事。

一三田道具屋単子金もの一件にて参る。

一中村五郎一書を出し早く出京あれがしと促しむ。

一松山へ丸薬を取りに遣す時一封を以分量の次第不同なき様頼遣候事。

七月廿七日晴天

［朱筆］
「本日」

一鎌倉行を為す。　朝八時十八分品川発の汽車に乗る。　井上定次召列候。　午後五時三十三分鎌倉発の車にて七時半品川着。

鎌倉着早々別荘に立寄り万事下知を下す、昼飯を三橋に於て食す、与八へ諸事依嘱之件あり、観音住持高橋参る」　渡辺厚とか云者夫婦列にて三橋に行逢ふ」再ひ別荘に至り有島武氏を彼の別荘に問ふ、同人頃は快方に赴けり。　車駅にて別る」柳谷氏一家昨日参り候迎、妻君見舞あり掛、帰途立寄置候」今朝　［朱筆］「横浜よりブラジル海軍士官二十余名と同軍す。　氏等横須賀行なり。　中にドンピドロの孫皇族某も見得たり」

228

帰り鎌倉より海軍士官某と同車、ブラジル士官の噂を聞く」横浜より鮫島武之助と同車、改正一件に付云々。

話合不日又当方を訪ふ筈」レジヤンドル氏と同車、四方山之積話を為す。込入たる事件は態と避て不言不語。

一此日前田氏田中章等相見得候由なり。

一「官設鉄道払下の利害」と題せる小冊院を経て達す。著者首藤諒氏なり」

一今夜梧園翁相見得居候。

一岡田同断倉行留主之事を申聞けむ。

一此日子供清風・清武・清介之三人歯医長谷川方へ遣すと云。貞子・文子墓参せりと云。

七月廿八日晴天日

一零時三十分頃休、六時前起上る。昨に比するも益快きを覚ふ、鎌倉行之草臥も無之のみならす、却て壮健を加ふ。

一終日要書類調分け取片付方に日を送る。終に外出散歩も不相叶候。貞子鎌倉行之支度に日を消す。

一吉田先生十時過参る、拙始め貞・文・清風・グラント治療を受く。拙子容体殊に勝ると申せり。

一田中章氏夕刻より入来、十時過る頃帰る。今両三日は滞在之筈と申事。

平元葉
（田中氏之恩人と云）は温厚篤実之人と申事、茨城の人なり、松崎先生の弟子なり。于今同家を後見し居ると云。

同人え、おんこふ（一位の木）の板を可遣と田中氏へ約せり。無他平元氏当時茶の間を造作し居、珍木を求むるとの事故なり。

一永山盛重（田実胤信の弟）入来、焔石製造会社設立之件に付、拙より三条公へ申込み花族連之賛成を求めんと

十　元老院議官・枢密顧問官時代

の事なり。右は程能く謝絶せり。[資紀][従道]樺山西郷辺より口出し有之候方万全なり、至当なり、又は[友実]吉井氏を芦の湯に

訪ひ頼み込にても可然何分生には早口受は難致に付、篤と致熟考置べし、云々等なり。

七月廿九日曇天月

終日取調ものに日を費したり。午後天晴上り好都合候事。[朱筆]「本日中村五郎来京草道一件に付相促し候。上京せり。少々眼病なり。」

鎌倉行之支度盛なり。夕刻より田中章氏相見得。楠大板弐枚あらゝき弐枚、駿河台平[本]元方より取に参候故、田

中氏宛にて為差出候。

一志村氏久井より相見得候。十時頃被帰候に付同伴にて拙は運動に出掛候。十一時半帰邸十二時半過休む。

七月廿八日午後十一時四十分頃天変あり。[朱筆]「九州一円大地震、但鹿児嶋長崎両県等より電報なし。多分無事なら

む。熊本佐賀大分柳川辺非常大震動、人畜死傷多く潰家等続々報道ありたり。九州の外異事あるを聞かす。原因

は阿蘇山破烈とも云へともいまた分らす。金峰山とも亦之を唱ふ。菟に角に近来未聞之地震なりき。」

七月卅日快晴炎甚、昨日より風なし。

一昇先生参る、文・清風・清成拙者并中村五郎にも治療を受け候。明後朔日より鎌倉行之つもり故相断置候。早

天前田献吉氏相見得候。鎌倉地所之義に付、長与専斎と示談之報告承り候。前田氏甚た真切故厚く相謝置候。

勿論同件は同氏醸出之件に有之候事。

[通庸カ]
一三島妻君相見得候へ共、取紛中に付面会相断候事。

一英人アルサル　ブレント氏来入、たしか始て也。陸海軍之御用承度に付誰が相当之人々へ紹介を頼むとの事な

り。篤と其人をも考置後日手状を認め可差出と相答置候。フリント　キルビーと云へる者に組合之由に候。一

向其スタトスや名誉等不聞及、多分格別之者共には無之哉に被察候。推するに海軍辺之買上ものゝテンダルを

36　「日記　次第不同万留　弐号」／吉田清成

入るゝ事出来候様致度との望に被察候。

一本日鎌倉行之荷物道一様相片付差立候[カ]まてに相成候。混雑無極候。子供等之為ならなくば何故にみなゝゝ如斯
苦労はせましものをと考候程なり。炎天と云ひ小共等の邪魔と云ひ不一方混雑なり、荷物大形大凡弐十余なり。

一拙子書類も大抵略今日にて片付終り候。

一前田氏[信義]の話に海江田氏今般の条約改正延期之熱心にて既に元老院にても衆へ説法ありたる由云々なり。外略す。

一草道一件に付書類を五郎取調候事。

七月卅一日快晴小風

一鎌倉行荷物は午前悉皆差出候。荷物惣数弐拾八個英行にして大凡千三百七拾行なりと云。
汽車運賃弐円七拾銭位、其外車賃蔵しき等にて惣〆五円余に及べり」

志村氏相見得十時過迄被話候。

昨日前田献吉氏入来、長与氏[専斎]と拙子鎌倉地所一件示談せし云々逐一承り候。

八月一日快晴炎甚

一品川を十二時十三分発車して貞始子共召列鎌倉へ向ひ、午後二字頃安着直に別業へ至れり。荷物等既に着し居
綱五郎を先着せしめ置たるに付好都合に候。

平野玉城（子供之先師）ステーション迄出迎。

一此夕芳川顕正にも着せりと云。

一廿年中に比すれは運搬の便数屋を加へ仕合なり。蒸気車之噂だにもなかりしに既に已に開設[カ]と相成剰へ車駅は別
業之近傍に設立し便宜申計なし。此模様ては日を追て繁昌之土地と相成事無相違。本年は長与氏も拙子より譲

十　元老院議官・枢密顧問官時代

り候地所に一棟を建てたり。四十坪足らすの一字也。

一夕飯前子供等召列海辺に至り子供浴水相始め候。此日暑気甚く東京を思ひ遣り候。当地にても八十七八度に昇れり。夜に入蝦沢山出人〔ママ〕を悩まし候。必竟風少きに基くならむ。此様子では志田町にも劣らす困却候。

一出入之井上方より酒野菜等、柳谷家より野菜肴等、三橋より何にか参りたる由。昨年に比すれは牛乳屋なぞ数多く相成り仕合なり。品も上等なり。

八月三日快晴　九十度位　昨今皆然

五時起上り六時半頃海水浴をなし長与氏と逢ふ。

一昼前有島武高橋新一外二人入来、昼の出来を進む。氏等例之通四方山之雑話は素より世の中の慷慨話相始り時を移たり。高橋氏は容体衰弱肺症之様子被見受、気之毒千万に存候。有島氏の脳病も昨今快く相見得摂養注意之様子に候。

午後再ひ子供等召列れ海辺に至り子供等浴せり。

一お貞少々服痛〔ママ〕の気味暑気当りと相見得候。下痢少しあり。持合之薬共相用しめ候。

昨日夕刻観音之住持高橋氏相見得候。当時当番之由にて早く帰り候。本日当人より手作之芋沢山進め候。

日々之諸新聞に条約改正之適否論配出すれとも、格別之名案とては無之哉に相見得候。実地と議論とは別なるものと相見得候。

八月四日晴天炎

一此日海岸の小屋峻〔カ〕る。

軒先の日よけに取掛る。

隣の中山見舞同人病状昨年と替る事なきか如し。午前十一時四十九分発の汽車より帰京す。二時過き帰宅昼飯

を為済一家会計取調書類検査せり。岡田非番にて参り居候故諸払向下知致置候。明日生年俸三ヶ月分を受取に

差出筈相約し且つ銀行用向之事を托す。

事状小切手三枚を相渡す。川西留五郎分、第二山形屋分、第三飼葉屋三部甚左衛門分。

志むら翁七時前後入来諸事致相談候。九時頃より少々散歩致候×。

八月五日晴天炎暑

帰京之用向万事相片付候に付、第二汽車より帰倉の途上高輪辺にて岡田令高氏名護屋より上京之処に出逢候故、

引返し帰宅せり。同氏は社用にて上京之由少々相談之趣も有之（小笠原島産最上之錦を利用せんとの企なり。

巨細は略す）。

十時頃志村氏枢密院会計局より帰り掛被立寄候。昨宵申合候通金子弐百七拾五円持参、内百円は岡田へ被渡候

由、百円は岩越渡残り七拾五円は拙者、直ちに相受取候、鎌倉へ持越之分。

十一時頃三人にて昼飯中相仕止拙は直と出邸、十二時十三分品川発の汽車にて鎌倉へ相向候。

午後二時半頃鎌倉着

此日大工両人参り日さし取付最中市五郎綱五郎其外も共に働く。六歩通出来上る。五時頃

家内中皆無事可記の珍事も無之候。お貞にも少々不快之処全く直り候様子、清介も同断仕合千万なり。

水浴致候。

八月六日晴天炎

食事進む事昨に異る事なし。

十　元老院議官・枢密顧問官時代

早天水浴此日南風少しありて快晴たり。

芳川有島の別邸を訪ふ。芳川は今朝帰京、有島は在荘、警保局の大浦と申人参り居候。暫時話し帰候。園部長

与氏ら暫く相話候。中山相見得候。子供如例水浴す。朝一度のみ。午後南風烈きか故なり。新論更になし。別に可驚異説もなしと雖事頗

昨今改正条約重脩按に関し、当否の説諸新聞紙に陸続相見得候。

る大事に渉るを以大抵記臆に留め略記候。

当月二日国元お須磨様より一封相達候。

八月七日晴天南風冷気と云を可也

子共早朝水浴す。

拙は十二時前同断。

長崎省吾より一封到達。

岡田彦三郎より同断。四日五日に委托之件、即三ヶ月俸給を受取三十三銀行へ八百五十円を預け、残り金所分

方之事云々申越せり。「日本」四日之百五十一号治安に妨害ありと被認停止を遂れり。改正一件に付余り無造

作に筆を廻し居候に付、多分右辺ならむと被存候。

「然る処本日之発行は矢張到達せり。紫溟会玄洋社などの有志者、松方大臣へ差出たる書取意見書大略と唱へ

て相見得居候。一応尤之識見も相見得候。井上毅なとも関係なして歟と被察候。論旨多くは一徹に出るものゝ

如し。

八月八日晴炎天

浴水如例皆無事。

234

36 「日記　次第不同万留　弐号」／吉田清成

貞此内より少々微恙服痛間々有之浴水も出来す。

海浜院にて玉突相始め候。　相手は医師勝見等なり。　雑虫多く夜間之運動も意に任す。

八月九日晴炎天

早天水浴為相済朝飯を仕廻九時二十分発の汽車より夫婦列上京す。　全くお貞治療之為に候。　十一時頃品川安着せり。　午飯為相済日吉町吉田師方へ押懸両人共治療を受たり。　お貞容体は格別之事に無之云々。

生容体は殆と平癒無病と申程に相成たり旨、目下之摂養注意専一なる趣承候。

帰り掛志村方へ立寄り候。　皆無事岡田に今滞在、今夜志村夫婦岡田参る。　麁飯を供す。　無人之事故何も意に任せす次第、十二時前夫婦列去る。　岡田一泊せり。　今夜近来の夜ふかし致（十二時半過頃迄）心持不宜候。

一午後序に八貫町小林なる時計屋に立寄托置候時計修繕催促致置候。

一お貞風月楼に立寄り、小供へ土産之為菓子数品相需め候。

此日非常炎天殊には鎌倉納涼後の事故殊更に相こたへ食事もす〻みかね候程に候。

八月十日晴炎天

一早天より志村翁入来、かせ之事。

一歯医長谷川方へ小切手を以払方取計置候。　弐拾五円也。

一午後匆々吉田師へ立寄り治療を受け直に新橋汽車場へ乗付、二時半発の汽車に投し無事鎌倉へ着せしは四時過なり。

一是より直に水浴せり。

今夜海浜院にて玉突相試候。

十　元老院議官・枢密顧問官時代

山田顕義氏同院へ滞留に付致面会候。談何れも条約改正論に渉り、数時相費候。内閣之論議等多少致聞取候。世間噴々之説も亦無理に無之様相聞得候点も不少候。拙予て心配せし通交渉公文「ヂプロマチックノート」なるものには不注意の文字文法等なきにしもあらさるか如し。少しく不熟之嗟なきに非らす。本条約之分は先つ可なりと可謂乎。何にせよ多少不注意之点有之様相聞得候けれとも、憲法に抵触云々の論は浅見と被存候。菟に角現物熟読翫味之上ならでは充分の当否は断言しがたし。

八月十一日曇天且晴
浴水如常皆無事。

一貞子共召列れ高橋良敬邸を訪ふ。手作の水瓜を進む。彼れ夫婦同道帰る。昼飯を進め談話数時間、両人は五時頃去る。

一植木屋市五郎帰倉す。本邸の水道全以出来候様子一安神に候。

一高橋氏之小児生れて四五月女子至て壮健為両人嬉敷存候事。

一今夕は少々風邪気、少々運動せり。

八月十二日曇且晴

一本日日さし落成せり。之れて大抵相凌き可申存候。柳島よりよしす弐拾間を取寄相用ひ候。壱間に付弐拾弐銭つゝ海浜院の中山世話致候。

一午前有島成氏入来、談弐時間、毎之通慷慨談多し。

一午後は益風邪気相募り候故、弐時間ほと相休候得共、所謂鼻かせ体にて心持不宜候。今朝の浴水は不得策と存候事。

236

（注）墨書。

37　「元帳」／吉田清成

〔表紙〕

明治二十二年七月下浣

元帳　　3882381号　　時計
〔朱筆〕
「ろ号」
不許他見　　吉田

明治22年7月26日〜12月24日

37　「元帳」／吉田清成

27　一金拾円
〔朱筆〕
同廿七日
「手元」
七月廿六日より

26　一金拾円
七月廿六日　　　　　　岩越

小川町加藤良助納ものゝありしとき渡す

此日井上をも召列鎌倉へ行く」

十　元老院議官・枢密顧問官時代

同日　　　　　　　　　　　　　　　　　外✓貞渡

28　一　拾円　　　　　　　　　　　　　貞渡

同廿八日　　　　　　　　　　　　　　　岩越

29　一同　拾円　　　　　　　　　　　　岩越

七月三十日　　　　　　　　　　　　　　岩越

30　一　金弐拾円　　　　　　　　　　　岩越

同卅一日

31　一　金弐拾円　下僕月給其外の為　　岩越

同日

32　一同　拾円　下婢同断其外　　　　　貞渡

八月一日

33　一同　拾円　　　　　　　　　　　　岩越

八月一日

34　一同　拾円　　　　　　　　　　　　井上定次
　　鎌倉行旅費の為

八月二日

35　一同五円
鎌倉別荘にて荷物運賃先払等の為
井上渡

八月四日
36　一金五円
本日用あり、東京行に付留守小遣用
井上渡

同
37　一金五円
右同断
お貞渡

八月五日
38　一金百円
〔智常〕
志村翁唯今帰宅の上直に右を相渡し候事
岩越

八月五日
39　一同弐百五拾円
但小切手（三十三銀行三十三号）を以岡田へ仮渡取計置候事。川西富五郎へ馬車代として可払渡分
岩越

同
40　一同三拾四円四拾弐銭
但右同断三十四号小切手、山形屋（呉服屋宮沢治平渡）、当五月六月買入もの代之内
岩越

同日

十　元老院議官・枢密顧問官時代

41　一同弐拾九円七拾銭
　但右同断三十五号小切手、飼葉屋三部甚左衛門渡、当六月七月分
　　　　　　　　　　　　　　　　　　　　岩越

42　一弐拾五円
八月十日
　但歯医師長谷川某渡、三十三銀行小切手
　　　　　　　　　　岩越渡

44　一金三円
八月十三日
　鎌倉にて小遣として渡、内壱円は前以小銭にて
　　　　　　　　　　貞渡

45　一金拾円
八月十四日
　大工払丸太竹代等取に参候節
　　　　　　　　　　井上渡

43　一弐拾円
八月九日
　但一時お貞渡に取計置たる分を更に井上渡に取計候事、一週間払の為なり
　　　　　　　　　　井上渡

44　一同拾五円
八月十九日
46
　　　　　　　　　　お貞渡

45　一同五円
同廿四日
〔朱筆〕
〔六〕
47
　　　　　　　　　　お貞渡

日付	記載	番号	宛・摘要
同廿八日		50	お貞渡
同廿六日	｀46 一同拾五円	48	井上渡
	一同拾五円	49	お貞渡
八月卅一日〔同廿七日〕	一同五円	49	お貞渡
	｀47 一金弐百円	51	吉田昇二郎へ貸渡す証文あり
九月三日			
九月三日渡	｀49 一金拾円	53	お貞渡
同四日			
	｀50 一金弐拾円	54	岩越
同五日	｀51 一同弐拾円	55	岩越
九月一日	｀52 一同弐拾円	56	岩越
	〔朱筆〕｀48 一同弐拾円	52	井上
八月七日	「之れは一時貞渡の分を更に井上渡に取計、お貞、本日生と帰京せし趣なり」		

十　元老院議官・枢密顧問官時代

一同弐拾円　　　　57　　　　　　　　　　　井上

　内五円三橋へ与へ、外拾弐円余諸払之為井上扱也

六月廿日より八月七日迄

第壱号より第五十七号迄

刀屋をも加算して

惣計壱千四百六十八円八拾四銭

〔朱筆〕
「九月九日帰京貞子共一同前十一時四十三分鎌倉発車、後二時前着品、井上外女五人召列」

九月十二日

一四拾五円　　　　　　　　　　　　　　　　岩越

銀行小切手三十九番、所得税前半季分貴島厳を以十三日に上納せしむ

〔注〕右上に朱で「此所に金百円銀行より引出元に立つ」とあり。

同十六日

一弐拾五円　　　　　　　　　　　　　　　　岩越

　壱円札にて　ランプ弐個代八円位学習院半季分等の為

同

一拾円　　　　　　　　　　　　　　　　　　貞渡

九月十六日夜

　但九月十一日風難破損に付梧園翁へ取替上候分

一拾円　　　子供四人本月分学資六円外小遣用　　　　　　　　貞渡

十七日

一拾円　　　　　　　　　　　　　　　　　　　　　　　　　　岩越
　　　風難之為やね葺替代内金として可払分

九月十八日

一三拾円　[朱筆]「三十三銀行小切手四十番を以同人渡に取計、○和歌山・奈良・福岡三県水害者へ救恤義捐金也、本日池上　岩越渡
　　緑太郎に命し枢密院へ納む」

同十八日

一拾円　　　　　　　　　　　　　　　　　　　　　　　　　　岩越

九月廿二日

一五円　　　　　　　　　　　　　　　　　　　　　　　　　　岩越

同廿三日

一五円　　　　　　　　　　　　　　　　　　　　　　　　　　貞渡

同廿五日

　小遣用
　　　此日馬丁佐吉暇遣すと云

一五円　此日椿苗七拾五本大久保の者より買求む。赤と白　　岩越

九月廿六日
一金拾五円也　　岩越

同廿六日
一同、壱円　野元彦次九月十月の学資　　岩越
〔三三〕

〔朱筆〕
「本日弐百円銀行より引出す。市五郎使之」

同廿七日　　岩越

一弐拾円
但屋ね払拾七円余ありと云　　岩越

同廿七日　　岩越

一三拾円
白木屋払三十円拾三銭也

同廿七日　　岩越

一五円　　小遣用

同廿七日　　貞渡

37　「元帳」／吉田清成

〔朱筆〕〔清成〕
「拾円　成」

一五円、、

同廿九日　　　　　　　　　　　　手元

一五円

一拾五円

同三十日　　　　　　　　　　　　岩越

一三拾円　　　　　　　　　　　　岩越

〔朱筆〕
一七拾九円弐拾弐銭
「四十三番小切手を以川西富五郎方払の分」　岩越

九月卅日

一弐拾円　　　　　　　　　　　　岩越

同日　　　　　　　　　　　　　　貞渡

一拾円

同日　　　　　　　　　　　　　　岩越

一弐拾円　　　　　　　　　　　　貞渡

一五円

同日　　　　　　　　　　　　　　岩越

志郎学資用

十月四日

一拾円　　　　　　　　　　　　　岩越

245

十　元老院議官・枢密顧問官時代

〔朱筆〕「十月四日弐百円銀行より引出す。市五郎使之」

十月五日　一百円　　　　岩越

十月五日　一拾五円　　　岩越

〔朱筆〕「但九月廿八日頃小切手四十一号を以小林時計匠へ払候分を「本払」之姿に取計候分なり」

十二日　一拾円　　　　　岩越

十月十四日　一弐拾円　　岩越

大工申出やね屋払其外の為

十四日　一五円　　　　　貞渡

十七日　一五円　　　　　岩越

十八日　一拾円　　　　　岩越

一五円　　　　　　　　　岩越

〔朱筆〕「十八日金百円銀行より引出、市五郎使之」

同十九日
一三拾円　　　　　　　　　岩越

同十九日
一五円　　　　　　　　　　貞渡

同廿日
一五円　　　　　　　　　　手元

同廿二日
一拾円　　　　　　　　　　岩越

同廿四日
一五円　　　　　　　　　　貞渡

同廿四日
一拾円　　　　　　　　　　岩越

十月三十日
一拾円　　　　　　　　　　岩越

一拾円
貞取次之事、此日雨森来家中、田中章来京

十月卅一日
〔朱筆〕
「此日百五拾円銀行より引取」

一金五拾円　　　　　　　　岩越

十　元老院議官・枢密顧問官時代

十一月二日　一金参円　　　　　　　　　　　　　　　　　　全人

同　四日　一金百円　　　　　　　　　　　　　　　　　　　全人

［朱筆〕「十一月一日」　一同百円　　　　　　　　　　　　吉田昇二郎

七日　一同百円　徂来書

一同四拾円　　　　　　　　　　　　　　　　　　　　　　　前同断

［朱筆〕前同断、岡田扱之
　　　　　　　　　　〔清成〕
「二重付記誤に付消す　成」

十一月四日　一金百円也　　　　　　　　　　　　　　　　　岩越

六日　一金百円　　　　　　　　　　　　　　　　　　　　　岩越

一同五拾円　　　　　　　　　　　　　　　　　　　　　　　岩越

八日　　　　　　　　　　　　　　　　　　　　　　　　　　岩越

一同四拾円　　　　　　　　　　　　　　　　　　　　　　　岩越

十日

37　「元帳」／吉田清成

一同弐拾円　　　　　　　　　　岩越

十一日　一同三拾円　　　　　　岩越

十四日　一同拾円　　　　　　　岩越

十一月十五日　一金弐拾円　　　岩越

十八日　一同拾円　　　　　　　岩越

廿二日　一同拾円　　　　　　　岩越

廿五日　〔朱筆〕「六」一同拾円　岩越

卅日　一同拾円　　　　　　　　岩越

同日　一同三拾円　　　　　　　岩越

十二月二日　一同拾円　　　　　岩越

十　元老院議官・枢密顧問官時代

一　同弐拾円　　　　　　　　　　岩越

同三朝　　　　　　　　　　　　　岩越

一　同五拾円　　　　　　　　　　岩越

四日　　　　　　　　　　　　　　岩越

一　同弐拾円　　　　　　　　　　岩越
　岡田の手を経

五日

一　同三拾円　　　　　　　　　　岩越

同日

一　同七拾円　　　　　　　　　　岩越

同日

一　同五拾円　　　　　　　　　　岩越

六日

一　同三拾円　　　　　　　　　　岩越

八日

一　同拾円　　　　　　　　　　　岩越

十二月八日

一　金拾円　　　　　　　　　　　岩越

十日

一同拾円　　　　　　　　岩越

〔朱筆〕「十日夜」　　　　〔朱筆〕「岩越」

一同拾円

　　市五郎貸渡の分」

十一日

一同三拾円　　　　　　　岩越

十二日

一同七拾円　　　　　　　岩越

十二日夜

一同五拾円　　　　　　　岩越

　右刀大小代、長谷川扱之

十四日

一同五円　　　　　　　　手元

十三日

一同五拾円　　　　　　　貞へ仮渡

十四日

一同拾円

十　元老院議官・枢密顧問官時代

十四日
一同拾円　　岩越
十五日
一同四拾円　長谷川　岩越
　本日より長谷川え会計事務次渡　岩越
十六日
一四拾円　　長谷川
十二月十六日
一五円　　　貞渡
十七日
一拾円　　　手元
十九日
一五円　　　長谷川
一弐拾円　　長谷川
廿一日
一五円　　　長谷川
廿二日
一拾円　　　長谷川
廿二日
一五円　　　長谷川

252

37 「元帳」／吉田清成

一五円		貞渡
廿三日		
一弐拾六円		
廿三日		
一五円		
廿四日		
一弐拾円		長谷川
廿六日		
一六拾七円		長谷川
廿六日		
一三拾五円		長谷川
廿六日		
一五拾円		長谷川
十二月廿四日	 十四五日頃留 廿四日留 ﹇朱筆﹈	岡田彦三郎へ渡、別記あり

十　元老院議官・枢密顧問官時代

一拾円

同日

一五円

〔注〕墨書。見せ消し、算用数字はすべて朱筆。吉田ほかの確認印多数あり。また一部に確認済を表すと思われる朱線あり。

志印

岡印

38　「日記　次第不同万留　三号」／吉田清成

明治22年8月13日〜9月2日

〔表表紙〕

明治二十二年八月十二日

日　記
　　　次第不同
　　　万留

〔朱筆〕
「三号」　　禁他見清成

八月十三日晴天

九時二十分発帰東京、昼飯後吉田国手へ出懸治療を受く、風邪気故なり。少々熱気あれとも格別は無之候。岡田令高参り合せり。同氏明日頃発京古護屋〔名〕へ帰るとの事。二時半新橋発にて四時半頃帰鎌、炎熱難堪候。

八月十四日

長谷寺坊主と鶴見相見得候。

此日陣幕休五郎見舞す。海浜院にて子供始四人故買取召列昼飯を為し、跡にて玉突共致し、陣幕は晩飯を与へ候後東京之様帰る。中村五郎へ一封を遣し呉との頼事あり、肯し置候。

山田顕義昨日海浜院へ来る。

〇八月十五日晴天

十六日

井上定次脚気にて相悩候故差返し吉田国手へ依嘱せり。

同便に岡田へ一封差立置候。今夜も玉突致候、有島氏相手なり。合角の勝負なり。子供皆無事。

十五日は格別可記之奇事なし。例の改正一件囂々、格別の銘案も不相見得、鳥尾なと余程名高く相成候半。或は後悔することもあらんか。側より見ると余計なことも沢山有之様被存候。

有島武氏へ百仏聖一棉進し候（吉田製也）。昨夜同人と戦ひ拙大勝ゆへ又明晩と約し置たる故、今夜一戦を挑みしに、三度にて拙勝負まけ。

八月十七日

岩越来倉す、野菜もの等持参の事。

〇子供等一同観音寺へ召列、帰りには大仏辺へ廻り暮れと雨に降られ窮せり。柳谷の女おくめも召列れ候。防主高橋と逢ふ。両三日之内囲碁を約置たり。

〇鶴見を過ぎる時一寸立寄置候。

〇三橋にて暫時休む。

今夜玉を十台位も突き運動に相成候。相手は半田の小栗、医の勝見、郵船会社の岩永等なり。拙大に勝利を得

十　元老院議官・枢密顧問官時代

たり。

風邪気故水浴は不出来。風もなく雨降りかけてよふ降らす寝苦敷夜に候。雑虫殊に蝦[ママ]には衆人困却せり。

夜半よりポチくヽ降つヽき仕合に候。

八月十八日雨天日

当地にて土用しけとて風もなきに浪の荒きを指して号けたるか、昨夜よりの降りもやゝつゝき、今朝少しは冷敷相覚候風は北風にて所謂「ナラヒ」なり。昨今浪荒く両三日中にはしけ可申と申居候所、降り照り定めなく戸外の運動は出来かね候。アルサブレント氏入来。兼て依頼之紹介状催促なり。仁礼[景範]中将へ一封相認遣候。別に用向之委曲は不知候付、同人より聞取可給と申入置候。

子供打揃大神楽を呼ひ大騒きなり。長与[専斎]氏一同、柳谷[謙太郎]氏一同多数の子供等集り賑々敷事に候。

井上定次より手状参る。経師屋雇[台]之事共委敷申参り居候。

午後には余程降り出し冷気相催候。諸作物之為愈以仕合なり。

八月十九日曇天月

九時二十分之発車にて帰京せり。

用向多端なれとも昇二郎[吉田]国手へ治療を受けたり。今晩は単身にて晩飯を喫せり。無類のこと共なり。

×散歩致候。

今朝は志村[智常]氏相見得候。皆無事之由。夕には雨。

八月廿日早天より大雨火

風雨烈敷、外行頗る難事に候。国中全般の模様被思遣候。作物の為には幸を得たる地もあるべけれとも、雨過は

不致やと懸念せり。

昼後吉田国手へ越し治療を得たり。風雨なれとも用も済たる故帰鎌せり。四時過着。風強し、皆無事。

八月廿一日風雨水

可記之珍事なし。両度の治療の為か風邪気も快く相覚候。

同廿二日半天木

子供毎之通浴水大元気。日暮之為玉突共致候。別に記事なし。

同廿三日晴天風あり金

有島・高橋両士来る、九時頃なり。終日談話且玉突等にて日を送り候。多少の調ものもありたれとも此の形勢故不能なり。高橋は少々不快なり。持病之肺症は実に難物故気之どくに存候。吉田国手へ引合せ候つもりなり。

同廿四日晴天土

早朝加藤三左衛門へ命して地網を引かせたれば沢山の漁獲あり。柳谷・芳川[顕正]・有島・長与なんどの家内□[虫損]を見物に招たれは多獲故一入之興を加たり。

獲ものは右四家は勿論、高橋・富田・平野・玉城・馬越[カ]へ進め候。四斗樽もて三四抔も取れ申候。太力の魚弐三[ママ]百鮨千余其外雑肴なり。

八月廿五日晴天日

早天より芳川顕正氏入来談数刻、何れも条約改正一件にて打つめなり。本日寺島副議長の命なりとて書記官共より召還状来る。国民身分法御諮詢相成たる故迅かに帰京せよとのことなり。

十　元老院議官・枢密顧問官時代

夕には子供等召列散歩せり。

海浜院にて玉突致候。日曜故外人数多繁に過きたり。

八月廿六日晴且曇月

本日植木屋市を帰京せしめ候。今朝は久々振海水浴奮発せり。別に支障なし。子供・貞皆同時なり。朝飯前を以至極妙とす。

昨日井上定次書類持来る故本日は調ものゝために寸暇を不得候。

夕刻ステーション迄小供等召列散歩せり。帰る頃（八時過）雨降らんと欲して下り得す。仕合せたり、昨夕と今日とに帰化法案弁右参照書類大体一読了。

八月廿七日曇火

九時二十分発帰京。

午後吉田へ出掛治療を受く。帰りに中村へ立寄り刀数本を見る。

志村午後相見得候。

夜更る迄調もの致一時頃相休み候。

同廿八日曇天水

九時より出院致し大抵出揃なり。日本臣民身分法に付総委員会、別に可記奇事無之候。今夜六時五拾八分之汽車にて帰倉致候。

同廿九日曇天木

七時十三分の汽車にて帰京、直に出院致候。本日を以質義会相了へ委員撰定相成候。即副島・佐野・福岡・吉
（種臣）（常民）（孝弟）

258

38　「日記　次第不同万留　三号」／吉田清成

田・鳥尾なり。

来月二日より右開会之筈に取極め候。

帰途吉田にて治療をうけ即ち新橋発車帰倉致候。

八月三十日金曇

有島等と玉突致候。本日は円覚寺へ差越之途岩倉と行逢候処、虫干は未なりとのこと承候故、建長寺へ立寄り銘

画数幅を見候。例年の土用干天気次第両三日中に致すとの事に候。帰りに雪の下の三橋へ立寄り昼飯を喫せり。[ママ]崔見弥三郎も召列候。貞始子供は素より召列候事。

建長寺へ金壱円香料として差出置候事。吉川氏のばゝとのも建長寺内に行逢候事。

同卅一日曇天土曜

鎌倉にては天気わるく別に記事なし。

皆無事。

壱番汽車にて上京、明宮殿下御誕辰に付赤阪王宮へ罷出候。但小礼服着用。

夫より王宮へ罷出此内拝領被　仰付候。

聖上　御写影之御礼申上候事。[ママ]

帰途吉田へ立寄候処幸在家にて治療を受け直と帰宅、昼飯仕廻直に発足、二時半之汽車にて鎌倉へ立帰り候。

此日吉田氏懇談に付金弐百円貸渡候事、別に証文あり。

外×の件も共に市五郎え下命候事。

九月一日曇日

十　元老院議官・枢密顧問官時代

夕刻五時三十分之汽車にてお貞召列帰京致候。明日より委員会始める故なり。筆女召列候事。七時過帰宅、電信

かけ置たれ共、明朝の事と解候哉にて、何の仕度も無之、わか家の思ひなきか如し。

今夜早々相休み候。

岡田相見得候。

九月二日曇小雨月

九時より出勤、委員会に列す。四時半引取帰りに吉田に立寄る。

貞にも同断也。且長谷川医師へ差越、向ひ歯一本を入れさせ候由。

国民身分法は三十条余あり。僅かに七条迄概定修正相済候。議論多く中両三日中には済さうに無之候。

〔注〕墨書。

甲号

39　草道家廃戸主及相続についての願書

明治22年8月

廃戸主及相続之義に付願

鹿児島県鹿児島郡加治屋町二百六番戸 士族吉田勇蔵方同居当時東京府下芝区白金

志田町十五番地東京府華族正三位子爵吉田清成方寄留

亡草道覚右ヱ門相続人士族

戸主　草道清武

39　草道家廃戸主及相続についての願書

右幼稚にして過半来疾病に罹り候故、万事不都合の場合不敢候に付、今般親戚協議致候処目下亡戸主適当のものも
無之候間、亡草道覚右ヱ門妻サワ戸主相続致し度候条御許容被成下度、此段連署を以て奉願候也。

　年　月　日

　　　　　　　　　　　　　　　　　　　　　　　　　　鹿児島県鹿児島郡加治屋町二百六番戸吉田勇蔵方同居士族亡草道覚右ヱ門妻

　　　草道サワ

　知事宛

乙号

右本県士族亡草道覚右ヱ門養子家督相続致居候処、病気等の為め先般廃戸主の義出願、其筋の認可を得候。然る
に今般無拠事故有之、親戚協議の上離縁実家へ立戻引取候条送籍被成下度、此段連署を以て御届仕候也。

　年　月　日

　　　　　　　　　　　　　　　　　　　　　　　　　　東京府芝区白金志田町十五番地東京府華族

　　　　　　　　　　　　　　　　　　　　　　　　　　　　　　　　　　　　　右後見人

　　　　　　　　　　　　　　　　　　　　　　　　　　　　　　　　　　　　　正三位子爵　　吉田清成

　　　　　　　　　　　　　　　　　　　　　　　　　　　　　　　　　　　　　親戚　　　　　何之誰

　　　　　　　　　　　　　　　　　　　　　　　　　　東京府下芝区白金志田町十五番地寄留

　　　　　　　　　　　　　　　　　　　　　　　　　　東京府華族正三位子爵吉田清成三男

　　　　　　　　　　　　　　　　　　　　　　　　　　　　　　　　　　　　　　　草道清武

　　　　　　　　　　　　　　　　　　　　　　　　　　鹿児島県鹿児島郡加治屋町二百六番戸吉田勇蔵方

十　元老院議官・枢密顧問官時代

同居　草道サワ

右　吉田清成

地元戸長宛

〔朱筆にて抹消〕
「丙号」

華士族相続法　明治六年一月二十二日
第二十八号布告

今般華士族家督相続の儀に付左之通被相定候条、此旨相達候事。

家督相続は必す総領の男子たるへし。若し亡没或は廃篤疾等不得止の事故あれは其事実を詳にし次男三男又は女子へ養子相続願出つへし。若し故なく順序を越て相続致す者は相当の咎可申付事。　六年第二百六十三号布告を以て全条改正

幼少にて家督為致候節は親戚又は他人にても相当の者相撰後見可為致事。

当主隠居致し実子又は養子家督相続致し候上其相続人多病或は不埒の儀有之歟又は病死致し最前の隠居壮健にて再相続願出候節は聞届不苦事。

但再相続人と可称事。

当主壮年なれとも疾病其外無拠事故有之養子致し候処、前当主疾病平愈又は事故相解候節再家督致し、右養子は実家へ立戻り候歟又は当主他へ縁付候共双方熟談の上願出候はゝ聞届不苦事。　九年第七十五号布告を以て次の一項を廃す

父兄伯叔総て目上の者子弟甥等の目下の家を継承するときは相続人と称し養子と称すへからす。

262

39 草道家廃戸主及相続についての願書

当主死去跡嗣子無之婦女子のみにて已を得さる事情あり養子難致者は婦女子の相続差許従前の給禄可支給事。
婦女子相続の後に於て夫を迎へ又は養子致し候はゝ直ちに其夫又は養子へ相続可相譲事。　六年第二百六十三号
右之通候条華族は管轄庁より正院へ相伺、士族は管轄庁に於て聞届可申事。　　　布告を以て追加

控

　　戸主疾病に付跡相続願

　　　　　　　　　　　　鹿児島県鹿児島市大字加治屋町二百六番戸吉田勇蔵方同居

　　　　　　　　　　　　　　　　　　　　　　　　草道清武

右過般来疾病に罹り候故万事不都合の場合不尠候に付、今般親戚協議の上養母サワ戸主相続致し度候条御許容被
成下度、此段連署を以て奉願候也。

明治二十二年八月

　　　　　　　　　　　　　　　　　　　　　　右養母　　草道サワ

　　　　　　　　　　　　　　東京府芝区白金志田町十五番地
　　　　　　　　　　　　　　　　華族
　　　　　　　　　　　　　　　　　　　右後見人　　　吉田清成　［朱筆］「印」

［朱筆］「控」

送籍願

263

十　元老院議官・枢密顧問官時代

東京府芝区白金志田町十五番地華族吉田清成三男

草道清武

右は家事上無拠事故有之候に付、今般親戚協議の上離縁実家へ引戻候条、送籍方御取計被下度、此段連署を以て奉願候也。

明治二十二年八月

右

鹿児島県鹿児島市大字加治屋町二百六番戸吉田勇蔵方同居

草道サワ

〔朱筆〕
吉田清成　〔朱印〕［印］

〔注〕墨書。

40　帝国臣民身分法修正案

明治（22）年9月

〔表紙〕

〈八月卅一日夜達九月一日鎌倉にて請取　吉田〉

〈修正擬案〉

〔朱印〕
秘

〈日本国籍法〉

〈帝国臣民身分法〉

帝国臣民身分法修正案

第一章　臣民身分の得有

第一条　左に掲くる者は出生に因り日本臣民身分を得有す。
〔第〕一　日本人を父とする正出子
〔第〕二　日本人を母とする私出子
〔第〕三　国〈籍〉〔民身分なき者と婚姻したる日本婦女の子〕
〔第二条〕
三　外国人を母とする私生子にして其の父たる日本人の〔法律上の〕認知を受けたる者〈国籍〉〔若は准正に因り日本臣民身分を得有す〕
四　日本帝国の領内に生れ父母共に知れさる者

第二条　外国人は第二章の規定に従ひ帰化に因り日本臣民身分を得有す。〈国籍〉〔程〕

第三条〔四〕　外国〔の婦〕女にして日本人の妻と為りたる者は当然日本臣民身分を得有す。〈国籍〉

第四条〔五〕　日本に帰化したる者の妻及〔帰化したる者の〕未成年の子は反対の正条なき場合に於ては日本臣民身分を得有す。但し其の子は成年の後一個年〔以〕内に第三十二条の申出〔願〕。〔五〕〔にして別に取除きたる者の外は総て〕を為すに因り外国の国民身分を撰択することを得。

第五条〔八〕　左に掲くる者は日本に住居するに於ては其の本国の法律に従ひ成年に至りし時より一個年〔以〕内に第三十二条の申出〔願〕を為すに因り日本臣民身分を得有す。
前項の規定は外国〔の婦〕女にして日本人の妻と為りたる者の未成年の子にも之を適用す。〔程〕〔宅を構ふ〕

40　帝国臣民身分法修正案

265

十　元老院議官・枢密顧問官時代

〔第〕一　第一条〔及第二条〕に掲けたる日本人にして其の親の身分の変更に因り日本臣民身分を〔喪〕失ひた〈父又は母〉〈し〉

る者

〔第〕二　親の日本に帰化したる時成年なりし外国人〈父又は母〉

三　日本帝国の領内に生れたる外国人の子にして又帝国の領内に生れたる者

第六条　国民身分なき者と婚姻したる日本女の子及父母共に国民身分なき者にして日本帝国の領内に生れたる者は日〔九〕〈ケツル〉〈日本帝国〉の領内に生れ父母共に知れさる者〈籍なき〉〈国籍を〉

本臣民身分を〔得〕有す。

第二章　帰化

第七条　左の条件を具へたる外国人は日本帝国に帰化するの願書を呈出することを得。〔十〕

〔第〕一　本国の法律に依り成年にして治産の〔不〕能力を有する事。「但し未成年者と雖其の父又は後見人の〔一切〕〈に罹らさ〉

承諾を得たる者は願書を呈出することを得」

〔第〕二　品行正しき事

〔第〕三　独立して生活するの資産又は技能ある事〈生計を立つ〉

〔第〕四　願書呈出前引続き満五個年日本に住居し仍引続き住居せんとする事〈五年以上〉

〔第〕五　願書呈出より少くとも二個年前に日本帝国に帰化せんとするの意あることを其の住居地の身分取扱役〔十〕〔地方長官〕

場に届出たる事

第八条　有益の発明を日本帝国に伝へたる者又は農工技術に付き著しき効益を日本帝国に起したる者其の他日本〔十三〕〔商其の他諸般の技芸〕〔及〕

〔帝国〕の為に功労ある者は第七条第四号及第五号の条件を特免す〔ることを得〕。

40　帝国臣民身分法修正案

〈十二〉
第九条　第七条第五号に依り帰化せんとするの意あることを届出たる後未た帰化せすして死亡したる者の妻〈子〉は
日本に住居するに於ては其の届出より二個年の後同条第一号乃至第四号の条件を具ふるときは帰化の願書を呈
出することを得。

〈十一〉
第十〈二〉条
〈前条〉
　第〈十〉七条第四号に記載せる期限の間に日本〈帝国〉を離るゝこと引続き六個月以上に及〈迄〉ふ〈雖〉ときは二個年を経
過せさる間は其の離れたる年月を扣除して前後の年月を通算す。但し日本政府の官用の為に外国に在る年月は
之を扣除せす。

〈四〉
第十一条　帰化の願書には保証人三名〈の〉〈を以て〉連署し願人の国民身分氏名職業年齢住所〈并に願人と共に日本臣民の身分を得〉〈十三〉〈仍引続き日本に住居し又は〉〈ヘイキル〉
日本政府に任用せらるゝ〈十二〉の意ある事を記載し並に第七条第八条第九条に掲けたる条件の証明に必要なる文書を
添ふるを要す。〈へ及左の件を証明すへし。〉

〈第一〉　日本臣民として憲法及法律を遵守し義務に服従する事

〈第二〉　従前所属国の身分爵位官職及其の他の地位を拋棄する事

〈五〉
第十二条　帰化の願書は之を現住地の地方長官に由り〈内務〉司法大臣に呈出すへし。〈内務〉司法大臣は願人の品行及其の他必
要なる事項を取調へ上奏して〈たる〉勅裁を請ふの後〈其の許可すへきものは〉地方長官を経て帰化証を付与すへし。
〈帰化の願を許可し又は許可せさる指令には理由を付せす。〉

〈六〉
第十三条　帰化人は帰化証を受領するの日に於て〈別に定むる所の式に依り〉〈天皇陛下〉〈日本帝国〉に臣従〈する〉の誓を為
すへし。帰化証は此の誓を為したる後に非されは効力を有せす。

十　元老院議官・枢密顧問官時代

【第十七条】　帰化証を付与せられたる者は日本臣民に属する一切の私権〈を得有し〉及第二十二条に掲けたる特

例其の他法律に反対の正条ある場合を除く外諸般の公権を得有し幷に一切の義務に服従す。】

【八】
第十四条　帰化の願を許されさる者は願書を却下せられたる日より一個年以上日本に住居するに非されは再ひ帰

化の願書を呈出することを得。

【九】
第十五条　帰化証には帰化者と共に日本臣民身分を得有する者を併記すへし。

〈右九月四日委員会にて済〉

【二十】
第十六条　凡日本帝国【内】に於て官吏に任用せらるへき外国人にして帰化の願を為したる者は第十三条を除く

【国籍】　【文武の官及其の他の公務】に【為】　【程】

外前数条の規定に依らす枢密院の議を経勅裁に依り帰化証を付与せらるゝことあるへし。

【但し領事又は公使館領事館の附属官たる者及学術技芸に依り任用する者又は日本政府一時の雇に係る外国人
は誠実に勤仕するの契約を為さしめ帰化国民たるの義務を免るゝことを任用状に記載することを得。】

【一年以上引続き日本の陸海軍役に服したる】　【削除すべき事に決す】

【二十一】
第十七条　左に掲くる外国人は日本に住居するに於ては第三十二条の申出【願】を為すに因り

【五】　【成年の後何時にても】

日本臣民身分を得有す。

一　一年以上引続き日本の陸海軍役に服したる者

二　日本の徴兵に際し外国の国民身分を申立さりし者

第十八条　帰国の意なく十個年間日本に住居する外国人は帰化の手続を為すへし。

【一旦此条は削る事に決せり。再考のつもり。】

【五】
第十九条　第二条第四条第五条第二号第三号第六号第十六条第十七条に依り日本臣民身分を得有する者は其の身

【枢密院の議を経裁可】　【九】　【二十】　【二十一】

分を得たる日より十個年を経たる後特に帝国議会の承認を得るに非されは両院の議員国務大臣枢密顧問及陸海

40　帝国臣民身分法修正案

軍の将官〔及両院の議員〕と為ることを得す。

　　第三章　臣民身分の喪失

第二十〔三〕条　左に掲くる者は当然日本臣民身分を〔喪〕失ふ。

〔第〕一　外国人の妻と為りたる日本人及其の未成年の子。但し当然其の夫及父の身分に従ふとき

〔第二〕二　外国人の養子と為りたる者。但し当然養親の身分に従ふとき

〔第三〕三　日本人を母とするの私出子にして其の父たる外国人〔の法律上〕の認知〔若は准正〕を受けたる者

〔第四〕四　外国に帰化したる者

〔第五〕五　日本政府の許可を得すして外国の官に就き又は恩給を受け又は兵役に服し又は軍隊に入りたる者。但し日本政府の命に従ひ〔期限内に〕外国の官職恩給又は兵役を辞したるときは此の限に在らす

〔第六〕六　戦時又は開戦せんとする時外国に滞在し日本政府の公布したる帰国の命令に従ひ期限内に帰国せさる者

第二十一条　外国に帰化したる者の妻及未成年の子は〔にして別に取除きたる者の外は総て〕反対の正条なき場合に於ては日本臣民身分を〔喪〕失ふ。

第二十二条　日本人にして本国を去りたる者は出立の日より起算して引続き十年間外国に住居するに由り〔日本〕臣民の身分を〔喪〕失ふ。但し此の年限は本人に於て若し旅券又は同様の証書を所持するときは其の旅券又は証書の満期の日より起算し、若し日本の公使館又は領事館に於て記入を受け又は本国の身分事務取扱役場に外国住居の届出を為したるときは、其の記入又は届出の後一年の終より起算す。

前項の期限は未成年者に付ては成年に達したる日より起算す。

269

十　元老院議官・枢密顧問官時代

身分の喪失は日本に住居せさるに於ては本人の妻及未成年の子に及ふものとす。

第二十三条〔六〕　日本人にして外国に移住せんことを欲し租税其の他公義務〔又は負債其の他民法上の義務〕なき者は除籍の勅許を願出ることを得。此の場合に於て戦時及第二十六条に規定する場合を除く外除籍を許可すへし。

第二十四条〔七〕　除籍証は其の交付の時より効力を生するものとす。但し除籍証を交付せられたる者其の交付の日より六個月〔以〕内に外国に移住し又は外国に帰化せさるときは其の効力を失ふ。

第二十五条〔八〕　除籍は反対の正条なき場合に於ては本人の妻及未成年の子に及ふものとす。〔別に取除きたる者の外総て〕〔又は〕

第二十六条〔九〕　左に掲くる者は除籍を許可し又は日本臣民身分を〔せす〕失はしめす。〔せ〕

〔第〕一　満十七歳以上三十四歳以下の男子。但し陸海軍現役を免せられたる者は此の限に在らす

〔第〕二　官吏及陸海軍現役の軍人

第二十七条〈二条〉　第一条に依り日本帝国臣民身分を〔得〕有せし者は一旦之を〔喪〕失ひたるも第三十二条の申出〔願〕を為し申出〔願〕後一個年〔以〕内に日本に帰国して住居を定むるに因り其の身分を回復す〔る事を得〕と改めて可也。〔三十〕〔し〕〔五〕

第二十八条　第二十〔三〕条第五号第六号に因り日本臣民身分を〔喪〕失ひたる者は正当なる弁明を為さゝる間は身分を回復することを許さす。〔四〕〔五〕〔し〕

第二十九条　第二条第三条第四条第五条第六条第十六条第十七条に依り日本臣民と為りたる後其の身分を〔喪〕失ひたる者は更に帰化の手続を為すに非されは日本人と為ることを得す。〔三〕〔四〕〔八〕〔九〕〔十二〕〔二十一〕〔臣民身分を得有す〕〔し〕

第四章　通則

40 帝国臣民身分法修正案

第三十（三）条 日本臣民身分を得有し又は回復したる者は外国の国民身分爵位官職及其の他の位地を保有せす。

【帰化証を付与したる者に対しては日本政府は総て外国の身分爵位官職及其の他の地位を併有することを認め
す。】

第三十一条 身分を変更するの効力は既往に遡らす。

〔四〕

第三十二条 身分の撰択、回復又は得有に関る申出〔願〕は日本に住居する者は其の住居地の身分取扱役場、外
国に住居し又は寄留する者は日本の公使館又は領事館に之を為すへし。

公正の法式に依り委任を為したる代理人を以て前項の申出〔願〕を為すことを得。

〔五〕

〔注〕コンニャク版の原文に朱筆（ ）で示す）及び鉛筆（ ）で示す）による修正あり。また、鉛筆で□囲み、修正を示す箇
所あり。見せ消しは、朱筆、鉛筆の両方あり。また以下に掲げるように、欄外等に多数の加筆あり。

①第一条〔第三〕の欄外に「婦は不用也」とあり。

②第三条の欄外に〝"Epso-facto"〟とあり。
〔五〕

③第四条の前に次の書き込みあり。

〈第五条 日本に帰化したる者の妻及帰化したる者の未成年の子は日本国籍を得有す。但し帰化したる者の未成年の子に
〈帰化願書に〉
〈別に〉して取除きたる者は此限にあらす。

前項未成年の子は成年の後一年以内に第三十五条の出願を為さすに因り外国の国籍を撰択することを得。

第一項の規程は外国女にして日本人の妻と為たる者の未成年の子にも之を適用す〉

〔前項…〕の一文に「可除もの也。之は先つ御預りと成る。九月二日」の書き込みあり
〔五〕
なり

④第四条の全体に鉛筆にて×を記す。 欄外には次の書き込みあり。

〈申出と出願とは少しく異る所あり。 願なれは間届けざる場合あるなり。 申出なれは之を必す容許する意味あるなり。 両
案の内いつれを可採や一疑題なり？拙案なり〉

271

十　元老院議官・枢密顧問官時代

⑤第五条の前に次の書き込みあり。

〔八〕

〈国籍〉
日本臣民たるの身分を得有し〈たる者〉及夫と共に帰化を得たる婦女〈もの〉

△

〔第六条〕〈外国女にして〉日本人の妻となりたるに因り
離婚することあるも又は寡婦となるも帰化の効力を失はす。」
〈△及夫の帰化に因り日本国籍を得有したる外国女は〉
〔第七条〕外国人の妻となり又は夫と共に外国に帰化したる日本の婦女離婚することあるか又は寡婦となりたるときは日本帝国に住居したる如何時にても第三十条の身分回復の出願を為すことを得。〉
〈此条は必要に非らす。三十条存するときは重復の憾あり、由て可削事也。〉
〈右九月二日荒増済〉

⑥第五条全体に鉛筆にて×を記す。　欄外には次の書き込みあり。
〈全除削〉
〈外国にて大凡成年に及ひし者は父母の下に居る事稀なり。独立地位を占むるを常とす。しかれは通常の帰化手続きを為さしむるを以最至当とするなり。〉

⑦第二章の前に次の書込みあり。

mental imbacility
civil in capacity ──如斯ものなるべし
civil disability
i.e. 1 economic incapacity
2 bodily disability
3 mental imbacility
民法上の能力　治産の力
起訴の権
其外

⑧第七条第一の欄外に次の書き込みあり。

〔十〕

〈但書以下は独逸の第八条に同様の備あれとも彼と我とは国柄の差あり。日本には其設を為すに不及」あれは後見人等の

40　帝国臣民身分法修正案

⑨第八条は、鉛筆にて全条削除の上、次の書き込みあり。

　〔十三〕
　〈別に改正案あり〉、下欄外に〈日本政府に於て……ありと見認める者は云々と改むる方確かなるべし。〉

身分国柄をも取調べさるを得、非常に手数を増すなり。　為除く方可然。〉

⑩第十一条の欄外に次の書き込みあり。

　〔四〕
　〈を明記したる宣言書を出すへし。〉

⑪第十三条の前に次の書き込みあり。

　〔六〕
　〈愚按陛下の尊称を加ふるを可とす。現に陶国帰化法第十四条に照すも同文あり。
　副島伯には法文には称号を加へざる方を主張せり。〉

⑫第十六条の前に次の書き込みあり。

　〔二十〕
　〈凡官吏に任せらるゝ為めに〉

⑬第十七条の欄外に次の書き込みあり。

　〔二十一〕
　〈修正案第八条を削たる上は成年後何時にても」の九字は不要用となる故に除くべし。　拙案〉
　〔原の五〕

⑭第十九条の前に次の書き込みあり。

　〔二十二〕
　〈枢密院の議を経、裁可を得るに非されは」を除く事に概決せり。九月五日午後〉

⑮さらに別紙二葉あり。その内一葉には欄外に「吉田」と墨書があり、もう一葉には裏に「吉田」と朱書がある。

　〔十〕
　第十三条　左に掲くる者は第七条第一第二第三の条件を具ふるときは帰化の願書を呈出することを得。

　第一　日本に功労ある者

　第二　日本に有益の発明を伝へ又は農工商の事業其の他学術技芸に付効益を起したる者

　第三　父母又は
　　　〈国籍を得有せしとき外国籍にありし者〉
　　　父母の一方日本人たる者

　第四　日本女を娶りたる者

　〈へ日本に住居す〉
　　九月三日修正案を起し同四日決す〉

　第十四条　帰化の願書には証人三名の連署を以て願人の国籍氏名職業年齢住所並に願人と共に日本国籍を得有すへき者の
氏名年齢及左の件を明記し願人之に署名すへし。

273

十　元老院議官・枢密顧問官時代

41　条約改正についての御前会議開催意見書／後藤象二郎

明治22年（10）月

第一　日本臣民として憲法及法律を遵守し義務に服従すること

第二　従前所属国の国籍爵位官職及其の他の地位を抛棄すること

帰化の願書には第十条第十二条第十三条に掲げたる条件の証明に必要なる文書を添附すへし。

第二十条　凡官吏に任せらるゝ為帰化の願を為したる外国人は枢密院の議を経勅裁に依り帰化証を付与せらるゝことある

へし。

前項の願書には願人の国籍氏名年齢住所履歴、願人と共に日本国籍を得有すへき者の氏名年齢及第十四条第一第二に掲

けたる事項を明記し願人之に署名し、其の願人を任用せんとする官庁を経て内閣総理大臣に呈出すへし。

公使館総領事館領事館書記生反訳官其の他附属官吏たる者、名誉領事及学術技芸に依り任用する外国人は、帰化臣民た

るを要せす。

条約改正の国家重要の一大問題たるは固より本大臣の贅弁を待たずして明瞭にして、此問題が輿論を惹起し全国

の人心をして恟々たらしむるは、亦貴大臣閣下の現に目撃する所とす。今や内閣に於て一定の方針を取り速に人

々を堵に安んぜしむるは最も必要の事に属す。本大臣去月廿八日を以て書を総理大臣黒田伯〔清隆〕に呈し、先つ露条

約に関し　御前会議を開かん事を請求したるに、黒田伯は山県内務大臣〔有朋〕の帰朝を待つて処分する所あらん事を約

したり。山県伯帰朝して既に週日を経るに黒田伯は未だ何等の決する所を見ず。本大臣去十一日内閣に於て黒田

伯に面し伯に質すに前日の事を以てせるに、伯は断言して曰く、条約改正は八月二日の内閣会議の決定に基き之

を断行すべく、其終局に至るまで復た閣議を開くを要せずと。夫れ八月二日の閣議に於て決定せるは左の一件の

みなりしは貴大臣閣下の記臆〔ママ〕する所なる可し。即ち大隈伯〔重信〕が外交告知文中外国出身云々は帰化外国人を云ふの意

なりとの事を外国政府に通知す可く、且つ其改正告知文を予め内閣に提出す可しと約諾せるの一事のみ。其他に

於ては
〔警〕
井上農商務大臣の発議に基き条約履行期限、即ち明治二十三年二月〇日の期限を延期する事、及び
伊藤枢密院議長の発議に因り条約改正の問題を枢密院に御下問なる可き事　の二事にして、此二事は議決には至
らざりし。

八月二日の内閣会議は実に上文に陳言するの外なし。爾来大隈外務大臣は其約諾したる外交告知文の修正文を内
閣に提出したるを聞かず。而して総理大臣黒田伯は改正談判の終局に至るまで復た会議を開くの必要なしと断言
したり。若し条約改正中重要の問題に関しても各大臣が意見を呈するに及ばずとなすならば、何の故に外交告知
文修正の事を閣議に付したりや。是れ本大臣の怪訝に堪へざる所とす。若し実に黒田伯は此重大なる問題を挙げ
て大隈外務大臣に一任し他の各大臣をして嘴を容れしめずとの事なれば、本大臣復た何をか言はん。只た本大臣
は国務大臣の職を尽して已まんのみ。然れとも重要の政務は天皇陛下の親しく聴き玉ふ可きものにして、内閣に
玉座の設あるは此に因るに非ずや。況んや条約改正の問題に関しては、曩に徳大寺侍従長を以て速に会議を開く
べしとの　勅意を黒田総理大臣に伝へ玉ひしは本大臣の親しく侍従長に聞く所とす。聖意既に此の如し、宜く速
に内閣会議を開き　陛下の臨御を仰ぎ御親裁に基き国是を一定せん事、本大臣の切望する所とす。斯に曩に黒田
総理大臣に寄送せし意見書写一通を呈示して以て貴大臣の瀏覧に供す。若し夫れ条約改正の全体の問題の如きは
内閣会議に於て本大臣の意見を縷陳し貴大臣の清聴を汗さんとす。貴大臣幸に諒焉、恐惶多罪

〔注〕墨書。

42 「久光親話紀を奉るに就て上申」／島津忠義・島津忠済　明治22年11月19日

十　元老院議官・枢密顧問官時代

久光親話紀を奉るに就て上申

臣忠義臣忠済誠惶誠頓首謹て白す。今春特別の　聖旨を以て故久光か国事上の親話を記し奉呈すへき　恩命を蒙り臣等に於て　聖旨の厚きに感し涙の下るを覚さるに至れり。況んや久光が霊魂に於てをや。誠に　聖旨の隆渥なる臣等唯々言なし。謹て　恩命に従ひ、平素臣等に訓誡せる数千言の中に於て国事上に関して必要緊急なる条項を摘抜し二篇を作り、乙夜の　御覧に供す。仰き願くは　聖念を垂れ玉へよ。臣等本紀を編述するに当り熟ら既往を鑑みて慚愧に堪へさるものあり。如何となれば　皇恩の隆渥なると先人の余光を受け、不肖の身を以て公爵の班を辱ふし、無涯の徳沢に浴するか故に、今日の際聊か微力を竭し奉答の心衷を表せんと欲すと雖も、浅見寡聞にして其言ふ処其施す処を明にすること能はず。常に無為に安して忠誠を欠くの責を逭れさるを愧つ。惟るに故久光は故斉彬の遺志を継紹し、聊か　皇命を奉し竭力する処ありしを賞せられ無限の　聖恩を蒙り一身の光栄のみならす、臣等に至りても其恩波に浴し今日あるを致せり。故に故久光居常臣等に訓誡するに唯　皇室保護　聖徳洽布の一点を以てし、身尚ほ職に居るの念頭を絶たす。只報答の義を欠く事なからん事を誓ひ、以て身家を顧みさるの決心なり。且故久光在世中平素事に触れ折に就て臣等を督励する毎に必す先つ　先帝の聡明英敏にましませしことよりして、中興の偉業を挙け玉ひし御事蹟を談すること懇疑を極め、感憤泣の下るを知らさること多し。其言たるや中古政権武門に遷り　朝威漸く衰へ稍虚器を擁し玉ひ、剰へ当時執政は僭上驕奢を極め、重要なる外国通信の大事も専断允容して、後ちに　奏上せし等の所為は　至尊を蔑如し奉るの甚しと謂ふべし。茲を以て先帝震怒に堪へ玉はす、

276

日夜御憂憤御寝食も安んせられす　烈祖の神霊に対せられ御申訳なしとて御位をすべらせ玉ふべしとまで憂念あ

らせられ、趣を奉承し臣子の情義黙々すべからざるを覚り、故斉彬は断然志慮を決し、意中を密　奏し周旋する

処ありしも、時期切迫し傍観坐視すへきにあらさるを念ひ、安政五戊午の秋上洛し　奏聞する旨あらんと其準備

に勤勉せしか、不幸にして天年を藉さす遽病に罹り臨終、故久光に遺嘱して志を継かしめたり。故久光は遺命の

重を荷ひ百方計画して、遂に文久二壬戌の夏名を出府に仮りて上洛し奏　聞する旨ありしに　叡感斜ならす。浪

士鎮撫の　勅命を奉し、是よりして公然国事に尽力することゝなれり。　先帝如斯　叡慮を煩はし玉ひ、其間数

年稍く大政復旧に垂々たるに臨んて顕著の日を見玉はさりしを遺憾とす云々に至りては、語塞り涙襟を濡せり。

臣等も又倶に言ふこと能はさるなり。是れ故久光か居常憂国の衷情を表するの言なり。之に依りて臣等も亦勤め

て事蹟を問ひ、或は思想を尋問し、他日　皇室に竭すの資とせんと、枢要の条項は書記して以て函に秘めたり。

名て久光親話と題す。其条歎数百条数千言の多きに及へり。其中現今の時勢に関して緊急と認めたる条項を撰択

して、以て二篇を作れり。是れ今回奉呈　天覧に供するものなり。伏て冀くは万機御施政上　聖考の一端ともな

るあらは、故斉彬・久光か霊魂如何はかり乎感戴せん。又臣等に於ても光栄何か之れに若かんや。然り而して臣

等迂愚の身方今の形勢に際し先人の遺意を継紹し、以て奉答の責を竭すこと能はさるを恐れ、兄弟心を協せ思を

潜め、日夜汲々として世態人情の変遷を察するに、内外の事難年月に頻迫し国家の先途実に容易ならさるの時に

臨めり。　然かるに臣等莫大の　聖恩を蒙り上は　先帝及ひ　陛下に報するの道を知らす。実に先霊を辱め家名を

汚すを免れす。是以て去る明治五年壬午夏鹿児島　御巡幸の際、故久光の奉呈したる十四ケ条建議の中当今の事

体に緊切なる条項に基き臣等の愚見を附記し、以て　叡覧に奉供す。仰き願くは乙夜の　御覧を賜ひ芻蕘の蕪言

万一採択を辱ふするあれは、　臣等先人の霊に告け聊か追孝の情を表するに至らんとす。冀くは臣等懇款の微志を

十　元老院議官・枢密顧問官時代

燐み、聖念を垂れ玉はん事を泣願する処なり。誠惶誠恐頓首謹白

明治二十二年十一月十九日

〔注〕墨書。

43　島津久光建議附書（写）

明治（22）年（11）月（19）日

正二位公爵島津忠義

従四位公爵島津忠済

久光建議の附書

一至尊御学問之事

久光建議説明の略に曰く　天子の御学問は他なし　皇国固有の大道を講明せられ御修身の学を先んぜられ、治国平天下の要旨を講究せられ、善悪曲直を明にし、忠邪の分を弁へ玉ひ、軽易の御挙動なく暁然として[ママ]道の正に趨せ玉ふに在り云々。親話記に曰、御成学の後は博く和漢洋古今の歴史を諳んじ玉ひ、万機の政務に就て時勢人情に則り古今に徴し御親裁あるを要とす云々。或は歴史は政務の亀鑑にして寸時も欠くべからざるは多弁を要せす。殊に維新の不図は開闢未曽有の大業にして、当時の世態も又内外の艱難ありて名状すべからざるも、此時に当り　先帝は不世出の明君に渉せられ、中古以来政権覇府に遷り　皇威は在れとも無きか如く、稍虚器を擁し玉ふも厭はせられす、夙夜国難の頻至を憂憤あらせられ千緒万端辛酸を嘗め玉ひ　聖慮を以て諭命を下させられしも、幕府の政弊積りて振わず。年月に統御の術を失ふを　叡聞ありて終に頼むへからさるを　叡断あらせられ、密かに有為の牧伯を御誘導ありて故斎彬等か如きにも密　旨を下し賜ひ、或は有志の人士を鼓舞

43 島津久光建議附書(写)

振作あらせられ数年の間一日の如く百方　叡意を脳し玉ひ[ママ]、遂に維新の大業成るに垂々たるに臨んて　崩御あらせられ、実に千歳の遺憾と申すも愚なる次第なり。　幸に　陛下の威徳天時人事に応感し年ならずして大業成るに及ひ、国家の基本定まり万民徳沢を蒙るに至りたる迄、前後の御事蹟は最も後世の模範となるは無論我国歴史中最大緊要の事蹟にして、古人の勲績を表し、今人の規鑑ともなるべければ　勅撰の体裁にして一大正史を御編製あらまほしく、然らは此間　王事に勲労ある面々は生死を問はす、如何許か　聖徳を奉仰なるべし。特に　先帝に対せられては御追孝の第一にして実に万世の亀鑑、天下蒼生の鴻益ならむ。是れ則ち実学御講習の一端ならん云々。　就ては此際　特命を以て御手許に一局を開かせられ　先帝に奉事し、兼て前後の実事に方れる親王方をして総裁に置かせられ、且つ現に国事に当れる旧公卿旧諸侯其他各藩当時時事に預りたる輩にして、在世の者を集めて編纂に従事せしめ、弘く彼我の事実を質議綜索して誤謬遺脱なき一大正史を編纂あらせられんことを希望す。　就ては我一家の事蹟より端緒を開き、親子共に前時の得失を顧慮すべし云々の趣、[臣]等に於ても其言の不可ならさるを信じ、去る明治十八年より一家の事蹟編集に従事したりしに、一昨二十年に及ひ更に嘉永巳[ママ]丑以来国事執掌の始末を編纂奉呈すべきの特命を辱ふし、一家の光栄何そ之に若かん。　爾来家人を督して日夜編纂に従事し、切に成功の期を急く処なり。　仰き翼くは此際　御手許に一局を設けさせられ、今後　特命を以て諸家に於て編纂奉呈したる記録は勿論、汎く諸士百家の記録を網羅して、一大正史及ひ当時国事に竭力したる輩の詳伝等御編纂あらせらるべき旨　勅命を下させられんことを奉翼望候。

立国本張紀綱事

久光建議説明の略に曰く、本条は立国の大綱にして則ち国体を揺揆せす　皇統一系万古革命なく、綱常明に礼

義を尊ひ、廉恥を重んし民心を維持し、政令正且つ大ならさるへからす云々。臣等本条に基き、現今の形勢を

稽ふるに　陛下登極爾来百事緒に就き、旧例古格当世に便ならさるものは宜しく時に従ひ機に応し作新改良あ

らせられ、或は遡りて　祖宗の遺典に則り、或は遠く範を海外各国に求め玉ひ、皇猷日に新に月に盛にして実

に千載の遺典挙らさるなきか如くなりしも、内外の機運頻迫し時宜利ならさること多く、亦臣僚中忠亮の誠を

失ふ者も尠からす。終に方今の人情形勢を馴致し、国本未た立たさるに人心の乖離を来し、官民和せす、民力

日に月に貧弱に陥り、細民に至りては殆んと流離顛沛凍餒に頻する者多く、加之人心浮薄に赴き軽躁利に趨り、

敦厚の風漸く薄らき一向外国の典章政令を模倣し、毫も国性に基き国基を立つることを知らす、外国の典範

に拠り国体を創造せんことを翼望するものゝ如し。是以て人心更に定着せす、各自偏辟の理論を主唱し、転々

煽惑を極め往々民政革命の暴論を口にするの気風を慕ふに遷遷したり。是に依りて紀綱振はす、制令訓諭頻繁

に過き、人民適従する処を知らす。為めに改廃常ならす。随て遵奉の誠心厚からす、年々違法の者幾万の多き

に及へり。此の如き形勢にして推移するときは終に何れの境遇に至らんとするや、実に震慄に堪へさるなり。

畢竟維新爾来国本確定せす、外国の文物に恋々として深く国家の大本を顧慮せざりしに起因せりと謂はさるを得

す。若し現今の姿に放任するときは遂に不測の変動を惹起し、恐れ多くも　皇室の尊厳を傷くるに至らんこと

を憂懼に堪へざるなり。仰き冀くは既往現今将来に徴し玉ひ、速かに巨僚を召して弘く諮詢を遂け玉ひ、国家

の大憲に基き　聖裁以て後来の国基を竪立し玉はんことを奉翼望候。

定服制厳容貌事

久光説明の略に曰く、服制容貌は内外の弁を明にし貴賤の等を分つ所以にして、正政の要典治国の大経、最も

忽にすへからざる云々。是を以て更に旧制に因て適冝の服制を定め、皇国の皇国たる本色を明にすべし云々。

本条に基き臣等現今の事態を稽ふるに、今や万国開市の途大に開け、致富の道便なるを以て国年月に富饒の域に進むべきの理なるに、僅々少数の人民にして一時の豪富を致したる者なきにあらざるも、概するに国民の多くは貧弱に傾き困頓凍餒の徒日々可に増加するの形況あり。是れ他なし。近来貴賤ともに華美に趨り、驕奢に流れ、国力民力の程度を顧みず、贅余の物品年月に輸入を増し、輓近に及ひ僅に輸出入の平均を得るか如きも依然金銀の濫出年々一年として絶る期なく、殆んと正貨の影を収め、全く紙片に変せんとするの虞なきを保せす。其他濫出の因由種々百端なるも、就中近来服制を彼に模擬するに至り毛布器玩の類々彼に擬するに及ひ、其費耗亦幾千なるを知らめに一層濫出の勢を促かしたるか如し。加之近頃女服髪飾の輸入巨多にして、之か為す。殊に恐れ多くも　皇后陛下の御服の如きは巨万の高価を以て外国に調製せられたりと伝へ、猥りに事実を構造して華奢を人に誇るの傾あり。聞く者も又羨望の念を絶たす、転々相下らざらんとするの勢を馴致し、一物を購ふには一物之に伴ふか如き事実ありて、金貨濫出の原因となり、人情の赴く処下之れに倣ふて通情にして、大小吏員の婦女、或は少しく生計のらしむるの媒介となるの傾あり。上の好む処下之れに倣ふて通情にして、大小吏員の婦女、或は少しく生計の途ある者は各競ふて洋風を模せんとするに傾向したり。就中婦女子に至ては外飾を事とするの情切なるか故、益貧弱に陥之を誡止するは甚た難しとする処なり。然かるに畏こくも曩きに　皇后陛下は　令旨を下し玉ひ、従来の女服醜猥に過くるを以て旧慣に基き着袴の制に復させられたき　御赴旨にして、固より欧米の風俗を模し奢侈を極めしめ玉ふの　御意にあらざりしも、伝ふる人は強て御誘導あらせらるゝものゝ如き説を為すに至れり。且つ伝聞に拠れは外国交際上不都合の廉あるか故、服制を改め外人の歓心を買ふの赴旨を以て　陛下より御誘掖あらせられたき云々の旨某大臣の上言に因りて、御否やなからも召させらるゝことゝなりたりと。或は某の大臣

十　元老院議官・枢密顧問官時代

か或る女官と密議して内外より迫り奉れりと処説喧雑聞くに堪へす。果して某大臣の上言実ありとせは、之れ

何等の言そや。国交上男女の服制を改めされは外国の親睦を保ち難しとせは、寧ろ交際を絶つに若かす。若し

外人を接遇するか為め彼の国風に模擬変更せされは障碍ありとせは、何そ独立の精神に乏しきや。素より本邦の風俗は野蛮

裸体の民にあらす。上下貴賤の序を失わす、式礼の服亦定制ありて乱れさるは遙かに欧米の制に超へたり。就

中従来宮廷の女服は外観の美飾優佳を極めたるは洋人にして、尚ほ且つ之を賞するもの多し。曽て海江田元老[信義]

院議官に聞くに、議官欧州巡回の命を奉し、偶々澳国の鴻儒スタイン氏に面談せしに、氏　皇国の風慣を賛美

して措かす、特に宮廷の女服は優美高尚世界に冠絶す。然れとも未た現に着服の女人を見ることなきを遺憾に

思ひたりしに　小松宮殿下御息所御同道澳都に御来遊ありしに、始めて宮廷女服を召せらるゝを拝見するこ

とならんと心喜しく、同感の者共打連れて御出迎に出てたりしに、豈に図らんや固有の女服を召さゝりしや、返す々々も残念に堪へさ

る次第なりき。故に諸人の失望言ん方なく、如何なれは国風の女服を召さすして欧州

の女服なりき。若し国風の女服を召せ玉ふものなりせは、如何計か諸人の欽仰も深かるべかりしに、然らさり

しを以て人々も種々の非評を伝へて聞くに堪へす。抑も国各々固有の服制ありて天然身体に相応するものなれ

ば、如何に立派に妝ひたりとも他国の服を着くるときは自らに身に添はさるの心持せり。故に御息所も国風の女

服を召せられしなは一層御体貌も優尚なるべかりしも、洋服なりしを以て毫も尊貴の御方とは見奉らす、誤て

下賤の婦女に比するの悪言を聞きしことあり。実に御気毒に存するなり。此の如き理由あるを以て一事一物国

風を廃改することは慎むべきなり。然かのみならす現今欧州の女服は身体の栄養に適せす、亦た経済上尤も不

利なり。故に当時已に女服改良論を唱ふるもの尠からす。今遽かに実効を見さるも一二世を経さる間には必す

欧州の女服は一変する期あるべし。之れ婦女は天性愚痴多く、容易に事を勘別するを得す。徒に世人の毀誉を恐れて強情を張るも、早晩感発するの期に至るや疑なからん。而して将来改良の女服は予め願望は日本宮廷の女服を以て世界中女服の模範たらしめんと欲す。故に議官帰国の後は、宜く洋風の女服を抑へ国風に復せられたし。聞く処に由れは近来　皇后陛下も洋風の女服を召さるとぞ。之れ何等の思召に出てしや知らざるも、国風を変するは国体を革むるの端なり。決して軽々しく思ふべからす。速かに旧に復せられ全国の婦女をして皆な範を陛下の御体貌に採らしめ玉はんことを願へり。之れ帝国は上範を示して下之に伴ふを以て本体とす。故に男子は　皇帝陛下を奉仰、女子は　皇后陛下を奉仰、座作進退皆上に倣ひ、身心一致、愛敬の情あるこそ希望する処なり云々と聞くことありて、大に感発するの情あり。外人に於てすら国風を保するの必要を説けり。何そ況んや帝国臣民に於てや。決して軽忽視すべからさるなり。然のみならす身体の生養に適し、往々外人にして我衣服を着くる者勘からす。然るを何の必用ありてか衛生不適経費莫大なる洋風に革むるとは、其理由を解すへからさるなり。然かるに猥りに俗を破り、国をして貧弱に導き、且つ衛生上不適なりとせは毫も彼の服制を羨むに足らさるなり。依て女服に於ては　皇后陛下を初め奉り、固有の服制に復せらるゝときは金貨濫出の一源を塞き、国俗をして華奢に流れしめず、民力を養長し、兼て国風を保守して国基を継ぐの道たるべし。仰き冀くは断然復旧の　令旨を発せさせられ、先つ一般の婦女をして篤く御趣意を奉承せしめられんことを。是れ故久光か平素仰望する処にして、亦臣等の熱望する処なり。須らく速かに　御裁決奉冀望候。

一　正学術事

久光建議説明の略に曰、夫れ漢土は古より学校を設け、才を養ひ、士を造る者必す聖賢教学の道を以てし、忠

十　元老院議官・枢密顧問官時代

信を主とし、礼義を先し、徳行純一言行一致経国の大才を養成するを要す云々。　皇国は固有の大道あれは相合一して以て国体を維持すべきなり云々。　臣等本条に基き考ふるに方今一大緊急の条項にして、一日も忽視すべからざるの要件なるのみならず、国家の盛衰強弱の本源は皆教育の基本立つと立たざるにあり。　仮令教育の制度周備し、智識を磨き才気を長すべきも、人情菲薄に流れ国体の如何んを弁せす、徳義を尊ひ廉恥を重んするの風習を破り、一身の利達に汲々し、国家を愛護するの念を失ふに至りては、将た学術正明なりと謂ふを得ざるべし。　聞く処に由れは、欧州各国大中小の学校に於ても悉く其国固有の学を基本とし、交るに技術の学を以ひ、国性を発達愛重するの設けなりと。　蓋し其国固有の学は乃ち建国の歴史にして国家の建礎を審明せしめ、国祖の勲蹟を感戴せしめ、一国独立の思想を各人の脳裏に浸染せしめ、而して後各方向を定め、何れの国の学に就くを要す。　是れ一身一家を経営し、各自百般の目的を貫徹するも畢竟国民協同富強の策を講究し、国体を鞏定し、国威を海外に輝かすに外ならす。　然るに現今我国の学制は主として範を外邦に採るに偏し、国学を授くるを以て本義とせず、反て外邦の学を本義とするものゝ如し。　是以て近来学識卓越と称する者も啻に外邦の学術に通達すると謂ふに過きす。　毫も国家の本体を明弁したる者を聞くこと稀なり。　此の如く年月に本を忘れて他に耽り国家の本体を重んせす、猥りに外国の体性に深酔して教ゆるに外邦の制教を以てし、導くに外邦の習俗を以てし、転々少壮を煽惑して年一年として人心軽浮に奔り、徒に他人の皮想を学ひて一身の本分を全ふせざる者蓋々として皆一般ならざるはなし。　今にして此風潮を挽回し、一日も速かに国家の本体を確立し、純然たる国家教育の大本を確立し理を審明し学制を一新し教育の方針をして確乎不抜の基礎を定めさせられ　陛下親く国民薫陶の　大命を総攬あらせられ、毫も他の施政と混同し時宜に従ひ変更伸縮するの関係を絶ち、純然たる国家教育の大本を確立し玉はすんは、今日の如き政務の弛張当務大臣の更迭に従ひ変転極きものとせは、如何そ国体を保存し国民愛

284

43　島津久光建議附書（写）

護の精神を発揮するに違あらんや。若し今日の姿に放任する時は爾来人心益々壊乱し、国礎年月に揺動するに及ひ終に誤国の因を開くに至らんや知るべし。是れ故久光平素臣等に訓戒し居常憂悶最も切なりし処なり。仰き冀くは速かに臣僚を召して弘く諮詢を遂け玉ひ、国体に基き国学を審明し　聖裁以て教育の方針を鞏定し、国民をして国家愛重の本心を養長あらせられんことを奉冀望候。

慎択人才事

久光建議説明の略に曰く、治国の要は賢才を用るより先なるはなし。然して人を知るは聖賢も難しとする処、故に之を毀誉に求れは愛憎に出つ、是を功状に考ふれは功詐横生す。其本を要するに至公至明にあるのみ。夫れ一君子を進むれは衆君子進み、一小人を進むれは衆小人進む。是れ治を致す者、人を用るに慎む所以なり。今や上　朝廷より下府県に至り登庸其人に非らす、政を蒙り国を誤り、上は　祖宗千戴の基業を敗り、下は生霊億兆の身命を拭ふ、其任に耐へざるの致す所なり。漢土宋の神宗韓琦富弼を棄てゝ王安石を用ひ、旧法を変革して終に靖康の禍乱を致したるか如き、是当今の明鑑なり云々。臣等本条に基き稽ふるに、維新の始め旧時の陋制を破り、家格門閥の制限を廃し弘く人才を登庸せられしは、実に時勢人情に応せられたるものにして、僅に二十余年を経へて今日の成蹟を奏したりと雖とも、往々乱雑に流れ、随て治平に馴れて情弊を生し、牽連因縁制すべからす。為めに世人をして情縁に流るゝの弊を歓せしむるに及べり。是れ維新草創の際勤　王の諸藩主として　朝廷に奉事し、万般の政務年月に繁劇を極め、勢ひ偏重に傾くは免れざる処なり。然れとも　聖明の治蹟固より万民に普及す。何人と雖とも才力を伸はし志望を達するに道なからんや。況んや輓近官吏登庸規則の設けありて情弊に流るゝの途を塞かれたりと雖とも、概ね下司以下の任用に止まり、要路の大臣に至て

十　元老院議官・枢密顧問官時代

は未た藩閥任用の情弊を絶つに至らざるの嫌なきにあらず。　固より　聖意を奉体して国政を預る者は義親疎を

分たす、情厚薄を問はざるべく、才力任に適する者に至ては何人を別たざるべきは論を俟たざるなり。況ん

や　聖意の在せらるゝ処は全国人民均しく　仰戴する処なれはなり。　然れとも既往の事に至ては亦た人情を傷

ふの跡なきを得す。已に国家の大憲を制定し立憲の政を布かせらるゝに及んでは、亦た従前の情弊を絶ち、人

民の冀望を満さゝるを得す。　然らは則ち政党内閣の組織に倣ひ大臣の進退も政党の推薦に出んとする乎、何そ

夫れ然らんや。官吏任免の特権は典憲の明文に基き動かすべからざるを哉。　然れとも後来依然人民の興望に逆

ひ、二三臣僚の意衷を以て官吏の進退を議するの弊を絶たゝ[ママ]るに於ては恐多くも　聖意を汚すの虞なきを保

せざるなり。　特に現今の形勢人情より推考するに、事茲に至るに及んては必す人心の乖逆を来すに至らん。之

を思ひ彼を惟へは先途の事決して軽きにあらざるを知るなり。　仰き冀くは　陛下至明を以て時勢の変遷を察し

玉ひ、　宜しく　聖慮を定め玉ひ、弘く巨僚に諮詢を垂れ、情義に泥まず勲績に偏せす、国務の才力を有する者

を撰抜して輔弼の責に服せしめ玉はんこと、尤も現今の急務なりと信す。　速かに　聖断あらせられて忠亮の臣

僚を挙け、国政に任し玉はんことを奉冀望候。

謹外国交際審可弁彼我之分事

久光建議説明の略に曰く、　外国交際は時勢止むを得さるに出つと雖とも、猶ほ彼我の弁に於ては是を厳明にし

是を待つに誠信を以てし、是に交はるに礼義を以てすべし。今や皇威稍衰へ西洋の勢猖獗、剰さへ都下に雑居

し、蹄輪相交はり屋室相望み、甚しきに至りては婚姻をも許され、彼我の弁あるを知らす。　歎慨に堪ゆべけん

や云々。　臣等本条に基き稽ふるに、外国交際は嘉永癸丑ノ年幕府締盟ノ条款其宜しきを失ひしのみならず、専

43　島津久光建議附書（写）

断允許ノ後奏聞に及ひし専僭上放恣の所為　先帝震怒国人憂憤鎖攘の説四方に起り終に幕府の罪を討するに及

ひしも、維新爾後世界の大勢を審かにせしより人情遽かに一変し、鎖攘の議は跡を収め和交通商年々に繁く一

時に人意を刺激せしより又彼我の分を弁別せす、取捨長短の説を誤まり彼の文物制度を摸倣するに恋々し遂に

今日の姿に転換し、甚しきに至りては彼を尊重し我を鄙下するの人情となり、一事一物外邦に求め外人に請ふ

に及ひ殆んと国権失墜の域に陥らんとす。之カ為め国性を傷け民情を害するの跡勘からす、豈に猛省せざるべ

けんや。剰さへ現今条約改正談判の説起るや可否の論蜂の如くに起り所在囂々頗る喧雑を極め、愚夫愚婦とい

へとも尚可否を唱ふるの勢を馴致し、終に今日云ふべからさるの結局を見るに至れり。臣等窃かに其情状を観

察するに、今日の論者は彼我何れも正鵠を失ふの論にして倶に国家を愛重するの念薄しと云はざるべからず。

故に今後国民にして彼我の分を厳にし交際の本義を審かにせずんは殆んと国家の大事を誤つに至らんとす。素

より宣戦講和の可否は　聖裁に存して敢て臣民の分として猥りに予議すべきの限りにあらずと雖も、一旦締結

成るに及んては禍福幸不幸を蒙むるは君民共に相同しく、実に至重至大永遠の利害禍福に関するは論を俟たざ

るなり。故に宜しく目下の人情を諮詢し玉ひ人意の帰向する処を慮り其宜しきを採り、以て　親裁あらせられ

すんは他日大患の基にして内外の至難之より起るや明かなり。因て目下姑らく時宜を与へ徐々に興論の帰する処

を鑑み玉ひ、専ら内国の進運を促かし真に彼我対等の国権を養長するの時に及んで後決行せられて何の遅き事

か之れあらんや。果して然りとせば後日外国交際上紛情を生ずるときは、国民一体となり其責に当るを以て禍

福利害君臣共に安んずる処あればなり。仰き願くは深く永遠の利害得喪を慮り玉ひ、速かに適任の者を挙げて

今回改正談判の処置を為さしめ、爾後慎重を専らとし決して軽しく計議に渉らしむることなく、内を充実して

然る後に外に対抗するの方略を定め、臣僚をして深く既往将来の大計を服膺せしめ玉はんこと実に目下の至務

287

十　元老院議官・枢密顧問官時代

なるべし。是れ居常故久光か内外交渉の至重至大なる所以を憂慮して臣等に懇諭する処なり。目下の事難に当り当時の訓戒を念ひ衷心切々思に堪へさらんとす。冀くは　聖念を垂れ玉はんこと伏して奉冀望候。

開言路之事

久光建議説明の略に曰、言路を開くは王道の要治安の源なり。虞舜は誹謗木を設け帝徳を広ふし、晋文は与人の誦を聴て以て覇業興れり。又大雅に芻蕘に詢ふの言あり、洪範に謀庶人に及ふの言あり。是れ聖賢の治を成す務を衆に詢ひ、敢て忽にせさる所以なり。今や議院の設けありと雖とも言路壅塞の患を免れす。普く士庶人の上書直言務めて上達することを命し玉ふべきなり云々。臣等本条に基 き考ふるに、現今言路の開通は之を往時に比すれは倶に論するの比にあらずと雖とも、深く其情体を察するに言路開通の名ありて言路貫徹の実を欠くの弊なきにあらず。今其一例を掲くれば、凡そ国事を建議するものは元老院に於て受収陳言するの道開かれたりと雖とも、其手続甚た煩縟を極め往々官司の手を経るを以て、中途為めに意思を撓め当初の趣意を達することを得ざることなしとせす。且つ聞く処に拠れは、適々建言せしものもあるも同院に於て二三議官の調査を経へ事柄に依り主務省に送致し、或は同院に留置き更に可否の議を下すことなし。故に幾十百回の建議を為すあるも只一片の陳情に止まり其効否に至ては固より知るを得す。徒に労苦して実効なしとせは人誰か忠実の誠を表する者あらんや。是に由り考ふるに、従前上疏建議にして幾千に上るべきも未だ敢て　陛下の親覧に奉供たること ありしや否や、是れ居常故久光か憂念する処にして、言路開通の名ありて実なきは寧ろ名なくして実あるに若かす。昔時人民官司に訴ふる者は死生予期すべからさるの艱難に頻せんも亦其目的を貫き、或は官司を進退し、或は冤横を伸雪したるの例は尠からす。此の如く言路開通の道備はらすと雖とも、反て下情上達の実効を

43　島津久光建議附書(写)

奏したるにあらずや。然れとも今日の如く言論の陳情容易なるを慢り、公私共に事を構ふの情況あるを以て一旦応答可否の議を允すに至ては、終に勢ひ制すべからざるに及はんこと顕然たりと雖も、又幾多の建言者中に於ては其事の精粗当否あるは言を俟たざるも、必す善悪の間人心の枉屈伸縮に於て参考の裕益あるは論を俟たざるなり。時に今後は時勢の推移自ら言論の箝束も年月に寛容なるに当りて、尚ほ下情上達せす人言欝塞するときは、仮令法制厳正なりと雖も瞑々衷中誹議を逞ふするのみならす、巧みに法網を潜り新聞に演説に著作に一層喧囂を極むるに至らん。斯の如くなるときは人情益隠険に赴くや疑なし。況んや議会開設の後は言論著作の自由自ら寛厳を異にするに及ひ、人民の上疏請願の権利も従て伸張を主とするに至りては、寧ろ名義を作為して事実を疎隔するの不可なるを知るなり。若し体裁に泥み情感を害するに及んては言路開通の実将たして何くに存するや。故に今後は務めて人意を感動せしめ徒に事を設けて官府の煩労を促かすか如き弊も、言を言ふものをして自ら戒飾する処を知らしむるに若かざるなり。故に今後国民の捧るゝ処の書にして、親覧に供すべきものは近侍をして親しく受収応答せしめ玉ひ、或は親しく召して　内謁を賜ひ務めて感戴の情を収め賜へば、人をして感激の心を深からしめ、一事一言皆な　聖念を留めさせらるゝものと聞かは人誰か恩徳を感泣せざるものあらんや。然かれば人々反求して志慮を凝らし決して軽々しく言を発せざるのみならず、又其陳言忠誠の真情に発するものとせば世事に効益あるや論を俟たざるなり。之れ言を慎み言を言はしむるの道なり。若し事の煩冗を厭ひ、或は従前の慣行に倣ひ徒に体面を粧ふに及んては反て要求強願に出つるもの多く、之を箝束するときは議論激烈に出て制すべからざるに及ひ終に其措置に窮するに至るべし。故に今後は飽まて弘く言路を開くと倶に、人をして情意を伸ばさしむるの道を定めさせられんこと政務の円滑を期し　聖恩の隆渥を感銘せしむるの要点にして、尤も今日の至務ならん。是れ臣等か先人の訓戒を服膺して特に熱望する処なり。冀くは速

十　元老院議官・枢密顧問官時代

かに巨僚に令して上下情意の貫徹する処を　聖裁あらせられんことを奉冀望候。

慎讞獄正賞罰事

久光建議説明の略に曰、讞獄は訴訟を聴断し情意を評決するを言ふなり。夫れ法官たるものは意を公にし心を

正ふし道を直し状を明にし、上に冤獄なく下に枉民なきを要とす。賞罰は国家の大典所謂紀綱是れなり。賞罰

正しからさるときは天下何を以て治安ならしむや云々。臣等本条に基き考ふるに、今や司法の大権確定して讞

獄の制亦備はり聴訟の法漸次に泰西の法規を準用して、公開裁判代言○弁護毫も冤枉の所為なし。之を往時に比

すれは人権を貴むの実蹟歴々徴すべしと雖も、一時に外邦の法制を模するに急にして只其形貌を取りて其実情

を穿たざる処なしとせす。　特に我国俗慣行の特異なるを問はす、一概に法理の可否を取捨するを以て、下民に

至ては反て典章の煩冗にして資力の足らざることを恐れて空しく横屈に沈むの情なしとせす。　特に昔時と違ひ

一訴を起し一訟を託するも起訴及ひ代言弁護の耗費に堪へす。　通俗訴訟を起す者は産を破り家を潰すの歎を聞

くこと勘からす。　一時健訟の風行はれ為めに彼我の情意を破り風俗を変し、現今往々人をして徳義を忘れ利欲

に流れしむるは蓋し讞獄の更革人意に適合せす、為めに来したるの弊俗と云はざるを

以て諄良撲朴の良民は横屈に安んし、奸譎隠悪の徒は巧に法網を利用して以て専恣を極むるの跡なきに非ざる

なり。　特に法官其人の如きも、重もに泰西の法律を研究したるも我旧俗慣習に諳熟せざる者勘からす。　為めに

典則に拘泥し、情意を参酌せざるの弊なきを保せざるなり。　故に往々冤屈を歎し横虐を怨むる者も少なしとせ

す。是以て近来益々越訴に出つる者多く法官は瑣末の差誤を自任し、訴人ハ亦上告の権を自負し、交々法衙を

煩はし法典を弄し年月に繁忙を極め転々底止する処を知らざらんとす。　是れ豈に紀綱振明なりと謂ふべけんや、

思はざるべからす。

又曰、賞罰の典讞獄の法、亦洋法に倣ひ刑典當を失するに至る云々。臣等本條に基き考ふるに、法は國の治安を維持するの要具なり。故に何れの國と雖も法制の備具せざるは國家紊乱の基なり。然れとも國各舊慣の法令ありて國民之に安んして之れか爲めに治平なれは假令法文備はらすと雖も亦其實行の力あるを貴しとす。故に凡そ法令を廃改するには其利を見るも其害を見ざれは改むへからす、其害を見るも其利存すれは廃すべからす。須く慎密覈査し以て其必要欠くべからざるにあらざれは決して軽忽に改廃すべからざるものなり。維新以來一時の風潮に促され僅かに二十有余年、其間百般の制度其便不便を問はす、挙て舊慣を廃改して泰西の主旨を遵行せざるはなし。固より民意に副ひ民利を増進するの意に出てたるべしと雖も、未た要せざるの法令を出た

し、未た害なきの法を廃し以て今日の不便を来せしのみならす、却て習俗を壊り人意を乱し法を施さんか爲め法を作るの弊を生し、法に重ぬるに法を以てし、殆んと底止する処を知らざるに至らしめ、益々民利を妨け國政を撓め、云ふべからざるの害毒を後世に伝へんとするの情勢あり。然るに教化普からす、民智未た深からす。上下倶に目前の理説に眩惑し、挙て欧米の文明に擬せんと欲し、終に今日の弊端を啓くに至りしは、畢竟彼我の弁識なきの罪なりと雖も、要路事を執る者に於て之を誘導馴致するの力足らざりしに由るものと云ふべし。蓋泰西諸國の文明と唱ふるは彼國の人情習慣に則り數百年來薫養化成の功を積みしものにして、一朝一夕の成蹟にあらす。然かるを一時に其風を移輸し彼の文物制度に摸倣し以て國民を風化し彼と競衡の街に立たと欲するは、素より一國の成立人情に背違するの過失と謂はざらんや。故に今日に於ては從來の法令にして民度に適せす徒法の實あるものは務めて之を参酌折衷して國情風慣に違はしめす、國民をして務めて遵奉の難を覚へざらしめ、又新法を施行せんと欲せは、審かに人情に適し民智に遠ざかざらんことを評定し、決して法を布くの

十　元老院議官・枢密顧問官時代

美を飾らす、法を施すの実を収め、民智の進歩に応して以て国家の治安を保維するの主旨を失はさらんことを欲す。是臣等か既往現今に徴して将来に冀望するの要領たり。仰き願くは深く　聖旨を垂れ巨僚を召して弘く諮詢し、存すべきは之を修正し廃すへきは之を漸止し、以て臣民をして一日も早く清明の治下に棲息せしめ玉はんことを奉冀望候。

軽租薄斂之事

久光建議説明の略に曰、凡そ乱を致すの原由は多端なりと雖も、重斂横税より甚しきはなし。細民何を以て堪ゆべけんや。貧民納税に耐へざるときは死を顧みす、衆を集め党を結ひ潰叛暴動に至る、慎まざるへけんや。今や農市の細民殆んと堪へざるに至れり。宜しく苛酷の税を免し蘇息せしめ玉ふべきなり云々。臣等本条に基き現今の事実を観察するに、維新以来百度緒に就き政務の繁劇内外に亘り年一年より煩多を極む。是以て爾後貢租も旧時の如くなるを得す。旧税を増課し新税を起し随て収納の法も厳密に赴き、殆んと其繁重に堪へざるの情況なきにあらす。特に税務を改廃するや概ね範を泰西に採り、取捨折衷亦国情に応せす、民智に適せさるの跡なきにあらす。為めに民力凋弊し、細民に至りては凍餒の域に沈むの談を聞くことあり。故に果して現今徴租の程度は民力に相応するや如何に至りては固より深く探究すべきの要領なるを以て、軽しく寛苛何れに存せざるはなし。畢竟現今の政務を執るに於ては亦昔時の如く軽租薄税到底国家維持の経費を支ゆべからすと雖も、熟ら民間の情体を鑒みるに減税軽租民力休養の論囂々噴々として、匹夫匹婦も之を口にするを知らすと雖も、　民心を擾乱し民力を凋衰せしむるの実蹟あるに至りては豈に何そ黙々すべき事ならんや。固より治国の要は人民をして生業に安んせしめ、国をして富強を致さしむるに外ならさるべし。然るを察せす猥りに税法を改

更新設して以て益々負担を重ねしむるに至りては、終に国家を空耗し人民を困頓せしむるものにして最も鑒み

ざるべからす。特に故斉彬か言に民富めは君富むの語は君たるものゝ遺忘すべからざるの語なりと。故久光は

始終此言を服膺し、臣等を訓戒せり。臣等も亦先人か訓誠の言最も世務に適切なるを感銘し、居常念頭に留め

て忘却せす、是以て現今の人情形勢に就て稽ふるに大に訓誠の適実なるを覚ふ。仰き冀くは　聖慮を垂れ目下

の民情を熟思し玉ひ、若し是語にして的実なりとなし玉ふに於ては、速かに臣僚を召して弘く諮詢を遂け玉ひ、

民力に応するの程限を審にし、全般の税法を改廃し以て納税の方法を簡易にし、人民をして課税の負担を軽か

らしむると俱に納租の煩冗を省き務めて民力休養の方針を以て国家維持の要領となし玉はんことを奉冀望候。

詳量出納事

久光建議説明の略に曰、地方の物を生するや数あり人力の物を成すや限りあり、是を取るに度あり是を用ゆる

に節あれは財常に足る。是に反するときは常に不足す。是を以て先王程を立て量入為出、如此なれは災変に遇

ふと雖民窮することなし。財の盈虚は唯節すると節せさるとにあるのみ。今や一般洋風を尊ひ侈大冨溢の政を

主張し、不急の土木を興し財用の盈虚を顧みす、量入為出を良法と謂ふを迂儒の常論とし、妄費濫出の暴政を

謂て姫偉の治法と称し外債を募り、或は華士族の家禄を減損せんとす云々。臣等本条に基き考ふるに、追年国

帑の支出増倍し、一年として財用の余盈を聞くことなく、常に財政困難の歎声上下に普及し一人も国家の富隆

を誇るを聞かざるなり。畢竟此の如く年々財用の欠乏を感し、当務大臣の焦慮を煩はせしは内外の事難常に堪

へす、臨時の支出以て定規の経費を耗消するの事歴夥からすと雖とも、亦猥りに泰西の文物を輸入し、無用の

土木を起し贅用の品物を購ひ、或は教導に託して外人を雇用するか如く、妄費濫出の源を為し転た財用を靡散

十　元老院議官・枢密顧問官時代

したるものなきにあらす。是以て国庫の支出に至ても往々中間政務の変更に伴ひ其程度を越ゆること多く、為めに当初の予算を紊乱し終に支ふべからざるに至り、数年来内外国債を募集し以て不時の急を凌くと雖も、年毎に費途増進して止まる処を知らす。是を以て幾回改革を施行し官吏を沙汰し務めて費用節減の挙あるも僅に一時の名聞を衒ふの形跡にして、未た数日ならざるに前時に倍するの失費を来たし、毫も実際の効験を奏したることなく、殆んと児戯に均しきの談を聞く事なきにあらす。故に幾回の改革も徒らに物情を害するに過きすして毫も政務の補益なきに似たり。畢竟此の如き弊習を生するは、要路大臣の責任軽く事を取捨するの情弊行はれたるに由るものにして、更に政務の方針を確立するに違なく、互に臨時の便宜を主唱し定限を顧みさるの致す処ならん歟。是れ乃ち国庫ノ財用を管理するに量出為入の傾向を為し、多く益々欠乏を来すも至る所以にして避くべからざるの宿弊なりとす。故に去る明治八年の冬故久光か捧けたる書中にも当時の施政上皆責任なし、故を以て事故あらは罪の帰する処なく渾て非を　天皇陛下に帰し奉る不臣の至と云ふべし。夫れ如此なは蒼生何を以て安堵し、国基何を以て鞏固ならんや云々の上言を呈したる所以にして、其本定まらさるを以て末終に乱るゝは免れざるの数なり。故に今日に於ては、宜しく本に反りて欠失を補ひ切に妄費を節約し互に当務の責任を貴ひ慎思猛省するにあらすんば、先途の事歴決して容易ならさるなり。若し来る明治二十三年帝国議会開設の期に及んては、歳計予算の如くは議会の詳決を要するに至らん。此の時に至り政府の弁理宜きを失せは遂に上下の争議を開くを免れす。加之前年の欠乏を咎め将来の節約を主張するに及んては、施政益々至難を感するに至らん。仰き冀くは　聖旨深く事態を鑑み玉ひ、速かに臣僚を召して理財の方法を釐革し、無用を省き贅用を減し、主として無用の官吏を免し不急の土木を廃し空用の外人を解傭し、勉めて節均を厳行し玉ふの　大詔を発しさせられ鋭意宿弊を矯正あらせられんこと、実に目下の急務なるべし。

294

43　島津久光建議附書(写)

須らく速かに　聖断あらせられんことを奉冀望候。

以上十条は故久光か明治五壬申ノ夏本県　御巡幸の際奉呈したる建議十四ケ条の中方今の世態上緊急の要条、及ひ故久光在世中各条に就て説明したる書面の略に基き、臣等現今の人情形勢に適切なる事由を附記し更に臣等の願望を列序し以て　聖覧に奉供す。且臣等方今は勿論将来を推究し前条の主旨を衍釈して、以て目下緊急必要なる条件と認むるものを左に復陳す。

第一　大臣其他枢要の官吏は大義を重んし責任を分ち同心協力して政務を尚議し　聖裁を賛襄すべき旨を誓はしめ玉ふべき事

第二　裁育の制度を改正し国体を明にするの学制を布き、更に文部の組織を更め玉ふべき事

第三　法律規則を簡明にし旧法を廃改し新法を制定することを慎み玉ふべき事

第四　国民の心意を安にし疑心を去り各職に務め業を励み上下の情意を通するの処置を設け、忠君愛国の志念を感発せしめ玉ふべき事

第五　税法を修正して民力を休養し、務めて物産繁殖を奨励し玉ふべき事

第六　政費を節減し諸有諸局を廃合し組織を更革し玉ふべき事

第七　官吏任用の適否を審査し職守を厳明にし、務めて冗員を減省せしめ玉ふべき事

第八　貴賤朝野の驕奢を厳戒し風俗敦厚廉節を重んせしめ玉ふべき事

第九　不用の土木を熄め贅用の品物を廃し質朴倹素を貴ひ、経費を補充するの方法を定め玉ふべき事

第十　官吏の弊風を厳戒せられ所謂上下隔意の弊を一洗し、和衷協同倶に国事に尽さしめ玉ふべき事

第十一　参政権を拡張し国民をして弘く国事に諮詢するの道を開き、相倶に報答の責を負わしめ玉ふべき事

十　元老院議官・枢密顧問官時代

第十二　言論著作出版集会結社の覊束を寛大にし、事を言ふ者をして隠険に流るゝの弊を杜絶し玉ふべき事

以上十二目は臣等先人の遺訓を鑑み目下の情況を観察して以て陳言する処なり。之を約言すれば、則ち国体民情に基かれ守るべきは固く守り革むべきは之を革め務めて国体を失はす民情に戻らす、所謂長を採り短を補ふの主旨に準拠して、以て速かに将来の政策を確定あらせられ、物情を鎮め民心を和し、以て国家の典憲を実行し上下一致盛に経綸を行ふの赴旨に外ならざるなり。若し今日に及んて速かに矯正の道を立つるにあらずんば将来国家の不幸を来さゝらんことを恐るゝなり。仰き冀くは　聖慮を垂れさせ玉わんことを奉伏願候。

〔注〕墨書。『明治天皇紀』第七によれば、42文書の附属書。

44　三条実美宛意見書／島津忠義・島津忠済

忠義忠済謹て案するに凡そ為政の要は大本を知るにあり。　大本とは何ぞや、乃ち国家維持の方針を確定するにあり。　故に国家維持の大本立たさるは恰も人にして方向なきに均し、何そ国権の独立を保維すへけんや。夫れ我皇国は東洋の表に立て古来淬然国基を維持し歴世悠久万古に秀つ。此国体を維持し此民生を安育し、以て永遠不替に国基を確立するは所謂帝国の国是にして臣民の志望なるへし。　故に苟も臣民たる者は国家をして海外と対立せしむるに止まらす、帝国の光輝を海外に宣揚し、海外万国をして欽仰の念を抱かしめさるへからす。　況んや明治元年三月五ケ条の御誓文を宣布し、中外をして国是を確認せしめ玉ふや、悉く国威を海外に輝かし玉ふの旨趣ならさるはなし。　故に上下一致協心同力以て　皇国の国威を発輝し国体を鞏立せんことは、固より登極の初め欽定し玉ふ　聖旨にして、亦列祖に対せられて遺伝の国土民生を統治し玉ふの　聖職なるへし。是以て我忠愛の

明治22年11月

296

臣子も又篤く　聖旨を奉承して賛翼の議を上るへきは其分にして決して其責を辞すること能はさるなり。維新以来時勢の変遷に伴ひ智識を世界に求め大に　皇基を振起し玉ひ、僅に二十余年間にして弘く世界の大局に達観し文物制度又旧来の陋習を破るに吝ならす、已に立憲政体の実施日も又遠からす。之れ百僚克く　聖意を奉体して時弊を矯め文化を進め、勧誘奨励以て今日に至れる所以なりと雖とも、往々進むに懦して繁褥（褥）に堪へす、終に方針を惑乱し、彼我確正の方向を踏ますして各個随意に己の欲する処を遂くるに鋭く、為めに国家の大本を忘れ国性を傷け、民情を破るの跡蹊しとせす。是以て形跡稍々文化を称し開明を唱ふると雖とも、其実を欠くもの多く国力日々に空耗し、民智日々に浅薄に流る、先途を顧みて目下の情勢を察する時、転々憂念に堪へさるなり。是れ全く当初思慮足らすして国性の異同を忘れたるに由るものにして、何を以てか帝国の大本を維持したりと謂はんや。故に今後国家維持の方針を一定し専ら国威を海外に発輝するの目的を貫き何等の事変に際するも確乎として世勢に動揺せす、飽まて　聖旨を欽奉し以て速かに帝国の基礎を竪立せすんは何の時か期すへけんや。若し国性を察せす漫に時務に応するの説を藉りて巧に策謀を用ふるに於ては、依然前轍を踏むの時か免れさるへし、慎まさるへからす。是以て内閣大臣は主として国基を鞏固にし　皇上の徳威を中外に輝かし玉ふことを誓ひ、身心捧て以て其責に当らさるへからす。若し一己の私に泥み経国の要を誤つときは、何の時か内閣必す其道に迷ふは影の形に従ふか如し。　加旃（ママ）　皇国の体は欧米各国と異なり政府の中心竪立するときは恰も衆星之に嚮ふか如し。　天下の人心皆之に集り、左指右揮亦背戻することなきは固有の国性にして東西慣行を均ふせさる処なり。　然るに人情風慣の異同を問はす遽かに欧米特異の制度文物を輸入し吾を化せしめんと欲す、国情に戻

内閣にして其議定まらすんは余響必す下民に及ふは彰乎として明かなり。是以て政其方を失せは人民の方針を確立し、以て国是を一定するの期あらんや。蓋内閣は政務の本原にして国家の安危動静皆其原を内閣の議に発す。　内閣にして其議定まらすんは余響必す下民に及ふは彰乎として明かなり。

297

十　元老院議官・枢密顧問官時代

り人意を害する者勘からす。互に意思を誤想し、官民交々相排戻し上下互に相疎斥し情意を傷け和情を破るに至

る。如此一国中隠然親疎の別を為し、均しく国家の利害を顧察せさるものゝ如き観を為すは果して　聖意を体認

したるものと謂ふへけんや。故に予め人心の趨勢を考へ人智の純雑を慮り、宜く実情を徴し、上下疎隔の意を解

き一致協同国事に当るの精神を表明し、先つ内閣大臣一体となりて内閣の基礎を堅め、各官吏一体となりて各省

院の基礎を堅め、各個人一体を為して全国人民の結合を堅ふし、今後世勢の紛乱を解き、以て将来の大計を確定

し　聖意をして永遠無際の徳沢を欽仰せしめ、立憲の基礎を厳立し上下心を一にして盛に経綸を行はんと欲せは、

宜く既往の失度を鑑み、現在の艱難を顧み、将来の安危を慮り、速かに内閣大臣心を一にして方針を定め、従前

の情緒を絶ちて更に立国の要旨を服膺せす、徒に旧功に泥み前言を重んし、目前の利喪に汲々して以て天下の大

勢を乱すことあらば、内外の事難果して何の時か底止せんや。若し大局の利害を暁らす、苟且の心慮を以て今日

を弥縫せは、再ひ天下紛乱の機宜遂に防くへからさるに至るへし。故に目下の急務は瑣末の政務を是非し局小の

政策を取捨するの時にあらさるなり。宜く内閣大臣の心慮を一定し、其職守を厳明し、以て国家に対するの責任

を保持するの外なきを信す。之れ目下唯一緊急の事件にして一日も速かに閣議を一定し、断然心慮を定め、其職

に当らるゝへし。若し今日の事難力に及はす、到底其任に堪へすとせは宜く後任を推薦し、以て上は　聖旨を奉

安し、下は万民を撫綏せらるにあらされは、何の時か帝国の徳威を海外に宣揚するを得んや。是れ忠義忠済平素

の志願にして又満腔の精神なり。冀くは閣下宜く前意を酌納して速かに裁決する処あれよ。若し採納更に質す処

あらんと欲せは遺漏を拾ひ、更に施政の要領を述へんことを期す。冀くは採否の応答を与られよ。期急を告け条

句意を悉さす宣く諒覧を乞ふ。誠惶謹言

明治廿二年十一月

正二位公爵　島津忠義

45　雑メモ／吉田清成

〔注〕墨書。

内閣総理大臣従一位公爵三条実美殿

従四位公爵　島津忠済

明治(22)年(12)月

埃及近世史

東海散士

京橋区三十間堀博文堂

壱円五十銭

右廿二の十一月廿七日

発売す

────────

明治二十二年十二月調査

有爵者

公爵　　十一名

〔ママ〕
候爵　二十八名

伯爵　　八十名

子爵　百五十名

男爵　百〇五名

合三百七拾四名

〔注〕墨書。

46　条約廃棄論批判の覚書／吉田清成

明治22年

万一にも泰西各国との締約調候後に至り、清国独り不肯旧約を墨守せんとするときは、右の他の各国は最恵国の

一章に依り彼れに利益ある分は清国の分に引付けんとする事の起らさるを保証しがたし（但海関税は泰西各国と

の間の分に従ふとあるからは、強て実場の憂ひはなきかもしれす）。併注意ものなり。

之を思ひ彼れを想へは杞憂千万なり。兎角条約破棄の決心（其結果如何は不問に措き）なからされは断行云々は

不安至極の事なり。

破棄之事は万々不可行。之れ諸外国を敵とし百戦百勝国家を維持し之れか威権を保ち能ふの力なくては不能事也。

此見認なくして口に強碪主義を唱へ、浅識の人々を煽動するは勇に似て至て非なる者、忠に似て不忠、愛国に似

て売国之実ある者なり。破棄の事類例至〔宣〕し。好しあるも場合の異なる事同日之論にあらす。古今万国交際上

の活劇史に疎く、浅学なれとも多才ある者共は往々心得違ひを為し、大事を誤るの例少からす。実に可憂の極な

り。天下を犠牲に供して己れの虚名を博せんと謀るものは国賊なり。嗚呼如何して此難局を救はんや。実に国家

危急存亡之秋也矣。

有感記す　廿二年夏

〔注〕墨書。

47　磯御邸宛請求書／堀之内勘五右衛門

明治23年1月29日

記

一御弓六張
　内
一七部半　壱張
　御代金壱円五拾銭
一七部　　壱張
　御代金壱円五拾銭
一七部　　壱張
　御代金壱円
一五部半　壱張
　御代金壱円
一五部　　三張
　御代金壱円つゝ
合金七円
右之通御坐候也。

十　元老院議官・枢密顧問官時代

48　島津忠義・島津忠済宛意見書／高崎正風・海江田信義・吉田清成・寺島宗則

明治23年4月24日

〔表紙〕

上

〔注〕墨書。

御執事方様
磯御邸
廿三年一月廿九日

堀之内勘五右衛門

春暖之期に罷成候間、益々御壮栄被為入候条奉欣寿候。小宮等も不相替無事送光罷在候間、乍恐御安慮被成下度候。拠、近頃唐突不遜には候得共聊か衷情言上仕候間、御明察被成下候得は小宮等之本懐不過之奉存候。其理由は時期弥々切迫議会開設も余月無之日々相迫り候間、上下倶に苟も志ある者は坐視傍観すへき時節に無之、各自憤励罷在候。特に同族中近来非常之憤発にて、過般より伯子男爵は議員撰挙規則の議事相開き毎会出席者も特の外多く、今日に於ては従来無為閑散に消過致候面々も昼夜の差別なく相励み候次第に御坐候。就ては御両公には是迄国家之大事に当りては御先代之遺志を継紹し御尽力之成績も顕著に被為在候処より御名勲も高く内外之推

戴も重く候而已ならす、公爵中高班に被為立候に由り同族之根軸となり一般之摸範とも奉仰候次第に御坐候間、尚ほ此際に至りても御両公には一層御協力親しく御周旋も被為在候得は、華族全体之方向も相定まり　皇室に奉対忠誠無此上御事と奉信認候に付、一日も早く御上京之義偏に奉渇望候。尤も御深慮も被為在候訳にて小官等より更に御促し申上迄も無之、旁々御情実には無之候得共、今日之場合片時も空しく難過存付之儘黙々罷過候ては衷誠を欠くに相当り難忍候間、一日も早く御上京奉待、御着の上は小官等も亦戮力同心篤鈍を啓ます尽力可仕と決心罷在候間、篤と今日之時態御明察之上速かに御上京被為遊候様奉希望候。若し又両公一時に御出京も不被為適候得者、忠済公御名代として寸時も早く御出京被為在親しく実際に就き御尽力被為及候得者、同族中に於ても如何計か感激も可致候。将亦た世に百聞一見に不若と申事も候得者、此際御上京被為在実際之御経歴被為重候時は時事益々御通達被為在候に付、爾後実況之御報道も審明に可被為行届と奉存候。実に今日は黙視すべからざる大事之場合にも候得者、何卒御家名に被為対御決断開、旁々両全之御事と奉存候。勿論小官等は承恩之情義を以て乍不及一臂相尽すの一心に御坐候間、速かに被為仰談此際忠済公御名代御上京之義速かに御決定被為在度為国家偏に奉希願候。尚ほ小官等之意思は詳細御家人中へも申談置候得共、何分時期切迫寸時も放却難致候間、一同申合せ愚見之次第不取合御伺申上候間、篤と御高察被為成下度偏に奉願上候也。誠惶謹言

　　　明治廿三年四月廿四日

　　　　　　　　　　　　　　　　　　　　　　　　　　　　　高崎正風

　　　　　　　　　　　　　　　　　　　　　　　　　　　　　海江田信義

　　　　　　　　　　　　　　　　　　　　　　　　　　　　　吉田清成

　　　　　　　　　　　　　　　　　　　　　　　　　　　　　寺島宗則

十　元老院議官・枢密顧問官時代

島津公両閣下

　奉呈

〔注〕墨書。

49　「旅行願」／吉田清成

明治23年7月18日

〔朱印〕「内閣批第」一一六〔朱印〕「号」

旅行願

明治二十三年七月十八日

小官儀病気療養之為近県へ旅行致度候間、二周間御暇賜度、此段奉願上候也。

内閣総理大臣伯爵山県有朋殿

〔朱筆〕「甲一一六ノ壱」

〔朱筆〕「願の趣認許す」

明治廿三年七月十九日〔印〕「内閣総理大臣之印」

〔注〕墨書。

枢密顧問官吉田清成

50　吉田清成宛議案送状／枢密院書記官

明治23年8月21日

写

一、増価競売規則

一、裁判上代位規則

一、財産委棄規則

一、弁済提供規則

右四件今般本院の諮詢に付せられ候に付、別冊議案四冊議長の命に依り及配付候。

追て会日の儀は更に及御通知候筈に有之候也。

明治廿三年八月廿一日

〔注〕墨書。

[朱筆]
「但し右議案四冊は当邸へ保存致置候。」

枢密院書記官

51　吉田清成宛東宮参賀申入／曽我祐準

明治23年8月25日

来る三十一日

皇太子殿下御誕辰に付、午前八時三十分通常礼服着用東宮御所へ参賀可有之、此段申入候也。

明治廿三年八月廿五日

枢密顧問官子爵吉田清成殿

〔注〕墨書。

52 「非分県再陳情書」／長野県下伊那郡飯田町住人二十四名　明治23年9月17日

東宮大夫子爵曽我祐準

非分県再陳情書

長野県南部七郡を分割し筑摩県再置の議を嚮に或る一部局の人民に於て主張し、既に上書請願等を為したるを以て不肖等之を不可とし、本年五月中其利害を具載上陳仕候処、其後政府に於て御詮議の上終に断然該請願を排斥せられ、当局大臣より其理由を挙示して将来の御方針を地方長官に論告せられたりと仄かに拝承仕候。実に本県下百有余万人民の幸福のみならず国家の為め慶賀に不堪候。抑も本県分割論の興るや嚮に上陳仕候如く県会議員等の些々たる軋轢に起因し、甲に諭し乙に説き竟に多少の同意を求めて上書請願仕候ものにして、至公至当なる御論達あるにも拘はらす目下尚又再願の為め上京仕候者有之、要するに内心該御論達に服するも表面之を止むるの機なく、公益を謀るに非すして、一部局人民の私約を貫徹せんとするに在りて、決して南部各郡の輿望に無之、今出京したる者を吟味するに概ね一種私益の為めに其身を供したるものにて、或は旧藩士族の代表者と唱へ、或は郡町村の惣代なりと云ふも、当地方に於て委託したるものに無之、既に分県の不可なる理由を示されたる上は到底御採用なきを確信仕候得共、万一分県の御詮議相成候ときは多数非分県論者に非常の激

52 「非分県再陳情書」／長野県下伊那郡飯田町住人二十四名

昂を与へ可申は勿論、不肖等に於ても亦地方の為め大に之に反対を試むるの不幸に遭遇するも難測憂慮仕候間、何卒出願人の性格御取調宜敷御裁捨あらん事希望の至に堪へす。　聊か現時の情況を具し謹て再陳仕候也。

明治廿三年九月十七日

長野県下伊那郡飯田町

牧　野　春　郎㊞

奥　村　収　蔵㊞

黒須藤三郎㊞

山　田　新　七㊞

大原六兵衛㊞

原　吉　郎㊞

安東欽一郎㊞

伊原五郎兵衛㊞

上柳喜右衛門㊞

黒　田　忠　一㊞

羽生加茂吉㊞

吉　沢　利　八㊞

秋田千代三郎㊞

野原半三郎㊞

小西利右衛門㊞

307

十　元老院議官・枢密顧問官時代

枢密顧問官子爵吉田清成殿

　　　閣下

〔注〕「島久改」用箋、墨書。

53　非条約論者および大隈重信らの扇動に関する抜萃書

〔朱筆〕
「抜萃書」

明治23年9月

今般フレザー其他か非条約論を唱出せしは、全く他に煽動者ありて然るものなり。其煽動者は昨年改正条約の大局に当りし大隈重信是なりと。

市　瀬　　信㊞

篠　田　知　哲㊞

皆　川　半　三㊞

杉山善九郎㊞

加藤純逸郎㊞

渡　辺　猶　人㊞

小林源一郎㊞

平沢喜七郎㊞

星　野　有　信㊞

大隈重信か内閣に関係を有する炭山にて裏面は大隈と結托し居る両国社なるものあり。足野吉二郎等が関あるものなり。而して筑前の炭山を同社にて買入んと種々手を廻したるは昨年中の事にてあり。此社は内部大隈の資本によりて運用活動をなすものなり。然る所昨年大隈は外務大臣として条約改正の衝に当り着々外国と談判を開くに際し、英人フレザーは窃かに大隈と相通し英国某銀行より資本を流出し、内地に於て筑前の炭山は勿論、目指所の数十ヶ所の地所を一千万円丈の地所を買入るゝ事に密約を大隈と結ひ、改正条約成り外国人内地雑居の上は、大隈は勿論其手下の周旋にて右の地所は英人の有に帰する筈となりしが、此密約をするに当り事成就の暁は一千万円の報酬として買入れたる外人中より拠出にて大隈に贈る事に談合を遂けたり。

然るに輿論は断行に非らすして中止にありし為め大隈の密謀も全く画瓶に属し、示来外務大臣の更迭後現任青木大臣は鋭意対等条約の方針を取り、漸く其歩を進めんとし日本新聞に記載する如き新条約案の要領を見るに至る。今日の勢を以て察すれは昨年大隈が執りたる所よりは数等の好果を得たるものゝ如し。爰に於てか大隈の意中甚た穏かならす。如何となれは今や第二流の人が対等に近き条約を結ふの勢あるにも拘はらす、其身第一流の人物を以て居なから青木氏に劣る数等の条約案を以て断行せんとしたるは、内に顧みて疚しき而已ならす朝野に向て合すへき面なきを知り、一は己れの失点を減却せんか為め、又一つにはフレザーとの約束の上に付思ふ旨もあり、窃に条約一条に付き此頃フレザーと書面の往来なしたる末、遂に此非条約論を居留外人の口より盛ならしめたるものなりと。

此義に付ては後藤大臣は今回条約改正の主任の内命もある事と云ひ金銭を厭はす充分取調をなし居り、谷中将も注意怠らすありと。

一両日前日本新聞紙上に此事に関する記事ありしは正に大隈と知て記載したるものにて、而してフレザー氏と大

十　元老院議官・枢密顧問官時代

隈が内約一件は動す可らさる事実ありと云ふ。

右の談話は去る廿一日新肴町開化亭に於て対等条約会の有志数十名会合の際、井上角五郎は後藤伯の内命を受け

て出席（本会よりは井上に通知をなさす）、頗る其の事に尽力するのみならす別席にて中西文二郎に已上の始末

を漏したり。　加之ならす今后政府に対する条約改正の方針に付ては角五郎擢てゝ其任に当る覚悟なりと断言した

り。　是は後藤伯に就て聞くの途あるが為めにして、且後藤も今後は此会に深く力を用ひ井上をして親しく其運動

に当らしむるものなりとの赴きなりと云ふ。

又谷干城・副島種臣・佐々木高行及長男高美等も隠然今回の対等条約一件に付ては内々往来密議する処あるのみ

ならす、　間接に該会の為めに力を添へたり。

但し同会には別に運動費と云ふものなき故へ有志者の義捐金を以てするものゝ処、副島・後藤等より多少寄付

する運もありしと云ふ。

以上抜〔朱筆〕「萃」

〔注〕墨書。

54　「出納簿」／吉田清成

〔表紙〕
二十三年十一月
出納簿
成

明治23年11月

〔朱筆〕「十二月廿八日改

〔朱筆〕「△」金百弐拾六円弐拾五銭六厘

銀行残金高　壱番より弐拾壱番に至る」

千百弐拾五円

内払

一金拾壱円弐拾五銭

　歩金は差引候分

入　十一月六日

一金拾円　　　図師崎より返済

二十三

十一月改

同五日

一金拾円　　　中村

同日

一同壱円五十銭　中村

六日

一同百円　　　中村

同日

十　元老院議官・枢密顧問官時代

一同五円　　手元

同日

一同五拾円　　中村

二十三　十一月

七日

一金弐拾円　　志邨

　　弐百五拾円の内返済

七日

一金五拾円　　中村

七日

一金百円也

右建築用之内として吉田昇二郎渡し、津曲和介使之

〔朱筆〕
「十一月七日

一金六百五拾円也

右百十九銀行へ預け入る

津曲和介使之」

八日

一金三拾円也　　中村

×

二十三

十一月九日

一拾円　　中村
　貞取次

十日　　中村

一五円　　中村

十三日

一弌拾五円　　中村

書棚十五円　油絵七円等
　津曲取次

同日　　中村

一同弐拾五円　　中村
畳屋高橋兼吉内渡の分

一同五円　　中村
　岩越取次

十四日

十　元老院議官・枢密顧問官時代

一同五円　　手元

十八日

一同五円　　中村

十八日

一同拾円　　中村

穴子取次

慈善会出品物割合右之通にて寺島夫人へ払之分

十一月十八日

一五円　　　中村

廿一日

貞取次

一五円　　　中村

〔朱筆〕
廿三日

△　内五円は中村渡廿四日

一九円　　　手元

是は元金種々之口を集む」、此日清国公使へ晩饗に行

十一月廿四日

本日中村をして百十九銀行より」○　〔朱筆〕金弐百円請取之事

314

残り四百五十円」

内払

廿四日

一金拾五円　　　中村

　　　玉美○狐亭払等

廿四日

一同五円　　　　中村

　　　津曲を経て渡す

△但之は別口手元より出す

××

一拾五円　　　　中村

　　　岩越取次

十一月廿七日

　　　フラネル類代

一弐拾円　　　　中村

　　　畳屋高橋兼吉内渡

卅日　　×

十　元老院議官・枢密顧問官時代

十二月一日
一金四拾円　　中村
　下郎共月給其外

同三日
一同拾円　　中村

同四日
一同拾円　　中村

一同弐拾五円　　中村

同日
百十九銀行チェツキ八番網屋惣右衛門払、兼定力一[ママ]振代弐尺弐寸

一同拾円　　手元

清国公使黎庶昌其外帰国に付、紅葉館にて送別宴会費（四日）幷同五日鹿児嶋人懇親会費、旧知事にも出会、凡て百人計なり、盛宴に候事

五日　✓

二十三

十二月六日
一金五拾円　　中村

［朱筆］〆百九拾円

外弐拾五円手形八番にて払

此弐百円の口残十円也

入

十二月六日

一　拾円　　　　十一月廿四日引当弐百円残

同日

入

一　弐百円　　　十二月六日第十番引出岩越扱之

右弐口〆

「元金弐百拾円也」

　　内払

六日夜

一　金三拾円　　　中村

七日朝

一　同七拾円　　　中村

［朱筆］
「十二月五日

一　同弐百円　　　中村

九番――大谷金次郎披見

切手――大谷義計渡大礼服代之内払

十　元老院議官・枢密顧問官時代

同七日

一同三拾四円五十銭　同

十一番　　白木屋大村和太郎、子供春着、絵絹

切手　　弐丈其外共」

二十三

十二月七日

〔朱筆〕
「一金弐拾弐円　　中村

切手　　中沢周蔵渡

十二番　　米屋豊前屋即

同八日

一金弐拾三円七拾五銭　中村

十三番　　本棚壱個〇書記椅子一、石炭入壱ケ

切手　　岡安正三郎方より求（芝烏森町一番）」

九日
〔朱筆〕
「一同三拾円　　中村

十四番　　宮沢治平（山形屋）

切手　　十月十一日織物等払」

九日

318

54 「出納簿」／吉田清成

一金拾円也　　志村

右弐百五拾円之内渡〆三拾円渡済

九日

一同弐拾円　　　中村

諸払用

十日

一同拾五円　　　中村

不在に付お貞取次、此日天機伺参朝

十三日

一五円　　　志村渡

同日

一同五円　　　貞渡

英人慈善会行

廿三　十二月十三日

［朱筆］
十四日

一金三拾弐円弐拾五銭　　中村渡

十六　　吉沢新平（琴平町樋職）新築樋一式の代十一月中旬

番

十　元老院議官・枢密顧問官時代

同日　　一同拾八円弐拾銭　　中村渡

十七　　一――　中沢周蔵（芝園橋側石屋）踏石三本代〇四円〇六円五十銭〇七円七十銭」
番　――

十五日　　一金拾円　　　　　　中村

十七日　　一同拾円　　　　　　中村

十五日

一同拾五円　　　　　　手元

建野公使出発に付横浜行一泊友人等と逢ひ入費多少かゝる、丼往来車賃等帰京掛高橋同車きつねにて昼飯を共
にし彼れに振舞
〔朱筆〕
「十八日」

一同　　　〔朱筆〕
　　　「六拾円」　　　中村

十八番　――　新築襖一式代の内四辻八幡側　神谷甚五郎払残少々あり」

切手　――

同日

新吉弟忠次

320

一同拾円　　　　中村

×

［朱筆］「二十三、十二月十八日　［墨書］此日有島氏快気祝にて紅葉館へ行松方始なり」

一金六拾円　　中村

第十九──大工川口伊三郎三拾七円三拾六銭

番切手──左官岡本倉吉弐拾円之処に剰して川口名前にて六十円払」

十九日

一金拾円　　　　中村

田中より進めの大形桐火針をとし代幷外四つ直し代等九円十五銭之払　加藤良助方

［朱筆］「廿日」

一金七円　　　貞渡　岡田扱之

［朱筆］「但郵便局預けに取計申付、尤外雑入三円ありし歟合せて十円となる」

廿一日

一金拾円　　　　中村

廿一日

一同三円　　　手元

廿三日

一同弐拾円　　中村

十　元老院議官・枢密顧問官時代

写真師其外

二十三年十二月

廿四日　　一金百円也入

　　　　　廿番小切手を以百十九銀行より引出す　中村使之

内払

廿四日

一金弐拾円　　　　貞取次、中村渡

廿四日

一金五百円也入

改

廿日

一金五百八拾円也　　元金

内払

廿四日

一金六円拾三銭也

古梅園にて墨筆数々子共其外歳暮之祝の為求む

廿四日

一同七円弐拾九銭五厘

かんな七、鋸五、ちやうなう二、のみ三、鋏一、其外、本町通油町炭屋七左衛門方右大工等へ与へ候為なり

一同壱円五拾銭

通り三丁目玉屋方にて眼鏡壱ケ求候事、自用

二十三年十二月

廿五日

一金拾九円五十銭　手元

歳暮付届家中男女給与之内なり、小札にて取払

×××

廿五日

一同六円手元にあり

廿六日

一同拾円貞扱之　中村

内五円 大五円 小

同日

一同拾円　中村

同日

小テーブル二ケ棚壱ケ、火鉢一ケ　五円札にて

十　元老院議官・枢密顧問官時代

一同百円　　　中村

五円札二十枚

同日

自分取計後中村へ申付くる吉田昇次郎謝儀　七月以来本月に至弐百度以上の治療　会計簿にあり

一同拾円　　　中村

自分取計後中村へ托す

同日

村瀬・玉田へ誂たる画謝儀と〆相払候分

預金内金渡の分　　志村氏

廿八日

一同拾七円

[朱筆]「弐拾円也」

一同拾円　　小遣用　中村

廿七日

一同拾円　　　中村

廿八日

二十三年十二月

一金弐拾円　五円札二　中村

廿八日

紺屋へ川西馬車屋等

同日

54 「出納簿」／吉田清成

一同拾円　　　中村
きつね払七円十四銭五厘

廿九日
一同百円也　　中村

卅日
一同五十円也　　中村
経師屋此日参る

〔注〕この間、十七頁白紙。

〔朱筆〕
「△次のページより此れに次く払の分」

二十三　十二月十五日
一金壱円　　横浜往来　建野を送る為一泊せり

十六日
一同五円余　此日友人等と取会入費を聞く
一同八円程
一五拾銭　　車賃数度
一拾銭　　　新聞紙等
一壱円　　　下人共へ遣す

十　元老院議官・枢密顧問官時代

十九日　　一金五拾銭　　衆議院にて昼飯

廿日

一金八拾七銭　　同断寺師分共

十九日

一同五銭

廿日

一同五銭　　車夫代

五百円の内より払ひ

廿四日

一壱円五十銭目鏡一　　三丁目玉屋

一七円弐十九銭五厘　　かんな七本其外

同日

一六円拾三銭　　墨筆其外古梅園

十一月十四日

一八拾銭　寺島・柳谷等と天一見に越桟敷代

十六日

一九拾銭　たばこ五百本代

[朱筆]
「廿一日」

一弐拾五銭　たばこ二十五本代

廿三日

一十八銭　のみ口六本代

同日

一弐拾五銭　たばこ二十五本代」

十二月

四日

一壱円七十銭　紅葉館清国公使其外送別宴

五日

一弐円七十銭　鹿児島懇親会　於同館

九日

一八十銭　巻煙草入一松田屋にて求め昇次郎医へ遣る

九日

一十銭　同所にてたばこ入修覆代

✓……三宴亭其外

十　元老院議官・枢密顧問官時代

〔朱筆〕
「△印之処に次く」
〔注〕墨書。

十二月十二日　米公使晩餐

55　尾崎朝景宛照会／枢密院書記官

本日御渡に相成居分傍聴券之内壱葉枢密院顧問官吉田清成へ御渡し被下度及御照会候也。

明治廿三年十二月六日

尾崎貴族院属殿

〔注〕枢密院用箋、墨書。

明治23年12月6日

枢密院書記官

56　外務大臣と枢密院の内談に関する手続き案

別啓

第一

顧問官中誰には談し其他は除くと云ふ訳にも至り難く、然らは顧問官は皆一同なり。英より出せし物を若し案上にて廻覧するとせは十分会得し能はさるに依り、コンニャク板にして配達し、少くとも二三日間を置いて会議するとすへし。尤名々の宅に配達するを厭はゝ出院して見るものとす。

明治（23／24）年

第二 此形は御諮詢には非すして外務大臣内談のものなり。院の官制には如此手続あらされとも、尓来条約改正及其他重要の事件を内詢あらんときは、例の通議場に出てゝ三読会を経多少を以て決するか如きは唯外面のみにして実功を挙るの用なし。　殊に条約は彼の同意なければは決定にはならさるものなれはなり。

第三 総委員会は議長を委員長の場に置き唯議事の間雑言するを制せしめ其儘にて他の委員同様自説を出さしむ。

第四 此議席には他の大臣も出席し各顧問の所言を熟聴し、大臣は従来の処分に違ふ所あれは之に答弁す。

第五 此委員会の結末は賛成者の多少を決する事なく内閣に於て其善を採り之を内奏して我政府案とす。

〔注〕墨書。

57

「清市に対し目的を立候以来続て外務省へ奉職後今日迄の概略」／町田実一

明治（23／24）年

清市に対し目的を立候以来続て外務省へ奉職後今日迄の概略

一、外国貿易を盛んにし富国の資を作るには近き清市に向つて始めさるへからすと望を起したるは、海軍主計官にて春日艦乗組中明治六年冬始て渡清致したる時に有之候。

一、同七年夏帰県希望を海軍長官其他え申述其後数回渡清致候へ共、迚も目的を達し得へき様に思はれす。依て

十　元老院議官・枢密顧問官時代

外務省え奉職清国に在勤候は、或は望を達する事もあらんと考へ、清市に対し既往九年間注意罷在候趣意と将来の希望を明治十五年上野、吉田の両太〔ママ〕輔え申述候処、幸ひ愚意採用致し呉れられ、同年夏朝鮮京城の変起りし際八月一日外務省奏任御用係被仰付始めて出仕致候。

一、京城変動処分として井上外務卿馬関え出張相成候節随行被命、八月二日名護屋丸にて出発、馬関え到着候処、清国の形勢視察として渡清被命、同船にて上海へ渡り夫れより芝罘（芝罘へ到着候処清国軍艦数艘に兵隊を積み韓地へ向け操出す最中に有之候。依て早速報道せしに該件に付ては生等の報告第一着なりし由跡にて承り候）・天津を経て牛荘に到り滞留、翌十六年六月帰京（滞留中奉天府より鳳凰城・鴨緑江・旅順口等の地方視察して旅行致候）。

一、同十六年十月香港領事代理被命十二月赴任、然るに清仏戦争中にて随分面働且平期書記生官金及人民よりの預り金〆三千余円を私借致し居りしを以て、之れを内済にて処分せし等は頗る困難にて有之候。

一、同十八年春漢口え領事館設立の事を外務省より政府へ上申相成候由伝聞候に付素志を長次官え申進候処、右書信外務省え到着の数日前既に南貞助氏へ漢口領事命せられたる由に候へ共、拙者の希望を御採用被下南氏香港在勤となり、拙者は帰朝被命同九月帰京、同十月領事に任せられ漢口在勤被命同十二月赴任、同十月帰任于今相勤居候。（廿年十月起程四川地方え旅行、廿一年一月帰漢）満三ヶ年以上在勤賜暇を得て廿二年夏帰京致候に付、在勤中三ヶ年間の実況に基き将来の意見等も申立候へ、及ふ丈の事を尽して清人との交際を厚くし、併て両国貿易殊に我商

一、外務省へ奉職を願たるは他事にあらす、の直輸出業を盛にし公益を起し度希望に有之候に付、拝命已来真に寝食を忘れ昼夜此事にのみ苦慮罷在候処、本邦歳月を経清国人の性質と清商の実情を熟知するに従ひ倍す直輸貿易の六つかしき事を悟り候のみならす、本邦

58　「無罪放免判決書之写」

近来の有様を以て考ふる時は生等何程心配仕候とも数年間に目的を達し本邦の公益を起す事無覚束、且本省にても近来痛く節倹を行はれ候処より、在亜細亜地方我領事館にて之れ迄領事在勤の場所も既に副領事又は代理にて事務取扱の事に相成候へ共、拙者のみ于今無事勤続致候義或は拙者積年の素志を御推量被下候ての事には無之哉と推察致候間、万一右様の事に有之候ては実に御高配を奉謝するに辞無之、去乍ら他との権衡も有之義に付自ら職を辞すると帰朝命せらるゝ迄在勤するの可否数日間篤と熟考仕候処、外務省へ奉職已来目的を変せず凡八年間在清刻苦勉励候へ共寸功を奏せさるのみならす、前に述し通り迚も数年内に公益を起すべき目途も無之候間、自ら職を辞し御賛助を得て他の公務に従事勉強するの至当なるを悟り、終に辞職の事に決心致したる義に有之候。

〔注〕「まちだ」用箋、墨書。

58　「無罪放免判決書之写」

判決書

〔表紙〕
無罪放免判決書之写

明治24年3月30日

福井県越前国福井市湊下町
五拾四番戸平民農元青森大
林区署長
林務官
　　　井　手　今　滋
　　　四十五年四ケ月

十　元老院議官・枢密顧問官時代

右井手今滋か官文書偽造行使被告事件に対し、青森地方裁判所於て刑法第二百五条に依り全法第二百三条に照し一等を加へ重懲役に処す可きものなるも、所犯情状諒すへきを以て全法第八拾九条・第九拾条に基き刑本に一等を減し軽懲役七年に処すと言渡したる裁判に服せさる被告人井手今滋か控訴を受理し、当控訴院公廷に於て被告人井手今滋の陳述、本院検事根岸敬の意見、弁護人一戸豊蔵・伊藤隆真の弁論を聴き審理を遂る処、被告人井手今滋は青森大林区署長奉職中、明治十七年四月七日青森県東津軽郡増川官林に於て檜末木合六千弐百本を青森町小館善兵衛へ代金千弐百四拾円にて払下けを為し、其代金納付後伐採の季節に後れ且木材の価額も漸次下落したる処より、払受人小館善兵衛は全年度中に木材の山出を為すこと能はす、既に取消願書をも差出さんとする景況に立至り、然るに被告人今滋は当時林政拡張の日に際し別途事業の用途多端なるか故に収入金額を増植せん事に苦慮し、可成丈青森官林中より雑木末木等を支払ひ来りたる折柄、小館善兵衛外五名より全十八年十月廿一日に至り、更に全官林に於て檜盗伐木及ひ根返り風折木と前に払下けたる六千弐百本とを加へ、壱本石数平均弐石仕上の見込にて木数壱万本を弐万石と見積り此代金弐千円に計算を立て、伐採事業の負担願書を差出したるに付、被告人今滋は六千弐百本の木材徒に取消し処分を為すに於ては仮令証拠金を取揚るも右は雑収入に編入すへき者にして別途事業の用途に充つ可からさるを慮り、六千弐百本の払下を維持する為め、旁全年十月廿六日に旧青森山林事務所に於て回議の上払下の許可を為し、依て全年十一月全官林に於て右願面の内檜根返風折立枯木并に末木共三千八百本の仮引渡を為し木数都合壱万本の高となし、其後全年十一月十八日右木数の外該官林中に全種の残木三千七百本有之見込にて、小舘善兵衛より其払下再願に依り全事務所に於て回議の上、全十八年十一月十八日に之か仮引渡の許可を為し右木数取調を為したるに三千七拾六本の外無之に付、全十九年二月中該木数を仮に引渡し受書を取り山撿印を為さしめたるも、三千七拾六本の分は官林中処々に切倒しあり、殊に木材

332

58 　「無罪放免判決書之写」

運搬の路次に散在したる者に付き壱万本山出の後悉皆引渡の処分に及ふへく、且壱万本の石数に減量する節は之を以て補足すへき見込なるか故に之を引残し、総木数壱万本は願人小舘善兵衛等に於て造材に着手し石量になし土場にて改めたる石数壱万九千百三十八石四斗七升を引渡し、残木並に三千七拾六本は其儘になしたり。此間被告今滋は他県下巡廻又は上京等にて三千八百本に対する引渡処分届の遷延せしに付、明治十九年六月九日即ち被告今滋か帰署の当日青森大林区署に於て檜末木四千五百本を小舘善兵衛外五名に代金七百六拾円にて払下の回議を為し、且此三千八百本の分は全十八年の会計年度中に編入せされば十八年度の別途事業の用度に充つへからさる理由なるを以て、此払下は十九年三月廿五日則ち十八年の会計年度閉鎖の期月を経過するに至りたる処、三千八百本の分は既に青森大林区署に於て払下会議の末全年七月十日に取消さゝるを得さる場合に至りたる故に、別に願人の請願書を要せさる筋合なれ共、三千八百本の分は六千弐百本と全局第弐課へ具情の添書を為したり。其後払受人小舘善兵衛外五名の者か木材引取り方遅滞に至り、会計年度閉九年三月三十一日付に記入し、全年七月十日に該四千五百本払下処分を山林局長に宛相届、其届方遷延の事故を全十鎖の期月を経過するに金千弐百四拾円の外四千五百本の分は代金未納となり、勢ひ金七百六拾円に対する払下を其の趣を山林局に届置きたるか故に、今単に四千五百本のみを取消すときは却て事緒分明ならさらんと慮を合せ石量払下の届書を差出置きたるに付、今更に小舘善兵衛より四千五百本に対する払下け願書を出さしめ、尚又右願書に全年九月付にて四千五百り、更らに小舘善兵衛より四千五百本に対する払下け願書を出さしめ、尚又右願書に全年九月付にて四千五百の取消願書を小舘善兵衛より差出させ、全年九月廿四日に右払下の取消を全署に於て回議を為し、全年九月廿五日取消処分済の届書を農商務大臣に宛差出し向きに仮引渡しに為したる三千七十六本の残木処分は未定中、被告今滋は解職となりたる事実なりと確認す。而て檜末木四千五百本の払下回議案は明治十九年六月九日青森大林区署に於て回議を開きたる際、主任者か事務匆卒の際三千八百本を四千五百本と取違へ之を起草したるに、被告井

333

十 元老院議官・枢密顧問官時代

手今滋に於ても之を等閑に看過したる実況にして、右価額七百六十円と記載しある項を三千八百本の代価一本に付二十銭の計算を以て之を参照すれば金七百六十円となる。此計算に依れば四千五百本は則ち三千八百本の誤謬たるは論を俟す。而て小舘善兵衛より差出したる四千五百本の払下願書丼に取消願書も前文回議案に基きたるものなれは、是又三千八百本の誤謬たるは明晰なりとす。

以上の事実なるに依り、被告人井手今滋か三千八百本及ひ三千七百七十六本の事実を陰蔽し、併て見込石数二万石の内四千本余に相当する石数の減少したるを取繕ふの手段を施し、終に檜末木四千五百本を代金七百六十円にて払下け后之を取消たりとの虚偽の事実を構造し、明治十九年九月廿一日にありて全年三月廿五日に溯りたる日付の檜末木四千五百本の払下願書及ひ全年九月付檜末木四千五百本払下取消願書の二通を差出さしめ共に許可の指令を為し、全年九月廿五日付を以て其旨の届書を農商務大臣へ差出し、則其指令書二通届書一通は被告今滋か其管掌に係る文書を偽造行使したるとの証憑は都て充分ならさるものとす。

右の理由なるを以て判決する左の如し。

明治廿四年一月十四日青森地方裁判所か被告丼手今滋に対し言渡したる裁判は不適当なるに付、刑事訴訟法第二百六十一条後段に依り之を取消、更に被告丼手今滋を全法第二百廿四条前段に照し無罪を言渡且放免するものなり。

但証拠品として押収したる帳簿丼に書類は刑事訴訟法第二百二条に依り各差出人に還付す。且公訴裁判費用は全法第二百一条に照し国庫の負担とす。

明治廿四年三月廿七日函館控訴院公廷に於て撿事根岸敬立会宣告す。

函館控訴院刑事部長　　西岡　逾明

函館控訴院判事　　　　横地　安信

59 「英国覆案に対する意見」／伊東巳代治

右原本に依り謄写す。

明治廿四年三月三十日

〔注〕活字印刷。

全　　中尾捨吉

全　　長安道一
　　　函館地方裁判所判事　石井喜兵衛
　　　函館控訴院書記　　　青木浩蔵

函館控訴院書記　　青木浩蔵

〔表紙〕

甲十一　　五月二日

英国覆案に対する意見

佐野顧問官殿

〔朱筆〕
「秘」

59
「英国覆案に対する意見」／伊東巳代治

明治（24）年5月2日

本案に対し当局者の修正あり。之に対しては愚見のあるあれとも今之を是非論弁するの用を見す。特に彼に対して未た協議を経へさるものなれば、其成否を期すへからす。仍て英国発題原案に付意見を陳ふるものとす。

335

英国覆案に対する意見

熟ら外交上の事歴を察するに、煩雑と紛争とに囲繞せられ今日に至る迄纏綿一日として満足の結果を奏したることなく、之か為めに内部の乖戻を来すに止まり、国家の安危殆んと之に伴ふの勢あるは世の普く知る所なり。之れ畢竟外交の枢機に通せさるか為めか、将た未た其時期熟せさるにあるか何れか其二を出つることとなかるへし。往年以来外交上の事端は起る毎に国家の汚辱を招き、国民の幸福を傷けたること枚挙に遑あらす。政府に於ても其屈抑に堪へす、幾回か之を雪くの挙に出たりといへとも、毎時失敗を重ね未た今日に至り其結果を見るを得す。固より当局者に於ても鋭意熱心努めさるにあらさるも、其事成らんとして成らさるは蓋其原因の以て蔽ふへからさるもの存するならん乎。

顧みるに明治八年始めて改正の議ありしも、僅に米国に対し其企望を達せしのみにして未た実行に及はす。爾後内部の紛擾姑く外事に及ふ能はす。稍く同十五年に及ひ予議会を開き更に改正上の一機軸を出すに及ふも、尚ほ百般の阻碍絶へす。稍く同十九年に至り正式の談判を開くも其事半を了するも、朝野の紛議起り事終に中途に破れたり。続て同廿二年に及ひ再ひ前規を続きたりしも、之れ又同一の紛議に倒れ遂に現今には及へり。斯く幾度か我より求めて事半に我より中止し、将に其挙動たる軽浮躁急毫も信用を置くに足らさるの譏を免れさるに至らんとす。是以て当局者は勿論、当時政府の人々に於ては海外各国に対し其体面を失ふのみならす、殆んと国の威信を失墜するならん。故に一次毎に其事の破るゝを聞くや慚憤殆んと堪へさるの感なきにあらさりしも、其咎誰にか帰せん。皆日本国民たる吾人の受くる所にして、独り当局者のみの失過ならんや。畢竟一般人民の思想未た外交上の利害に熟通せす、上下協同の力足らさるの結果なりと云はさるへからす。此の如き経歴にして一次々々に煩難を加へ稍く今日に及ひたる次序なれは、敢て難を責めて事を強ゆるの本意にあらす。徹頭徹尾協同補益し

て以て速かに外交上の問題を一結せんことは、固より満腔の熱望なりといへとも、如何せん機宜最も我に不利に
して、其事断して将来の幸運にあらさるを信す。仍て左に本官の所思を陳へて以て諸君の再考を請ふ。

本回英国提出案を閲するに、概して前回提出案よりは一歩を進めたるの感ありといへとも、特に異なる所は法権
に関する事項を拆て之を議定書に移したるに過きす。細に其条款を精査するときは反て前案に劣る少しとせさ
るなり。故に之を看過するときは通商及ひ航海条約に係る条文中互相の利益を保維したる所なしとせさるも、概
ね其他の条款に至りては又頗る思考を要する所勘しとせす。之れ固より前案より胚胎し来れる結果にして、所謂
歴史付の条款なるへきを以て直断して之を改削するを得さるの情実あるならむ。故に忍ひ得へくんは忍ひて以て
今日茲に一帰局を結ふは実に国家の為め望むへきこととなるへきも、熟ら現在の情勢を鑑み民心の趨勢を察するに、
今後国歩の艱難は日一日と相加ふるの情況なるは何人も知る所なり。此時に当りて只目下の急要に迫られ軽々に
此大問題を果断するは実に再考を要すへき事なりとす。若夫行懸の情義に絆され目前の毀誉に泥み軽卒に決行す
るに於ては、其事固より尋常の理に違はさるにせよ為に国民の意想に逆ふに及んては、仮令各国に対して締約を
果すも後日之か実施に臨みては意外の阻碍を生し、只に内部の紛乱を醸すに止まらす、延ひ外交上の難題を引起
すに至らさるを得んや。特に本年より議会の開設ありて政務の煩難は従前に倍徙するものあり。此時に当りて只
表面の道理を推して事万一乖戻を生するに及んては如何政府は独り国民の怨怒を招くに止まらす、又各国の凌侮
を来すこと、或は今日の形行に一任するよりは最も峻激なるものあるへし。勿論昨二十三年中前当局者の後を承
け、更に各国に対して改正の発題を提出するに当り、現当局者の諮問に対し聊か意見を陳へたり。当時当局者に
問ふに、今回の新発題を以て条約締結を遂け得るの見込なるや否やを諮ふに当り、現当局者は答て曰く、先つ其
結果を遂け得るは万一を期するならむと、然らは可なり、故に無止の点のみに関し修正を求めたるに過きさりき。

337

十　元老院議官・枢密顧問官時代

尓来数閲月間隠顕其経歴に就き聞かさるにあらさりしも、期する所は全く当時当局者の意思と均しく締約の成らさらんことを企望したりき。然るに去夏英国政府は我要求に応して一の覆案を作り之を提出し、粗ほ我要求に吻合するの傾向ありと伝ふるに至れり。惟ふに当初本官の期する処は、既往の失敗を鑑み将来の安危を慮り、断然行懸りの条約改正事件を中止し従前より引続きたる関係を絶ち姑く内部の妥安を図り、徐ろに数年を期して新に談判の緒に就かんと欲し献策する処ありしも終に用られす。衷心遺憾に堪へさりしも亦止むを得さりしなり。然れとも伝ふか如く英国政府の発題は稍々妥当にして、我又之を拒むの口実なきに困むの情況に遭遇せりとせは、実に僥倖中の不幸と謂はんのみ。〔傍点朱筆〕然れとも彼全く我要求に応せは勿論我に於て今更違拒すへからすと雖も、熟ら英国覆案を熟閲するに、決して我要求の要点に応せしの跡なきか如し。加之我に取りて最可避の件を彼より要請する一にして足らさるか如し。仮令之より談判上多少修正を加ふる見込ありて彼之を容るゝにもせよ、本体已に定りて動かされは、仮令末節の修正加はるゝとも到底彼に利ありて我に利なきの条約たらさるを得す。幾度之を更改潤飾すと雖も決して完全なるを保すへからす。実に条約改正の事業たるや一時の情意に任すへきものにあらす。深く其影響の及ふ処を察せは転た其事の重且つ大にして軽視すへからさるを感すへし。故に前日に可なりと認めしことも今日に至ては不可を認め大小軽重大に其趣を同ふせさるを覚れり。故に今に至て尚ほ前日の意思を以て判定を下すこと能はさるなり。仍て彼の覆案に基き利害の関係を概述すへし。

　一　通商及ひ航海条約の事

通商及ひ航海条約中の条款を総括して之を現存条約に比せは〔傍点朱筆、〕、蓋輸入税率の若干を高め新に嚬税を課するの外一も得る所なし。其条款を叙すれは第一条一、二、三項及ひ第十一条の如し。各条皆従前に比して多少収入を増殖するを得へきなり。且つ第十九条（終了期限を約するは無期限に幾分か利便を加ふるに似たれとも、一便あれは

一難加はるものにして、従前条約有効期限の未定なりし時に異ならさるの不便なしとせす、即ち十二ケ年の期限を以て条約終了に帰するに当り預め之を改約するに違なきに及んては再ひ旧約を復活せしむるものなりとす、可考）の如く条約終了の規約新たに加はるを以て、今後改正事業に対しては幾分か我国権を張るに便なるを。此等の条款は固より現存条約に比して我に利益あるは勿論なりと雖も、一方に得る処多けれは随て一方に費す処多きは普通の条理なり。故に今日海関の収益幾分を増加するの道ありとて一概に其利益のみを頼み難し。必すや我に得る処あれは又彼に酬ゆる処なきを得さるなり。果して然らは得る所多きに準して之を得るの用意従て整はさるを得す。例すれは海関の組織其他百般の方法手段必す又今日の儘に過すへきにあらす。要するに税率改正若くは頻税賦課等の収益ありとするも之れ只其員額を唱ふるに止まり、現に我国庫の余贏増加すへしとは信せさるなり。曩に我当局者の税率増加の案を作りしは、畢竟条約改正の後に及ひ自然其準備に関する費用の多きを以て之を支弁補充するの趣意に出てたるものなれは、縦令今政府に於て支用の権を有し毫も他人の容啄を容さすと雖も、到底彼の好意に酬ゆるの精神なかるへからすとの論者も少しとせす。然れは偶々収入を増加したりとも再ひ外国人の為め支弁するに至ては、恰も税率増加の口上を贈りて之に増倍する処の利益を攫収せらるゝものと云はさるを得す。反て堂々改正条約案中条章譲与の口実を以て事毎に己の欲する処を要請せらるゝに及んては、我何を以て之に答へんとするや。特に数年前に於て当時の情勢に則し発題したる方案をして今日の現況に推し及さんと欲するは、豈に時期を誤るの嫌なしとせんや。已に数年来時勢の変遷に伴ひ民業も又一変して往時の情態にあらず。此時に当りて尚ほ数年前に作為したる方案を執りて今後十数年間に施行せんと欲するは、実際の須要に応すへからすと断言すへきなり。特に目今外国貿易上の変動に随ひ一般の民業頗る衰弊を極め、年に月に惨況を現せんとらすと断言すへきなり。此時に当りては宜しく列国の所為に做ひ大に民業保護の趣意を達するにあらされは、到底国家の危殆を現せんす。此時に当りては宜しく列国の所為に做ひ大に民業保護の趣意を達するにあらされは、到底国家の危殆を免る

十　元老院議官・枢密顧問官時代

へからす。故に今日は区々たる税率増加に安んして之を数年の後に延すは最も不可とする所なり。是を以て一日

も速に海関税権を回復するの趣意を貫かすんは今日の衰弊を免るへからす。縦令税率増加を約し得たりとも、到

底貿易上の平衡を維持すへきものにあらす。反て之れか為め損害を来すに及んては、我独り其損害を蒙るに終ら

んのみ。本条約の有効期限は十二ケ年間に止まるとするも、今日の現況に照し来れは我国経済上の衰弊は此長年

月を待つに妨けなしとするや、実に一日寸時を待つへからさるの感想あり。故に今日軽々小利に安んして条約改

正を遂けたりとも、彼は益々口実を高めて税権回復の期を延緩ならしむるの虞なしとせさるなり。故に通商及航

海条約に対しては寧ろ今日は之を擱き姑く時機を待ち、数年を期し純然海関税権の恢復を以て外交上の一主眼た
〔傍点朱筆〕

らしめんことを期するの趣旨なりとす。尚ほ細に条款に就て可否の意見は別に論する処あらむとす。

　　　一議定書の事

議定書に関しては最も慎思熟考を要すへきなり。且つ国家の為め安危利害を感するに至ても亦最も重大なりとす。

固より本条約にあらさるも已に議定書に明記するに至ては其効力は多少の差異ある事なし。其条章六項ありと雖

も、其要旨は領事裁判権廃止と内地開放即ち外人雑居、通商航海の自由、不動産所有権及旅券制度の拡張の規約

に係るなり。其細目の約款に至ては後年更に其規約実施の時に於て又定約する処あるへきも、大体已に確定規約

に係るを以て一旦之を約定するに至ては之を動かす事を得さるのみならす、領事裁判権廃止に就ては実に熟慮を

要すへき内地雑居之に伴ふの関係存すれは、決して軽忽に其可否を断定すへきにあらさるなり。如何となれは

夫れ領事裁判権の廃止は我に必要とするか、勿論必用なりとす。然れとも之に伴ひ来る処の内地雑居、不動産所

有権の報酬を以て比較するときは固より九牛の一毛だも及はさるなり。如何となれは領事裁判の制は開国の当初

彼我国情の差違あるより之か衝突を避けんか為め、我より好んて我国権の一部を挙て彼に委任したるものにして、

59 「英国覆案に対する意見」／伊東巳代治

我国に於ては安政条約に於て始めて生したるにあらす。遠く徳川始祖の英吉利国人に対する公約中に於ても、尚ほ交互所罰の権を分任したるの先例あり。決して我国独り海外各国の凌圧に抑へられ為めに此初例を開きたるにあらさるは又多弁を要せす。然るに世人往々埃及、土児胡等諸国の例を引き其事例の類同なるを口実とし、遂に治外法権と称し恰も居留地を以て外属の邦土と見做し領事裁判と相混視して其弊を論するものゝ如し。豈に誤感の甚しきにあらすや。畢竟領事裁判は国状人情殊異なるより一時の便法として交互相約したるものにして、固より我国権を屈抑したるにあらさりしも、積弊遂に往々不当不正の事あるに至るも之れ全く其制度方法の不善なるにあらす、我国状民度の特異なるの致す所なるや知るへからす。然るに世人は往々領事裁判の実況を究めす、其虚影に驚き其声聞に魘へ、自ら好んて治外法権の名称を甘んし其弊害汚辱の甚たしきを論する者あるも、其実際の事に至ては実に瑣少にして又顧眄を費すに足らさるなり。即ち五六年間の交渉訴件を調査するに平均百二三十件に過きす。其事件に至ては概ね僅々たる金銭貨物の貸借訴訟に過きす、又多くは我国人の直に帰するものゝ如し。蓋し従前に於ては我国の損害汚辱を受けたる事件なしとせさるも、当時未た外交の方法整頓せさるより公私を混同して往々国際上の問題に上ること多かりし所以にして、皆彼我の情意相通せさりしか為めなりとす。然るに世往々此等の口実を作為して領事裁判廃止に沈酔するものあるも、蓋其名に驚きて其実を知らさるの徒たらんのみ。此の如き瑣末なる領事裁判権にして之を今日に廃止せんと欲せは、事実上又道理上内地雑居を允さゝるへからさるや勿論なり。【傍点朱筆】然るに内地雑居に比せは領事裁判は何れを重しとするや、更に一弁を費すに足らさるへし。今若領事裁判を廃止せは断して内地雑居を許さゝるを得す。然るに現今の国状民情にして之を允すの利害果して如何そや。今議定書中の条項に就き細に査閲せは利害の関係自ら詳明なるへしと雖も、仮りに其大体に就き之を論するも、目下の国状に於ては百害ありて一利なきを証するの事実ありと信す。【傍点朱筆】仍て其所由を陳へん。

341

十　元老院議官・枢密顧問官時代

第一項領事裁判の廃止は少くとも五ケ年を経過し、其際日本の諸法典及諸法律にして満足に十二ケ月間の実施を確めたる後に実行すべし。然らされは何時までも其実施を確むる迄は実行を延期する事。

領事裁判廃止の事たる今日より少くとも五ケ年を期し、其際に至り諸法典・諸法律の実施効果の如何に由るものにして其事たる先つ今日に迫りたるに非らされは、従来茲に切論すへき要なきか如しと雖も、畢竟五ケ年を期す〔傍点朱筆〕るは其真意の存する処我我国をして外人待接の準備を整へしむるか為め此若干年の猶予を与ふるに限らす、反て彼をして我管轄に服せしむるに当り、予め我をして彼の所望に応せしむるに基くものにして、要するに我をして強て彼の所望に伴随せしむるものと判せさるを得す。而して其裁判権廃止を実行するは我諸法典・諸法律の実施を験する事一ケ年間にして満足なりと思考せは始めて其約を履むへしと約するものにして、仮令今日此規約を結ふも我諸法典・諸法律にして悉く実行を遂くるに至らすんは、此規約果して何の時にか果さんや。仮令五年の後又は十年の後に至るも、我国状民情にして法典の実施を阻碍するの事実ありなは如何、彼は其実行の結果不満足なりとの口実を設けて百般之を違拒するに及んては裁判権廃止の期は今後何の時にあるを予知すへからさるなり。〔傍点朱筆〕然るに事の成否を鑑みす、漫に予期すへからさる事を予期して外交上の規約に明記し、万一其約束を履行するに及んては其事態は如何そや。只国の不信を海外に流すに止まらす又事の疎略を国民に謝せさるを得さるへし。特に前回改正にして官民の不満を買ひ遂に紛乱騒擾を来せしは重に法典編纂又は裁判官採用等の公文に存す。今回の議定書に於ては固より其旨意異なりと雖も、年限を約して我法典・法律の実施を予約し裁判権廃止を期するは其主意に至ては前後軽軽ならんや。況んや今日は立憲政治の時にして一国の法制悉く議会の協賛を経さるを得す。仮令新法典已に発布ありて来明治廿六年の実施を期するも、万一興論の反対起り、或は其実施期限を延し、或は其条款を修正するに当り議会之を容るゝに及んては、廿六年の実施も又今後数年の後に至るへ

342

59　「英国覆案に対する意見」／伊東巳代治

し。已に本年商法延期の実例に徴せは又多弁を要せす。然るに五ケ年間を経過し一ケ年間満足の実歴あるにあら

されは廃止せすと云ふに至りては、只我に無上の難題を負はしめ独り坐して其利を受くるの心意にして、我に対

して寧ろ非常の煩冗を嫁したるものと云はさるを得ず。特に我法典・法律の実施を験するは、我にあるか将た彼
〔傍点朱筆〕

にあるか云はすして彼に在るを覚るへし。果して然らは仮令我国に於て飽まて本規約を果さんことに熱中し百般

の法令期年ならすして実施するとも、満足なりとの一言を以て此規約を果すの権は彼にあり。若夫故意執拗我要

望を容れさるに及ふも我亦之を強ふるの辞あらんや、思はさるへからさるなり。況んや目下人心の趨勢を察する

に今後何等の方向に帰着すへきか未た先途の成行を予知すへからす。此の如き危急切迫の時に当り漫に外国に対

して此等重大の関係ある規約を締結するは、仮令今日に於て其計図を得たりとするも、将来を顧慮せは為めに内

外紊乱の媒介を醸生するの原因と謂はさるを得す。豈に再思せざるべけんや。

第二は四項あり。

一項は条件なしに日本全国を開くことは領事裁判権廃止の日より実行せらるへき事。

二項は領事裁判権廃止の日より両国の版図間には互に通商航海は充分自由たるへき事。

三項・四項は内地開放に関する準備の事項なり。其事柄は本章中に併論するを以て別に贅せす。

第二は第一の裁判権廃止の結果にして我に裁判権を収め外人をして我管轄に服せしむるに至りては必す外人に雑

居を許すは自然の結果にして又怪むに足らず。固より英国の覆案には「条件なし」の文義あり。然れとも不動産

所有権を允さす、又内国人同様の権利を与ふるに若干の制限を置くが如き制裁を設くへきは勿論なるべし。故に

或は今日の事体に及んでは万止を得すんは領事裁判を廃止せしめて若干の制限内に内地雑居を許すも又避くへか
〔傍点朱筆〕

らさる事たるも、現今我国状民度に照らし其軽重を較慮するときは一日も措くへからさる必用あるにあらす。只

従前よりの行懸に於て、止を得す空名にして実利少き領事裁判権と、重大にして危害多き内地雑居と相交換するか如きは尤も我国先途の利害に照らして執らさる所なり。今若現今の国状民度を考察せす啻一時の行懸に託し、若くは目前の体面に泥みて軽々に速断し、此一大問題を決するに及んては、終に回復すへからさるの患害を貽すに至るへし。今日に於て内地雑居を允すの弊害を叙すれは其条件一二に止まらすと雖も、其最も著しきものは左の如し。

　一民業の占奪を免れさる、事〔傍点朱筆〕
　二社会の情勢を変せしむる事〔傍点朱筆〕
　三政務の実施を難からしむる事〔傍点朱筆〕

以上三項の事実は必す免るへからす。其他公私倶に予想外の結果を呈するや知るへきなり。断して事物の情状今日の比にあらさるへし。顧みるに現今の国情は如何、人心未た定着する所なく、随て物論紛起し更に先途の成行を確知すへからす。加旃民力凋弊に傾き経済上の変動従ふて底止する所なく、為めに益人心の紊乱を重ぬるの勢あり。此の如く内治の急務一にして足らす。僅に其整理に汲々たるの今日に当りて更に国情民風特異なる各国人民と、混在せしめは其現状如何、只我実益上の競争輸贏あるに止まらす、一層今日の人心を挑発して殆んと収拾すへからさるに至らしめん。然るに世人往々内地雑居を以て憂とせす、反て外資輸入、民業隆盛等の所論を楯とし今日に之を決行するの必用なるを論する人あり。又不動産所有権を禁せは内地雑居を厭はすと断言する者あり〔傍点朱筆〕、之れ彼我の情勢を弁せさる皮想論のみ。少しく顧みて民間の現況を察せは、外資輸入は我国民の利たるや、随て民業隆盛に至るへきや、必す其事の言易くして行難きを知るに難からす。特に不動産所有権を允さゝれは内地雑居に伴ふ所の弊害挙て避くるを得べしと信するは、只其虚声に泥みて其実効を弁知せさるの浅見なり。

彼、外国人にして内地雑居を望むは豈に独り不動産所有権を望むものならん。仮令土地の如く又其他不動産にして其所有権を禁ずるも其使用権を制するを得ざるべし。其名義に至まらんや。仮令土地の如く又其他不動産にして其所有権を禁ずるも其使用権を制するを得ざるべし。〔傍点朱筆〕百般の事業又は不動産の所益にのみ止ては之を賃借地と称し之を所有地と称するも、其実利を享くることに至ては将た何の区別かあるや。現に居住地借地権は九十九ヶ年間にして継続の自由あり、又新民法の永借地権は五十ヶ年間なり。所謂所有地権との差は僅に名義上の称のみ。況んや将来を鑑みるに、仮令今日若干の制限を約するも、一回内地を開くに至りては直接間接外国人の余力我国政上に影響を及ぼし、期年ならずして其制限を解くの要求を起すに至るべし〔傍点朱筆〕。故に一歩を譲りて、百歩を得るの目的已に立つ、何ぞ鎖々たる土地所有権の有無に拘泥して雑居の利源を放却することあらんや。故に一旦内地雑居を允すの議を決せば宜しく大に開きて大に入るゝの覚悟なかるべからず。何ぞ区々名義上の制限を設けて之に安んじ反て彼此の交渉を繁くし、政務の煩雑を開き求めて事端を繁くすることを欲せざるなり。豈に再思せざるべけんや。

第三　内地を開くまでは旅券方法を拡張し一旦受領するときは、満十二ヶ月間は国内何の地へも至るを得べき旅券を外務省、若くは開港場ある各府県より交付せしむること。

旅券に関し必要なる諸規則は英国代理官と日本外務大臣の決定する所に依らしむ。

本条は内地雑居を実施する迄先つ彼の得んと欲するの要求にして、今日の場合に立ち我に於て本案に同意を表するときは、　旅行規程等に関して厳密の制限を加ふるにせよ其大体に於ては之に応ぜざるを得ず。而して之を允すの可否に至りては固より多弁を要せず。外国人に取りては現実の利益たるや固より論なきのみならず、数年後に及び内地雑居の暁に至ては彼か為め準備的の旅行を為すの利便を与ふるものにして、一時に内地を開放し急慌相率ひて定住の地を求むるものに比すれば、　其利益豈に少々ならんや。〔傍点朱筆〕然るに我に取りては全国到る所外

十　元老院議官・枢密顧問官時代

国人の探見跋渉を経ざるなく、国内の利源概ね彼の占奪に帰するの先蹤を造るものにして、已に現今狡猾の徒に、ありては往々遊覧保養に仮託して各地を巡行し、巧に営利の策を講するものなしとせず。仮令旅行に関し多少の制限を置くも、固より監禁其自由を束縛すべからざるを以て、一旦全国交通の旅券を交付するに於ては其波及する所何ぞ今日の現状に止まらんや。然のみならず今後旅行規程の如き彼我協議を経て決定するの要求なるに於ては、彼の要望決して瑣少の範囲に止まらんや。特に外国人旅行の自由を与ふるに至りては、主として多少の改正を経、又修飾を加ふべきは地方大小官衙の掌務にあり。言語不通の外国人踵至するに当りては、勢ひ之か措置の方規を定めざるを得ず。執務益々煩重を加へ経費弥々増加するに至りては、其利を受くるは独外国人にして、其弊を受くるは我国民なりとす。仮令数年の後に至りて内地を開くも其根基既に成るに至らは、将た内外人雑居の後を俟て、始めて其利害を判するを要せんや。故に内地雑居に代へ今日より内地旅行の自由を寛ふせしめんと欲するは、決して無為の旅行を為すのみの本意ならんや。其抱蔵する所の結果に至りては必す国民の不利を醸すに至るや期すべきなり。豈に再思せざるべけんや。

第四・第五は固より条約に規定するの要なし。特に論弁を要せずと思考す。

前項所論の如く議定書に基き今後外交上の規約を結ぶものとせば、立どころに其反響を受くるに至るや期すべきなり。仮令前後多少の緩急ありとするも一旦是等の規約を以て其羈絆を受くるに及んでは、国家の不利之より大なるはなからん。故に、今日の際領事裁判廃止、内地雑居允許の問題は只現時の利害を以て軽卒に論断すべきにあらず。必すや国家百年の大計を慮り以て之か適否を判するの必用なるを知るなり。

〔傍点朱筆〕

此の如く我国条約改正の問題は純然たる通商条約に均しからず、実に千載の国是を一変するの一大重事に関するを以て、是を一時の便否に託して軽挙に出つべからず。特に昨年二月覚書を発するに当り其書中に叙して曰く、

346

59 「英国覆案に対する意見」／伊東巳代治

帝国議会の開設に臨みては爾来帝国の立法事務は議会の協賛を要すべきを以て、新条約に適当且完全なる実行を為すに必須欠くべからざる許多の法律を制定することに対し、之を確然保証する能はざるを以て更に修正を提出するの趣旨と為し、爾後条約改正に対する方法中、一は無定限に延期すること、一は議会の協力を得るに足るべき幾分の修正案を提出することの二ケ条中、政府は改正事業の為め費したる許多の日子と貴重なる労力とを以て是迄進みたる功程を空ふせざらんことを熱望して、第二の方案を執ることを明言したり。然るに今や英国政府は我要求に対して一の修正案を提出し、粗ほ我要望に副ふたりとて時期を鑑みず国情を察せず遽かに之に応して改正の談判に及はんとするは、当初発議の際に当りて我予期する所の企望に相反するの嫌なしとせんか。前回の改正会議と今後の改正会議とは事体決して同じからず、仮令憲法上の通義犯すべからざるもの存するも、公議を執り輿論を酌み政務を執行するの今日に至ては、宜しく民心の趨勢を慮り先途の利害を考計せざるべからず。然らずんば彼れに約する所あるも我に行ふ事能はざれば、如何独当任者の煩難を加ふるに止まらず、延て国政上の阻得を醸さん。況んや外国条約の如き一旦規約を了すれば、我より恣に之を解くことを得ず。万一障害を生するに至りては挙て全国民の利害に関するものなれは、最も民情を察し時機を鑑み、慎思熟考を加へずんば、必ず内外乖戻の紛擾を惹起するに至らんとす。且つ前回我修正議提出の趣旨たるや、議会の協力を得るに足るべしと予期せり。今後も又同しく議会の協賛を経ずんば百般の法律制法も其存廃を決すべからず。〔傍点朱筆〕然るに政府独今日の現況に対し其信認する所を以て可なりとし、深く国民の興望を顧察することなく、反て其意思を推断して、外国政府と規約を締ぶに及んでは、必す従前に均しき紛難を来すや知るべきなり。仮令条約上の規約遂くるを得す、外国に対して威信を欠くは其責政府にあらずとするも、国民の失過は結局一国に帰す。〔傍点朱筆〕万一、政府人民条約上の権義に関して憲法上の解義を異にし互に其不当を抗論して乖戻の情益々募るに及んては、政府は外国に対して親愛の誼

十　元老院議官・枢密顧問官時代

を表すべきも、人民は之を疎悪するの結果を生ぜんとす。特に立憲政治を施行するに及んでは国論の勢力益々強大なるべきを以て、自然各派各党の政議亦人心を煽起するに力あるをや。若し一歩を誤り人心の乖戻を招くに及んでは、恐らくは条約改正の名実相反するの結果を見るに至らざるを得ず。是以て熟ら時宜人心の如何を観察するに、今日に於ては此問題を決すべき時にあらず。姑らく内地の整理を務め、人意相和し、国論相協ひ、改正の方針一途に出つるの時を待つに若かず。仮令今日強て改正の議を決するも、内部の整理完から

〔傍点朱筆〕

ざれば、領事裁判権の如き之を撤去せしむるは幾年の後にあるや予知すべからず。今日の如き人心乖忤の時に当て、内外に対して事難を結ぶに之を撤去せしむるは幾年の後にあるや予知すべからず。今日の如き人心乖忤の時に当て、内外に対して事難を結ぶして国家の利福にあらざるなり。反て人心の反抗を招きて予期の目的を空ふすることあれば、外に対しては国威を欠き、内に対して威信を失ふに至り、独り政府の不利なるのみならず実に日本帝国の汚辱を招くこと恰も往時安政条約の余弊今日子孫の煩累を貽すに均しく、現時の人は後世子孫に対して豈に其失害を貽すの責を辞するを得べけんや。固より今回改正案は其条款悉く不当なりと云ふにあらず。其危害を与ふる点に於て峻且激なるを以て其余響する所国利を欠き、民益を損するあり。之を強て実行するに及んでは、国信を顕章し国威を光耀するの目的は反て之を汚損するの不幸を招くに至らざるを保せず。蓋し政府の本意は旧来受くる所の国家の損害を賠ひ、民人の幸福を保するにあらん。決して人心を挑発して国安を害するの意あるにあらざるや明かなり。然れとも如何せん之を今日に実行せんと欲せば、反て人心の悖戻を来すを免れざるをや。故に此際外交上の紛糾を解くには、断して従前の行懸を絶ち、数年間は条約改正の施設を慎み、堅く現存条約の範囲内に於て其約束を厳行し、彼我毫も仮借する所なからしめ、務めて人心を治め国論を養ふに於ては、人々自然外交上の志念を喚起し、之を達せんことを欲望せば、全国合同其帰向を一にするに及ぶべし。〔傍点朱筆〕此時に当り始めて其方針を公示し万口均しく之を賛成するに至ては、政府は輿論の援助を得、人民は政府の指導を得て相倶に其

348

志望を達するや、必す一挙手一投足の間にあらんのみ。固より時運の進度は人心を啓発するものにして、社会の

秩序も自ら定まる所あるを以て、数年の後に及んては人心の要望何ぞ今日に安せんや。之れ我人民の地位

進歩するときは海外人といへども自ら我に対するの感情を厚ふし、今日に於て踟躇するの情念を去るや已に前回

以来一回毎に我要望の各其歩を進むるの結果に徴して明かなり。故に仮令今日再ひ之を延期するも後来之を遂く

るの妨碍を為すものと信するは浅見の至なり。【傍点朱筆】我国論一定し国是堅立せは、何時を問はす我要望に応せん。之れ

列国交通を望むの実情、必すしも義の為めにあらす、利の為めにあるを察するに難からされはなり。

然れは如何して可ならん。国議未た熟せさる所ありとて今回の改正案を退けて、姑く延期を約するのみ。時幸に

英国政府は今回の改正案にして、我之に応せされは今後十ヶ年間は改正談判に応せさるの議ありと、之れ我か望

む所なり。政府は姑く内治を整へ人心を定むるの時期を予定して、若干年間の延期を約し、従前改正事業の関係

を絶ち、徐らに国論を収めて、更に其期に及んて堂々新案を提出するの議に決せんこと実に切望に堪へさる所な

り。

〔注〕コンニャク版。『秘書類纂』外交篇中巻四九〇〜五〇九頁に類以のものあり。

60 吉田清成宛賛成依頼書／日本諸新聞切抜通信舎

明治24年5月9日

謹啓、弊舎諸新聞切抜通信事業開始之儀御披露のため先般規則書相添へ御賛成下され度旨相願ひ、尚又其後御参

考のため新聞紙上の記事を切抜き御通信申上置候に付ては、御手数ながら此際御賛成の有無御一報相煩し奉り度、

因て不敬を顧みず更に此段相伺ひ候。匆々頓首

十　元老院議官・枢密顧問官時代

明治廿〔四〕年〔五〕月〔九〕日
〔墨書〕
「吉田清成」様
〔墨書〕

〔注〕活字印刷。

61　病床日誌A／吉田清成

明治24年5月13〜24日

日本諸新聞切抜通信舎印

五月十三日

后二時半吐血、一オンス斗り。其後しばく〜せきの出る毎に少しつゝ血まじる。合して半オンスに不足。食慾如常。今夜十一時頃、ビル三オンス程呑む。菓子二オンス位、喫煙如常。八時頃人力車にて永田町迄急行。

十一時半過迄談話之際、常に喫煙。せき一両度。少々血を見る。

五月十四日午前

零時十五分帰宅。手紙二通認め、新紙并手紙等に時を消し、一時十五分、床に就かんとせしに、俄然咳嗽相催し、吐血始る。十分程は不ゝ治、濁血鮮血交々出る。凡そ水呑コップ一個ほど、即壱合余と覚ふ。

三時頃松山先生来診△肺臓には目下弱点を不見出、多分ブロンキアル、ヘンムレーヂ（ホォルスト　ステーヂ）△脈少く不常　体温七度五分　なるべし云々。動体を堅く禁せらる。吐血の二オンス位を送る。甲の剤は四時半頃一度、七時過一度、十時過き一度、用ひたり。又五時半に之を用ゆ。

八時松山氏来診。肺無事。熱なし。体温七度余。脈七十五六歟。出血を改めつれば、何のトレースもなく、

薬二種を得。甲は出血防き剤、乙は咳嗽止めの剤と云。未用ゆるの要をみず。

61　病床日誌Ａ／吉田清成

唯鮮血のみなりしとの事。　矢張機〔ママ〕かんし一部分に破烈〔ママ〕を来たしならむ。　未ゝ確とのことにてありき。　動揺を

堅く禁せらる。

食事九時頃ビーフチー二オンス程。　十一時オーツミールにミルク一合を化し用ゆ。　イチゴ、砂糖にて十四五個。

さしみ（マグロ）一血〔皿カ〕　各之を食す。

食事四時過る頃ビーフチー二オンス、トースト二オンス余。　ミルク壱合〔但ボッター付〕。　氷片時々含めり。

熱　三時半、体温八度二分。　脈八十三四なりき。　自診。

朝より暮にいたり、咳嗽の為めに苦します。　一時或は二時間に出血少々つゝ。気分如平常。

通事昨今今ゆるみたる方。　胃弱は満性〔ママ〕なり。　昔年は一層よからす。　昨今年に至り、平順に趣きたれとも、時あり又

十八年ノ事也。　起る事あり。　胃の左の部に痛所あり。　十年此方時あり起りて不自由を感す。　執筆最之れに障るものゝことし。

先年は薬を以治する事不能、終に針治方を以て、輙く之れを治したる事ありたり。　目今も亦此痛み起り、間

々苦むなり。

五月十四続き

后七時過き実吉安純先生来診。　。。。

熱八十三分弱〇脈八十三四度〔ママ〕〇肺無異条〇気かんしの或部分の血くわん破れたるに相違なけれとも、いよ

ゝどの点と云事も判然せす。　右は上胸に少々斗り弱点あり。　左は肩の辺に少々物云ひあるが如し。　併之れ

も慥には不分との事。　薬剤を調合書を為して、松山方に取に遣す。　間なく来る。　矢張止血剤なり。　之れを一

度用ゆ。

食事ミルク壱合、ソープ、ビーフチー、ビスケット五六ケ、之を各相用ゆ。　十一時頃寝床につく。　朝方三時頃目

十　元老院議官・枢密顧問官時代

食
熱
用水ゆを塩
△十五日

覚む。出血する事（黒色）半オンスに足らす　△亦氷を胸に当て、前肩をひたして安眠す。五字目覚む。

五字半熱温七度五分。

六時前ビーフチーニオンス以上之を用ゆ。

九時頃、オーツミール、ミルク一合、ベリー壱皿。

医
午後二時食事。尋常。前田氏見舞、不逢。川村氏見舞、暫時逢。他見舞人は不逢。寺師へは逢ふ。暫時也。

六時頃、実吉先生見ゆ。矢張肺には申分なし。左の肩に少々欠点あるが如し。尤気簡肢付庸の小血管破れた

るに相違なきが如し〇氷袋を用ゆるにも不及との事〇

食
食事尋常〇温度高点八度に不及。

日
十時頃より寝入る。両度電信手紙等にて被起、甚た安眠を妨けたり。

十六
前三時頃目覚。吐血少し斗り。再ひ休み五字に到る。薬とビーフチーを用ゆ。実吉松方来診。変なしと云。

温
前六時、三十八度五部。十時、八度六部半。后二時、八度七分〇五時半、八度七分。八時半、八度七分。

十七日
三時頃、吐血少々つゝ、三四返。五六時頃にも同断。六時薬を用ひ、再ひ寝入る。八時前目覚む。温前七時、七度九分。

食
八時半頃、ベリーを食す。

九時半前、オーツミルとミルク壱合用ゆ。ヒーフチー三オンス程之を飲む。食味如常。月もの喰ひ安し。

医
吉田先生、九時半過来診。今日は治療は見合せの方可然との事にて、治療せす。別に変なしとの事。

薬の為めか、大便不通なりしか、未明少々ありしゆへ、少しは快く相成る。昨に比すれは今日は少々労れあ

るが如し。気分不宜、殊に頭痛絶えす。

61　病床日誌Ａ／吉田清成

本日は昨日と違、寒暖七八度も下れり。不愉快なり。寺師来つれとも不逢。

吐血後直に塩水をコップ一つ呑込めり。

前四時より八時迄安眠、氷を胸部に当たり。

五月廿三日夜より、廿四日六時に至る

一三先生会診後、異条なし。

一咳嗽は皆無と云ふも可なり。

一マツトルは如是、極少々なり。

一八時頃より安眠。廿四日前五時半に至る。

但其間時々眼覚め、薬用、体温斗り等にて少しの間覚めたりと云ふか如しと雖、続睡を妨けざりし。

一今朝眼覚めて爽快なり。

一発汗少しつゝ終束。之れ平常と同断と云ふも可なり。

一前十時半より安眠、十一時四十分頃迄。

一後三時半時間程まどろ寝。

一終日食味、至て宜しき中、唯喰過きむ事を恐る程なり。

一頭の重さも激剤之割合には感せす。平常少々勝りて、左耳鳴あるが如し。以上。

His Excellency

The Russian Minister.

I would personally & long before this have paid humble homage to His Imperial Highness had I not been taken by sudden illness which still confines me to bed ever since 13 th. I feel exceedingly sorry that Highness The Grand Duke has been directed soon to proceed to Uradiwostok without giving us the long cherished pleasure of wellcoming[ママ] him to our Capital. It is indeed impossible to find words to express the feeling caused by the deplorable emergency which have so deeply wounded our hearts. Now that pray represent my humblest sentiment that long live the Crown Prince the future Emperor of all the Russian is our humblest ernest desire and prayer!

Viscount Yoshida
Privy councillor

〔注〕鉛筆書。英文は挟込草稿。

62　病床日誌B／吉田清成　明治24年5月19日〜6月5日

〔温度表省略〕

五月十九日

体温　后九時三八、七。全十二時三六、一。

脈搏　全上一〇二。全上七八。

62　病床日誌B／吉田清成

呼吸　后九時三〇。全十二時二四。

薬用　后九時丸薬。全十一時四十分水薬。

摘要　七時頃より熟眠中盗汗非常に発す。九時検温するに三十八度七分を示す。十二時に至るも尚ほ安眠。時々腹鳴す。十時頃二三回の咳嗽、泡沫状の咯痰〔喀カ〕在るも、赤色を見ず。

此日午後一時より六時の間、体温三九七乃至四〇、七を示し、午後九時に到り三八七、となりたり。

五月二十日

体温　前二時三六、三。全五時三六、五。全八時三六、二。〃十時三六、二。后一時三六、六。全四時三七、二。

〃七時三七、八。〃十時三八、一。

脈搏　全上八四。全八時七八。〃十時、后七時七八。

呼吸　前三時二四。

薬用　前一時丸薬。全五時丸薬。全七時水薬。全十時丸薬。全十二時水薬。后二時丸薬。〃七時丸薬。

飲食　前一時牛乳三ℨ、牛肉茶三ℨ、ビスケット二個。全七時半スープ三ℨ。全八時イチゴ一皿。十時牛乳四ℨ、

パン少許、スープ五ℨ、オートミル少許。十二時牛乳五ℨ、刺身少許、飯二碗。〃五時スープ三ℨ。〃八時オツ

トミル二碗、牛乳六ℨ、スープ三ℨ、ヒスケット三個。

大便　前十二時半一行。全八時半一行。后三時十五分一行。

小便　前十二時半一行。后一時半一行。〃三時半一行。〃八時半一行。

摘要　至極安眠。更に咳嗽なく、時々醒覚あるも、直ちに就眠。六時半醒覚后異状なし。午後六時□□に変状な

く、胸部を診するに左肺先部后部に著しき水胞音あり。隠音等の打度に比較的に濁音を生す。又心臓下部に摩擦

十　元老院議官・枢密顧問官時代

音あり。其他異音なし。発熱なきを以て平穏なり。

終日変状なく、爽快の状を呈す。咳嗽二三回に止まり、咯痰[咯カ]あるも極少量の暗赤色を混するのみ。后八時頃より

就眠に臨み、全身かい痒の為め、初睡を妨げしを以て敢て安眠を得ず。

五月廿一日

体温　前一時三八、四。〃四時三八、七。〃五時四十五分三八、九。〃八時三八、三。〃九時半三八[ママ]、六。后一時

三八四[ママ]。后三時四〇、五。〃四時四〇、五。〃六時四〇、三。〃八時半三九、五。〃九時五十分三七、六。后十

二時三七、〇。

呼吸　后十二時一八。

脈搏　后八時半一〇八。〃十二時八四。

薬用　前〇時二十分丸薬。〃五時丸薬。〃十時水薬。〃十一時丸薬。后三時二十分解熱薬。

飲食　前一時牛乳五瓦、スープ四瓦、ヒスケット三個。全七時半オットミル一碗、牛乳六瓦、スープ三瓦、イチ

ゴ一皿。正午飯二碗、スープ五瓦、刺身一皿、ツユ一碗。〃十時スープ三瓦。〃十時半牛乳三瓦。

大便　后十二時半軟便快通。

小便　前一時一行。〃六時半一行。〃十二時半一行。后三時一行。〃五時一行。

摘要　前様にして終夜なりし故、今朝に至りても爽快ならず。七時半飲食后初めて就眠甚だ安静なり。前夜中咳

嗽咯痰[咯カ]稀発し、五十分余にして醒覚后、二三回の発咳同時少量の血痰を見る。但し暗赤色。后二時半頃迄異状な

かりしも、二時四十分より俄かに悪寒を発し次でせん慄を来す。直ちに検温、四十度九分を示す。因りて解熱剤

を用ゆ。□120となり、極めて微弱なるを以て、カンフルキニーネ各〇、一を毎三時に用ふ。三時より睡眠非常の

62　病床日誌Ｂ／吉田清成

盗汗咳嗽咯痰なし。后一時実吉先生御来診。〃八時松山先生御来診。

明治廿四年五月廿二日

体温　前三時三六、五。〃六時半三六、三。〃十時半三六、二。后一時三六、一。〃六時五十分三六、七。〃十

一時十五分三七、一。

脈搏　前三時七八。

薬用　前〇時十分丸薬。〃五時半丸薬。〃十時水薬。〃十一時丸薬。后一時半水薬。〃三時半丸薬。五時半水薬。

〃七時丸薬。九時半水薬。十時半丸薬。

飲食　前二時牛乳五ℨ、スープ三ℨ、ビスケット一個。后一時半オットミル二碗、牛乳五ℨ、スープ三ℨ、パン一片。〃八時オットミル一碗、牛乳五

個、イチゴ少許。后一時半オットミル二碗、牛乳六ℨ、スープ三ℨ、卵一

ℨ、スープ三ℨ、ヒズケット二個。〃十二時牛乳三ℨ、スープ三ℨ。

大便　前一時下痢。〃八時下痢。后二時半下痢。

小便　前一時一行。〃八時一行。后二時半一行。十時十五分一行。

摘要　続眠にて一時に至り、醒覚后、二三回の咳嗽、同時に血痰を混ず。二時再眠、盗汗絶へず。十一時俄かに

咳嗽と共に咯血凡四ℨ許。十一時四十分より十二時半に至るの間、安眠。始終盗汗甚し。醒覚后は時々血痰在り。

他に異状なくして、十二時に及ぶ。前八時松山先生来診、后三時実吉先生来診。

五月廿三日

体温　前一時半三七、五。〃四時三七、九。〃五時半三七、八。〃八時半三八、四。〃十一時半三八、七弱。后

一時半三八、七。〃三時三八、七。〃六時三八、五。〃九時半三八、三。

十　元老院議官・枢密顧問官時代

脈搏　前四時七二。

薬用　前一時五十分水薬。〃五時五十分水薬。〃七時十五分規那丸。〃九時半規那丸。〃十一時半水薬。后〇時

半キナ丸。〃三時半水薬。〃五時二十分兼水薬。

飲食　前六時半スープ三〇cc、〃七時イチゴ一皿、〃九時オートミル一碗、牛乳六〇cc、卵黄一個。后一時パン一片、

スープ三〇cc、牛乳六〇cc。〃四時ビーフチー二〇cc。〃五時四十分イチゴ一皿。〃七時半オートミル二碗、牛乳五〇cc、

パン少許。

大便　前一時半下痢。〃七時快通、一行。〃六時半一行。

小便　前一時半一行。〃七時一行。后〇時四十五分一行。〃六時半一行。

摘要　一時過まで不眠なれども二時に至り就眠。三時半に醒覚、麦湯を飲用して再眠。暫時にして醒覚。四時過

より軽眠。六時全く醒覚、爽快の状なりし。時々血痰在るのみ。他に異状なく、后七時半に至り就眠。甚だ安静。

盗汗甚し。

五月廿四日

体温　前二時三八、二。〃六時三八、三。八時三八、一。十時三八、〇。十二時三八、〇。后二時三八、四。〃

四時三八、一。〃六時三八、二。〃八時三八、一。〃十時三七、五。〃十二時三六、七。

薬用　前五時五十分水薬。〃八時半兼水薬。〃九時五十分水薬。〃九時規那丸[ママ]。十二時規那丸。后一時五十分水

薬。〃五時兼水薬。〃五時五十分水薬。

飲食　前六時半牛乳五〇cc、ビーフチー三〇cc、ハン一片[ママ]、イチゴ一皿、オートミル一碗。〃十二時パン一片、ヒー

フチー三〇cc、イチゴ一皿、魚肉少許。〃二時半牛乳五〇cc[ママ]。〃七時半牛乳五〇cc、スープ五〇cc、ビーフチー三〇cc、オ

ーツミル一碗、卵黄一個。

大便　后一時半快通一行。

小便　十時四十五分一行。后一時半一行。〃七時一行。

摘要　続眠甚だ安穏。二三回の咳嗽少しく暗赤色の血痰を混するのみ。他に異状なく五時に至り醒覚、頗る爽快なりし。后六時実吉先生御来診。后八時就眠。十二時に至るの間、三四回醒覚あるも、先づ安眠なりし。盗汗は例の如し。

五月廿五日

体温　前三時三七、七。〃五時三十分三八、一。〃八時半三八、三。〃十二時三八、二。〃六時三八、七。〃八時三八、三。〃十一時三七、三。

脈搏　前三時七八。

薬用　前一時半水薬。〃五時半水薬。〃九時十五分規那丸。〃九時三十五分水薬。〃十時半規那丸。〃十二時規那丸。后二時水薬。〃五時半水薬。

飲食　前一時牛乳六瓦、麦湯四瓦。〃五時十五分ビーフチー三瓦。〃六時半オーツミル一皿、ミルク五瓦、卵黄一個、イチゴ二十五個。〃十一時半イチゴ一皿。后一時パン一片、ビーフチー三瓦、牛乳六瓦、スープ五瓦、魚肉少許。〃六時オーツミル一碗、パン少許、牛乳五瓦、スープ五瓦。〃五時ヒスケット三個、ヒーブチー三瓦半。

大便　前四時四十分快通一行。后二時半一行。

小便　前一時一行。〃四時四十分一行。〃九時一行。〃十二時半一行。后二時半一行。〃八時一行。

摘要　一時頃より后は軽眠。二三回の暗赤色の血痰在り。五時に至り全く醒覚、益々爽快。前九時半松山先生御

十　元老院議官・枢密顧問官時代

来診。后一時十五分実吉先生御来診。后八時就眠。甚安静。盗汗減少して無きが如し。后七時頃少しく頭部の右

側部に疼痛を訴へらるも甚しきにあらず。

五月廿六日

体温　前二時三七、二。〃三時三七、五。〃五時三七、五。〃八時半三七、七五。〃十一時四十分三八、五。后

三時三八、二。〃五時三八、五。〃八時半三八、二。〃十一時三七、四。

薬用　前一時水薬。〃四時四十五分水薬。〃七時半規那丸。〃九時水薬。〃十時兼水。〃十一時五十分規那丸。

后一時水薬。〃三時兼水。〃五時水薬。〃九時半水薬。

飲食　前一時ミルク四ℨ。〃五時十五分ビーフチー三ℨ。〃七時オートミル一碗、ミルク六ℨ、イチゴ二十四五

個。十二時半パン一片、卵黄二個、ビーフチー三ℨ、魚ウシヲ半碗、牛乳六ℨ、イチゴ一皿。后七時牛乳六ℨ。

オーミル一皿、ビーフチー三ℨ、パン少許。
〔ママ〕

大便　前九時硬便一行。后二時軟便快通。

小便　前一時一行。〃九時一行。后十二時四十分一行。三時半一行。

摘要　左乳下第六七肋間に於て、尚摩擦音あれとも以前よりも減少せり。続眠二三回の咳嗽血痰少量あるのみ。

至極安静。四時半に醒覚后異状なし。后九時半就眠安静なり。

〔五月〕
廿七日

体温　前二時三七、〇。〃四時半三七、四。〃八時半三八、〇。〃十一時三八、二。〃三時三八、四。　五時半
〔ママ〕

三八、三。〃八時三八、一。十一時半三七、三。

薬用　前五時水薬。〃八時半3丸薬。〃九時水薬。〃十時半兼用水。后一時水薬。〃五時半水薬。七時半3丸薬。

62　病床日誌B／吉田清成

后二時3丸薬。

飲食　前六時半オーツミル一皿、イチゴ一皿、牛乳五ℨ。〃十一時半イチゴ一皿。〃十二時牛乳六ℨ、ビーフチー三ℨ、卵黄二個、魚ウシヲ一碗、パン少許。〃三時イヂゴ［ママ］一皿。八時二十分オーツミル、卵黄、ヒズケット、ヒーフチー。

大便　前七時快通一行。后一時一行。

小便　四時半一行。〃九時半一行。后一時一行。〃三時半一行。〃五時半。

摘要　連眠四時に至り醒覚。異状なし。終日爽快、后九時四十分に就眠。今日丸薬三粒を用ゆ。

五月廿八日

体温　前二時半三七、〇。〃六時三七、九。〃九時三八、三。〃十二時三八、二。后三時三八、三。〃六時三八、一。〃十時三七、五。

薬用　五時半水薬。〃八時半3丸薬。〃十時半水薬。后一時半兼用水。〃二時3丸薬。〃二時半水薬。

飲食　前六時ビーフチー三ℨ。〃六時半オーツミュル［ママ］一皿、ミルク六ℨ、ビーフチー三ℨ、ビスケット一片、卵黄二個、イチゴ十個。〃十一時イチゴ一皿。〃十二時ハン［ママ］一片、スープ五ℨ、ヒーフチー三ℨ、卵黄一個、牛乳三ℨ。后六時半オーツミル一皿、ビーフチー三ℨ、スープ二ℨ、ヒスケット一個。

大便　前七時半硬便一行。

小便　五時半一行、十時半一行、〃四時半一行。

摘要　昨夜九時四十分より就眠。安静にて前一時に至り醒覚。少量の盗汗在り。暫時にして再眠。五時二十分醒覚后、爽快なり。終日変無し。今日丸薬三粒を用ふ。

十　元老院議官・枢密顧問官時代

明治廿四年五月廿九日

体温　前一時三七、五。〃五時半三七、二。〃十時三八、一。〃十二時三八、四。后三時三八、五。〃六時三八、

○五。〃九時三七、九。十二時三七、八。

脈搏　后九時八三。

薬用　前一時4丸薬。前六時水薬。〃七時十五分4丸薬。〃十時兼水。〃十一時半水薬。后一時十五分4丸薬。

〃五時四十分水薬。〃六時十分4丸薬。〃八時半兼水。

飲食　前五時二十五分ビーフチー三3。〃八時オーツミル一皿、卵黄二個、スープ五3、パン一片、イチゴ一皿、

牛乳六3。〃十二時牛乳五3、ビーフチー三3、パン一片、卵黄二個、イチゴ一皿。后四時二十分ビーフチー二

3、カステーラ一片。〃六時二十分オーツミル一皿、ビスケット一片、ビーフチー三3、スープ四3、卵黄二個、

ミルク六3。

大便　前一時半一行。〃十時一行。〃二時半庸一行。[ママ]

小便　前一時一行。〃八時一行。〃十時一行。后三時一行。〃八時一行。

摘要　昨夜九時就眠にて、一時に至り醒覚。二時に安眠に就き、五時二十分に全く醒覚后、益々爽快なり。安眠

中少しく盗汗在り。二三回の咳嗽咯[喀カ]痰中に極微の血腺。但し暗赤色なり。后七時半より八時半に至るの間睡眠、

少量の盗汗有り。

ヒーフチー十一3、ミルク十七3、スープ九3、卵六3、〆四十二3

五月三十日

今日丸薬四粒を用ゆ。

体温　前三時三七、三。〃六時三七、四。〃九時半三七、八。〃十二時三八、五。〃三時三八[ママ]、五。〃六時三八

一。〃八時三八、五。〃十二時三七、七。

脈搏　前六時十分七六。

薬用　前六時半5丸薬。〃十時水薬。后一時5丸薬。〃三時水薬。〃六時5丸薬。〃十二時水薬。

飲食　前六時ビーフチー三ℨ。〃六時半ミルク四ℨ。〃八時半ミルク五ℨ、イチゴ一皿、ヲーツミル一皿、卵黄

二個、パン一片、スープ三ℨ。后二時牛乳六ℨ、パン一片、ビーフチー三ℨ、牛肉少許、イチゴ一皿。

〃六時ビーフチー二ℨ。〃七時オーツミル一皿、ビイフチー二ℨ、ビスケツト二個、スープ四ℨ、卵黄二個、ミ

ルク六ℨ。

大便　前八時軟一行。后一時半一行。七時一行。

小便　前八時一行。后一時半一行。

摘要　終夜熟眠、五時四十分に醒覚、爽快なり。咳嗽は稀発。咯痰[喀ヵ]褐色少量を混するのみ。

内用　丹□○、六。おひや○、六。

くすりに□□各四、○。

余は九○、○、一日分。

兼用　結列○、四五。

右丸とし一日分。

此外結列吸引法

今日丸薬五粒を服用す。ビーフチー八ℨ、ミルク廿一ℨ、スープ七ℨ、卵六ℨ、〆四十二ℨ。

五月卅一日

体温　前三時三七二、[ママ]前五時三七、四。前八時三七、五。〃十二時三八、四。〃三時半三八、三。[ママ]〃六時三八、三。〃十時三八、一。

薬用　前五時半5丸薬。〃十一時半5丸薬。后一時二十分水薬。〃五時半5丸薬。〃八時水薬。

飲食　前〇時二十分ビーフチー三ℨ、卵黄二個、イチゴ一皿。〃五時半牛乳三ℨ、ビーフチー三ℨ。〃十一時半ミルク二ℨ。〃五時半ビーフチー三ℨ、オーツミル一皿、スープ四ℨ、サシミ少許、卵黄二個、スープ三ℨ、パン少許。〃六時半ビーフチー三ℨ、オーツミル一皿、スープ四ℨ、ビスケツト一片、卵黄二個、ミルク六ℨ。

大便　前六時半庸便、后一時半軟便、〃十時一行。

小便　前〇時十分一行。〃六時一行。[ママ]〃十時一行。

摘要　異状無し。ビーフチー十二ℨ、ミルク廿三ℨ、スープ十ℨ、卵六ℨ、〆五十一ℨ。今日丸薬五粒を服用す。

六月一日

体温　前一時三七、七。〃三時三七、五。〃五時半三七、四。〃八時三七、七。〃十一時三八、一。〃二時三八二。〃四時三八、一。〃六時三七、八。〃八時三七八、[ママ]〃十一時三六、九。

薬用　前六時6丸薬。〃九時水薬。〃十一時四十分6丸薬。〃二時水薬。〃五時半6丸薬。

飲食　前五時四十分ヒーフチー三ℨ。[ママ]〃六時ミルク五ℨ。〃七時半ミルク五ℨ、オーツミュル一皿、スープ四ℨ、卵黄二個、トースト少許、ロースビーフ少片。[ママ]〃十二時パン一片、ビーフチー三ℨ、スープ四ℨ、ミルク六ℨ、牛肉少許、卵黄二個。〃五時ミルク三ℨ。〃五時半ミルク四ℨ。〃六時オーツミル一皿、ミルク六ℨ、ビーフチ

一三匁、卵二個、スープ四匁。

大便　前七時硬便一行。正午軟一行。

小便　前七時一行。后一時一行。〃七時一行。

摘要　昨夜十時より就眠。今朝五時に醒覚。益々爽快なり。本日体重を取りしに、十二貫八百九十五匁（匁）を示す。

但し正重なり。

今日丸薬六粒服用。ミルク二十七匁、ビーフチー九匁、スープ十二匁、卵黄六匁、〆五十四匁。

六月二日

体温　前二時三七、三。〃六時半三七、三。〃九時半三八、一五。〃十二時三八、六。后二時三八、五。〃三時

半三八、四五。〃五時半三八、三。〃八時半三七、九。〃十時半三七、七。

薬用　前七時6丸薬。前九時半水薬。〃十一時二十分水薬。后一時半6丸薬。〃五時水薬。〃七時四十五分水止。

十時水薬。九時半丸薬。（ママ）

飲食　前八時半オーツミュル一皿、ミルク六匁、スープ四匁、卵黄二個、パン一片、イチゴ一皿。〃十二時ビー

フチー三匁、ミルク六匁、スープ四匁、卵黄二個、パン一片、牛肉少片。六時ビーフチー三匁、ミルク九匁、ス

ープ五匁、卵二個、パン少片、オーツミル一皿、バナ一個半。他にミルク九匁。但し薬用三回分なり。

大便　前七時一行。〃十一時一行。

小便　前七時一行。〃十一時一行。后三時一行。

摘要　昨夜安眠、少しく盗汗有り。六時半醒覚后、少しく不快の状なりし。今朝より時々咳嗽咯痰有りて、中に（咯カ）

少量の血痰を混ず。但し鏽色なり。四時より五時半に至る迄安眠。其后は頗る爽快なり。十一時半就眠。

十　元老院議官・枢密顧問官時代

ミルク三十ℊ、ビーフチー九ℊ、スープ十三ℊ、卵六ℊ、〆五十八ℊ。

六月三日

体温　前二時半三七、三。〃七時半三六、九。〃十時三八、一。〃十二時半三八、三。〃五時三七、九。〃八時三八一［ママ］。

薬用　前五時十五分丸薬。〃十時水薬。〃十一時半丸薬。后二時水薬。〃五時半丸薬。「ミルク六ℊ。」［ママ］

飲食　前五時ビーフチー三ℊ。〃五時十五分ミルク三ℊ。〃七時半ミルク六ℊ、スープ五ℊ、パン一片、卵黄二個、ヒーフチー三ℊ、オーツミルク一皿、卵黄二個、イチゴ一皿。〃十一時半ミルク三ℊ。十二時二十分パン一片、刺身少許、スープ五ℊ、ミルク六ℊ、牛肉三片。〃六時ビーフチー三ℊ、ミルク六ℊ、スープ五ℊ、パン一片、オーツミル一皿、バナ、一個、卵二個。

大便　前六時一行。后一時半一行。

小便　前六時一行。后一時半一行。〃八時一行。

摘要　ミルク三十ℊ、スープ十五ℊ、ビーフチー九ℊ、卵六個、〆六十ℊ。

［六月］四日

体温　前三時三六、九［ママ］。〃五時半三七三［ママ］。〃八時半三七、八。〃十一時半三八、一。〃四時半三八、四。〃八時三八、一。〃十時三八、二。

薬用　五時十五分6丸薬。〃八時水薬。〃十一時十五分丸薬。后二時水薬。〃四時止水薬。〃五時二十分丸薬。〃十時半止薬。〃九時十五分水薬。

飲食　前五時ビーフチー三ℊ。五時十五分ミルク三ℊ。〃七時ミルク九ℊ、スープ二ℊ、卵二個、オーツミル一

皿、イチゴ一皿。〃十一時十五分ミルク三ℨ。〃十二時パン片[ママ]、ミルク六ℨ、ヒーフチー三ℨ、スープ五ℨ、卵

二個、牛肉二片、ベナ[ママ]一個。后七時二十分ビフチー三ℨ、ミルク七ℨ、卵二個、スープ五ℨ、パン少許、オー

ツミル半皿。

大便　前五時半軟一行。后一時一行。〃八時一行。

小便　前五時半一行。后一時一行。〃五時一行。

〔六月〕
五日

体温　前二時三七六。五時四十五分三七、二。〃九時三七、二。后一時三八四[ママ]。〃四時三七、七。〃七時三七、

九。

薬用　前六時7丸薬。八時半水薬。十二時丸薬。后三時水薬。〃六時7丸薬。

飲食　前六時ミルク三ℨ、ビーフチー三ℨ。〃七時ミルク六ℨ、パン一片、卵二個、オーツミル一皿、スープ五

ℨ。〃十二時ミルク三ℨ。〃一時[ママ]ミルク三ℨ、スープ五ℨ、卵二個、イチゴ一皿、オーツミル半皿。〃七時オー

ツミル一皿、スープ五ℨ、ミルク六ℨ、パン一片、ビーフチー三ℨ、卵黄二個。

大便　前七時一行。〃十二時一行。

小便　前七時、〃十時、后一時。

摘要　終夜熟眠益々爽快なり。八時半松山先生来診にてケレヲソートの注入、一等を肩胛関部に行ふ。

今日より丸薬七粒を用ゆ。

〔注〕東京慈恵医院用箋、鉛筆書。

十　元老院議官・枢密顧問官時代

63　「廿四年辛卯五月病痾中当座備臆簿」／吉田清成

明治24年5月26日〜6月7日

〔表紙〕

廿四年辛卯
五月病痾
中当座
備臆簿翠

六月一日　晴　風

卅日体量　十二貫八百九拾五匁

外風袋

　　　七百弐拾五匁

但綿入一枚　フラ子ル褌一　湯上り一

紐一　足袋一足

　　総量

　　十三貫六百二十匁

12,895匁
　　725
13,620

六月八日　一日に比し四十五匁の減量

体量
　十二貫八百五十匁
外風袋八百五十匁
総量十三貫七百匁

13,700
－　　850
12,850

六月廿三日月曜日

体量
　十三貫弐百匁
内　衣類
　六百六十匁
差引
　純量十二貫五百四十匁

五月廿六日
前四時半睡覚
今日は晴天、昨は風雨

一　五時ビーフチー三ᵍᵣ。

十　元老院議官・枢密顧問官時代

一　四時四十五分止血水薬。

一　六十時食事例之通。
　　〔ママ〕

一　オーツミール一皿

　　　　　廿と壱ろ

一　トースト　少々

一　ミルク生　六ろ

一　七時過松山先生来診、無異状、昨に比すれば宣布方。

一　前田献吉氏来訪。

七時過より八時頃迄。

一　寺師氏九時来訪。

一　井上要之助来訪。

韓城より帰国以来始て面会、沈石田の古掛地壱幅、印財一個、土産として贈る、前是唐錦一疋同断。

△右には報酬を要するなり。

一　体温

五時　　三七、五〇

八時半　三七、七五

十一時半　三八、五〇

后三時　三八、二〇

370

一田中章氏午前十一時頃来訪、昨夜山梨県より着京の由。久々振面会嬉敷候。同氏至て元気、同家一同も無事と云。お清同断。

一岡田令高二時頃来訪、是亦嬉し。

一田中氏へ有成家近・国行等之名刀を一見せしむ。

一昨日午後柳谷・有嶋両氏に午後暫時宛面会す。

有嶋武氏へ秘密書を貸す。

同氏より真の志にて無類の「妙薬奇応丸」なるものを五包贈残す。誠に信切なり。〔左に親の書き入れ〕

例の改正一件に付ては助復を口嘱す」かれ云に、此義に付ては既に充分に御切出しの上、事皆生きて居るから全く心配すること勿れ、我々満分尽力すべし」何分にも保養専一、一日も早く全快を祈る云々等にて辞去る。

一五時半頃　実吉先生来診、無異状と云へり。昨に比すれば又少々快気の方に趣けりと。薬剤も昨今日と同断にてよろしとのこと也。キナエン八3を午前二回に服用すべし。若発熱の萌もあらは又少々加へて可也との事也。

一体温

后八時半　三八、二〇

露皇太子の御遭難を痛み悼みてよめる。

醜のなしゝ

此禍事や

十　元老院議官・枢密顧問官時代

〔朱筆〕
「うらやすの」
　日のもとの
〔朱筆〕
「くにゝるひなき」

〔朱筆〕
　代々例なき
「きすならめやも」
　瑾となりけむ

此御災難に罹らせ玉ふことの御親皇帝皇后両陛下之御許に聞えし時は如何はかりの御悲歎に沈ませ玉ふらむと思
ひ遣り奉りて
たらちねの親のこゝろにくらふれは
うみの深さも物の数かは

時正に九時半睡を催す。

五月廿七日晴天
昨夜九時半過寝入、十二時過覚む。少々発汗ありし故令伝婆掛之」又寝る三時覚む」又同断四時頃覚めて再ひ不眠。

一体温　四時半　三七、四〇
　　　　五時　止血水薬

一四時半小水一行沢山出る。

一松山先醒七時半来診キナ丸を止めて

○結利屋丸を与ふ、三粒つゝ三回々一日分
止血剤は本の如し、無異条而已ならす快方に上進せるが故此変更を為す云ふ」但廿三日午後を以橋本・実吉・

松山三先生会診之時に此変更に予定しありしなり申聞候。

一体温前八時半　三八、〇〇

一本日別にかわる事なし。

一川村氏来訪庭より返る。　半時間程対話。

大山綱昌　大山巌　柳谷　其外見舞之由。

一勝安芳君より流芳遺墨其外贈らる。　手紙添ふ、親切なり。　先生脊上に腫物発し困難之由申来る。　併し昨今快方
之由。

一今夜至て安眠暁に及ぶ」　眼覚めて東雲日已紅」朝より爽快なり。　即廿八日也。

一昇二郎先生前十一時頃来診、治療に手を下ださす食事し帰らる。

五月廿八日晴天、　四時半頃より夕立烈く六時頃迄降続よき滋なり。

一寝起爽快故終日同断なり。

一此日より熱度も平常の方に傾けり。　昨日より此萌ありたり。

一食事平常。

十　元老院議官・枢密顧問官時代

一薬用無更。

一実吉先生四時頃来診、無異状のみならす血出止めり。最早氷嚢を用ゆるに及はすとまて云はれたれとも矢張続 【行の上部に○印あり】

ひて用ゆ。

一前田氏八時頃見舞、昨日鎌倉へ行けり之話。

一岡田・田中両氏親切にも看護を助く。来客の接待を引受の事。

一本日　皇后陛下御誕辰に付宮中開宴あり。病気ゆへ貞も参内不叶。乍恐陛下には少く御不例にて謁見は不被 【行の上部に○印あり】

仰付候由なり。

一右に付本日夕は御祝として類中幷来合せの朋友等打寄祝杯を傾けたり。 【醒カ】

一今夜安眠八時より明け四時半迄但五更過暫時睡む。

五月廿九日晴天

昨の夕立にて空気冷、朝は六十二三度にて昼時分漸く六十八度位なり。ちと冷に過きる心持せり。

一此日熱度最高点、后三時三十八度五分。

一丸薬四丸つゝ四度服用す。

○橋本・実吉・松山の三国手先生后五時に揃会診を遂く。充分に止血せりとのこと。外万端存分に快方に赴けり。故に此所にて気長く心静かに禅道を行ふべしとの事なり。煙草は不宜無他咳嗽を起すに至るときは又不量の出来事に及ぶも不被測が故なりと。三人共満足の意を表して去れり。今夜岡田・田中氏等同断之由。

三人共柳谷氏を亭主分として酒肴茶飯等を進む。

五月卅日晴天土曜日

此日体温最高点十二時　三時　八時　三十八、五〇なり。

○本日より丸薬五粒つゝ三度服用。

一水薬如故」ガーグル弁吸入薬等用ゆ。

一力士鈠山見舞一時間程余噺して去る。

一岡田・田中例之通万事を助く。

一本日は気分少々不勝の感ありしも格別の事には及ばざりし。少々草臥たる心持なり。

一本日お貞、后四時より寺嶋氏を訪問す。宗則先醒病嵩み来るを以、終に昨夕橋本先生を招き診察を請たりと云

（前是使者を以此義を頻りに勧告せし所同案にて折角其日を以橋本国手に申遣したりとの事也）。

本日手紙を遣し云々申入れし趣有之候処、返翰来る。是を以之を見れば執筆之気力は有之ものと見得候」其中

に卅一日を以赤十字社病院へ行くとのことあり。

一今夜八時少々過より九時半迄安眠。

一十時過より又安眠、一時頃覚め又寝入りて五時十分に睡む、爽快。
〔醒ヵ〕

一松山先生朝八時頃来診、無異と云へり。

一体温高点三八、五〇。

此四五日は前八時過より午後三時頃迄之間高点多し。

一実吉先生二時頃来診、異条なしと云へり。昨に比すれは能き方なりと。

十　元老院議官・枢密顧問官時代

五月卅一日晴天日曜

一体温最高点三八、五。

一此日食事大ひに進む。

△本日より結利屋ソート丸六粒づゝ服用す、但三回。

一本日用ひたる滋養物品壱升に及ぶ。　即六十オンスなり。　此位なれは充分なる旨、松山先生申聞けり。　内ビーフチー十3以上なり。

一雷権太夫九時頃より来訪、午後四時頃閑話せり。

一午後実吉先生来診。　無異条のみならす昨に比すれは勝れりとのことなり。

一田中氏例之通、岡田氏今日不見得。

一今夜安眠八時間余。
［ママ］
一

六月一日快晴　七十度位
〔醒カ〕
一五時半睡む体温三十七、四。

一六時丸薬　六粒。

△此日より六粒つゝ三回。

一止血薬軟なる分三回旧の通。

一西の海八時前より来訪、十時半帰る。

376

「廿四年辛卯五月病痾中当座備臆簿」／吉田清成

一田・岡田・柳谷・吉田二郎等来訪。

一実吉先生三時半来診、昨に勝れりとのこと。

一本日は意外に気分も宜布熱度三八、二を不昇。食事美味あり。

一外に異事なし。

今夜安眠。

六月二日晴天　火

一六時覚む　体温三七、三。

一本日は少々気分不宜、熱度も后三時には三十八度六分に上りたり。

多客の故かと思ふ。

一食事其外同前日。

一松山先生八時過来診。

△無異条此日より水薬は痰を切る等の為め向けたり。止血剤は不用とのことなれとも本日少々残物の出血ありし

故又々少く相用ひ候。

一田中・岡田・柳なと入来。

一今夜早刻より安眠、五時過に及ふ。

六月三日曇天午後雨

十　元老院議官・枢密顧問官時代

一五時過暝めて気分爽快なり。
〔醒カ〕

一薬食事如常。通事同断無申分。

一后三時に至り三十八、三を以最高天とす。
〔点〕

一岡田・田中見舞三時過より両人別にて水難救済会の大角力見に出かけたり。五時前後より雨益強く降りつれ共
夫迄に皆相済候由にて、西の海・劔山・小錦・八幡等今日を盛りの力士共皆上出来なりとの報告なりき。

○露太子遭難に関し政海大に騒ぎ、前きに青木大臣辞職之御聴届になり、又山田司法大臣・西郷内務大臣辞表
を呈し、去る一日御許容被為遊、田中不二麿を司法大臣に、品川弥二郎を内務大臣に、大木喬任を文部大臣に
（芳川氏辞職）任せられたり。伊藤博文を枢密院議長に任せらる」前是大山陸軍大臣辞表を呈す。之を許し大
将に任し兼任枢密顧問官、尋て高嶋中将を陸軍大臣に任し玉ふ」此一更迭は陛下西京御駐輦の時既に親任式有
之候事、先つ異例なり」

一今夜安眠盗汗少々あり。

一降出せる雨降つゝきて朝に及ぶ。

六月四日終日降雨

一五時に眠覚む、体温

一咳嗽不繁なれとも血痰少々つゝ出る。

一気分は至て勝れたり。

一食事其外如常。

378

一実吉先生午後早々来診、昨よりも胸の様子宜しとのこと。止血剤あらは可用とのこと也。血痰は残物なるゆへ

出つべきものなり。風薬の為めに被促たるならむとのこと。

一松山氏不来、吉田も」

一例の通田中・岡田終日枕辺に出没す。

一谷の川来る。

△此日体温四時十五分三十八度四分に上る。之れ夜来の降つゝきに北風を加大気至て滋ひたると対客多話と書も

のに余り骨を折過きたる等にて俄然昇たるものならむと想像せり。

△八時には又三八、一〇に下れり」此日榎本大臣へ一書を遣し就任を賀し、併条約改正案に対す意見書二冊共差

遺候。

毎日くけふもあすも体温食事薬用切隠通ひ等にて蓐を友としてぐつくして居らさるを得さるなと退屈千万

云はん方なし。嗚呼病には罹らぬやうに兼て注意せざるべからす。

△此両三日は日に六十オンス位の滋養物を服用せり。医師の申すにも之れにて沢山すぎるなりとのこと。通事よ

きゆへ胃の弱はるやうすもみえす。尤ペプシネ時々用ひる事。

△昨日今日と左の肋骨にからしを張るなり。あばら迦れの痛所も同断。少く快し。

一今は后十時なり。風雨朝より不止、中々止みさうのもやうもみへす。入梅の先触なるべし。

六月五日雨降る金

薬用食事等如例別に異事なし。

十　元老院議官・枢密顧問官時代

実吉氏後早く来診、少々昨に勝れりとのこと。色の付たる痰は終日吐出せりと雖、別に案するに不足とのこと也。

中村五郎家内引連れ石河県岩手県大林区署へ更任途上昨夕着京す〔より欠カ〕金沢より四日路なり」

田中・岡田其外来訪。

一此日少々眠る。

体温最高点三八、四。

夜亦安眠暁に至る。

六月六日半天土

一体温　三八、四〇に至る。
　　　但午後なり。

一此朝来来訪人に接し后後四時頃には余程草臥たり。

田中・岡田・吉田昇二郎・斎藤五郎・松山先生・柳谷氏等代る〳〵相見得困却致し候。之形にても親切も病人の身に対しては不親切と相成候半歟と思ふ斗に候。

一斎藤神戸より昨日十二時発今朝八時着一泊の上は大ひに安心せりとのことに候。今夜六時出発品川より出般又〔ママ〕神戸に向く、おしけ同伴。

之れより屯田の徴兵召連れ直ちに北海に向け発船之つもり。五時暇を乞別袖す。

田中章氏明七日未明出発山梨県へ滞るを以て今夜便宜の所へ一泊致度とて三時半過暇を告げて去る」去るに臨

63 「廿四年辛卯五月病痾中当座備臆簿」／吉田清成

み左の品を贈る。

一延寿国時の刀一振　二尺五寸位在銘白拵入[ママ]

但本阿弥成善より昨年中買求置候分

一細上布白飛白　一

一刀油

一実吉先生本日は不来。

一松出先生后四時過き来診。

一昨五日結理屋の注謝を「手打かけ」の辺になせり。本日も至るも跡痛みて苦しき故今日は断りたり。[ママ]

一九時より安眠七時に至る、大いに休む。

六月七日半晴日

一朝岡田令高来訪、本日出発帰阪するとて暇を告けて去る。

一西村茂樹氏へ一の長文を送る幵書類二個も」

一此日より臼井氏外客接対の為め来る。

一本日朝来気分殊之外快爽なり。

〔注〕鉛筆書、表紙は墨書。原文書のページが変わる毎に、前日の続きの旨、冒頭一行記載あり。下書きメモ一葉あり。

十　元老院議官・枢密顧問官時代

64　大津事件に関する上奏／東久世通禧他十二名

明治24年6月1日

〔表紙〕
上奏

上奏

一今般の大変事第一に講究すべきは、露国皇太子殿下接対は、単に一皇族の旅行として之を待たん。我政府は我国の大賓として国賓を以て之を待てるに非すして、只た我帝室の一つ賓客として之を待したること先年独逸皇孫の来遊と同一視したるか如し。聞く、万国の例規に依れは、皇太子は皇帝と同待遇を為すものゝ如し。現に墺国へ露国皇太子殿下の来遊せられたる時も露帝同様の待遇なりしやに承る。果して然りとせは、津田三蔵か無礼を働く前、既に我か政府は露国に対し君主国と君主国との交際の礼を欠きたるに非らさるか。若し此礼を欠きたりとせは、其大礼を欠きたる、我帝国政府は其責任を負はさることと相考候。

一今般の事実に先んし露国公使館へ匿名の投書を為したるものあり。公使之を外務大臣に具陳し、陸路上京の危険を案し、海路東上の事を陳す。同大臣断乎として危険なきを答へ之を請合たりと。是より前き露国公使は、日本法律には自国皇室に対する不敬を罰する条は備はれとも、外国に対する法律なきを以て緊急命令を以て其欠を補はんことを乞たるとき、外務大臣は之に対し決して危険なきを断言し、且つ若し其事あれは我皇室に対する律を活用すと答へたりと。司法大臣も亦然り。前総理大臣も亦然りと承りたり。此活用を公使に請合たりと云ふ説はあり間敷説なれとも、万一にも此の事ありとは政府か三蔵を待つに常人律を以てしたるは、露国を欺きたるものなり。我帝国政府は其責任を負はさるべからさるものと思考仕候。

一今般露国に対し礼を失したるは、実に我国にして国際公法に聞きの致す所とせば、三蔵か挙なきも猶ほ当局者は其責任を欠きたるものとす。況んや其行政官に属する警察吏にして此暴人を出す、是れ日本政府の大過失なり。日本政府の過失如此。其れ大にして政府其責なしとせば、大臣は今後如何なる失策あるも責に任せすへきものなからんとす。是れ臣等の解し難き所に御座候。

一露国皇太子殿下を救ひ奉り、三蔵に刀傷を負はしめたる車夫も尋常の法律を以て論するときは、法官の尋問を経さるへからす。然を其事なくして直に勲章を与へられたるは、露国皇太子殿下を救ひ奉りたる功の偉大なるに依るなるべし。既に常律を破て直に車夫を賞す。而して三蔵を擬律するに至ては却て常人謀殺の律を以てす。又常人犯を所断するに大審院を開く、前後甚貫連せす。是臣等か甚解し難き所に御座候。

一今般の事に付、英人、独逸人等の助言あるも猥りに信用すへからすと存候。彼等は他国の政略上より発する言を信用して、飽くまて敬礼を尽し、露人の怨を解くに注意せさるへからす。英独人等の政略上より発する言を信用して、飽くまて敬礼を尽し、露人の怨を解くに注意せさるへからす。露国の政略は遠大なり。今日の至穏甘言を頼み之を後年に保つ可からすと相考候。

一露国今日の事変に対し平穏を示すも、他日日本の国難に際会せば、其の時こそ今日の報酬を謀ること彼の国既往の歴史に徴して明なり。セバストホール敗軍の時の条約は、仏国敗軍の機に乗して忽ち破壊したり。又英仏連合軍の北京を陥るゝに当りて、忽ち其機に乗し支那に迫り東シヘリヤを割取りて露国の版図に帰したり。他日若し我れ危難あるときは、其機に乗して報復を計るも未た知る可らす。是歴史の証明する所決して一時の事として安んすへからす。我れ只礼を尽し義を重んし隙の乗すへきなき様注意すること肝要と相考候。

383

十　元老院議官・枢密顧問官時代

一勅使御派遣の事は国際法の上に是非共是れなかるへからすとは識者の主張する処にして、臣等亦希望仕候処に御座候。而して政府は忽ち決し、又忽ち止む。其理由とする処を伝聞するに、彼れより断り来れは、推して行くも却て彼れの感を悪敷なすの恐れあり。故に止められたりと。我の行くは我か礼なり。彼れの一応辞するも亦礼なり。我れ若し彼れの言儘にせは、是れ我れの礼を欠くなり。公法学者の論より言へは、此事は単に露国と日本の関係而已と考ふるは大なる間違ひなり。日本は実に古今未曽有の事を為し、未曽有の歴史を作り、万国公法の未た曽て見さる一条を加へたり。今般の事の礼を得ると得さるとは、公法上を汚と輝との岐路にして、日本か世界の公法学者の罪人となる歟又は手本と成る歟の分るゝ処なりと。臣等も実に此説を賛成するものに御座候。罪人の処刑と当局者の罷免とを断行して後ち直に勅使御派遣有らせらるゝ事を希望仕候。前陳数条之次第に付、今日の御所置国家重大事件と相考候。因て政府責任之帰する所を明瞭にし、併て勅使御派遣の義至急御施行有之度、謹て上奏仕候。恐惶謹言

明治廿四年六月一日

従二位伯爵　　東久世通禧

従二位子爵　　谷　　干城

従三位子爵　　黒田清綱

従三位子爵　　河田景与

従三位子爵　　海江田信義

正五位子爵　　日野西光善

従三位男爵　　千家尊福

従三位男爵　高崎五六
従三位　山口尚芳
従三位　伊丹重賢
従三位　三浦安
従四位　西村茂樹
正五位　富田鉄之助

〔注〕羅紙、墨書。

65　病床日記

明治24年6月6日〜7月19日

六月七日より日
〳〵〳〵〳〵

六月廿三日
「山吹の事」〔虫損〕「□の事」「樋を直す事」「物品会計を厳にする事」「玄関用筆紙墨の事」

△看護夫は五月十九日より六月六日迄十八日間

△山田磯解雇す。

十　元老院議官・枢密顧問官時代

六月六日　土

后十時半　三七、四〇

　　　此日夕刻迄に看護夫△

○同　七日　日

前四時十五分　三七、二〇

七時二十分　ビーフチー三ʒ

七時半　丸薬六個

同　　　ミルク三ʒ

体温同　　　三七、一五

八時半　大便一行軟

九時　　食事

一卵黄　　二個

一スープ　五オンス

一ミルク　六ʒ

一オーツミール　少々

一パン　少々

一イチコ　二十個

一サトウ　三ʒ

十時──────含嗽

十一時──────水薬

十一時半より后一時頃迄吸入薬

后十二時半　丸薬六

同　温度　三八、一〇

后一時半食事

一ビーフチー　三ℨ

一ミルク　六ℨ

一スープ　五ℨ

一卵黄　二個

一焼牛軟製　一片

一オーツミール小一皿

一イチゴ　十四五ケ

一サトウ　三ℨ

一四時大便一行軟

一四時半実吉先生来診

一后五時前　水薬

一五時二十分　丸薬六

十　元老院議官・枢密顧問官時代

一五時体温　　三八、〇〇
一五時十分より同半頃まて吸入薬
一五時四十分より六時十五分迄からし張付　胸部二ヶ所
一六時二十分より七時まて同断脊左肩の部一個服部[腹]一個
一七時小便一行
一七時五分食事
一ビーフチー　　三ℨ
一ミルク　　六ℨ
一卵黄　　二個
一スープ　　五ℨ
一オーツミール　一皿
一パン　　小一片
一サトウ　　一ℨ
一バナ、　　半個
一后八時五十分より九時半迄盗眠
一〃八時半温度　　三八、四〇
一〃九時四十五分　丸薬六
一〃十一時　　三七、五〇

65　病床日記

一十一時十五分　水薬

一十一時半大便　一行軟

一十二時より休み五時に至る

六月八日

前五時　　　　　　三七、〇〇

一〃五時半　ビーフチー三ℨ

一〃六時　　丸薬　六個

一同　　　　ミルク　三ℨ

一〃六時半　ミルク　三ℨ

一〃六時半　大便一行

一七時食事

一卵黄　　　二個

一ミルク　　六ℨ

一ソープ　　四ℨ

一オーツミル　一皿

一サトウ　　三ℨ

一イチゴ　　二十個

一八時　　　ペプシネ

十　元老院議官・枢密顧問官時代

一十時　　　　　　　　　　　　　水薬
一十時半　　　　　　　　　　三七、七〇
一十一時　　　　　　　　　　丸六
一十一時半　　　　　　　　　含嗽
一后十二時半食事
一スープ　　　　　　　　　　五ℊ
一玉子　　　　　　　　　　　二ツ
一牛肉　　　　　　　　　　　一片
一ミルク　　　　　　　　　　五ℊ
一オーツミール　　　　　　　少許
一鯵　　　　　　　　　　　　小一疋
一パンバツタル　　　　　　　一片
一サトウ　　　　　　　　　　一ℊ
一后二時　　　　　　　　　　丸六
一三時十五分　　　　　ビーフチー三ℊ
一同朝鮮飴　　　　　　　　　小二片
一三時半より五時半まて吸入薬
一三時半　　　　　　　　　　水薬

一四時　　三八、一〇

一五時半　　丸六

〆　丸二十四

此日体重を取る　即十二貫八百五十匁也。

去る一日の量に比すれば四十五匁の減。

─────

一食事六時半

　　如前日

　　外に鶏刺身少々

一七時　　ペプシネ

一八時半　　大便一行

一八時五十分　水薬

一九時より　眠る

十一時半　　三七、三〇

─────

六月九日

一前四時　　三七、四〇

一五時　　丸六ヶ

十　元老院議官・枢密顧問官時代

一七時半食事

　　如前日

一七時二十五分　　ペプシネ

一九時　　　　水薬

一九時半より十時半頃迄吸入薬

一十時　　　　丸薬六個

一后二時　　〃　六〃

一六時半　　〃　六〃

一十時　　　三八、五

一后一時　　三八、七五

一三時　　　三八、六〇

一六時　　　三八、六〇

─────

一后十二時二十分食事

一后七時半食事

　　例之通

「一終日のミルク三十3即五合なり

65　病床日記

一后四時　　大便一行

一三時頃　　水薬

一九時半　　水薬

一九時　　　大便一行

一十時十五分　三七、七〇

一之れより休み安眠明朝六時に至る

六月十日　曇微雨、水

一六時覚む

一六時半　　　三六、七〇

一六時四十五分　丸六

一九時　　　三七、八〇

一七時半　　　大便一行

一八時食事

一ミルク　壱合

一玉子　弐つ

一スープ　五ろ

其外如例」

十　元老院議官・枢密顧問官時代

Milk ————————	30
Beef Tee ————	12
Soup ————————	15
6 Eggs ———————	18
Butter 1 ろ = ——	3
	78

6|78
13合　即壱升三合なり

十日

一十時　丸六個
外別紙にあり略す

十一日

六月拾一日

五時半　すむ
九時半　〃
三時　　〃
十時半 ⎫
　　　 ⎬ 丸薬六個つゝ
九時　すむ ⎭

三時半　すむ

十二時　すむ ⎤
　　　　　　 ⎥水薬
十一時　すむ ⎦

五時半　すむ ⎤
　　　　　　 ⎦嗽合
八時

吸入薬 ⎰十一時半より十二時四十分まて
　　　 ⎱六時半より七時、后十一時頃少々

五時半　　　　三六、九〇

八時半　　　　三七、四〇

十一時　　　　三八、一〇

四時半　　　　三七、八〇

七時　　　　　三八、二〇

十一時　　　　三七、二〇

食事朝

一五時半ビーフチー　　四ℊ

一　〃　ミルク　　　　三ℊ

一七時半ミルク　　　　六ℊ

一卵黄　　　　　　　　二個

十　元老院議官・枢密顧問官時代

一スープ　　　　　三3
一バツタル　　　　1 3
一パン半片
一オーツミール　　一皿
一イチゴ　　　　　二十個
一サトウ　　　　　三3
一ペプシネ　　　　三分

后十二時半　　大便一行
六時　　又少々

○此日服用せし滋養物は七十3内外なり。

五時半すむ
六月十二日　曇
十時　〃　　｝ミルク二合
二時半　〃
十時半　〃　　丸薬六個つゝ

65　病床日記

九時　すむ）
三時　同　　）水薬
十一時半同　）

含嗽｛六時五十分
　　｛五時四十分頃より七時前迄

吸入薬｛五時四十分頃より七時前迄
　　　｛又八時前後二十分間

体温
前
五時　　三七、二〇
八時半　三七、四〇
十時半　三七、七〇
三時　　三八、二〇
五時半
十一時半　三七、九〇

十　元老院議官・枢密顧問官時代

純

○本日の滋養物は七十オンス以上なり。

前

六時前　大便一行なし

十二時　同断

松山・実吉両先生后後[ママ]各自に来診、共に快方なりと喜色ありたり。もう不遠よくなりますなとの言葉もありき。

我も亦斯くは思へり。

此日快爽なりしも夜十一時に至り俄に模様替りとなり咯血せり。大凡五ℬ計之出血なり。

十日午后に鮮血を少々つゝ両度に見、十一日午前両度、十二日前両度都合三日之出血には頗る当惑せり。而して今夜の出来事に及び不思儀[ママ]千万に思ふなり。

⊕愚見は外に記置

六月十三日　晴、土

・一五時覚む

・五時十分　すむ

・九時半　すむ

・一時　すむ 〕止血剤

・五時　すむ

水薬

・九時半　すむ）

后三時松山先生来診、静寧冷法を専らにせよとの命なり。

七時　すむ）
十一時半すむ）丸薬六個つゝ
三時半

之より一両日止めとのことなり。　代りにキナヱン丸を服用のつもり。

十一時　すむ）
二時　すむ）風水薬
七時　すむ）

一体温

五時半　　　三七、〇〇
九時半　　　三七、四〇
十二時二十分　三八、一〇
三時　　　△三九、〇〇
五時　　　三九、四〇
八時半　　　三八、四〇

十　元老院議官・枢密顧問官時代

此体温の上りしは昨夜略の反動なる由故に規那園を服用する事にせり。

一后五時十五分　キナ丸四粒

一　八時半　キナ丸四粒

十三日

ん跡の心持わるからす

大便前八時十五分極軟一行

后十一時五十分一行

一実吉先生へ人を遣す（早天）。是非今朝早々来診を乞。

前十時来診、同人も稍々ビックリ被致たり。昨夜松山先生より得たる止血薬を四度服用すべしとの事。

△結利屋丸は十八粒に減しても可しとの事。

食事も少しは扣へる方可然との事。

松山先生不快に付外診不叶との事にて代診入来、実吉先生と同時なり。

松山氏三時来診、ケリオ丸を止め喜那丸を与ふ。

本日食事は一体に扣へたれとも純滋養物は七十オンス内外を服用す。

65　病床日記

胸部痛所の呼吸咯血前よりも却て安らきたりと松山先生申されたり」　実吉君もやゝ其口気ありき」

一昨十二日昼前伊藤博文氏見舞、直に居間に通り半時間程雑話別袖す。　此機を不迦予て承居候海江田氏身上の件を話す。　伊藤伯云く定数之なきを如何せん、又東久世も帰院せねばならぬ勢と成り居り彼是心配最中の趣云々承候」

尋て安藤則命氏身上に関する訟を開談せり。之に対しては云へる様彼一件に□□□〔虫損〕最早疾く解したる事也と。因て恩給令云々の苦情にも談及し置たり。　細事は略す」

一有嶋武氏五時来訪、機密摺ものを返す。唯一輿論誘導の要用を解きCustoms Lawsに関する分は受持整頓之義を以せしに、氏正に肯んして暇を告けしは六時なりき。

六月十四日　晴天、日

一前六時十分覚む

△一時半頃せきの為めに目覚む。　此時咯血あり。　二オンス位と覚ゆ、随分苦痛を感せり。　五時早々強き塩水を九オンス位呑込みたれは吐血も随て止みぬ。　血は重もに濁色を帯ひたり。

一前二時　　三七、九〇

一六時半　　三七、八〇

十　元老院議官・枢密顧問官時代

一　九時半　　三七、八〇

一后十二時三十分　三八、六〇

一　三時　　三九、二〇

一　五時　　三九、三〇

　　此処でキナ丸四ツ用ゆ。

一七時十五分　三八、四〇

一　九時

一三時四十分　すむ　散薬

一七時半　すむ　同

一十時半　　同

一六時十五分　すむ^{止血}　水薬

九時半　すむ　同

十二時半　すむ　同

五時　すむ　同

八時　　同

一十一時　　風水薬

ん之れは当分用ゆるに及ばすと松山氏命せり。

雑

一前二時頃　大便沢山たり
一二時半　ビーフチー　二オンス
一七時　ビーフチー　四ℨ
一七時半　ミルク　四ℨ
一八時　又大便少々
一十時食事
（ミルク　七ℨ
　玉子　弐つ
　スープ　鶏　四ℨ
　パン　ボツタル　少許
以上
一后一時半食事
（イチゴ　一皿
　ビスケツト　一片半
　ビーフチー　四ℨ
以上

十　元老院議官・枢密顧問官時代

松山氏云、今日は食事は格別勉強して沢山服用するに不及と。

一九時頃松山先生来診、先生自云して云、咯血前よりは呼吸の工合は安らかなり、不思儀なる[ママ]もの哉。或は前に滞居しものゝ為めに呼吸も不充分なりしならむ。唯血行は却てさわやかに呼吸の出来るやうなりしものなら[虫損]□。

此説昨日と同断。

世九度に昇らは可用とてキナエン丸薬三度分即十弐粒を与へられたり。

先つ当分風水薬は不用、止血剤丈け昼夜に五度服用すべしとの事。

一実吉先生三時来診、其当時少しばかり咯血ありたり。又六時に真に少し同断。実吉氏散薬を三度用ひべしと。故に之を用ひたり」アヘン入之薬の由」

△后十一時頃純乎たる咯血ありたり（単一度）。跡は少し出血ありて格別の事に至らす。尤直に塩水を壱合呑込めり。

六月十五日　曇半天、月

七十八度

前四時過目覚む。

四時半単行咯血ありたれとも跡は格別なし。

404

一五時半　ビーフチー　　　四3

一七時　ミルク　　　　　　六3

一八時半食事如常

六七時　すむ　同 `'`

四時　すむ　同

十二時　すむ　同

九時　すむ　同

前五時　すむ　止血剤

体温

一四時四十五分　　　三八、九〇

此所にてキナ丸四つ用ゆ。

一六時十分　　　三八、七〇

一八時半　　　三八、七〇

一十時半　　　三八、四五

二十二時半一時　三八、三〇

一四時　　　三九、二〇

十　元老院議官・枢密顧問官時代

一五時半　　　　　　三九、一〇
一七時半
一九時半　　　　　　三七、八〇
之れより安眠、暁三時目覚。
一十二時　ビーフチー　四3
一十二時半　ミルク　　六3
一十二時半食事
（ビーフチー　　　　弍3
　ミルク　　　　　　六3
　玉子　　　　　　　二つ
　スープ　　　　　　少々
　パン　バッタル　　少々
　イチゴ　　　　　　一皿

一実吉先生一時半来診、異なる診断なし。松山先生差図之通にて可然との事也。
成り丈け早目に転地御養生可然、却て其方可被宜との事被申居候。いつれ当月一抔を経過せざれは不能談なり。
一前七八時頃大便一行
一后一時過又一行少々
一此日昨日と同じく全然清静を旨とし身体の労動を禁し常に平臥して大便食事診察等の外更に起上らす。殊に氷

囊弍個を間断なく胸に当て摂養せり。

一后十二時頃より出血出痰も至て少なく仕合なり。

○税所愛之助本日より当方へ引戻し候事。

后八時食事如常

六月十六日　半天、火、七十六度

一三時目覚む。

一四時より眠　五時過頃覚む。

体温

一六時　　　　　　　三七、〇

一三時四十五分　　　三七、九

一后十二時四十五分　三八、二五

一十時四十五分　　　三八、五〇

一八時　　　　　　　三七、五〇

一六時　　　　　　　三七、四〇

一三時　　　　　　　三八、三〇

十　元老院議官・枢密顧問官時代

一　八時　　　三八、三〇

一　十時　　　三八、〇〇

一三時　　　　すむ　止血剤

一六時半　　　すむ　同

一九時四十五分　すむ　同

一后一時　　　すむ　同

一四時　　　　すむ　同

一七時　　　　すむ　同

一十時大便一行　軟

△此日朝より鮮血を見ず。稀に少々つゝ痰に交りて濁色のものを見しのみ。先つ此分にては出血は止りたるならむかと思ふなり。

───────────

岩手の依藤忠夫氏来訪せしも不面会。

○本日は如何なる栄誉の日ぞ、恐多くも畏き御辺より至微病状御尋として交肴壱台下し賜り思食の旨身に余りて難有感泣の外無之候事。侍従長手状写

拝啓　陳は貴官御病臥之旨被　聞食為御尋交肴壱台下賜候間御伝申進候。敬具

明治廿四年六月十六日

侍従長侯爵徳大寺実則

枢密顧問官子爵吉田清成殿

六月十七日　曇、水

一昨夜十一時就眠、今朝未明三時覚め又不睡。

一前三時　　すむ　水薬

一七時半　　すむ　同

一十時半　　すむ　同

一一時半　　すむ　同

一四時半　　すむ　同

一七時半　　　　　同

体温

一前三時　　三七、七〇

一六時　　　三七、八〇

一十時　　　三七、八五

一十二時　　三七、九〇

一二時　　　三八、四〇

一五時　　　三八、五〇

一七時　　　三八

十　元老院議官・枢密顧問官時代

一前三時半　大便硬

一三時過出血を始め続ひて血痰少々つゝ七時に及ぶ。然れとも分量においては些々たる事なり。

一八時前

松山先生来診、外に一種の止血剤を調ふべしとの事也。

因云米国発明の薬にて榛の木の渋皮を蒸溜したるものゝ由。

但無害の薬なりと、痢の妙薬なりと。

昨日交肴下賜之御礼として前田献吉氏代つて内参す。前九時当邸を発す。

而して十時半頃帰宅相成、徳大寺侍従長へ厚く御礼の執奏を申出、殊に昨今まての病状等委細に被話呉候処、伯爵にも不一方安堵之旨申述、且つ此趣は直ちに御上之御聴に奉入候様可致の事被申述候由。尤拙者へ伝言も有之候。

大事之期節と存候間折角無手抜様摂養有之度云々を以てせり。

因日想ふに宮中辺にては病状余り不勝との感ありしものゝ如し。近日宮内大臣次官等其外総理大臣榎本大臣山田中将等続々見舞有之しなり。皆不能逢事。

一本日は又　内親王常宮殿下より鮮魚一台賜り身に余る有りかたさ筆紙に無被尽候。即刻志村氏に依頼して拙代理として御礼に参殿被致候。

六月十八日　木

一　午前六時過目覚む気分よし。　昨夜は能く安眠せり。

一　午前七時　　　　　　三七、六五

一　〃　七時十五分　　ミルク壱合

一　血痰少々つゝ出つ、新出血なし。

一　午前七時　　止血剤　一

一　〃　八時　　新止血剤

一　〃　十時　　同断

一　午前九時半吉田昇次郎氏来訪。

一　午前十時十五分　三八、六五

　　これは食後早々なりしによる。

一　午前八時半　　大便一行

一　〃　九時　　食事

　　　　如例

一　正午　　　　新水薬

一　午後拾弐時十五分　三八、四〇

一　〃　壱時過　　大便少々

一　〃　弐時半　　　　三八、五〇

一　〃　四時半　　　　三八、一〇

十　元老院議官・枢密顧問官時代

一　〃　五時　　水薬

一　〃　六時半　　三八、一〇

一　〃　七時　　水薬

六月十九日　金

一午前五時半覚む。

一同時　ビーフチー　　四3

一同時　三七、八〇

一〃六時　　新水薬

一〃八時半　旧水薬

一松山氏来診、新水薬の功力を加ふ。

一七時　大便一行　極軟

一九時　食事

　　食味不宜

一九時半　大便少々

一十時　　新水薬

一九時半　三八、二〇

一黒田氏見舞、玉子持参。

65　病床日記

一海江田氏より玉子拾弐参る。
一十一時半　兼用水薬
一同時　　　三八、三〇
一同時手足の瓜を取る。[ママ]
一午後壱時　新水薬
一三時　　　兼用水薬
一弐時　　　三八、四〇
一四時十五分　新水薬
一四時半　　　三八、三〇
一六時半　　　三八、一〇
一九時半　　　三七、八〇

六月廿日曇　土、半天
一午前六時覚む。

一〃　六時十五分　　三七、六〇
一〃　　　　　新水薬
一〃　七時　　ミルク壱合
一〃　七時半　大便庸

十　元老院議官・枢密顧問官時代

一　〃　八時十五分　　三八、二〇

一　〃　八時半　　食事
　　　　　　　如常

一六時十五分　　三七、六〇

一八時十五分　　三八、二〇

一一時半　　　　三八、九〇強

一二時半　　　　三八、四〇

一二時五十分　　三八、四〇

一四時四十五分　三八、二〇

一七時　　　　　三八、六〇

一十時　　　　　三八、〇〇

〇九時半　　ケリオ丸四粒

再ひ始めて日々十二粒つゝ用ゆる事。

一六時十五分　　止血剤

一九時半　　　　同

一十時半　　　　兼用水薬

一十二時　　　　止血水薬

一二時四十五分　兼用水薬

一三時半　止血水薬

一六時半　止血剤

一九時半

一前七時半　大便

一十一時頃同断

　　ん痢血少々交る。

一后四時過　同　少々

一前八時半食事

ミルク　　　　七ℨ

玉子　　　　　弐つ

スープ　　　　五ℨ

パンバツタル　少々

オーツミル　　一皿

ビーフチー　　五ℨ余

外七時にミルク　六ℨ

以上

昼飯

十　元老院議官・枢密顧問官時代

后一時食事

ミルク　　　　　七勺

玉子　　　　　　弐つ

スープ　　　　　五勺

オーツミール　　一皿

ビーフチー　　　四勺強

イチゴ　　　　　二十個

　　　以上

△四時少々烈く咳嗽起る。尋て出血始まる。新血の如く思はる、如何。

直ちに塩水を五勺呑こみ氷嚢を胸部に当つ。

因日

胸部一種の呼吸の音は咳嗽ありし後はしばらく止む。又た咳嗽は何時も吐血の種なるがごとく覚ゆ。

一昨今呼吸短にして永く内に引くことは中々難渋、殊に直に咳嗽を醸生するの恐あり。何れに原因ありや。

一本日橋本先生を聘す。

一后五時橋本・実吉・松山の三先生相揃診察を始めたり。橋本先生云く、いまだキツチリ癒へ切らぬ所あるから血も時々出るであろう、又熱も急には全去にいたらざるべし、夫故右辺は含み置きて成丈け静かに気長く養生の外なし、人によりては僅々つゝの出血は一ヶ月もつゝく事あり、何そ少々つゝ数日間の出血を気にするに足らざるものなり云々。

「カンシヤク」は一番にわるし、成りたけおさえてださぬやうになされ、又話は大にさわるゆへ之れも余程気を付けてひかへめにするを好とす云々」

外略す

六月廿一日　雨天、日

六時十五分前覚む。

廿二日前十二時二十分　三八、三〇

九時半　三八、四〇

五時　三八、五〇

三時　三八、二〇

十一時十五分　三八、五〇

八時十五分　三八、二〇

六時　三七、七〇

前六時　新水薬

十一時十五分　同

三時　同

十　元老院議官・枢密顧問官時代

十一時　　同

前八時　　ケリオ丸四つ
十二時半　同四つ
四時半　　同四つ

前七時二十分　大便
十二時　　同

ん痢血を見る。
〔肛カ〕
屁門側のものより出血の様子あり。

二時　　再大便
随分下る、之より腹のぐわいよし。

食事
六時半　ビチー　　三ぷ
七時　　ミルク　　五ぷ
八時半　ミルク　　六ぷ
　　　　玉子　　　弐つ
外にミルク三
　　　　スープ　　五ぷ

（パンバツタル少々
　　　　パン半片

同后一時　ビチー　　　　五ℨ
　　　ミルク　　　　　　四ℨ
　　　玉子　　　　　　　弐つ
　　　スープ　　　　　　四ℨ
　外にミルク　　　　　　三ℨ
ん丸薬服用の為
　　イチゴ　　　　　　　二十個
昼前後水飴を相応に用ゆ、子共へも相応に遣候事。

前八時半松山先生来診」試験せし吐ものには何も悪きもの見得不申、多分此日より用ひのケリオ実効なるべしとの事に候。

此日出血更になし、あやしき血痰様のもの朝の間に少々見得たれとも終日咳嗽も血痰も至て稀なりけり。

大雨十二時半頃来る、直に止めりと雖一種騒きの基となれり、爾来降つゝき鬱陶敷天気なり。

夜の食事八時過昼の分と大凡そ同し略す。

十　元老院議官・枢密顧問官時代

此日午前午後とも睡眠多ふし。〔ママ〕　九時半より十一時半、后三時頃一時間程
又六時半頃より八時頃まて
又眠り且つ覚め十一時に至る。

　六月廿二日　半天、火

五時半覚む。

○体温

五時四十五分　　　三七、六〇

九時半　　　　　　三八、三〇

十二時　脉搏八十六七　三九、〇〇

一時半　　　　　　三八、八〇

二時半　　　　　　三八、八〇

四時　　　　　　　三八、八〇

六時半　　　　　　三八、二〇

○丸薬

六時　　　ケリオ丸三粒

十時　　　すむ　同

420

二時　　すむ　同

六時　　すむ　同

○水薬

七時半　　すむ　新水薬

十一時半　すむ　同

三時半　　すむ　同

七時半　　　　同

○兼用レモネー水薬

后五時　　すむ　同

○大便

七時一行軟

九時過同断

四時過同少々

○食事

六時十五分　ミルク　六ℨ

八時半　　ミルク　五ℨ

同　　　ビーフチー　四ℨ

同　　四ℨと認　卵黄　二つ

十　元老院議官・枢密顧問官時代

同　　スープ　　　　四ℨ

同　二ℨと認　バツタル　一ℨ

同　　パン　　　小一片

同　　オーツミル　一皿

　　合二十五ℨ

后十二時　　　　　　ビチー　四ℨ

一時　｛ミルク　　　六ℨ

　　　玉子　　　　　二つ

　　　スープ　　　　四ℨ

　　　バツタル　　　一ℨ

　　　パン　　　小一片

　　　オーツミール　一皿

　　　イチゴ　　　　少々

実吉先生后三時頃来診、無異事趣被申聞。

少々下痢の気味ある故如何と云ければ日外用ひしレモネー水薬を可用との事也。直に松山薬局より取寄。

此日少々血痰出る。みな古き濁色のもののみ、熱度少々高過きる心持せり。食欲には少しも障なきが如し。

師匠の千代に常盤津四つ五つ語り置きたり。別に草臥の種にもならざりしが如し。両三日前にては之を聞くの元気なかりき。此間盗眠あり。

十時頃床に次く。

六月廿三日　半晴、火

五時十分睡覚

○体温

三時半　　　　三七、八〇

五時半　　　　三七、六〇

十時　　　　　三八、五〇

一時　　　　　三九、〇〇

四時　　　　　三九、二〇

　脉搏九十一、二

体温は如之上れとも気分上格別の苦みを不覚。

五時半　三八、四〇」

十一時半　三八、五〇

○水薬レモネトアヘンチンキ含入の分。

△止血水薬は今日より取止めの事。

十　元老院議官・枢密顧問官時代

九時二十分　すむ　水薬

十二時二十分　すむ　同

五時半　すむ　同

九時　すむ　同

松山先生八時前来診、無異条旨云々」止血剤を止めレモネ剤にアヘンチンキを少々加ふる事にしたり」出血はや

みたれとも少々下痢の気味あるゆへ之を止むるの法なり。

○丸薬　一日十六粒の割

前六時　すむ　丸四粒

七時半　〃〃　同

四時半　すむ　同

一時　すむ　同

十時　すむ　同

○食事　結利屋

前四時　ビーフチー　三ℨ

五時四十分　ミルク　四ℨ

八時半　ミルク　六ℨ

同　2＝バツタル　正一ℨ

З9＝玉子　二個

ビチー　　三З

オーツミル　一皿

パン　中一片

肉茶六З

牛乳十З

玉子六З　　合純滋養物二十四З也

牛酪二З
〔酪力〕

ん此バツタル硬体一Зミルク何Зに当るや不詳。

バツタル一Зの正味は三、四、Зのミルクと劣る事なかるべしと思ふなり。可糾。

△ビーフチーの力　三Зの肉茶は十二Зの牛のスープに劣る事万々なかるべしと思、後日可糾。

○食事

昼飯は朝の分と大抵同じ。

二十Зの純滋養物は服用せり。

夕飯同断

んタピオカ　プツヂングを少々加ふ。

二十四ℊ純滋養物服用せり。

合計六十八ℊ也

内肉茶十二ℊ以上

牛乳三十四ℊ以上

玉子十八ℊ以上

スープ十二ℊ以上

バツタル若干ℊ

六月廿四日　晴天、水

四時半覚む」合九時間程安眠せしなり」

○丸薬

五時　　　すむ　ケリオ丸四つ

十時半　　すむ　同

二時半　　すむ　同

六時半　　すむ　同

○水薬　下痢止めの方

八時半　　すむ　水薬

十二時　　すむ　同

四時半　すむ　同

八時　　すむ　同

○キナエン　　十二個

后十時

○体温

五時　　　　三八、○○

八時十五分　三八、七○

十二時半　　三九、○○

四時半　　　三八、六○

六時半　　　三八、七○

九時半　　　三八、九○

○食事

五時　ミルク　四ʒ

七時　肉茶　　四ʒ

九時　ミルク　六ʒ

　　　玉子　　弐個

　　　スープ　六ʒ

十　元老院議官・枢密顧問官時代

合滋養物二十六 $\frac{3}{}$

オーツミル　一皿

パン　　少々

バツタル　少々

十二時　ビーフチー　　四 $\frac{3}{}$

　　　　タピオカプツヂンク　一皿

二時　　ミルク　　六 $\frac{3}{}$

同　　　ソーダビスケット　一片

同　　　イチゴヂヤム　少々

后四時頃　カステイラ　小一片

一松山先生七時半来診無異条」バツタルを扣へたる方可然かとの事。

一実吉先生三時半来診。高熱を征伐せすんば余り連日の三十八度以上も為めに不良なりとて、喜奈遠を命し呉たり。不知松山先生は同意するや否や」今夕六ゲレインを用ひ明朝同断のつもり。

実吉先生云く、本局部の方は無事なれとも気管枝カタール少々起り居れり、夫れが為めに或は此高熱を来すも亦知るべからすとの事。

アイスクリーム三縁亭より取寄せたれとも不出来故拙者は不〔虫損〕□たしか返したる由なり。

六月廿八日　曇、日

四時半覚む。

五時半　肉茶　三ゟ

八時　ビスケット　一ッ
　　　ミルク　六ゟ
　　　玉子　三つ
　　　ビーフチー　四ゟ
　　　パン　少々
　　　バツタル　少々つゝ
　　　ゼリー
　　　オーツミール　一皿

水薬
六時二十分　すむ　水薬新
十一時半　すむ　同
四時半　すむ　同

十　元老院議官・枢密顧問官時代

散薬二度（今日より二度減ず）

九時半　　すむ　散薬

五時半　　すむ　　同

廿九日前一時　　すむ　　同

体温

五時　　　　　　三八、五〇

十一時二十分　　三八、九〇

二時　　　　　　三八、五〇

六時十五分　　　三九、〇〇

昼食事夕同

大抵如常

今日より玉子三個を増加せり。合て一日分九個也。

大便

八時前一度、午後二字半一行、皆極軟

八時半松山先生来診、病院等の話あり」午後二時頃実吉先生来診、無異条」

六月廿九日　月

一年前六時覚む。

一〃六時十五分

ミルク　　　　　六勺

水飴　　　　　　少々

一〃九時　　　　食事

ミルク　　　　　六勺

玉子　　　　　　三ケ

ビーフチー　　　五勺

オーツミール　　一皿

パンバツタル　　少々

午后二時半　食事

ミルク　　　　　五勺

玉子　　　　　　三勺

ビーフチー　　　五勺

ドウミヤウシ　　少々

十　元老院議官・枢密顧問官時代

　　〃　九時　食事

玉子　　　　　三つ

ビーフチー　　五3

アスキ　　　　少々

カンツメアンズ　一ツ

散薬

午前壱時

午后十一時三十分

水薬

午前七時十五分

午后壱時十分

　〃　八時半

丸薬

午后六時三十分

大便

午前壱時過　七時　十時半

午后三時　十一時半

体温

午后四時

松山先生来診

午后四時

十一時　　三八、三

午后五時三十分　三八、三

七時　　　三八、五

午前一時　　三九、四

三時半覚む。

六月三十日　晴天　時あり微雨、火

四時〃　ビーフチー　四ℨ

五時半　ケリオ丸　　四粒

七時五十分　散薬　　ん前日新に調製の分下痢止め剤と云。

65　病床日記

433

十　元老院議官・枢密顧問官時代

十一時　水薬

結利屋

五時半　ケリオ丸　四

十二時　　　　　同四

七時　すむ　　　同四

散薬下痢止め

七時五十分　散薬

一時　すむ　　　同

六時半　　　　　同

此所で薬法更る。

水薬

十一時　すむ水薬

四時半　すむ　　同

七時半　　　　　同

大便

前五時頃一行軟

十時頃一行同

65　病床日記

一時頃一行少々同
五時頃一行極軟

体温
前四時十五分　　三八、〇〇
同九時半　　　　三八、二〇
后三時　　　　　三九、四〇
后四時半　　　　三九、三〇
七時半　　　　　三九、四〇
十時頃　　　　　三九、四〇

食事
四時　　ビーフチー　四ℨ
五時半　ミルク　　　六ℨ
十二時　ミルク　　　四ℨ
一時〃　ミルク　　　六ℨ
二時〃　ビーフチー　四ℨ強
三時半　玉子　　　　弐個七ℨ
同時　　スープ　　　六ℨ

十　元老院議官・枢密顧問官時代

パンプツヂンク　少々

七時　ミルク　四3

新散薬

橋本、ベルツ、実吉、松山諸先生一時半会診」ベルツ氏のみ主任診察を施し外は略せり」胸部何れの点に於ても

痛所なきにはちと驚きたる模様なりけり」ベルツ氏の指南にて新散薬出来せり。四時毎壱包。

新々水薬

后五時半　すむ　新々水薬

九時半　眠不覚して用ゆる事を得ざりき。

ベルツ先生聘せしは橋本先生の注告に原因し、柳谷氏昨廿九日ベルツ氏へ面会依頼せしなり。

七月一日　晴、水

六時覚む。

前二時　散薬

三時半　三八、六〇

四時　ビーフチー　五3

同時　水飴　一3

四時大便一行　軟

65　病床日記

○散薬

前二時　すむ　散薬

六時半　すむ　散薬

十時半　すむ　新散薬

二時半　すむ　同

六時半　すむ　同

十一時半　すむ　同

○結理屋丸

七時半　すむ　丸四個

十一時半　当分中休み下痢を止るを

三時半　第一とする故なりと。

○水薬

九時

一時　右同断

五時

体温

三時半　　　三八、六〇

十　元老院議官・枢密顧問官時代

七時　　　　三九、二〇

一時十五分　三八、八〇

但十二時に解熱丸薬を用ゆ。

四時　　　　三九、四〇

十一時半　　三八、六〇

食事

四時　ビ、チー　四ℨ

　　　水飴　少々

七時半　ミルク　七ℨ

　　ん石灰水入

九時半頃　玉子　三つ

同　肉茶　三ℨ

同　ミルク　六ℨ

同　んラキム水入

同　カステラ少々

后一時半　肉茶　三ℨ

　　ミルク　六ℨ

玉子　三個

スープ　四ℨ

五時半頃　セイゴプーヂング　少々

肉茶　四ℨ

同　水飴　一ℨ

八時　ミルク　四ℨ

十時　肉茶　三ℨ

スープ　五ℨ

玉子　三つ

ドウメウジ　少々

ミルク　六ℨ

腹太く不用

大便の事　皆水瀉なり

前四時　一行　軟

九時　一行　同少々

一時頃　一行　同

四時　一行　同

薬の功能更に不見得がごとし。

十　元老院議官・枢密顧問官時代

松山先生九時頃来診、薬方に変更を加ヘケリヲ丸幷賢胃水薬を中止せよとの命」代ふるに二種幾奈丸を一日三回用ゆべしとの事、少しく熱を解かむとの見込なり」此頃の高熱は一つは庄［肛カ］門の腫物の為めにも相生し候事に存すとの事也。拙も同感なり。

幾那丸二種　　各二粒つゝ

十二時　すむ　丸　四個

四時　　すむ　丸　四個

八時　　すむ　丸　四つ

七月二日　半天　木

六時覚む。

六時　　　　散薬

十時五十分　同

二時　　　　同

六時　　　　同

十時　　　　同

八時　　　キナ丸薬

440

十二時　　同　　　　同

三時　　　同

――――――

体温

九時過　　　　　三八、六〇

六時二十分　　　三八、〇〇

二時半　　　　　三八、二〇

八時半　　　　　三八、八〇

前四時　　　　　三八、〇〇

八時半頃松山先生来診、無異事」九時頃昇先生同断、貞治療を受く」依て生云く従前之薬四種共何の功なし、実吉先生四時頃来診、無異事、乍去下痢は是非止めなければならぬ云々」故に奇応丸を用ゆる格護[マヽ]なりと」先生同意せり。

食事

同　　　ビーフチー　　四3」

后一時　　卵黄　　　　三個

九時　　　ミルク　　　六3」

〃　　　　水あめ　　　一3

四時半　　肉茶　　　　四3

有感記す。

下痢を止むる薬は容易になきものと此度始めて発明せり。可戒事也。

○大便の事

七時　　一行　水瀉

八時　　又　少しぐあい能き分もあり。

三時　　一行　極水瀉

十時十五分　一行　毎の通

△　水瀉且食物之実夥し。

此夜九時頃奇応丸五粒を服用す。

五時　ミルク　　五ざ

十時　ミルク　　五ざ

同　　ビ、チー　四ざ

同　　水あめ　　少々

七月三日　金

体温

午前七時　　三八、一

正午　　　　三七、二

442

午后四時半　　三八、八

〃十一時　　　三七、八

丸薬　　前六時半　奇応丸七つ

午前九時半　　前七時　　同　五粒

午后四時　　　后七時

〃十時
　　七時半

食事

午前八時　ミルク　　　六勺

〃九時　　ビーフチー　四勺

　　　　水飴　　　　　少々

　　　　葛　　　　　　少々

　　　　玉子　　　　　二ケ

午后二時　ビーフチー　三勺

　　　　ミルク　　　　四勺

　　　　オーツミル　　少々

十　元老院議官・枢密顧問官時代

　〃　七時　罐詰林檎　少々

　〃　八時　ビーフチー　四3

　　　　　　　飴　　少々

　〃　九時　ミルク

　　　　　　　　　六3

大便

午前二時

　〃　六時半

午后二時半

　　十二時

大便の模様少々変れり。

一午前六時奇応丸七粒を服す。

一午前九時松山先生来診。

　七月四日　土

体温

午前五時半　　三八、〇

正午　　　　　三八、八

444

65　病床日記

午后三時半　　三八、三

〃　六時廿分　三八、八

〃　八時四十分　三八、七

薬用　前七時　奇応丸　七粒

后八時　同　　五〃

午前十時　丸薬

午后四時半　〃

〃　十一時　〃

食事

午前〇時廿分　ビーフチー　三勺

〃　飴　少々

〃　五時　ミルク　六勺

玉子　二ケ

〃　九時半　ビーフチー　三勺

スープ　三勺

飴　少々

十　元老院議官・枢密顧問官時代

午后一時　鑵詰桃　少々
　　　　　ミルク　六ℊ
午后三時
　　　　　ビーフチー　四ℊ
〃　六時
　　　　　飴　少々
　　　　　葛　少々
〃　九時
　　　　　ミルク　四ℊ
　　　　　ミルク　六ℊ
　　　　　ビーフチー　四ℊ
一ミルク　　　　二十二ℊ
一ビーフチー　　十四ℊ
一卵　　　　　　六ℊ
一スープ　　　　三ℊ
　　　　　計四十五ℊ

大便
午前四時半
〃　七時半
〃　十一時半

午后一時十五分

〃　六時半

〃　八時

〃　十時半

一午后八時……………

一午前五時半奇応丸服用

七月五日　雨天、日

四時半覚む。

五時　大便　軟

六時　ミルク　壱合

　　　　　　　　六3

体温

午前六時半　　三八、五

　　十一時　　三八、三

午后二時　　　三八、五

十　元老院議官・枢密顧問官時代

五時半　三九、一

薬用
午前九時　丸薬
午后五時　〃
十時十五分　〃
午后二時半　奇応丸七

大便
午前五時　一行
午后一時廿分　〃
〃九時　〃
飲食
午前六時　ミルク　六3
十時　ビーフチー　三3
葛　少々
鐘詰桃　少々
午后三時半　葛　少々

65　病床日記

〃　六時　ビーフチー　四ℊ

　　　飴　少々

九時半　ミルク　六ℊ

惣料

一ミルク　十二ℊ

一ビーフチー　七ℊ

　　　計十九ℊ

一葛　少々

一飴　少々

一鑵詰桃　一回

七月六日　月

体温

午前十一時　三八、五

八時半　三八、四

正午　三八、八

午后三時半　三九、一

六時　三九、三

十　元老院議官・枢密顧問官時代

脈搏

午前一時　　八〇、
正午　　　　七八、
午后三時半　壱〇〇、
六時　　　　八六、

呼吸

午前一時　　二四、
正午　　　　二〇、
午后三時半　二三、
六時　　　　二三、

薬用

奇応丸　午前二時
　　　　七時半
午后八時

450

65　病床日記

塩規丸　————————————

午前十時

午后一時半

六時

散薬

午前四時半

午后九時

飲食

午前二時　ビーフチー　四ℊ

　　　　　葛湯　　　　一碗

八時半　　ミルク　　　六ℊ

十時半　　ビーフチー　四ℊ

　　　　　葛湯　　　　一碗

午后二時　ミルク　　　六ℊ

三時半　　ビーフチー　一ℊ半

十　元老院議官・枢密顧問官時代

卵　　二ケ
鑵詰桃　半個
五時半　ビーフチー　二弖
十時　葛湯　一碗

大便
午后九時　多量
十一時半　〃
午前〇時半　中量
四時　〃

小便
午前〇時半　中量
〃四時〃
〃十一時半〃
午后九時〃

一昨夜安眠を得て午前〇時半に醒む。尓後僅に軽眠、午前三時頃より毫も眠らす、時々少量の咯痰あり。

65　病床日記

一大便は極軟稍水様なり。

一午前十一時半に便通同質一回、正午頃より午后壱時過迄睡眠を得たり。

一本日は前日より気分快なり。

一足部寒冷を覚ふ。

一午后二時半松山先生御来診、散薬を御方せらる。

一午后三時過より鈍赤色を混したる咯痰あり。夜に入りて止む。然れとも咯痰時々少量宛あり。

〔ママ〕
六月七日　火

体温

午前一時半　　三九、〇

七時　　　　　三九、一

正午　　　　　三八、五

午后三時　　　三九、六

六時　　　　　三九、六

十時　　　　　三九、一

脈搏

午前一時半　　九〇

十　元老院議官・枢密顧問官時代

　　　　七時　　　　　九　六
　　　　正午　　　　　八　六
　　　　午后三時　　　九　八

呼吸
　　　　午前一時半　　　二三
　　　　七時　　　　　　二〇
　　　　正午　　　　　　一八

薬用
奇応丸　午前六時半　九時半
塩規丸　午前十一時
　　　　午后三時

454

散薬
　午前八時
　午后一時
　五時半

飲食
　午前二時　ビーフチー　三ℨ
　七時　　　ミルク　　　六ℨ
　十時　　　ビーフチー　三ℨ
　　　　　　葛湯　　　　一碗
　午后十一時　ビーフチー　三ℨ
　正午　　　ミルク　　　五ℨ
　　　　　　ミルク　　　四ℨ
　　　　　　ビーフチー　三ℨ
　　　　　　葛湯　　　　一碗

大便
　午前九時　多量
　午后二時　中量

十　元老院議官・枢密顧問官時代

十二時　　〃

小便

午前七時　　多量

一昨夜十時頃より午前一時過迄安眠を得たり。

一午前二時過より軽眠は三時頃に至り全く醒覚今朝に至る。

一今朝も亦一時間余睡眠し午前九時便通多量軽軟水瀉様、但し通利前に服痛［ママ］ありし。

一時々喀痰少量僅に鈍血を混す。

一午后二時極軟中量。

一午后三時三十分松山先生来診。

一夜に入り就眠十時頃迄安眠せり。

七月八日　水

体温

午前六時　　三九、〇

十時　　　　三九、一

正午　　　　三八、三

65　病床日記

午后三時　三九、〇
六時半　　三八、八
十二時　　三八、六

呼吸
午前六時　二四
正午　　　二四
午后三時　二四
六時半　　二〇
十二時　　二〇

脈搏
午前六時　一〇六
正午　　　一〇〇
午后三時　一〇〇
六時半　　九六
十二時　　八六

十　元老院議官・枢密顧問官時代

薬用

奇応丸
午后九時

塩規丸
午前〇時三十分

十一時

午后三時半

散薬

午前八時半

午后二時半

水薬
午后十一時

葡萄酒
午前六時四十分

午后一時半

四時三十分

飲食

午前五時十五分　ビーフチー　　三ℨ

六時　　ミルク　　四ℨ

十一時卅分　葛湯　　一碗

ビーフチー　　三ℨ

午后四時三十分　葛粉製　　少許

醬油汁及野菜

五時　ビーフチー　　三ℨ

ミルク　　四ℨ

大便

午前四時半　　多量

八時半　　〃

午后六時　　五ℨ

九時半　　四ℨ

十　元老院議官・枢密顧問官時代

十時半　一〇

小便
午前四時半　多量
午后三時　五〇
　　九時半　三〇
　　十時半　一〇

一昨夜十二時過続て屢睡眠を得今朝五時半全く醒覚、但し今朝少々盗汗の徴あり。咳嗽は身体動揺の際微発するのみ、咯痰も時々少量宛咯出す。色前に同し。

一便通は多量質前の如し。

一午前九時半松山先生来診。

一　〃　十時半実吉先生来診。

一尿は濃琥珀色を徴す（透明）。

一午后六時大便酸臭帯黒春黄色全く水様中に白色粘液状のものを混す。

一午后八時十五分より咯血を始め同九時頃に止之（三〇余暗赤色）。

一　〃　十時松山先生御来診、処方せらる。

一　〃　九時半便質前に同し。

65　病床日記

七月九日　木

体温

午前六時　三七、九

十一時　三七、四

午后三時　三八、二

六時　三八、七

九時　三九、四

十二時　三九、七

脈搏

午前六時　一〇〇

午后三時　八六

六時　八六

九時　一〇八

十二時　一〇八

呼吸

午前六時　二二

十　元老院議官・枢密顧問官時代

午后三時　二四
六時　二二

薬用　水薬
午前五時半　十一時半
午后二時　六時半

飲食
午前一時　ビーフチー　三〇
六時　ビーフチー　三〇
九時半　ミルク　三〇
十一時半　ミルク　三〇
午后三時半　葛湯　一碗
五時三十分　ミルク　三〇
麦湯　少許
八時三十分　葛湯　一碗
ビーフチー　三〇
十時三十分　ミルク　三〇

大便

午前五時半　　　　四𢦏

　　七時

　　九時

午后二時　　　　　三𢦏

　　十時　　　　　　九𢦏

小便

午前五時半　　　　四𢦏

午后二時　　　　　三𢦏

　　十時　　　　　　九𢦏

一昨夜十時頃より頻に便通を催し屢便器にて取り或は自利する事もあり。

一五時半に一回四𢦏許、質前日に同じ。

一今朝四時十五分頃より咯血三十分間許にして止み（三𢦏許鮮紅色）、昨夜来今朝に至る迄咯血及ひ便通の他度々就眠せり。

一午前九時松山・実吉両先生来診。

一午前七時及ひ九時の便は緑色の粘液状にて少量。

一四肢は始終冷を感す。又倦情も覚ふと云ふ。

十　元老院議官・枢密顧問官時代

一此日は朝より口中の乾燥増し口渇引飲絶す飲料を好む。
一便通の催しも大に減し腹鳴も減したるものゝ如し。
一午后七時半橋本・松山の両国手御来診。

七月十日　金

体温

午前三時　　三八、九
六時　　　　三九、八
九時　　　　三九、三
午后参時　　三九、五
六時　　　　三九、七
九時　　　　三九、二
十二時　　　三九、三

脉搏

午前三時　　八六
六時　　　　一〇〇
午后三時　　九六

六時　九二
九時　一〇〇
十二時　一〇〇

呼吸
午前三時　一八
六時　一八
午后三時　二〇
六時半　二四
九時　二二
十二時　二四

薬用　水薬
午前〇時半　六時半
午后二時半　六時

散薬
午后〇時半　四時半

十　元老院議官・枢密顧問官時代

十時 ｜

飲食

午前壱時半　ビーフチー　一勺半

五時　葛湯　一碗

六時　ミルク　三勺

九時　葛湯　一碗

午后一時半　ミルク　四勺

ビーフチー　三勺

六時　葛湯　一小碗

ビーフチー　三勺

九時半　ミルク　五勺

小便

午前一時　六勺

四時三十分　五勺

六時半　五勺

十時半　八勺

病床日記　65

一一昨夜喀血及ひ便通繁き為め安眠せす。昨日も終日少しも眠らす。

一昨夜十一時頃不快の感覚（悪寒ならんか）、由て胸部の氷巻法を去り十二時の体温上記の如く、且つ喀血の傾きあらんかを感して不眠を来し（但し此際再ひ氷巻法を行ひ氷薬及ひ食塩水を服す）、然れとも腹鳴便意漸減して時々軽眠に就き今朝に至る。喀痰は極少量にて血痰絶へす、皮膚に湿潤を帯ふるのみ全く発汗せす。一昨夜来聴覚過敏口中乾燥口渇飲引前日に同し。

一今朝より屡々睡眠を得下痢全く止み午后六時頃悪寒あり。此日始終睡眠勝、夜に入るも同し。口中乾燥依然として渇は減し皮膚は乾燥して発汗少もせす、時々腐色性血痰及粘痰を排出す。折節腹鳴便意あるも放疵［ママ］して暫時焉る。便通一回もなし。

午后五時　　六ろ
十一時　　　八ろ

七月十一日　土

体温

午前三時　　三九、〇
　六時　　　三八、三
　十時　　　三八、九
午后壱時半　三九、三

十　元老院議官・枢密顧問官時代

脉搏

三時半	三九、五
六時	三九、八
九時	三九、三
十二時	三九、二

午前三時	一〇〇
六時	一〇〇
十時	九二
午后六時	一〇〇
九時	一〇〇
十二時	一〇〇

呼吸

午前三時	一八
六時	二〇
十時	二〇
午后六時	一八

65　病床日記

九時　　　一八
十二時　　一八

薬用　水薬
午前七時　　六時
午后十二時半

散薬
午前九時半
午后三時　　九時半

飲食
午前二時　ビーフチー　二勺
七時半　　ミルク　　六勺
十時　　　ビーフチー　三勺
十一時　　葛湯　　一碗
　　　　　葛湯　　一碗
午后壱時半　ミルク　五勺

十　元老院議官・枢密顧問官時代

四時半　ビーフチー　三℥

七時　葛湯　一碗

　　ミルク　三℥

大便

午前一時半　三℥

九時半　自痢

午后四時半　極少量

小便

午前一時半　三℥

七時　八℥

十時　八℥

午后三時半　多量

四時半　〃

一前日来睡眠勝

昨夜より今朝迄も喫食両便通の他始終睡眠、偶々醒覚すれは全身不和を訴へ稍嗜眠状、睡中は絶へす魔夢に迷

さるゝと云ふ。今朝四時頃に発汗か盗汗か皮膚に微潤せり。咳嗽なく咯痰は至つて少し。

一午前壱時頃便通帯灰黄色極軟便少量。

一午前九時松山・実吉両先生来診。

一此日も終日睡眠せり。敢て咳嗽は在らさりしも咯痰の分泌は稍多し。

七月十二日　日

体温

午前三時	三九、〇
六時	三八、八
九時	三七、七
十一時	三七、七
午后三時	三八、八
六時半	三八、九
九時	三八、八
十二時	三九、一

脈搏

午前三時	九〇

十　元老院議官・枢密顧問官時代

六時　　　　一〇〇
午后六時　　九四
九時　　　　九六
十二時　　　一〇〇

呼吸
午前三時　　二二
六時　　　　二〇
午后六時　　二六
九時　　　　二三
十二時　　　一四

薬用　水薬
午前七時　　　六時
午后〇時半

散薬
午前十時半　　午后三時半

十二時半 ─────

飲食
午前一時　葛湯　五g
　　　　　ビーフチー　二g
七時　ミルク　五g
九時　ビーフチー　三g
十時　葛湯　一碗
午后壱時半　ビーフチー　三g
　　　　　　葛湯　一碗
三時半　ミルク　五g
十時　ビーフチー　三g
　　　葛湯　一碗

小便
午前一時半　八g
五時　五g
十一時　多量

十　元老院議官・枢密顧問官時代

午后五時
十時半　　〃
　　　　七三

一昨夜九時半頃より十一時半頃迄少く皮膚湿潤せり。然れとも其后は前の如く乾燥す。口中乾燥同し。

昨夜より今朝に至るも屡睡眠咯痰も少し。

一前日より右季肋部に微痛ありしも、昨夜来今朝に至り漸々同部より後方に蔓延し疼痛も増悪せりと云ふ。

一前八時半頃松山先生来診、聴診及案診して疼痛部に判創膏軟膏を貼用すへく命せらる。

一今朝八時頃より九時頃迄非常に発汗し尓来終日皮膚を湿せり。

一午后一時半頃実吉先生来診、療法松山先生に同し。

七月十三日

体温

午前三時　　　三八、五
六時　　　　　三七、七
九時　　　　　三七、一
十一時半　　　三七、二
午后三時半　　三七、五
六時半　　　　三七、八
九時　　　　　三七、七

65　病床日記

十二時　三八、〇

脉搏
午前三時　九〇
六時　九〇
九時　八〇
午后六時半　九四
九時　八八
十二時　八四

呼吸
午前三時　二四
六時　一六
九時　一六
午后六時半　一八
九時　二〇
十二時　一八

水薬
午后六時半
九時
十二時

十　元老院議官・枢密顧問官時代

午前八時半
午后二時半
九時半

散薬
午前十時半
午后五時
十時半

飲食

午前七時　　ビフチー　　三勺
　　　　　　葛湯　　　　一碗
十一時半　　ミルク　　　五合
午后壱時半　ビーフチー　三勺
　　　　　　葛湯　　　　一碗
六時　　　　ミルク　　　五勺
七時半　　　ビーフチー　三勺
　　　　　　葛湯　　　　一碗

65　病床日記

此日よりミルク一回にセリー酒二茶七を混用す。

合計　ビフチー　三ℨ

　　　　ミルク　　十ℨ

　　　　葛湯　　十八ℨ

大便

　午前七時半　　三ℨ

　午后二時　　　三ℨ

小便

　九時半　　　　七ℨ

　午后二時　　　三ℨ

　午前六時半　　十ℨ

一昨夜睡眠すれとも屢身思不安の情あり。絶へす皮膚湿潤す。睡眠中は咯痰の排泄する罕なり。

一今朝より非常に発汗す。

一午前七時半便通帯灰春黄色軟、且つ塊にて三ℨ許り。

一午前八時半松山国手来診。

十　元老院議官・枢密顧問官時代

一此日終日発汗多く午后に至り二時間余安眠。

一口中乾燥止み右季肋部の疼痛敢て変化なく夜に入り少しく緩解すと云ふ　（但し芥子入琶布を貼用す）。

七月十四日

体温

午前三時　三八、〇

六時　三八、一

正午　三八、一

午后二時　三八、七

五時　三八、一

十時　三八、一

脈搏

午前三時　九〇

六時　八四

正午　九〇

午后九時　八八

呼吸
午前三時　二〇
六時　二二
正午　二四
午后九時　一八

水薬
午前八時
午后一時

散薬
午前十一時
三時
六時

飲食
午前三時　ミルク　一五瓦
七時　ミルク　五瓦

十　元老院議官・枢密顧問官時代

十時　ビーフチー　三ℨ

葛湯　一碗

午后一時半　ミルク　五ℨ

四時　ビーフチー　三ℨ

葛湯　一碗

合計　ビーフチー　三ℨ

ミルク　十五ℨ

ビーフチー　六ℨ

葛湯　十二ℨ

小便

午后〇時半　多量

午前五時　七ℨ許

七時　〃

一昨夜も屢睡眠すれとも魔夢の為に安眠にあらす。午前三時頃より軽眠尚甚しく罕には軽眠中僅に譫語を交へる事あり。今朝右季肋部の疼痛大に減退すと昨夜来今朝迄咳嗽咯痰少しもなく今朝七時頃に至り少許を咯出す、又時々腹鳴を聴く。

一午前八時松山先生来診。

480

一八時過より折節腐敗性血痰及ひ又鮮紅色の血線状を混したる痰少々排出す。

一前日より発汗の量少なし。此日別に変化なし。

一午後七時実吉先生来診。

一同九時就眠。

七月十五日

体温

午前三時　　　三九、〇

六時　　　　　三八、〇

九時　　　　　三七、六

正午　　　　　三八、六

　　　　　　　三七、七

　　　　　　　三八、五

　　　　　　　三七、九

午后十一時　　三七、二

脈搏

午前二時　　　六六

十　元老院議官・枢密顧問官時代

六時　　　　　八四
正午　　　　　八四
十一時　　　　九二

呼吸
午前二時　　　二〇
六時　　　　　二〇
正午　　　　　二〇
午后十一時　　二〇

薬用　散薬
午前九時　　　一四
　　　　　　　一四

飯食
　　　　　　　一四
午前一時　葛湯　一碗
　　　　ビーフチー　三3
七時　ミルク　五3

482

十時　葛湯　　一碗

午后十一時三十分　ビフチー　三ℨ
　　　　　　　　　ミルク　　五ℨ
　　　　　　　　　葛湯　　　六ℨ
　　　　　　　　　ビフチー　三ℨ
　　　　　　　　　ビフチー　三ℨ
　　　　　　　　　葛湯　　　一碗

大便
　午前五時　　　　　　　四ℨ
　正午　　　　　　　　　三ℨ
　其後二回合計九ℨ許

小便
　午前五時　　　　　　　七ℨ
　正午　　　　　　　　　不分明

一昨夜も前夜の如く屢睡眠午前一時過より何となく睡眠不安の状、罕には譫語を交へ皮膚は絶へす湿潤を帯ぶ。

十　元老院議官・枢密顧問官時代

一今朝五時便通質同前日四ʒ許。

一咯痰も少く血線状混せす。

一午前八時松山先生来診。

一午前十一時頃より時々腹鳴あり。

一正午の便は下痢にて凡そ三ʒ許り、其后二回（尿共六ʒ許、一回は同三ʒ許）。

一此日終日眠を絶たす脱汗。

七月十六日

体温

午前三時　　　三八、〇

　　六時　　　三七、一

　　九時　　　三七、六

　　正午　　　三七、九

午后二時半　　三八、一

　　五時半　　三八、〇

　　九時　　　三八、五

　　十二時　　三八、五

65　病床日記

	脈搏	
	午前三時	九〇
	六時	八四
	九時	七六
	正午	八〇
	午后九時	八八
	十二時	九二

	呼吸	
	午前三時	二二
	六時	二二
	九時	二二
	正午	一八
	午后九時	一八
	十二時	一八

水薬	
午后六時	

十　元老院議官・枢密顧問官時代

十二時半

飲食

午前七時　ミルク　五ℨ

十一時　ビーフチー　三ℨ
　　　　葛湯　一碗

午后〇時半　ミルク　五ℨ

四時半　鶏卵　一個
　　　　ミルク　四ℨ
　　　　ビーフチー　三ℨ

十二時　ミルク　五ℨ
　　　　ミルク　十九ℨ
　　　　ビーフチー　六ℨ
　　　　葛湯　六ℨ

計　卵　一個

大便

午前十時　自痢　一ℨ

正午　二3

午后一時　二3

小便

午后一時　七3

正午　七3

十二時半　六3

一此夜も睡眠して発汗を催し今朝に至り軽眠、罕には譫語し咋夜来折節腹部雷鳴す。咳嗽咯痰共になし。

一午前十時の便痛自痢一3許り帯黒黄色。

一正午頃一回二3許り何れも臭気甚しからず、但し下痢性なり。

一午前十一時半実吉先生来診。

一此日昼間は少しも眠らず、気分も稍々快を訴ふ。然れとも時々腹鳴あり。口中乾燥せさるも口渇ありて飲料を望む。

一夜に入り十時過より就眠。

七月十七日

体温

十　元老院議官・枢密顧問官時代

午前三時　　三八、一
六時　　　　三八、二
九時半　　　三八、二
午后四時半　三九、〇
七時　　　　三八、八

脈搏
午前三時　九〇
六時　　　九〇
九時半　　九〇

呼吸
午前三時　一八
九時半　　二四

水薬
午前九時
午后壱時半

六時半

散薬
午前十一時
午后五時半

飲食
午前七時　ビーフチー　三ℊ
　　　　葛湯　一碗
午前十時　ミルク　五ℊ
　　　　紅茶
午后〇時半　卵　一ヶ
　　　　　ミルク　四個
午後三時　ビーフチー　三ℊ
　　　　パン　少々
〃七時　ビーフチー　三ℊ
　　　　葛湯　一碗
十一時　ミルク　五ℊ

十　元老院議官・枢密顧問官時代

計　ビーフチー　九瓦
　　ミルク　　　十四瓦
　　葛湯　　　　二回
　　紅茶　　　　少々
　　麺包　　　　少々

大便
午后二時　　少量

小便
午前八時　　七瓦
午后二時
六時

一昨夜安眠せす。口中乾燥し午前三時頃より漸く就眠、今朝五時醒覚后稍爽快なる由。
一午前八時尿通あり。　透明稀褐色。
一午前九時松山先生来診。
一午后大便一回少量稍下痢性。

一此日体温昇騰するも神思不快を訴へす。暫時客来人と談話を催す。夜に入り異状なし。咳嗽咯痰少く発汗は極少量悪寒もなし。

七月十八日

体温
午前一時　三八、五
四時　三八、四
七時　三七、七
十一時　三七、六
午后二時　三八、五
四時　三八、五
七時半　三八、八
十一時　三八、一

脈搏
午前一時　九〇
四時　八八
七時　八八

十　元老院議官・枢密顧問官時代

十一時　　　九
午后七時半　一〇〇
十一時　　　八〇

呼吸
午前四時　　二二
七時　　　　一八
十一時　　　二〇
午后七時半　二四
十一時　　　三三

水薬
午前九時
午后二時半
十一時

散薬
午后〇時半

65　病床日記

飲食

六時　　　ミルク　　　五ℨ

午前七時　ミルク　　　五ℨ

十時半　　ビーフチー　四ℨ
　　　　　ミルク　　　四ℨ
　　　　　卵　　　　　一個
　　　　　葛湯　　　　一碗

午后二時半　ビーフチー　三ℨ

四時　　　ミルク　　　五ℨ

七時　　　ビーフチー　三ℨ
　　　　　葛湯　　　　一碗

計　　　　ミルク　　　十四ℨ
　　　　　ビーフチー　十ℨ
　　　　　葛湯　　　　十二ℨ
　　　　　卵　　　　　一個

大便　　　　　　　　　一個

十　元老院議官・枢密顧問官時代

午后一時　軟便　中量

小便

午前九時　　　八3

午后壱時

────

一昨夜も睡眠し始終発汗、暁方に至り尚ほ増す。今朝気異状なしと云ふ。咳嗽咯痰少し。

一午前七時松山先生来診。

焼酎を以て全身を拭浄する事毎日なり。

一午後に至り実吉先生来診。此日終日別に変化なく気分も亦良し、時々来人と談話を試む。午後七時頃に少く呼吸困難の状なれとも暫時にして忘れ眠に就く。但し〇〇〇ならんか。

七月十九日

体温

午前三時　　　三八、〇

　　五時　　　三七、九

　　八時　　　三七、七

　　正午　　　三八、〇

午后二時　　　三七、七

八時　　三七、八
十二時　三八、八

脈搏
午前二時　一〇〇
五時　　　八六
八時　　　八八
正午　　　八八
午后八時　九〇
十一時　　一〇〇

呼吸
午前二時　二二
五時　　　一六
八時　　　二〇
正午　　　二〇
午后八時　一八
十一時　　二〇

十　元老院議官・枢密顧問官時代

薬用
午前八時　散薬
十時　水薬
午后二時半　散薬

飲食
午前二時　ミルク　五勺
七時　葛湯　一碗
九時　ミルク　四勺
　　　卵　壱ケ
午后壱時半　ビーフチー　三勺
　　　葛湯　一碗
四時　ミルク　四勺
　　　卵　一ヶ
十一時半　ビーフチー　三勺
　　　葛湯　一碗

計　　ミルク　　十三ℨ

　　　ビーフチー　九ℨ

　　　卵　　　　二ケ

　　　葛湯　　　三回

大便

午前七時半　軟少量

　十一時　　〃

午后二時　　少量

小便

午前二時　　十二ℨ

　七時半　　少量

　十一時　　少量

午后二時　　〃

一昨夜より今朝迄静穏にして安眠を得たり、発汗も多量ならす。

一午前七時半少量帯黄青色の軟便通あり。

十　元老院議官・枢密顧問官時代

一午前十一時に又少量質同前。

一午后二時同々。

一此日異状なし。時々咳嗽あるのみ。咯痰なし。終始腹鳴を多く。

一医薬は其効なくと云ふに由り散水薬共患者の意に任せ強て投せす。只朝夕二三回のみ、他時に売薬丸を用ふ。

〔注〕本来横帳であったものが綴じ紐がはずれ同折にて一括されている。

66　「廿四年五月より御床臥中御薬及御飯食物御手扣」／吉田清成

明治24年5月28日～8月2日

五月廿八日　晴天微風

○丸薬　前八時半、后二時、后八時。

○水薬　四時間毎（五時半、九時半、后一時半、后五時半、九時半。）四時半毎　前五時半、十時、后二時半、后七時、

○兼用水薬　前九時半、后三時半、后九時。

○食事　前六時半、十二時、六時、

○含嗽　前十一時、后四時、八時、

五月廿九日

○前七時十五分、后一時十五分、七時十五分、丸薬。

〇〃五時四十五分、十一時三十分、后五時三十分、水薬。

498

「廿四年五月より御床臥中御薬及御飯食物御手扣」／吉田清成

○〃十時、三時三十分、八時、兼用水薬。

○〃九時三十分、后三時、八時三十分、含嗽。

○〃九時三十分三八、二。后十二時三十分、三八、四〇。三時半、六時三十分、体温。

○〃八時三十分、十二時、六時、食事。

五月廿日

昨夜七時より八時半頃眠る」十時半迄覚む」十一時寝入り廿日五時四十分覚む（〆八時間）」爽快。体温　六時三七、四〇。脈搏　六時十分七十六度。六時ビーフチー三ℨ。六時半　丸五粒、ミルク四オンス

一食事七時半、ミルク五ℨ、オーツミール一皿、スープ五ℨ、卵黄二個、トースト少々、ローストビーフ軟肉小片一。后二時三八、二。四時三八、一。

六月一日

五時半三七、四。五時四十五分ビーフチー三ℨ。六時丸六個。同時ミルク五ℨ。七時前大便一行硬、小便一行。

七時松山来診、滋養、五十三ℨ及べりとて驚きたり。

六月四日夕

一后四時十五分体温三八、四〇に上る。思ふに朝来の降つゝき北風の烈き等にて空気大に滋ひたると対客多話及ひ書きものに少く骨を折りたる等にて斯く昇りたるものか。一八時三八、一〇に下る。一五時半より七時迄休む。一九時十五分、用水薬。一十時より同半まて吸入薬。一十時半体温三八、二〇。

食事七時二十分、一ビチー三ℨ、一ミルク七ℨ、一卵黄二ケ、一スープ五ℨ、一パン少許、一オーツミール半皿、

十　元老院議官・枢密顧問官時代

一サトウ半ℨ。

一大便八時半一行軟。一十時半止血薬。

六月六日

前四時半三七、二。五時半大便一行、小便一行。六時丸薬、ミルク三ℨ。前七時半ミルク四

ℨ。スープ四ℨ、卵二個、イチゴ一皿、サトヲ二ℨ。〃十一時半三七、八。十二時スープ四ℨ、ミルク六ℨ、オーツミール一皿、卵黄二個、〃十時

半丸薬、ミルク三ℨ。六時丸薬、ミルク三ℨ。四時半ビチー三ℨ。〃八時水薬。〃十時

牛肉三片、ビーフチー三ℨ、パン一片。后二時三八二。〃二時十分水薬。〃四時三八、三。オーツミール一皿、

小便一行。后六時半三八、三。〃五時半丸薬、ミルク三ℨ。〃六時半スープ三ℨ、ミルク六ℨ、オーツミール一

皿、卵二個、牛肉一片。

六月廿八日　雨天　日

四時半覚。五時三八、五〇。五時半肉茶三四ℨ、ビスケット一片。六時二十分すむ水薬新。十二時半すむ水薬。

四時半すむ水薬。さんやく九時、三時、八時すむ散薬。

二日

四時三八、〇〇。四時半ビチー四ℨ、水アメ一ℨ。六時散薬。七時大便一行軟。八時半三八、八。九時ミルク六

ℨ。八時丸薬。六時散薬。六時二十分三八。

四時半ビチー四ℨ、水アメ少々、クツ少々。

七月三日

一二時大便模様少々異る。一六時半大便同断。一七時三八、一〇。一八時ミルク六ℨ。一九時半丸薬。十二時

三七、二〇。一九時ビーフチー四ℨ、水アメ少々、クツ少々。一二時玉子二個、ビーフチー三ℨ、オーツミール

66 　「廿四年五月より御床臥中御薬及御飯食物御手扣」／吉田清成

少々、ミルク四ℨ。一二時半大便模様更り。一四時丸薬。一四時半三八、八〇。一七時リンゴ少々。一七時半全

丸薬。一八時、ビーフチー四ℨ、アメ少々。一九時ミルク六ℨ。二十時丸薬。二十一時三七、八〇。二十二時大

便。二十二時二十分ビーフチー三ℨ、アメ少々。

七月四日

一四時大便。一五時ミルク六ℨ。一五時半三八〇。一七時奇応丸。一七時半大便。一九時半玉子二個、ビーフ

チー三ℨ、スープ三ℨ、アメ少々。二十時丸薬。二十一時半大便。二十二時三八、八〇。二三時鐲詰（鐲カ）モ〻少々。

一時十五分大便。一三時ミルク六ℨ、ビーフチー四ℨ、アメ少々、葛少々。一三時半三八、三〇。一四時半丸

薬。一六時ミルク四ℨ。一六時二十分三八、八〇。一八時奇応丸。一八時大便少々。一八時

四十分三八、七〇。一九時ミルク六ℨ、ビーフチ四ℨ。二十時半大便。二十一時丸薬。

七月十一日

十一時半ビーフチー四ℨ、ミルク四ℨ、玉子一個、葛湯。十二時半散薬。一時大便、小便。二時三八、五。二時

半水薬。三時ビーフチー三ℨ。三時半奇応丸五。四時ミルク五ℨ。同三八、五。六時散歩。七時ビーフチー三ℨ、

葛湯。

七月十二日

七時ミルク五ℨ。十時ビーフチー三ℨ、葛湯。十時半散薬。十二時小便。十二時半水薬。◇十一時三七、七〇。

一時半ビーフチー三ℨ。一〃葛湯六ℨ。一時四十五分実吉先生来診右肋骨ノ痛ニハ格別意ヲ止メス。一三時三八、

五。一三時半散薬。一四時ミルク五。

七月十三日

十　元老院議官・枢密顧問官時代

六時半奇応丸、葛湯。七時半ビーフチー三ℨ。

十四日

六時半奇応丸、七時ミルク五ℨ。八時半水薬。十時ビーフチー三ℨ、葛湯。十時半散薬。一時水薬。二時ミルク六ℨ。二時三九、二〇。三時散薬。四時半ビーフチー三、葛湯。五時三八、六〇。六時散薬。七時小便五。七時半小便、葛湯。〔ママ〕

七月十六日

六時奇応丸五。七時半ミルク五ℨ。九時半ビーフチー三ℨ、葛湯。十二時半ミルク五ℨ。一時奇応丸五。二時半三八、一〇。三時半散薬。四時半玉子一、ミルク四ℨ、ビーフチー二ℨ半。五時半三八。六時水薬。八時奇応丸五。十時散薬。

七月十七日

六時奇応丸七。七時ビーフチー三ℨ、葛湯。十時ミルク五ℨ。十一時半散薬。十二時半玉子一個、ミルク四ℨ、紅茶。一時半水薬。二時大便少々、小便、水薬。三時ビーフチー三ℨ、パン。四時奇応丸七ツ。四時半三九、一〇。五時半散薬。六時半水薬。六時小便。七時ビーフチー三ℨ、葛湯。十時半ミルク四ℨ。十二時奇応丸五ツ。

七月十八日

七時半奇応丸七。八時ミルク五。九時水薬。十一時半ビーフチー三ℨ、ミルク四ℨ、玉子一個、葛湯。十二時半散薬。一時大便、小便。二時三八五。二時水薬。三時ビーフチー三。三時半奇応丸五。四時三八、五〇。同ミルク五。六時散薬。七時ビーフチー三、葛湯。十二時三九、五〇。

七月十九日

二時ミルク五ゎ。六時奇応丸八ツ、七時ヒーフチー三、葛湯。八時散薬。九時ミルク四ゎ、玉子一個。十時水薬。

十時半大便、小便。十二時半ミルク五ゎ。一時半大便、小便。二時奇応丸五。二時半三八、一〇。三時半散薬。

四時半玉子一個、ミルク四ゎ、ビーフチー三ゎ。五時半三八。六時水薬。七時奇応丸五。九時半散薬。

七月廿日

六時奇応丸五。二時ミルク四、玉子一個。八時散薬。十時ビーフチー三ゎ、葛湯。一時半奇応丸十。十二時大便、

小便。二時ミルク四。

七月廿一日

六時大便、小便。七時奇応丸十。七時半ミルク三、玉子一個。十時十分葛湯、ビーフチー三。十二時半奇応丸十。

一時ミルク四ゎ。二時小便。三時散薬。四時三九、二〇。四時半葛湯、ヒーフチー三ゎ。七時散薬。八時ミルク

四ゎ。九時奇応丸十。九時半小便。

七月廿二日

五時半葛湯五、ビーフチー三。六時半奇応丸十。八時半ミルク三、玉子一個。一時葛湯五、ビ

ーフチー三。二時半小便。三時散薬。三時半ミルク四ゎ。四時三九、一〇。六時半ヒーフチー三、葛湯。七時三

八、八〇。七時半散薬。一時三八、五〇。

七月廿六日

十一時ミルク四ゎ。十二時三八、五〇。二時散薬。三時葛湯。四時三八、六〇。八時半三九、三〇。七時過尿屎

通。十時三九〇、一一二、一八。

七月廿七日

十　元老院議官・枢密顧問官時代

三時ヒーフチー二℥。三時半散薬。四時奇応丸十。　五時半一二、一八、三八、八〇。　六時散薬。　六時半ミルク

四℥。　七時半大便自利。　八時水薬。　八時半三九〇、一一〇、一八。　奇応丸十粒。

七月廿八日

午前一時三九六、一二〇。　八時葛湯六℥。　一時半尿通二℥。　五時奇応丸十二。　六時ミルク四℥、七時水薬。　八時

半ビーフチー二℥。　九時半散薬。　十時奇応丸十二。　十一時三八、八〇。　十二時水薬。　一時三九、一〇。

一時半奇応丸十二。　二時ミルク四℥。

七月廿日

一六時奇応丸五。　一一時奇応丸十。　一七時半奇応丸十。

廿一日

七時奇応丸十。　十二時半奇応丸十。　八時奇応丸十。

廿二日

六時半奇応丸十。　十二時奇応丸十。　九時奇応丸十。

七月二十三日

七時奇応丸十。　十二時奇応丸七。　八時奇応丸七。

七月廿四日

六時半奇応丸七。　十一時奇応丸七。　七時奇応丸七。

七月廿六日

六時半奇応丸十。　十一時半奇応丸十二。　六時奇応丸十二。

66 「廿四年五月より御床臥中御薬及御飯食物御手扣」／吉田清成

七月廿七日

五時奇応丸十三。 十一時半奇応丸十三。 四時奇応丸十。 七時奇応丸十。

廿八日

五時奇応丸十三。 十時奇応丸十三。 一時半奇応丸十二。 六時奇応丸十二。

廿九日

五時奇応丸十三。 五時半奇応丸十五。 十時半ミルク四る、セリ。 二時奇応丸十五。 三時葛湯少々、ビーフチー少々。 三時半三九、一〇。 六時奇応丸十五。

三十日

五時半ビーフチー一る。 六時奇応丸十五。 十時奇応丸十五。 一時奇応丸十五。 六時奇応丸十五。

七月三十一日

五時奇応丸十五。 十時奇応丸十五。 十二時奇応丸十五。 六時奇応丸。

八月一日

五時奇応丸二十。 十時同二十。 二時同二十。 七時同二十。

二日

五時奇応丸。 十時同二十。 一時半同二十。

〔注〕メモ四十枚が、「廿四年五月より御床臥中御薬及御飯食物御手扣」とある封筒にまとめられている。その内、月日が明らかな二四枚分を載せた。

十　元老院議官・枢密顧問官時代

67　病床記録／吉田清成

明治24年6月28日〜6月30日

六月廿八日医師不来故に午後一時半文子清風召列[連]吉田方へ行（病後初ての外出なり）充分の治療を得大に功ある

を覚ふ。帰邸後益快爽、四時半帰る。帰途大脇氏（野津方森元丁二丁目廿四番）え見舞かゝとの不在野津妻女の

みあり。暫時話して去る」此日大脇氏午前見舞生梧翁与園中運動中故不知故に不逢

之より貴島氏へ立寄る留主なり。矢の羽の事を頼むとの事を申残せり。

梧翁庫の要書類を引出し置たり。　同人五時半頃去る」

六時過る頃夕飯を取る。引わり二杭。鯛潮蒸二。　同テリヤキ半。百引一個。ウナキ少々。甘味大し

アラメ少々。　前マテラ一食中　ウヰルモツ一食

岡田陪食す」銀行え手紙二通を出さしむ」勇蔵方へも同断。

七時十五分発して寺島氏へ行不在八時すぎ帰邸に付万緒話合（構成法二読会は本日を以了る重罪裁判控訴の件の

み未完故に七月二日を以委員会を開筈云々」十時三十分去帰」令夫人病痾之由を聞く）

午後

十一時十分百井聖。葛ねり（前田氏北海道の分）少々食す甘味あれともひかへたり」気分益快爽明案百出して不

寝三字を聞く迄に小水四度」マ印を一用ひ眠る三字半なるべし八字四十分に起されたり」汗なし

管なし」第一松山丸薬を用ゆ水。湯を以上下拭ひ焼酎を以同断。朝飯ビーフチー一3。オーツミル二。半熟二。

ステーキ少々（之ハ始てなり）

（九時より照りあがる）

十一時視力を試むるに非常に進めるを覚ゆ。近来稀なる事共なり。寒暖計七十六度南方の風一部晴天。

貞十一字に発し寺島夫人を見舞十二字に帰る。　十七年製の梅干小樽一、青梅若干、を進むと云。

午後一時「ペ」を用ひ後食す。引割三。汲もの生爪入二。カレー半。フキ少々。マデラ一。

〔注〕66と同封のメモ。年は不明により、別途載せた。

「六月卅日三時半ソンデイ伊印を問在宅。」 〔朱筆〕

（吸ナラン）

68　「殖民意見書」／榎本武揚

〔表紙〕

「殖民意見書」

殖民意見書

明治（23）年

五洲を歴遊するに到処皆西人の栖息せざるはなし壮哉と謂ふへし。其故を原するに他なし漏れ夙に殖民の要を認め人に先だつて鞭を着せし結果に外ならず。蓋し殖民の要二あり一は経済に属し一は政略に属す。而して其国家を利するや一なり。夫の人口と地積の権衡に基きて見を立つるものは単に経済上に属し、国民をして固陋の見を破り利源を海外に探りて一局面に区々たらしめざるは重に政略上に属す。此二者は我邦の現今と将来に向て共に其必要を覚ふ。請ふ先つ次の二例を挙て以て之を証せん。夫れ我邦は古より農を以て国を立て土肥へ雨足ると称すれとも試に今新たに開墾に従事する者を見よ、概ね七年後に至り漸く年五六朱の純益あるを以て例とすべきにあらずや。然るに目下我人民の雇はれて布哇国甘蔗耕地に在るものは毎月一人十五弗の給銀を領し而して毎月約ね七弗を貯蓄す。現下其数一万余人に達せしを以て毎年約七十余万円の金を本国に輸送するは当局者の知る所なり。

十　元老院議官・枢密顧問官時代

試に問ふ我邦開墾に従事する者能く斯る給銀を農夫に給し得べきや否、又問ふ我邦の小作人にして毎月能く六七円の貯蓄を為し得る者ありや否、斯れば我邦農業の利は布哇国甘蔗耕地に遠く及ばざるを証すべし。是故に我邦細民の為に家計の豊を計らば本土に力耕せしより彼地に移るを以て得策とす。将た我邦目今一般の急務は殊に殖産興シ業以て民力を養ふに在りて夫の政談理論の如き不生産的の事業に貴重の時日を徒費すべきにあらず。今設し真の有志者奮起して我純良の農民数万人に新利源を海外に得せしめば忽ち相率て彼岸に到り以て遂に新日本を天の一方に創立するの機あるべし。是れ決して夢想にあらざるなり。

殖民の要は大率是の如しと雖とも之を実施するは易事にあらず。先つ第一殖民会社なる者を創立し之が資金を募らさる可からず。第二何の国を以て最も我殖民に適当とすべきを究めさるべからず。而して第一を以て最も難しとす。今仮に我民一万人を最近米国の歩頭に送るに少くも毎額五十円を要すべきに三十万乃至五十万円の資本を備へざる可らず。斯る資金を農業の収穫より戻入るゝと聴けば兼て農業は薄利なりと臆断せる我邦人は入社する者あらざるべきも深く慮むに足らざるなり。然るに予が聞く所を以てすれば目下幸に前二者相抱合して本来の目的（即ち殖民）を達し得べき機会あるに似たり。墨是哥国「テフアンテペク」名地鉄道の布設事業なり此鉄道は墨是哥湾と太平海を連絡するの一線路にして其距離大約我七十五里に過きざる可し。墨是哥政府は数年来該鉄道を布設せんと計画したりしも資本家を見出し能はざりしが目今の大統領「ジヤス」氏の治声漸く内外の信用を繋き遂に昨年より独逸国より弐百七十万「ポンドステルリング」の資金を募り得たり。而して墨是哥の豪商「サルファドル、マロー」名なる者該鉄道布設の請負人コントラクトルとなり現に三千人の役夫を発して工事に着手し猶数多の役夫を要するを以て「サルファドル、マロー」氏は我日本人を雇入ん為め全権委員「フォーゲル」氏なる者を横浜に出張せしめたり。「フォーゲル」氏は数月前神奈川県庁に書を致して我役夫八千乃至一万人を

508

68　「殖民意見書」／榎本武揚

募集することを請願せしが外務省は別に考ふる所ありて其挙を拒めりと云ふ。爾後「フォーゲル」氏は数次余を訪ひ来り必らず自家負担の目的を達せんと尽力せり。同氏は頻に本邦人民が自ら殖民会社を創立して役夫を供給せん事を希望し之に対して彼国鉄道会社〔即ち「サルファドル、マロー」氏の会社なり〕より大約左の約束を結ばんと書面を以て申出たり。

一役夫は「テフアンテペク」鉄道工事に用ゆる者にて一日十時間労働する事。

一尋常の役夫一日の給銀七十五銭の事但し神奈川県庁へ出せし書面には此給銀六十銭たり。

一尋常の役夫三十人を以て一組とし毎組小頭一人を置き而して其給銀は一日一弗より少からざる事。

一役夫一組中に炊夫一名を置き而して其給銀は役夫と同様の事。

一日曜に働くものは雇主と相談にて別に給銀を取極むべき事。

一役夫には小家（ハウス）、薪水及医師を無代価にて給する事。

一役夫「サリナ、クルズ」して「テフアンテペク」鉄道の附近に在りしより給銀を受る事。

一役夫は着後各自の任所に赴く為めの鉄道又は馬車は無賃にして需用物品の運賃も亦同く無賃のこと或は役夫の中帰国する者あるときは「サリナクルズ」迄も自身も需用荷物も共に無賃の事。

一役夫は毎月八百人乃至一千人づゝ鉄道会社の傭汽船にて出帆すべき事。

右は「フォーゲル」氏より出せし商議の大要にして弥結約するに至らば猶多少の修正を要すべし。但し役夫の洩海賃は殖民会社の負担に係るを以て殖民会社は役夫の給銀中より毎月若干円を差引かさるべからす。

偖殖民会社なる者を組織するに先だつて必要なる件は先づ第一前陳の約条を鉄道会社に於て正当に履行し得るや否を慥むる為め墨是哥政府より相当の保証書を得ざるへからず。余は之が為め別紙甲号を「フォーゲル」氏に致

墨是哥の湊名横浜より一直線に着岸の地にに上陸する日より

509

十 元老院議官・枢密顧問官時代

したるに彼より乙号の答書を得たり。此答書に拠ば墨是哥政府は鉄道工事請負人の私務に関する事柄に対して保

証するを得ずと拒絶し、もし日本政府より直接の問合せあらば答ふる所あらんとの意味判然たり。斯れば予が今

より凡そ一ケ月前に青木外務大臣に向て此件に付駐米代理公使に電令して直接に華盛頓府駐札の墨公使に掛合

はれん事を請求したる返電を待つの外なし。只憾らくは今に何たる返電なし。

右の外猶一事予め探知すべきは「テファンテペク」地方の気候たる北緯十七度より十八度に亘る熱帯の地たるを

以て衛生上の実況如何是なり。「フォーゲル」氏の言に拠ば鉄道会社は此鉄道に沿へる両側の地数百万「ヱーク

ル」約我壱千二百坪を既に買入れ以て将来地価の騰貴を予期せる一事にても其衛生上有害の地たらざるを証すべし

と。然れとも是れ未だ以て遽に信を措く能はざるに似たり。

以上記する所は専ら鉄道工事の為に役夫を移すに限れる者の如しと雖とも其実は然らず。即ち此役夫が労力を以

て貯蓄せし資金を以て彼等の為に同国に於て膏腴の地を買ひ若くは同国政府より借受けしを以て我邦に比すれば

数倍有利の農業を興さしむるに在り。但し右の役夫中には同国に住居するを好まずして帰国する者も必らずある

べしと雖とも利の在る処は衆の赴く所なるを以て一旦有利の殖民事業が我邦東方の彼岸に興るを見れば必らず相

率て移住する者あるに至らん。

抑も目下我邦民の為め殖民の事業を興すへき適当の地は南米「ブラヂル」国に如く者なかるべきは地理家及遊歴

家の通論にして之に次く者を墨是哥国とす。同国は其面積七十五万英里と称す故に大約我邦より五倍余の大さた

れとも其人口に至ては僅に一千万に満たざるを以て殆んど我が四分一に過ぎず故を以て彼政府は他国人の来住を

奨励するに汲々たるは彼国移住民条例に就ても其一班を見るに足れり。将た其国の気候は土地の高低に由て甚だ

しき差ありと雖とも全土五分の三は熱帯に位するを以て甘蔗、藍、烟草、椰子哥菲木綿「ゴム」其他有利の菓実

510

草木類よりして暖帯地方に生長する穀類も亦皆繁殖すと称す。就裡太平海沿岸の地方「サン、ブラス」「マンゼ
リラ」等の如きは木綿及び「ゴム」樹等自然に繁茂して恰も雑木の観を作すと云ふ。只惜むらくは地理学家の記
する所に拠に東西共に沿岸の低地は概ね風土病多くして他国人の住居に適せずと。然れとも之に反して三
千五百尺乃至四千五百尺の高原に至ては季候極て健康にして各種の農業に適し而して一年平均の暖度は華氏六十
四度に過ぎずと云ふ。此他地味物産政治風俗等の詳に至は茲に贅せず。

客歳桑港の土地会社は本邦人石神国太郎なる者に托して墨是哥国内既成未成の開墾地并せて数百万「ヱークル」
の売却の周旋を我邦に計れり石神なる者は幼より米国に遊び墨是哥国も一覧せし者にて其売地の図面並に所産物等
の詳記を携帯し来て現に東京に在り。伊は我人民を此新地に移住せしむるに熱心なりと雖とも未た相当の手段を
得ざるを以て過般来余に就て教を乞へり。予は伊の齎らし来れる書類を閲読せしに頗る偉大の事業に属するを認
めり。又仏人「サルターレル」氏は曽て南米諸国を歴遊し「ブラジル」国に我人民を繁殖せしむ
るの要を起草して我農商務省に送りしことあり。同氏も亦予と同感にして今般「テフアンテペク」鉄道布設の役
夫を我より輸送し以て行々墨是哥若くは「ブラジル」に於て殖民の計を為すの極を好機会たるべきを賛称し既に
数日前に私費を以て墨是哥国実見の為め横浜を発せり。氏は三四月後に帰来る筈なり。
倩前陳の大要を約言せしに目下単に世間に向て殖民の我邦経済上に必用なるを声言すとも恐らくは自ら資を卸し
て会社を設立せんと企つる者は甚だ稀なるべし。殊に近日南米白露礦山会社なる者の失敗を知らざる者なければ
所謂薫蕕同類視する者無きを保すべからず故に今利益自前に在る役夫輸送の事業を殖民会社中に寓し先づ以て本
社を東京に置き墨是哥鉄道会社と約を結び更に支社を各地方に置き毎月八百乃至一千人の役夫を募り其支店に於
て渡海費を負担せしめ凡そ一万人の数に至て止むを要す。

而して役夫の渡海費毎額約ね五十円の前借は役夫領給

十　元老院議官・枢密顧問官時代

の日より相当の利子を附し月賦を以て完清せしむるときは（譬へは毎月二十二弗半の給料中より十弗を差引く）

役夫は五六ケ月を出ずして全給を手にし得べし。而して渠等は其月給中より毎月毎額十弗を貯ふるを得べし。然

らは則役夫は彼地着後十八ケ月を経れば一人に付苟も壱百弗即ち一万人にて一百万弗を貯へ得べきを以て之を以

て彼地に於て相応の土地を買ひ若くは借り以て農商業に従事せば十年を出ざる中に彼地に一個の新日本町村を創

出し得べし。況や此際本邦より各種の需要品を彼地に輸出せば必ず貿易上の一新路も従て生すべし。而して彼地の粗造物産

を我に輸入し我は精製若くは各種の目的を以て彼地に移住する者あるを期すべきおや。頃日墨是哥鉄

道会社は前記の社員「フォーゲル」氏を以て更に次の約条を申出たり。

「サルファドル、マロー」氏は日本より来墨の役夫にして六ケ月間「テフアンテペク」鉄道工事に従事せし者

には農業に適当する良地二十五「ヱークル」我十町歩を次の割合を以て貸渡すべし。

初年及二ケ年目迄は　　無賃

第三年目には　　壱「ヱークル」毎に二十五「セント」借料

第四年　　同　　全

第五年　　同　　全

第六年　　同　　七十五「セント」全

第七年　　同　　一弗二十五「セント」全

第八年　　同　　一弗七十五「セント」全

第九年　　同　　二弗二十五「セント」全

第十年　　同　　二弗七十五「セント」全

512

十ケ年後即約条済の期に至らば地主と借地人との間に商議次第地主は開墾地一「ヱークル」に付十弗にて売渡すべし。右の開墾地は何れも「テフアンテペク」鉄道に沿へる土地にして「サルファドル、マロー」氏の所有に属す。

又未開墾地にして材木又は貴重の材料を産する樹木又は何物たるを問はず其地に属する天産物は其品物の二割五分を地主たる「サルファドル、マロー」氏に納むるときは其余は渾て借地人の有に帰すべし。但し収納物には運搬費を要せず〔ママ〕」

墨是哥鉄道会社は至急に役夫を要する趣を以て一日も早く我殖民会社の設立を希望し既に本年八月九月の二ケ月中に弐千五百乃至三千人の役夫を輸送するに於ては渡海費（彼は六十五弗と申出たり）を幾分か減却し又殖民会社に向て初度の航海には出帆前に五千弗第二回の船は四千弗第三回の船には三千弗第四第五第六回迄の船には毎船一千弗即ち共計壱万五千弗を給与し而して其払渡は横浜に在る印度澳斯答刺利及支那銀行と称する店より出すべしと書面を以て申越せり。

以上記する所は目下墨是哥殖民案の実況なり。予は偏に我国家の為め我人民の為め此際我政府より墨是哥政府へ直接の問合を為し更に適当の官吏と農学士両三名を撰み一日も早く彼国に派遣し以て殖民案の利害得失して如何を攻究せられん事を希望に堪へず。此等の使事は蓋し往復五ケ月を以て足るべし。

因に云ふ墨是哥の銀礦に富めるは夙に天下の知る所にして現に毎年純銀の輸出高は四千万弗に下らず同国「アラモ」地名に於て近頃一大金礦を発見せし事に関し本月三日横浜出版「ヂヤツパンガセット」に左の一節を掲げり。

〔注〕コンニャク版。

十　元老院議官・枢密顧問官時代

69　三十三銀行失敗始末

元第三十三国立銀行重役種子田誠一が失敗の原因なりと云ふを聞くに、抑も第三十三銀行は従来川村伝兵衛等が発起にして最初より伝兵衛頭取となり、創立の当時は営業堅固にして社会の信用も宜かりしに連れ面白く貸し出したる結果、銀行の営業危きを来したる折柄、谷元道之等供謀し種子田を重役に撰挙し、為めに種子田も大に奮発し、営業上整理を主眼とし、三四年間の星霜を経て漸く恢復の気運に向ひ候処、種子田も又最初の轍に陥入、伝兵衛供々貸出方に注意行届かざるより、遂に大失敗を惹起し、如何とも無詮方、故に種子田思ふに正金銀行株主たるを幸ひ、原六郎を追出、自然該行頭取に成んとの計策を企謀し、該株主を語らひ、若し頭取に成る能はざる時は、副頭取に園田（現今頭取）を盛り立て而して三十三銀行の維持を講ぜんと胸中に包蔵し、企謀の如く原六郎を排斥せんも、原身方全く斥くるを好まず、取締役に置く可しと、反して種子田は重役にも不相成仕合に立至、無拠日本銀行へ泣附、二拾万円を借入んと伝兵衛供々企望したるに、豈図ん、原六郎は日本銀行株主中多額者なるにより、敵打ちの時機熟せりと窃かに歓び、日本銀行頭取其他重役に蜜謀し、日本銀行に於ては表面上川村伝兵衛・種子田誠一に対し申聞けるに、川邨・種子田両氏が財産資力限り裸になつて投げ出す可し、果して断決せられたる時は真に丈夫の所為なり、果して然る時は日本銀行は第三十三銀行営業維持金として金弐拾万円貸与すべしと。是に依て川村・種子田両氏の財産は総へて日本銀行へ、就中川邨が如きは腰に差し居る煙草入迄投け出したりと云ふ。両三日経過するや否、裁判所より執達吏両氏へ向ひ投け出したる財産に悉く封印せりと。爰に於て初めて川村・種子田も目が覚め、日本銀行より一杯喰つたと悲歎に沈みたりしは跡の祭り。故に種子田は直に家族を引纏め熱海へ、川村は三井銀行より一ケ月拾五円の借家を求め衣類其他朝夕家財道具及小使金迄恵与せりと。

然に商人社会の評を聞くに、種子田は資金壱万贃壱万五千円位は所持し居る、反して川村は煙草入迄投げ出したる始末、誠に気の毒千万、然りと雖とも長者なり、種子田は今紳士なりとの評説に有之候。

右蜜[ママ]探記事は証拠を徴揚したるものに非す。依之信疑の如何を保証するものに非す。単に御参考に供するのみ。

〔注〕墨書。明治25年閉店前後と考えここに収録。

十一　年代不明

1　金銭受取に関する覚書／吉田清成

明治（　）年7月（15）日

百円元

内払

七月五日　中村

一弐拾円　中村

一四拾円　中村

　　　　留五郎払

同日

一五円　　貞渡

十三日

一五円　　貞請取

十四日

一弐拾円　中村

十五日

一拾円　　貞

〔注〕墨書。

2　支払いメモ／島崎

明治（　）年8月15日

覚

八月八日

一拾七銭五厘　　中飯壱

一五拾銭　　　　御泊弐

一壱円　　　　　御酒肴

一廿五銭　　　　人力車

九日

一三拾七銭五厘　中飯三

一四銭　　　　　人力車

一三銭　　　　　生玉子

十二日

十一　年代不明

一　八銭　　砂ト

一　廿五銭　　西瓜壱つ

一　三拾七銭五厘　　カステイラ

一　廿銭　　桃

一　壱円五拾銭　　御泊六

一　六拾弐銭五厘　　人力

一　八拾七銭五厘　　ブランデ

一　拾八銭五厘　　あんま取かへ

十三日

一　五拾銭　　中飯四

一　七拾五銭　　御肴

一　弐拾五銭　　砂ト

一　廿五銭　　琥珀糖

一　拾八銭　　足袋壱つ

一　八拾銭　　かんさらし氷

一　弐円廿五銭　　流行人力

〆拾壱円三拾三銭

右之通

4 度量衡改革についての吉田清成覚書

〔注〕墨書。

上

八月十五日　　　　　島崎

3　椎野正兵衛領収書

証
〔異筆ペン書〕
Duplicate

一金弐拾円　白茶縮面緑入
　　　　　　子供上着式弐枚

右正に請取申候也。

十二月廿二日

椎野正兵衛〔印〕〔朱〕

上

〔注〕半紙、墨書。他二ケ所にも同一押印あり。

明治（　）年12月22日

4　度量衡改革についての吉田清成覚書

覚書

一定額之度量は第一大蔵省其余諸省へ一具つゝ、政府議事院へも備置御定之規とすへき事。

明治（　）年

519

十一　年代不明

一尺と定るは何に賦依する所なくは不出来、仏之ミートルの如きは即地球の大円図を四つに割り其一分を一千万分に分て其一分を以一ミートルとす。右は曲尺三尺に少々長し。

一現今之処は造幣寮諸病院学校為替会社等之用のみを新度量にかへ、其余は急に改革しかたき事情もあれば、先可成現今之儘にて差置、其内度量製造家之取締を厳粛にし当座之患を避るに足るべし。

〔注〕墨書。

5　横浜港石炭積入場所調

〔欄外朱筆〕
「横浜港石炭積入場所　　同港税関調」

百拾二番　　　　米国海軍物置所

山手百拾七番　　英海軍物置所

右地区は熟れも海軍所用の為め貸渡置候ものに付、軍艦用の石炭を貯蔵致候義も可有之事。

山手八拾七番　　太平洋郵船会社石炭置場

同百八拾三番　　仏国郵船会社同断

右は特に石炭置所として地区を貸渡すものに付同所に於て揚卸致候事。

右の外は別に石炭置場の名義を以地所貸渡候者無之候得共、往々私有地内に石炭貯積致候ものも有之由、差向き著しきものは左の通に有之候。

520

横浜　三番　　米ウイルキン、ロビンソン社

同百拾八番　　米ラングフェルドマイアヤ社

同百拾七番　　米グレー社

　右等は特に揚卸場を許可致候事は無之、近辺の共同物揚場より揚卸の由に有之候事。

〔注〕外務省用箋、墨書。

6　英米との通商条約に関するメモ／吉田清成

〔鉛筆書〕
「ドンゼイ之事を可取調事」

女王 1859 July の条約に女王と掲く、可調事。

日本公使総領事の何方を不問旅行の一儀を掲たり。　実に可笑事也。

英は千八百五十九年五月一日に神奈川を開くに決す。

米は千八百五十九年七月四日に同断。

──────────

Trade Regⁿ. II The impⁿ. of opium being prohibited etc. etc. $8 〔カ〕 15

〔注〕ノート、ペン書。裏面に英単語の練習跡あり。

十一　年代不明

7　英金俸給高に関するメモ

一　英金千三百九拾八封度拾八シリンク壱ペンス　　半ヶ年百八十日分　俸給高

内

英金六百拾八封度拾壱シリンク弐ペンス

　但此英金は為替券にて米国へ御持越しの分米金三千弗に当る分但壱ホントに付米金四弗八拾五セント替

差引残

英金七百八拾封度六シリンク拾壱ヘンス

此洋銀四千六百拾壱弗八十四セント

此金五千七百四拾三円三拾四銭壱厘

　但壱弗に付英金三シリンク九ペンス替　洋銀相場壱円三十八銭替

〔注〕外務省用箋、墨書。

8　華氏気温表

〃 17	〃 16	〃 15

8　華氏気温表

〔注〕気温表。在米時代のものか。

Date	July 25	〃 26	〃 27	〃 28	〃 29	〃 30	〃 31	Aug 1	〃 2	〃 3	〃 4	〃 5	〃 6	〃 7	〃 8	〃 9	〃 10	〃 11	〃 12	〃 13	〃 14
7a.m.		74°														76°					
9a.m.		77°	78°		73°	71°	67°		74°	77°				73°	75°	80°	78°				
10a.m.		76°	77°		72°	69°	70½°			77°	76½°	77°									
11a.m.	78°								78°						77°						76°
12m.														76°							
1p.m.	79°			75½°					80°		78½°	78°	78°	78°							
2p.m.	80°		78°						81°									76°			
3p.m.	79°			77°	76°	73°		73°	82°	81°					83°	84°	79°		78°		
4p.m.			79°						83°		77°										
5p.m.	78°															85°					
6p.m.		75°		73°														76°			
8p.m.		74°		74°										77°							
9p.m.	75°																				
10p.m.	73°																				
11p.m.	73°									77°	76°										
12m.n.																					

十一　年代不明

9　条約締結に際しての国是確定意見稿

条約締結の事たる独り道理的且権理的のみに拘泥すべきものに非す。交渉国是的一種無定規の則を利用せざるべからす。何をか一種無定規の則と云ふ、無他地理上成立上国各固有之質を存すれは、甲と乙と丙と丁と一として国体民情を同ふするものなきが故なり。甲に理利あるもの必すしも乙に利ありとせす、皆各異るなり。是故に国各宜交渉之国是を断定するは国交上の秘訣たり。我国の如き何そ一部皮表上の権理を争ひ尋て来る所の大害を不顧、却て他の一部の権理にして国利民福上須臾も不可忍の急務を放棄するが如きは自家撞着之詐を不免のみならす、既往現今の実際を見て以将来の成果を察せざるの最甚きものなり。夫れ豈交渉国是の宜きを得たりと云ものならんや。

〔注〕墨書。

10　人名表

有栖川宮

一投機商等既往地所を大早計にも買込、雑居の事一日長しと首を伸べて待つの情あるは之皆人の知る所、卑屈千万なれとも咎むるも益なからん云々。
一地所の俄に膳貴するは害目前国益なりと論する人もあれとも附帯の災害は眼中になきが如し。
一地価しば〳〵高低するは国家財政上に大害あり云々。

524

10　人名表

両大臣

大隈

寺嶋

伊藤

井上

西郷

河村

田中

榎本

上野

中井

○鍋島

伊達

英公使

米公使

魯公使

○イタリヤ公使

大鳥

十一　年代不明

青山〇大久保
〇青木
〇浅田
〇吉田次郎
〇高木

〔注〕墨書。

11　人名表

〔異筆〕
「井上
上野」
寺嶋
岩倉具視
大隈重信
大木喬任
西郷従道
川村純義
山田顕義

11　人名表

〔注〕墨書。

野津鎮雄

大山　巌

榎本武揚

松方正義

青木周蔵

蜂須賀茂韶

鍋島直大

長岡護美

野津道貫

樺山資紀

松邨淳蔵

吉原重俊

宮本小一

花房義質

塩田三郎

中井　弘

十一　年代不明

12　人名表断片

三条実美

伊藤博文

黒田清隆

伊達宗城

石橋政方

桜田親義

鄭　永寧

前田献吉

〔注〕墨書。

13　政治体制に関するメモ／吉田清成

「門閥を廃す○颺（オーカゼ）○」「諸価沸騰す○錠と○「乍憚御省慮」○「澳地利」〔淫雨降続○諸藩より版籍返還○開拓○研学○学課○万機東京より被発○今般大基礎相立○諸候伯〔ママ〕并中下大夫に至る迄○概略○被為渉○伎倆○擢用〔ママ〕○掄選（エヘム）○騰踊○函館屯集之匪徒○傭○漸次（やうやく）○繁殖す○僅少○接待○花旗国（アメリカ）歟○違作○

〔注〕ペン書。

14 「島津家譜歌」

〔表紙〕
「島津家譜歌」

高祖忠久号得仏

御元祖豊後守忠久頼朝卿長庶子にて、法名得仏道阿陀仏浄光明寺殿と申なり。

始領三州曰島津

忠久始めて薩隅日三州を御拝領にて、島津と名乗らせたり。

二世忠時称道仏

二代の祖は大隅守忠時なり。法名を道仏仁阿弥陀仏浄光明寺殿と申なり。

此時上古其風淳

此忠時之御時代は上代の時分にて、人の風儀淳に有りたる也。

三世久経称道忍

三代之祖下野守久経なり。法名道忍義阿弥陀仏浄光明寺殿と申なり。

攻亡礼部安我民

久経之御代に礼部と申すものを攻亡ぼして御領内之民共を安らかになせしとかや。

給黎町田其孫子

久経の舎第常陸守忠経之子に給黎左京亮宗長、町田五郎忠光あり。給黎は子孫なし。町田嫡家は町田主計家也。

〔弟〕

十一　年代不明

伊集院亦骨肉均

町田之弟侍従房俊之子に伊集院図書助久兼あり。　嫡流伊集院十右衛門也。

忠宗道義建長間

四代之祖上総介忠宗也。　法名を道義仲阿弥陀仏浄光明寺と殿申也。　建長之間とは建長年号の頃と云事也。

都鄙謂之為歌人

都はみやこ、鄙はいなか也。　都も鄙も此忠宗之御事を歌人と云へり。　兼て歌之御達者なるゆへなり。

其子貞久名道鑑

五代の祖は上総介なり。　法名を道鑑道阿弥陀仏浄光明寺殿と申なり。

舎弟六人国為隣

貞久の御舎弟六人ありて、国中皆隣とせり。　六人左右は左に有り。

和泉孫子今殆尽

和泉下野守忠氏は貞久の次弟にて、子孫断絶せりとなり。　今又後嗣ありて嫡流島津因幡なり。

佐多新納共相親

和泉の弟に佐多三郎左衛門忠光、其弟に新納近江守時久あり。　佐多嫡流島津木工、新納嫡流は新納四郎なり。

樺山北郷今猶盛

新納の弟に樺山安芸守資久、其弟に北郷尾張守資忠あり。　樺山嫡流は樺山左京、北郷嫡流は島津筑後也。

其中石坂跡独泯

北郷の弟に石坂九郎左衛門久泰あり。　子孫なきゆへ独つくとあり。　貞久より和泉、佐多、新納、樺山、北郷、

14　「島津家譜歌」

石坂迄兄弟七人、是を七人島津といへり。

道鑑有子号川上

五代道鑑之御子、他腹の長男に川上越前守頼久あり。嫡流は川上一学也。

子孫至今更説説

説説とは多き事なり。子孫今に至るまて栄へ多しと云ふ事なり。

氏久齢岳六代主

六代之祖陸奥守氏久也。法名は齢岳玄久即心院殿と申也。即心院は志布志にあり。又三郎と申名は此人より始れり。

創建即宗迹未陣

京都の即宗院は氏久の御寺にて、其跡未陣すして今にあると云事也。

元久恕翁創福昌

七代之祖は陸奥守元久也。法名を恕翁 忠福昌寺殿と申也。此御代に福昌寺を建られたり。

一子為僧戴烏巾

元久之御子は出家を遂られ、福昌寺三代の住持にて、仲翁和尚と申也。烏巾とは僧のかぶりもの也。

八代之祖陸奥守久豊は、元久の御舎弟にて御家督也。法名を義天存忠恵灯院殿と申也。

有弟久豊号義天

挑恵灯来尚循循

久豊之御寺恵灯院也。恵灯院を挑け来るとは、恵灯院住持今にをこたらすつゝいて勤をなすと云ふ也。循循

531

十一　年代不明

とはつゝら心と見へたり。

忠国大岳其諱誉

九代の祖は陸奥守忠国なり。　法名を大岳玄誉深固院院殿と申也。

深固院古栽松筠

忠国の御寺深固院は古き寺にて、松筠を栽てありと云也。

舎弟撫夫薩摩守

忠国之御舎弟薩摩守用久あり。　法名松[ママ]道存と云へり。　嫡流断絶、庶流は島津矢柄島津仲大田大野吉利寺山等也。　此家を薩州家と云へり。

題橋豊州武威純

用久の弟に豊後守季久あり。　後に越後守と云へり。　法名を桂道題橋と云へり。　嫡流は島津内膳也。　此家を豊州家と云へり。

出羽伯耆亦叔季

豊州の弟に出羽守有久、其弟に伯耆守豊久あり。　出羽は大島盛太夫元祖、伯耆は義岡弾正元祖なり。　叔季とは兄弟也。

有五兄弟徳已均

忠国より薩摩守、豊州、出羽、伯耆まで兄弟五人の事を云へり。

忠国宗子称天勇

宗子とは長男の事也。　忠国の他腹の御長男に相模守友久あり。　法名を天勇玄機常球寺殿と云へり。　寺は田布

施の常球寺也。

不嗣父位異天倫

父の位を嗣すとは、天勇は他腹ゆへ家督を嗣れす、天倫を異にすとは別に家を立てられたる事と見へたり。

大年登公天勇子

天勇の子に相模守運久あり。斎を一瓢斎といへり。法名は大年道登大年寺殿也。寺は阿多大年寺也。

斎名一瓢徳不貧

斎を瓢と名つけて、一つ瓢簞と申心なれとも、徳は貧くなしと云事也。

立久節山民具瞻

十代の祖は陸奥守立久也。法名を節山玄忠竜雲寺殿と申なり。

竜雲廟古猶薦蘋

竜雲寺御廟所は古き事なれとも猶蘋を薦とは今以て祭をなすと云事也。竜雲寺は市来にあり。

忠昌円室諱玄鑑

十一代の祖は陸奥守忠昌也。法名を円室玄鑑興国寺殿と申也。玄鑑は文字ちかへり。

寺名興国近城闉

忠昌の御寺を興国寺と名つけられたり。城闉に近しとは城近くあると云事也。

忠治蘭窓名津友

十二代の祖は又三郎忠治也。法名を蘭窓津友寺殿と申也。御寺は薩州吉田津友寺なり。

忠隆興岳不終晨

十一　年代不明

十三代の祖は又六郎忠隆也。忠隆は十二代忠治の御舎弟にて御家督也。法名を興岳隆盛院殿と申也。晨を終

らすとは早く御逝去の事と見へたり。

勝久主国国将滅

十四代の祖陸奥守勝久也。勝久は十三代忠隆の御舎弟にて御家督也。法名を大翁妙蓮と申す。勝久国の主と

為て政道善らす、国滅ひんとなり。

幾殺忠臣自沈淪

勝久幾人も忠節の臣下を殺されたり。自沈淪とは勝久身の沈となれり。

欲譲貴久以国家

勝久国家を貴久に譲りあたへんとせしに

国乱其約皆不真

国中乱れて国家を譲る約束も皆真にてあらさるなり。

貴久老父問誰某

貴久の御親父誰某となれは

一瓢之子称日新

一瓢之御子相模守忠良斎を日新と申せし人にて貴久の御父也。法名梅岳常潤左家菩薩、梅岳寺殿と申也。梅

岳寺は伊集院にあり。日新寺は加世田にあり。

日新無由散鬱憤

鬱憤[ママ]をいきとをりの事なり。日新いきとをりを散せらるゝにせんかたなき也。

534

14　「島津家譜歌」

更揚義兵無異論
きっと義兵をあげ、国中を征伐ありしゅへ、異論なしとは異儀を申ものなかりしと也。

従是三州諸家士
是より薩隅日州の士も

仰見貴久悉称臣
貴久を仰見て十五代の君となし、陸奥守貴久斎を伯囿と申也。三州諸家悉く臣下となり。

辛未林鐘二丁三
林鐘は六月の事也。元亀二年辛未六月二十三日なり。

正是大中辞世辰
貴久の法名を大中良等庵主林寺殿と申す。辞世辰とは御逝去の時也。辛林林鐘二十三日御逝去と云ふ事也。

海潮修梵南林寺
梵を修すとは仏の法を修行する事なり。海の潮の音のする所に貴久の御寺南林寺を建られ、僧侶修行をすると云事也。

香烟不断目輪困
輪困とはめくりめくると云事也。南林寺殿に捧る香烟は不断に立ちめくりて有と云事也。

義久治国猶超古
十六代の祖修理太夫義久斎を竜伯と申し、法名を貫明存忠庵主妙谷寺殿と申也。国を治められし御勲功は古へに超るほと有と云ふ事也。

535

十一　年代不明

是時六国臣伏臻

臣伏とは降参と云事也。　此義久の御時御勢ひ強きゆへ、　肥筑豊之六ヶ国降参して臻ると云ふ也。

以歌鳴世是余事

世に鳴とは世間に名高き事也。　余事とは外の事也。　義久歌道に名高き事は外の軽き事なり。

惟徳被民民帰仁

題目は義久の恩徳民に被て民は御仁徳になつけり。

令人景慕何至此

景慕とは大にしとふと云事也。　義久の徳人人大にしとう事、　何として此ほとに至るや。

遐齢猶祝八千椿

義久の御よはいを八千歳迄栄ふる椿の木ほとにいつれも祝せり。　遐齢とはよはいの事、　椿は八千年に花さく
めでたき木也。

新創妙谷預修善

義久新たに妙谷寺を建られまへをきより義根を御修行ありしと也。　預とはまへをきの事也。

碧瓦朱甍畳魚鱗

碧瓦はみとりの瓦、　朱甍はあかきいらか。　妙谷寺御建立あつて、　瓦つき見事にして魚鱗を畳ねたるよう也と
云事。

舎弟義弘兵庫頭

十七代の祖兵庫頭義弘宰相惟新と称せり。　義弘は義久の御舎弟にて御家督也。　法名を松齢自貞庵主妙園寺殿

536

14　「島津家譜歌」

と申也。舎弟は御舎弟の事也。

武威振世重千鈞
　義弘の武威勢世上に振ひ渡て、其重き事千鈞の重さあると云事也。千鈞は別して重き事を云。

匪啻誉声動我国
　誉声とははほまれの名と云事也。義弘の誉れと申は、我日本国を動すまてにあらす。

朝鮮八道誦名頻
　朝鮮の八道まても義弘の名を唱へ申事しきり也。

帰依三宝修妙円
　三宝とは仏法僧の三宝とて、寺には三つの宝あり。義弘其三宝に帰依在て伊集院の妙円寺御寺になせりと也。

無人不道希世珍
　希世の珍とは希代の珍しき人と云事也。義弘の御事を希代之珍しき人と云はぬはなし。

久保朝鮮撫軍日
　久保朝鮮撫軍日。久保は朝鮮に渡り軍兵の下知をさせらる、日比と云事也。撫軍とは軍の下知する事也。

惜羅微恙化作塵
　義弘の御子又一郎久保あり。久保は惜哉微しの恙にかゝつて、朝鮮にて塵となれり。法名を〔ママ〕恕参大禅定門皇徳寺殿と申なり。御寺は谷山皇徳寺。

家久多年在朝鮮
　十八代の祖中納言家久御舎弟あり。久保早世ゆへ家久御家督なり。家久は多年朝鮮に御在陣也。

537

十一　年代不明

擅施武威似有因

家久朝鮮にてほしいまゝに威風武功を振施せりと云事。

国務余力嗜儒学

家久国之御政道御務之余力に儒学を嗜ませられたり。余力はひまの事也。

其本不乱壱修身

国政之本になる御身を壱らに御修行有て乱れさるようになさせられたり。

就中心学探其頤

就中家久は心地の御学問を御工夫なされたりと也。頤を探るとは工夫する事也。

禅教入門博両輪

御学問の外に仏法にも御心をよせられ、教を受させたもう。両輪儒仏の二つか。

細大不捐芸非一

細事も大事も捐置れすなされたるゆへ、御芸能一方にあらす。

揮剣揮筆共彬彬

御剣術も御手跡も共にそろはせられた。彬々とはそろうた事也。

琉王来降何歳月

琉球王来て降参せしは何れの年月そなれは

慶長己酉在薐寅

慶長十四年己酉五月なり。薐寅とは五月之事也。

538

14 「島津家譜歌」

光久生元和二年　大樹懇懃加首巾

正保丁亥当霜月　王子犬追親族臻

吾君命運幾多少

当家の運命は幾くほとそと云ふに

孫子枝葉億万春

枝栄へ葉しけりて子々孫々億万年の春まて目出度く栄へんと也。

歴代歌解本終

綱久明暦発江府　自是帰国隔歳巡

綱貴承命修東叡　元禄七月越数旬

吉貴享保壬寅夏　大磯館楼望海浜

継豊婦人竹姫君　享保己酉結婚姻

有弟与分続狡　吉貴微意不遠親

宗信逝去号慈徳　万民如父涙霑巾

更無継子立久門　無為自治大平辰

吾君命運幾多少　孫子枝葉億万春

歴代国号歌

粤稽盤古生太荒嗣者天地人三皇伏羲炎帝暨軒轅堯舜相承五帝昌夏商周周秦西東漢後漢魏呉三国判入于魏魏禅晋晋

539

十一　年代不明

遂平呉天下定擾晋室者十七国以後朝分為南北南為東晋居金陵宋斉接踵又梁陳北則五胡並後魏東魏西魏復如蝟西禅于周東禅斉周滅斉兮随躡梯随復平陣始一統未幾唐興歴数永唐終五代多更変梁唐晋漢周相戦更兼列国勢瓜分宗祖登基始大奠金拠汴梁宗南渡北遼西夏兼侵侮駆淦滅宋是胡元滅滅元伝十六祚清代明兮億万世試問古今甲子計自堯至明皆可求四千一年真悠悠

〔注〕墨書。

15　「人は同等なる事」

人は同等なる事

万人皆同じ位にて生れながら上下の別なく自由自在云云とあり。今此義を拡て云はん。人の生るゝは天の然らしむる所にて、人力に非ず。この人々互に相敬愛して各其職分を尽し、互に相妨る事なき所以は、もと同類の人間して、共に一天を与にし、共に与に天地の間の造物なればなり。譬へば一家の内にて、兄弟相互に睦しくするは、もと同一家の兄弟にして共に一父一母を与にするの大倫あればなり。

〔注〕墨書。

16　「藍壺の法」

藍壺の法

16 「藍壺の法」

藍に酸素を奪易き質を供する物と、酒及石灰を調和し青精を白精に変したる溶解液に製し、此の中に布匹、毛布、緞綢の類を漬て染め、太気に乾し自然に藍色を生せ令る也。

毛織類及ひ絹布を染る法分量如左

藍八斤　　炭酸加里十二斤

糠三斤半　　茜根三斤半

水六斗六升

糠は麦糠を良とす。

右四品の内、先つ炭酸加里、糠、茜根の三品を六斗六升の水に和して九十度の暖度に烹、細末にしたる藍粉を和し、更に熱湯を加へ、然る后克く之を撹交せ、三十分時を経て蓋を明け之れを撹交る事如前、再ひ蓋を覆ひ、又十二時にして如此する事数回、其液翠色を帯ひたる菫色に変し、其表面に銅色様の痕青色の筋反美なる藍色の泡を生するに至る時は染壺の全出来たる也。大抵四十八時にして出来揚る也。

此の染壺にて藍其酸素を奪れ、白精に変する物は糠と茜根の所為にして、炭酸加里は其白精を溶解する為也。

凡二十五六日間染たる上は、新に藍粉、炭酸加里を可加也。

〔注〕墨書。

十一　年代不明

17　藍の製法

藍に酸素を奪易き質を供する物と酒及石灰を調和し、青精を白精に変したる溶解液に製し、此の中に布匹、毛布、緞綢の類を潰て染め、太気に乾し自然に藍色を生せ令る也。

〔注〕墨書。

18　「桐樹発生地」

桐樹発生地

一福島県岩代国安積郡月刑[ママ]村大字浜路五百九拾四番地村社稲荷神社境内に生す。

一年数詳ならす、凡八九十年以上。

右実地に就き取調候也。

〔注〕墨書。

19　公債買入に関する覚書

日本郵船会社株式券状弐百株也

此代価金壱万四千四百円也

542

但壱株に付金七拾弐円

右郵船株に対する配当金年壱割弐分と見做し之を実価に対照すれは

壱ケ年八分三厘三毛三三

又右弐百株の代金壱万四千四百円を以て整理公債証書を買入るときは左の額を得へし。

一整理公債証書額面金壱万四千五百拾六円拾弐銭九厘

但百円に付金九拾九円弐拾銭の割

右公債利子を買入代価に対照すれは

壱ケ年五分〇四毛〇三弐[余]よに当る。

又五分金禄公債を買入るときは

証書額面壱万四千七百三拾九円

但百円に付金九拾七円七拾銭

右利子を買入代価に対照すれは

壱ケ年五分壱厘壱毛七七余による。

〔注〕第百十九国立銀行罫紙、墨書。

20　吉田清成宛農地経営に関する報告／岡田彦三郎〔カ〕

〔欄外〕「御地所御買入為成候に付畑之壱と通左に申上候。」

十一　年代不明

○御注文相成候品丼に出来候品朱にて星打申候。

　　農具入用之品

○作鍬弐丁○鎌弐丁○天秤棒三本○まんのふ鍬一丁○まんか壱丁○くまて弐丁○竹ふふき○草ふふき○むしろ五
〔朱丸〕　　〔朱丸〕　〔朱丸〕　　　　　　　　　　　　　　　　　〔朱丸〕〔馬鍬〕　　　　　　　　　〔朱丸〕　〔朱丸〕〔箒〕

十枚○四斗樽五つ○羽うちた壱組○竹ふるい弐つ○み二枚○さる三つ○大ばん切おけ壱つ○金ばん枡壱つ○壱斗
　　　〔朱丸〕

おけ壱つ○種まきの節小ざる二つ○叺俵縄○かり込ばさみ壱丁○花ばさみ壱丁○糞四両持込丼に畑へかけし分
　　　　　　　　　　　　　　　　　　　　　　　〔朱丸〕　　　　　　　〔朱丸〕

○人足四人作切すいに記有之候事。
〔朱丸〕

右之通是非入用に相成可申事。

　　作糞丼百性日雇人足之事
　　　　　〔ママ〕

○一冬もの種まき附之節　灰弐両
　　　　　　　　　　　　糞壱艘四両入六両也

一寒中糞養　壱艘　四両

一春ひかん種まき附　壱艘四両

一夏もの種まき附　　灰弐両
　　　　　　　　　　糞養は内にて間合申候

〆凡金十六両

　　人足雇之事

一冬ものまき附之節畑ふかなへくらいは壱反壱人半位にして壱町二反此人足十八人但壱人一日十二匁
　　　　　　　　　　　　　　　　　　　　　　　　　　　　　　　　　　　　　　此代弐百十六匁

右畑作を立糞養いたし種まき附迄壱反に付壱人。

此人足十二人此賃壱匁二分にして百四十四匁也

右作切人足寒中迄に壱度に六人此賃銀七十弐匁也

544

春ひがん前作切人足壱度六人此賃金
同断

夏もの種まき附壱反壱人位相懸り可申此賃金同断

夏もの作きり壱人にて弐反は切可申此賃銀
百四十四匁

右之外夏冬之もの取込人足何人相懸り候哉見込無之。

但しいつれも一日壱人十二匁之賃銀之事。

一夏物草取人足壱反に付壱人にて十二人此分いつれも女。

是は壱人金弐朱つゝ位之事〆壱両弐分之見込に御座候。

惣雇人足高金壱両弐分と七百二十匁

此金十三両弐分也〇糞幷に人足賃銀共合して二十九両二分也。

右乍序申上候。志村様へ申上置候御決答無之候事。

一当時畑に相成居候所凡壱丁弐歩有之候事。内麦小麦そら豆ゐんどふ豆少々有之、此外大方菜種に御座候得共いつれも是迄糞養不足、手入も届不申哉、外々之畑よりも出来不宜候。殊には都てまき時も延引致し候由に御座候。

一是迄之御門番至て作物等は好、尤農家出生故田畑には心を用へ候故、番人且右等之差配人之御積りにて差被遣候事。

右いつれも同人之見込之事。

〔注〕墨書。用箋・筆跡などより岡田と推定。

21 家政に関する覚書／吉田清成

一諸税払高取調記載置の事。

　但期日迄も記置の事。

一月々諸会社抔へ義捐の金額同断の事。

一月々諸会社抔へ義捐の金額同断の事。

　但新聞紙も此内にあり。

一傭男女月給右同断。

一米味噌醤油其外毎月速かに可相払分同断。

一郵税切手葉書買入置き現金同様に取扱の事。

　但し別途に取扱の方法相立候方甚便なるべし。
　　　　　別帳の事なり

一成るべく郵便を以用を便し人の勤を省き候事。

一毎月卅日迄には必す諸通帳を差出す様確と諸向へ達置の事。

　但通帳は成丈け数少き方可然。

一前月の諸払は毎月五日六日七日の間に可丈可片付事。
　　　　　　　　　　　　　　　　　　　　　　成

一小仕を以諸方へ買ものに遣す手帳は毎月改製すべし。

一小仕を以買ものせし分に対し請取なきものは後日不都合の種也。

一下郎共の為掟書を取調の事。

　但一週間一度なり二度なり邸の都合を以自由に為致候方か之れも吟味もの。

一　下郎抒衣服其外の制度を定置かずば追々緩み、終に不可拾取之会計と相成可申注意之事。

一　毎月期節に後れざるやう邸苑の手入を為す為めに、予め見込を立てしめ書取置の事。

〔注〕墨書。

22　買入品に関する覚書／吉田清成

一　御家流手の本買入方の事
　　尊円風を云
　　ん石ずりものにて宜布候。
　　ことうたの本を云

一　諸稽古本并きやうげんの類買入事之事

一　万反物買入方の事
　　ん拙者下知すべし

一　西洋服を命する事
　　ん大倉店へ

一　履の類を命する事
　　ん伊勢勝店へ

右之外種々略す。

其他万出版物

547

十一　年代不明

清風分は概ね不掲載といへとも二三ケ条左に

一　西洋服を誂之事

一　巻煙草入十斗買入之事

一　墨紙筆買入之事

一　翻訳書万種買入之事

一

家財片付方之事

一　第一家財を総て改め

〔注〕墨書。

23　吉田貞買入品に関する覚書／吉田清成

お貞の分

一在米之日本着物は悉皆持越之事

三通か四通程新に揃方申付之事。

不用之品は他に譲り可申。

548

一、通俗の本多数買入之事

前太平記　太平記　太閤記　三楠実録　通俗外史　源平盛衰記　其他品々

近世の分

地理書　究理書　万国史

〔注〕墨書。

24　支払覚書

記

一金拾壱円
右九月三十日
尾仙渡し

一金三円六拾弐銭五厘
八月廿四日
縞八丈壱反代
いせ屋久八渡し

小以金拾四円六拾弐銭五厘

一金壱円六銭弐厘五毛
右十月五日
駒下駄壱足

一金弐円九拾銭八り
同月十五日
笠次郎様品々代
菊屋彦兵衛渡し

小以金三円九拾七銭五毛

一金三円五拾八銭弐厘五毛
仕立物代
右十二月廿一日
尾川や渡し

十一　年代不明

一金五円四拾弐銭五厘　　同日　小間物代
　　　　　　　　　　　　　　　柳や治兵衛渡し

一金拾五円四拾五銭五厘　同月廿三日　両国柏屋払

一金九円三拾九銭　　　同　横浜富貴楼払

　小以金三拾三円八拾五銭弐厘五毛

　合金五拾円四拾四銭八厘

右計算帳書載度相成候分

外金弐拾九円拾四銭六厘　　不足
　　　　　　　　　　　　立替相払候分

二口

　合金八拾壱円五拾九銭四厘

　　内

　金三拾円　　　　古瓦三千枚

　金六円五十銭　　ガラス

　金九円五十銭　　〔ママ〕練化石三千五百枚

　金五円五十銭　　運賃

　〆弐拾四円五拾銭

差引

〔注〕墨書。

550

25 刀装具目録

一、初代　甚五　　鉄象眼
　　　　　　　　　鉄かわらけ鍔
　　小柄　矢竹切

　　目貫　野晒らし

一、西国より　長富備前守へ送る

　　目貫　クルミ　鞘　アイザメ

一、新光　上下差し

　　甚五鉄輪　目貫五三の桐

短刀

一、正宗親　定宗歟　小柄丸に五三の桐

〃

一、定紋付

〃

一、五三の桐　三所物

一、五郎入道正宗　惣今振

刀

一、拵かけ　兼音

十一　年代不明

一、上下差　目貫　人物

一、助定歟目貫　葵

一、先祖遺物　鞘鮫

　　　　目貫しゝみ　並武念

短刀

一、鎮克手製　針を以打

　　目貫龍

弐号

脇差

一、黒柄〔ク〕　此身は幾度研とも不滅真に鋼入居べし

　　目貫糸巻

〃

一、目貫　犬コロ　革柄

〃

一、兼長　在名

　　目貫　袋

短刀

一、獣目貫　アイ鮫鞘

25　刀装具目録

刀

一、菊水目貫　獣五分刻み

　　小柄　赤銅人物

　　　　　さや蠟色

一、上下差

　　目貫龍赤銅

　　　　鍔甚五

一、目貫獣　大刻み鮫

　　小柄虫

　　鍔天龍

短刀

一、目貫富士山　さや朱みぢん〔ヵ〕

第三号

刀

一、鬼丸作り　イカ物作り

刀

一、三才作　柄茶色革

　　　　　細身

十一　年代不明

太刀作 _{上等}

目貫野晒し　巻の皮〔カ〕

一、初代　助定　五百円
　鍔自分工風
　袋に顔

刀
一、兼定　鉄鍔扇
　小柄銀矢切り
　譲りもの　柳鮫

刀
一、鮫鞘　不思議なる身
　身に鈕彫　一分刻み
　鍔傘

刀
一、上下差　琉色
　目貫葵　鉄鍔兜

刀
一、茶色柄　刻鞘鮫

刀

一、鞘溜ぬり

　　　　　　　　研出し

　　杉を弐つに割る　笹の香と号

太刀作り

一、助定黒作り　陣刀

　　赤銅高級鍔

第四号

〔注〕墨書。

26　松植木代金メモ

御持込共代金十二円也　高さ壱丈五尺、　廻り三尺

御持込共代金八円也　　高さ一丈五尺、　廻り二尺二寸

御持込共代金七円也　　高さ一丈五尺、　はゞり一丈八尺、　廻り二尺二寸

〔注〕三本の松の絵に右の説明あり。絵は略す。半紙、墨書。

十一　年代不明

27　書状文例／吉田清成

御第五月書す

文章

今般貴君儀何官え被命候由承知いたしめで度、当今文明之御世盛に有之英才御登用に相成無此上国家之美事と存し候。何卒御勉職可被成、今日為御欽御参堂可致処、不得止事用事出来に付、近日面接を期し候。先は当賀以使[カ]此鯛入貴覧候。御叱留可被下候也。

雲章忝拝誦いたし候。如仰不存寄某官被命難有奉存候。若年之小生何用にも薄気之もの故心痛いたし候。往々御教示被下度奉希願候。殊に見事之鮮鯛被懸御心頭に忝賞納いたし候。早速参堂万々御礼可申上之処今日は来客中に付草々拝答申上候也。

　　月日

　　〔注〕墨書。

吉田清成略年譜

****一般事項はゴチック体で表記した。
****旧暦表示の項目については、新暦換算した日付を（ ）内に補った。
****年齢は数えで表記した。
****推定にとどまる箇所には〔カ〕を付した。

【弘化二年（一八四五）】 一歳

二月一四日（三月二二日）、鹿児島藩士吉田源右衛門の四男として生まれる。

【元治元年（一八六四）】 二〇歳

六月に創設された薩摩藩の洋学養成機関「開成所」に入る（蘭学専修）。

【元治二年／慶応元年（一八六五）】 二一歳

一月一八日（二月一三日）、吉田ら留学生を含む薩摩藩英国派遣使節の人員が決定する。二〇日（一五日）、一行は鹿児島城下を出発し、以降約二ヶ月間羽島の商人宿で便船を待つ。

三月二二日（四月一七日）、薩摩藩英国派遣使節一行一九名がグラバー商会所有の蒸気船オースタライエン号で串木野郷羽島浦（現、鹿児島県いちき串木野市）を出帆する（吉田は変名「永井五百介」を使用する）。

四月一日（四月二五日）、香港に上陸し、五日、英国P＆O汽船会社の大型蒸気帆船に乗り換え、慶応元年四月一一日（五月五日）、英領シンガポールに入港、インド、スエズ等に海路立ち寄る。スエズ～アレクサンドリア間は鉄道を利用する。

五月二八日（六月二一日）、英国サザンプトンに入港し、同夜、蒸気車でロンドンに着く。

六月七日（七月二九日）、長州藩士山尾庸三らとロンドン郊外のベッドフォード鉄工場・近代的農業技術を見学し、市長と会食する。

六月二八日（八月一九日）頃、畠山義成と二人でロンドン大学ユニヴァーシティ・カレッジ法文学部デヴィッドソン博士の家に預け

られる。

八月中旬（一〇月初旬）、三カ月ほどの予備教育のあと、薩摩藩留学生がロンドン大学ユニヴァーシティ・カレッジ法文学部に聴講生として入学する。

一二月一五日（一八六六年一月三〇日）、ロンドン大学教授ウィリアムソン博士に留学生らの後事を委託する旨の契約を交わして新納刑部・五代友厚らが帰国する。

【慶応二年（一八六六）】二二歳

一月二一日（三月七日）、薩長同盟。

夏、留学生のうち六名が相前後して帰国する。

夏季休暇中、鮫島尚信と英国各地を訪ねた後、下院議員ローレンス・オリファントに同行して米国へ旅行し、ニューヨーク州アメニアでトーマス・レイク・ハリスに出会いその教義に傾倒する。

八月上旬（九月中旬）、薩摩藩第二次派遣留学生一行が米国渡航の途中にロンドンに立ち寄る。

【慶応三年（一八六七）】二三歳

春（四月上旬カ）、鮫島尚信・松村淳蔵・畠山義成とともにドーヴァー演習に義勇兵として参加し、中井弘がこれを観戦する。

吉田・鮫島以外の薩摩藩留学生がロンドンを訪れたハリスに会う。

五月二一日（六月二三日）、薩土盟約。

六月九日（七月一〇日）、吉田ら五名の連名で大久保一蔵（利通）・伊集院左中に宛てて「建言書」を起草する。

七月（八月）、鮫島・森有礼・松村・畠山・長沢鼎とともにロンドンを出発し一四日（一三日）、米国ボストンに着きアメニアにあるハリスの新生社へ向かう（まもなく新生社はブロクトンへ移る）。

一〇月一四日（一一月九日）、大政奉還。

558

吉田清成略年譜

【慶応四年／明治元年（一八六八）】二四歳

三月一四日（四月六日）、五箇条の誓文。

一八六八年五月、吉田・畠山・松村がハリスとの意見の相違から新生社を脱退し、ハリスのもとを去る（のち、ニュージャージー州ニューブランズウィックのラトガース・カレッジに入学し、政治経済学を学ぶ）。卒業後、実務研修のためにニューヨークおよびハートフォード両市で銀行保険業務の取扱方を修得する。

下半期になって、米国滞留が承認され、改めて官費留学生として海軍専攻が決まる。

【明治二年（一八六九）】二五歳

二月下旬〜三月上旬（四月上旬〜中旬）頃、ワシントンに帰着（カ）。

五月一八日（六月二七日）、戊辰戦争終結。六月一七日（七月二五日）、版籍奉還。

【明治三年（一八七〇）】二六歳

五月二八日、米国留学生学費配達方（兼留学生監督）を命じられる。

一二月、帰国する。

【明治四年（一八七一）】二七歳

二月一一日（三月三一日）、大蔵省奏任出仕、御用のため大阪出張を命じられる。一五日（四月四日）、造幣寮開業式。

三月一八日（五月七日）、参議大隈重信とともに、各国条約改定御用掛を命じられる。

五月九日（六月二六日）、大蔵少丞に任命される、従六位に叙せられる。一三日（三〇日）、御用のため大阪出張を命じられる。

六月二七日（八月一三日）、大久保利通が大蔵卿となる。

七月一四日（八月二九日）、廃藩置県。二八日（九月一二日）、租税権頭に任命される。

九月二七日（一一月九日）、横浜出張を命じられる。

一〇月一八日（一一月三〇日）、大蔵少輔に任命される。

一一月一日（一二月一二日）、大蔵大輔井上馨とともに「内国税法改正見込書」を正院に上申する。一二日（二三日）、岩倉使節団横浜出航。二四日、御用のため大阪出張を命じられる。

一二月一二日（一八七二年一月二二日）、正五位に叙せられる。

【明治五年（一八七二）】　二八歳

二月、正院が三〇〇〇万円外債募集・家禄削減案を内決。一二日（三月二〇日）、外債募集のための理事官として米国派遣が決定する、岩倉使節団の大久保利通・伊藤博文が一時帰国（〜六月一七日）。一八日（二六日）、米国郵船アメリカ号で横浜を出帆する。

三月一一日、サンフランシスコに着く（森有礼が出迎え）。二四日（または二七日）、サンフランシスコを出発する。

四月五日、ニューヨークに着く。七日、ニューヨークを出発する。八日、ワシントンに到着し、岩倉具視らに面会する。一五日、ワシントンを出発する。四月一六日、ニューヨークに到着し、デロングに面会する。一九日、ワシントンに着く。二四日、ニューヨークに着く。

五月三日、ロンドンに向けてニューヨークを出発する。一三日、ロンドンに着く。

六月二一日、ロンドンを出発してフランクフルトへ向かう。二九日、フランクフルトを出発し、パリへ出張する。

七月八日、ロンドンへ戻る。一四日、リバプールへ向かう、岩倉使節団一行ロンドン着。一五日、大久保・伊藤と面会する。

八月二七日、リバプールへ向かう。岩倉使節団一行もロンドンを出発し、リバプール他へ向かう。

九月三日、ロンドンへ戻る。一五日、正院（「内閣」）の決定を通知する九日の電報を受領。一二日、フランクフルトへ出張する。

一〇月一日、ロンドンへ戻る。九日、岩倉使節団一行もロンドンへ戻る。

一一月一六日、岩倉使節団一行がロンドンを出発しパリに着く。

560

吉田清成略年譜

【明治六(一八七三)】二九歳

一月一三日、イギリスで二四〇万ポンドの外債募集契約に調印する。

二月一〇日、公債募集成功の祝宴を催す。一七日、岩倉使節団一行パリを出発。

四月八日、ロンドンを出発しパリへ向かう。一六日、ロンドンへ戻る。

六月一八日、ロンドンを出発し、リバプールに着く。二二日、島津久光建言。

七月二三日、木戸孝允横浜着。二八日、地租改正条例布告。

八月八日、東京に帰着。

九月、「一八七三年恐慌」がアメリカにも波及し、南北戦争後の経済成長止まる。一三日、岩倉具視ら帰国。

一〇月一二日、大久保利通を参議に任命。二四日、陸軍大将西郷隆盛、参議・近衛都督辞任。二五日、副島種臣・後藤象二郎・板垣退助・江藤新平、参議辞職。参議大隈重信に大蔵卿兼任を命じる。

【一八七四(明治七)】三〇歳

一七日、民撰議院設立の建白書。

二月一日、佐賀の乱始まる、御用のため横浜に出張し、二日、帰京する。四日、御用のため横浜に出張し、五日、帰京する。六日、台湾出兵決定。

三月二〇日、御用のため横浜に出張し、二二日(カ)、帰京する。

四月一七日、大蔵卿大隈重信の長崎出張中の代理を命じられる、御用のため横浜に出張し、一八日、帰京する。

七月二三日、造幣寮出張を命じられる。

九月九日、特命全権公使に任命され、三等官月俸を下賜される。一〇日、アメリカ在勤を命じられる。

一〇月一八日(または一一月五日)、従四位に叙せられる。

一一月五日、フィラデルフィア博覧会御用掛を命じられ、「出品場所其外諸事取調ノ上見込可申出事」とされる。九日、出発する。

561

【一八七五（明治八）】 三一歳

二月一一日、大阪会議。

三月四日、日本で長女和華子が誕生するが、一一日に幼没する（妻貞は志村知常の次女）。

四月一四日、漸次立憲政体樹立の詔。九月二〇日、江華島事件。

【一八七六（明治九）】 三二歳

二月二六日、日朝修好条規調印。

四月、条約改正に関してアメリカ政府と交渉するよう訓状を受ける。

【一八七七（明治一〇）】 三三歳

二月一五日、西郷隆盛らが兵を率いて鹿児島を出発し、西南戦争が始まる。

六月一日、万国郵便連合条約に加盟。

九月二四日、西郷隆盛自刃（西南戦争終わる）。

一一月、次女文が誕生する（のちに三井武之助と結婚）。

【一八七八（明治一一）】 三四歳

二月六日、勲三等に叙せられ、旭日中綬章を下賜される。七月、外務卿寺島宗則が関税自主権回復を目的とする条約改正方針を決定し、九日以後、欧州各国駐在公使に訓令する。

三月二二日、米国国務長官またはその委員と商議し、改定条約調印の全権を受ける。一四日、大久保利通暗殺。

五月、条約改正交渉が開始される。

七月二五日、米国国務長官エヴァーツとの間に、日米条約・協定などを修正し日本に関税自主権を認める約書に調印する（一八七

562

吉田清成略年譜

九年二月七日、改定条約を批准し、一時帰国を許され、帰国中は一等書記官吉田二郎が臨時代理公使として事務取扱を命じられる。

九月二〇日、改定条約を批准し、批准書を交換、七月一日公布する）。

一二月二六日、一時帰国する。

【一八七九（明治一二）】三五歳

一月、前アメリカ大統領グラントが世界周遊旅行の途中、夫人・子息を伴って日本に立ち寄るとの報が届き、国賓として歓迎することとなる。

二月一二日、条約改正取調御用掛・滞京を命じられる。二八日、病気療養のため四週間の予定で熱海へ湯治に出発する（のち、期間の延長を申し出る）。

四月七日、帰京する。一四日、グラント滞在中の接伴掛を命じられる。一五日、グラント迎接として長崎出張を命じられる。

五月七日、長男清風が誕生する（のち貴族院議員、子爵）。

六月二一日、接伴掛として、同従二位伊達宗城（旧宇和島藩主）とともにアメリカ軍艦リッチモンド号で長崎に着いたグラント一行を迎え、「海路恙なかりしを祝し面会の日を楽しませらる」旨の勅語を伝える。二六日、グラント一行が長崎を出航し軍艦金剛の先導で、二九日、神戸港に着く。途中、金剛が海戦演習を行う。悪疫流行のため京摂巡遊の予定は取りやめる。

七月三日、グラントが横浜に着き、右大臣岩倉具視・参議伊藤博文・同西郷従道・同井上馨が東海鎮守府に迎え、御料汽車で新橋に移動し、接伴掛吉田・伊達が馬車に陪乗して延遼館（現、浜離宮恩賜庭園内）に向かう。四日、グラント・夫人・子息・アメリカ公使ビンガムらが御料車で参内し、天皇・皇后、熾仁・嘉彰・貞愛・能久四親王の出迎えを受け、太政大臣三条実美・右大臣岩倉具視・外務卿寺島宗則・宮内卿徳大寺実則とともに接伴掛吉田・伊達も待立する。七日、天皇がグラントとともに陸軍飾隊式を観覧したのち芝離宮でグラント夫妻を饗する。吉田も陪席し、食後に天皇の通訳を務める（※この日グラントが日を期して天皇と親しく話をすることを請うため、グラントが話そうとする内容を予め知っておく必要があるとの宮内卿徳大寺の命を受け、吉田は随行の書記デヨングらより内聞した）。

一四日、グラントの日光遊覧への同行を命じられる。一七日、グラント一行に同行して日光へ行く。一八日、接伴掛吉田・同伊達に加えて、政府の実権者の参議兼内務卿伊藤博文・参議兼陸軍卿西郷従道・外務大輔森有礼も日光に遣わされる（※二七日、伊藤らがグラントと懇話し、グラントが天皇に陳情しようとする内容の概要を了知する）。三一日、帰京する。

八月一〇日、浜離宮でグラントと天皇との会見を通訳する。一二日、グラントの箱根宮ノ下温泉場・塔ノ沢行きへの同行を命じられ、同行する。一九日、グラントと天皇が帰京する。三〇日、グラントが帰国の告別のために夫人・子息・米国公使ビンガムとともに参内する。三一日、明宮嘉仁親王（大正天皇）誕生。

九月三日、グラントが離日し帰国する。一〇日、参議兼工部卿井上馨が工部卿の任を解かれ、外務卿兼任を命じられる。

【一八八〇（明治一三）】三六歳

一月二八日、条約改正取調の御用済につき滞京の任を解かれる。

二月四日、妻等を任地に帯同することを許される。一〇日、一四日の便船で米国へ出発の予定のところ、御用のため次便まで滞京を命じられる。

三月二四日、一等年俸を下賜されることになる。二七日、勲二等に叙せられ、旭日重光章を下賜される。

四月一日、アメリカ赴任のため東京を出発する。一〇日、アメリカとの難破船及び難民救助費用償還の約書批准交換の全権を委任される。

六月一三日、次男清純が誕生する（海軍中将・男爵の井上良智の養子となり、のち、海軍大佐、貴族院議員、男爵）。

七月七日、アメリカ大統領に面謁する。

九月二八日、日本橋区箔屋町出火の節、罹災者に金二五両施与のため、木杯一個を下賜される。

一二月一七日、一八八一年一月一日にワシントンで開会する万国衛生会に政府代議員として出席を命じられる。

【一八八一（明治一四）】三七歳

564

吉田清成略年譜

一〇月一一日、大隈重信免官を決定（一二日発表）。

一〇月一二日、国会開設の詔。

【一八八二（明治一五）】三八歳

一月二八日、帰国する。

七月六日、外務大輔に任命される。二三日、壬午事変発生。

八月二日、外務卿井上馨の不在中の代理を命じられる。一九日、アメリカ在留特命全権公使の任を解かれる。三〇日、済物浦条約。

九月二七日、外務卿井上馨の不在中の代理を命じられる。

一二月二五日、病気療養のため三週間の予定で熱海へ湯治に出発する（のち、さらに三週間延長する）。

【一八八三（明治一六）】三九歳

二月八日、帰京する。一一日、病気療養中の兄吉田十郎が九日に鹿児島で死去したとの報に接し忌引きする。一九日、除服出仕。

五月二一日、外務卿井上馨の不在中の代理を命じられる。

七月一四日、議定官を兼任する。一八日、夏季休暇中、約四週間の予定で墓参のため鹿児島に帰省する。

八月一二日、帰京する。

【一八八四（明治一七）】四〇歳

二月、三男清介が誕生する。二三日、スペイン勲章「イサベルラカトリック大綬章」佩用を許される。

三月一〇日、元老院議官鷲尾隆聚・同長岡護美・同海江田信義・榎本武揚とともに延遼館で相撲を催し、天皇が臨席。

四月二一日、条約改正議会副委員を命じられる。

五月一六日、ポルトガル勲章「コンセプション大綬章」佩用を天皇から許される。

565

六月二三日、清仏戦争事実上開始。
七月七日、華族令制定。二八日、北海道出張を命じられる(一〇月一六日免除)。
八月二〇日、イタリア勲章「ノーロンヌ大綬章」佩用を許される。
九月二四日、栃木・福島両県への出張を命じられる(一〇月二一日出発、一一月一日帰京)。
一一月六日、外務卿井上馨不在中の代理を命じられる。
一二月、甲申事変。二一日、外務卿井上馨を特派全権大使として朝鮮派遣中の代理を命じられる。

【一八八五(明治一八)】 四一歳
一月三日、特派全権大使井上馨が漢城に着く。一九日、井上が帰国する。
二月七日、病気療養のため二週間の予定で熱海へ湯治に出発する。二四日、帰京する。
四月一五日、ハワイ王国勲章「クラオンオフハワイ大綬章」佩用を許される。一八日、天津条約。
五月七日、ロシア勲章「神聖スタニスラ第一等勲章」佩用を許される。一一日、ベルギー勲章「レオポール第二等勲章」佩用を許される。
七月一六日、病気療養のため三週間の予定で伊香保へ湯治に出発する。二七日、一八九〇年に東京で開催されるアジア大博覧会の組織取調委員を命じられる。
八月一九日、伊香保から帰京する。
九月二六日、農商務大輔に任命される(議定官は兼任のまま、農商務卿は西郷従道参議)。
一〇月二三日、佐賀県外七県連合綿茶砂糖鯣繭生糸織物共進会褒章授与のため佐賀県(ついでを以て長崎県)出張を命じられる(二九日出発、一一月一八日帰京)。
一二月一一日、条約改正議会副委員の任を解かれる。二二日、第一次伊藤博文内閣成立。

吉田清成略年譜

【一八八六（明治一九）】　四二歳

一月八日、千葉県下総国種畜場実況視察のため出張を命じられる（九日出発、一二日帰京）。

二月五日、ペルシア勲章「獅子太陽第一等勲章」佩用を許される。二七日、各省官制を公布し、各省の組織及び職責・権限を定める。

三月四日、農商務次官兼議定官に任命される（農商務大臣は谷干城）。二三日、大臣から各省官制通則第九条中制限外の職務一切を委任される。二六日、勅任官一等に叙せられ、上級俸を賜る。

五月一日、外務大臣井上馨が第一回条約改正会議を外務省で開催。六日、一府六県連合水産共進会褒章授与のため千葉県へ出張を命じられる。一九日、徳島県で開催の四国連合砂糖茶葉烟草紙織物共進会褒章授与式執行のため出張を命じられる。二七日、徳島県出張のついでを以て徳島・愛媛・広島・岡山四県を巡回することになる。

六月二五日、農商務省掌管の場所視察のために群馬県へ派遣される。

九月六日、農商務省所管の山林その他事業視察のため静岡県下巡回を命じられる。二〇日、従三位に叙せられる。

一〇月一六日、アジア大博覧会組織取調委員の任を解かれる。

一一月四日、広島県で開催の京都府外七県連合繭糸綿織物紙茶共進会褒章授与式執行のため出張を命じられる。

【一八八七（明治二〇）】　四三歳

五月九日、特旨によって華族に列せられる。勲功によって子爵を特授される。一四日、東京府貫属を命じられる。

七月三日、谷干城農商務大臣が条約改正に反対する意見書を提出する。二六日、元老院議官兼議定官を命じられる。勅任官一等に叙せられる。

【一八八八（明治二一）】　四四歳

四月三〇日、黒田清隆内閣成立、枢密院官制公布。

567

五月一〇日、枢密顧問官に任命される（議定官は兼任のまま）。三一日、白金志田町の自邸で相撲などを催す。

一〇月二〇日、正三位に叙せられる。

【一八八九（明治二二）】四五歳

二月一一日、大日本帝国憲法発布。

一一月二五日、大日本帝国憲法発布記念章を授与される。

一二月二四日、第一次山県有朋内閣成立。二七日、勲一等に叙せられ、瑞宝章を賜る。

【一八九〇（明治二三）】四六歳

七月一日、第一回総選挙。

一一月二五日、帝国議会開院式。

【一八九一（明治二四）】四七歳

五月六日、第一次松方正義内閣成立。

七月三一日、危篤となり、特旨をもって位階を進め従二位に叙せられる。

八月三日、死去。四日、天皇から祭祀金二〇〇〇円を賜る。五日、葬儀への勅使として遣わされた侍従子爵綾小路有良より幣帛を下賜される。

（諸先行研究、本研究会の成果をもとに、西山由理花がまとめた。）

568

京都大学史料叢書（第一期）『吉田清成関係文書』全七巻の完結にあたって

『吉田清成関係文書』第一巻の刊行は、一九九三年十二月、今から二十五年前にさかのぼる。刊行に際して、大久保利謙氏と梅渓昇氏より、次のような推薦の辞を賜った。現在となっては貴重なパンフレットに記された文章であるため、その一部を抜粋する。なお、肩書は当時のままである。

「推薦の辞」　歴史家　大久保利謙

吉田の残した膨大な文書は、次男井上清純によって一応整理され、京都帝国大学に寄贈されたという。筆者が往年、吉田と同郷人で幕末英国留学を共にした森有礼の全集編纂の際に、京都大学関係の某君の御斡旋で特別な提供を受けて、書翰篇に吉田宛文書一〇通を収録する事を得たという憶い出がある。

「明治国家の形成過程を語る第一級史料」　大阪大学名誉教授・仏教大学教授　梅渓昇

このたび『吉田清成関係文書』全七巻が出る。この挙を聞いて、まず思い起こすのは、かの名著『明治初年条約改正の研究』（一九六二年）の著者下村冨士男先生が、この関係文書閲覧のためしばしば東京から京都へ足を運ばれ、お目にかかるたびに、京都大学国史研究室の方でなんとか早く公刊してもらえないかともらされていたことである。ここに研究室関係者のご尽力でよう

569

やく近代史研究者長年の渇望がいやされることになったのは嬉しい限りである。

吉田清成（一八四五〜九一年）は、薩摩藩の出身で、幕末から明治初年にいたる英米への留学から帰国した後には大蔵省入りし、少丞・租税権頭・少輔を務めた。ついで駐米公使・外務大輔・農商務大輔・同次官を務め、さらに晩年には元老院議官・枢密顧問官を歴任した。大久保利通の腹心であり、大久保が暗殺されなかったら、閣僚にもなった可能性がある人物である。

吉田は、大蔵省時代には七分利付外債募集の理事官として、また駐米公使時代には、条約改正の発端をなす、いわゆる吉田・エバーツ協定締結の当事者として、その名を日本近代史上にとどめている。なお、吉田はこの協定に思い入れをもっており、調印した際のペンを大切に保管していた。

この吉田のもとに送られた多くの政治家・官僚・知友からの書翰や手もとに保存された書類などの膨大な史料が、昭和初年に京都帝国大学文学部国史研究室へ寄贈された「吉田清成関係文書」（以下、「吉田文書」）である。

「吉田文書」は、清成旧蔵の来翰、書翰草稿、関係官庁文書、外債募集理事官・駐米公使当時の記録、壬午事変・甲申事変・清仏戦争関係記録、農商務省関係の財政経済・地方行政書類、清成晩年の日記・文書、写真など約四千点にのぼる多彩な史料からなる。「吉田文書」は、幕末の留学生たちの動向に光をあてるものとして、また明治前期の政治・経済・外交の歴史に新たな事実を提供するものとして、大なる意義を有しているといえよう。

「吉田文書」を利用した最初の研究は、三浦周行（京都帝国大学文学部教授）のものであろう。一九

570

二七年一二月読史会大会講演をもとにした、三浦周行「新日本の大恩人ゼネラル、グラント」（『日本史の研究』第二輯、一九三〇年、岩波書店）の中に、三浦が吉田の次男の井上清純男爵より吉田関係の文書の閲覧を許された旨の記述がある。また、三浦の遺稿となった「明治時代に於ける琉球所属問題」（『史学雑誌』第四二編七・一二号、一九三一年七・一二月、のち『日本史の研究』新輯三）もこの吉田家の新史料を先駆的に利用したものである。近代までを視野に入れた日本法制史・日本中世史の泰斗としてだけでなく、古文書原本の蒐集に大変尽力した三浦を介して、それらの文書が国史研究室へ寄贈されたものと思われる。

しかしながら「吉田文書」は、その受け入れに際して作成された簡単な目録を除いては、十分な整理がなされないまま、戦後も研究者によって広く利用されることなく半世紀近くの年月を閲してきたのである。

この「吉田文書」の整理・解読作業は、一九七八年春から、京都大学研修員であった明石岩雄と大学院生の伊藤之雄・高橋秀直によって始められた。まもなくして、その当時京都女子大学教授であった山本四郎が加わり、さらには、新たに大学院に進学した鈴木栄樹・松延秀一らも参加し、吉田清成関係文書研究会と呼ぶようになった。

ところが、一九八〇年春にいたって、「原敬関係文書」が、盛岡市にある原敬の盛岡別邸の倉庫から発見され、研究会に関係していたメンバーが、同文書の整理・解読作業にも従事することとなった。「原敬関係文書」の刊行作業は、一九八三年半ばには山を越え、書翰篇刊行のめどもついた。この間の経緯については、伊藤之雄「原敬文書の発見と意義」（『日本史研究』第六七〇号、二〇一八年六月）を参

571

照されたい。

　その後、吉田清成関係文書研究会の方では、新たに松下孝昭・飯塚一幸・豆谷浩之・西山伸らが加わった。また、「吉田清成関係文書を中心とする明治前期外交・財政史研究」なる研究課題（課題番号：五六三一〇〇五五　研究代表者：山本四郎）のもとに、一九八一〜八三年度の文部省科学研究費補助金総合研究（Ａ）を得ることができた。この科研費では、明石に加え、朝尾直弘・井口和起・池田敬正・伊原沢周・岩井忠熊・後藤靖・芝原拓自・高久嶺之介・堤啓次郎・中村哲・久野修義・松尾尊兊の諸氏に研究分担者になっていただいた。

　第一巻刊行にこぎつけたのは、一九九三年のことであったが、以来、その時々の研究会には次のようなメンバーが新規に参加してきた。田中智子・岸本覚・大石一男・落合弘樹・井口治夫・谷川穣・小山俊樹・奈良岡聰智・森靖夫・平松良太・齊藤紅葉・久保田裕次・萩原淳・西山由理花、および筆者の京都女子大学教授時代の教え子である水野貴久子・竹村房子らである。とりわけ、田中智子・大石一男の二人には、その後の事務局の労多い役割を担当していただいた。

　当初は月に四回（半日）から二回（二日）、その後は月に一回（二日）、約四十年以上にもわたって開かれてきた本研究会には、以上のほかにも少なからぬ人たちが参加してきた。それぞれのお名前はここにはあげきれないので、各巻凡例末尾の一覧をご覧いただきたい。

　さらには、研究会のメンバーを中心として、山本四郎編著『近代日本の政党と官僚』（東京創元社、一九九一年）と同『日本近代国家の形成と展開』（吉川弘文館、一九九六年）の二冊の研究書を刊行することもできた。

筆者の百歳を前にして、『吉田清成関係文書』全七巻を完結することができたことには、感慨深いものがある。研究会のために尽力してくれた諸氏のおかげである。本史料集が、広く研究者に迎えられ、活用されることを期待してやまない。

二〇一八年八月三十一日

山本四郎

編集・解説

吉田清成関係文書研究会（代表・山本四郎）

京都大学史料叢書　**16**

吉田清成関係文書七　書翰篇　書類篇３５

平成三十（二〇一八）年十月十日　発行

定価‥**本体二一、〇〇〇円**（税別）

編　者　京都大学文学部日本史研究室

発行者　田中　大

印刷所　株式会社図書印刷同朋舎

発行所　株式会社　**思文閣出版**
京都市東山区元町三五五
電話（〇七五）七五一ー一七八一㈹

ISBN978-4-7842-1917-9 C3321　　　　　　　　Printed in Japan

京都大学史料叢書　吉田清成関係文書

※本史料集は、京都大学文学部日本史研究室が所蔵する「吉田清成関係文書」を翻刻した。
※書翰篇は、日本文書翰を吉田清成宛書翰・吉田清成書翰・第三者間書翰に分類し、次のような政官財界の主要人物の書翰を収録する。

青木周蔵・浅田徳則・伊藤博文・伊東巳代治・井上馨・岩倉具視・上野景範・大久保利通・大隈重信・大鳥圭介・大山綱昌・岡田令高・海江田信義・川村純義・北代正臣・日下義雄・熊谷武五郎・黒田清隆・五代友厚・西郷従道・斎藤修一郎・三条実美・渋沢栄一・高平小五郎・寺師宗徳・寺島宗則・徳大寺実則・得能良介・中井弘・花房義質・松方正義・柳谷謙太郎・吉田二郎

吉田清成関係文書1	書翰篇1	本体13,000円
吉田清成関係文書2	書翰篇2	本体13,000円
吉田清成関係文書3	書翰篇3	本体13,000円
吉田清成関係文書4	書翰篇4	本体15,000円
吉田清成関係文書5	書類篇1	本体19,500円
吉田清成関係文書6	書類篇2	本体21,000円
吉田清成関係文書7	書翰篇5・書類篇3	本体21,000円

●思文閣出版●　　（価格は税別）